PROFESSIONAL IRONPYTHON

PROFESSIONAL

IronPython™

John Paul Mueller

Wiley Publishing, Inc.

Professional IronPython™

Published by
Wiley Publishing, Inc.
10475 Crosspoint Boulevard
Indianapolis, IN 46256
www.wiley.com

Copyright © 2010 by Wiley Publishing, Inc., Indianapolis, Indiana

Published simultaneously in Canada

ISBN: 978-0-470-54859-2

Manufactured in the United States of America

10 9 8 7 6 5 4 3 2 1

For general information on our other products and services please contact our Customer Care Department within the United States at (877) 762-2974, outside the United States at (317) 572-3993 or fax (317) 572-4002.

Wiley also publishes its books in a variety of electronic formats. Some content that appears in print may not be available in electronic books.

Library of Congress Control Number: 2010921245

This book is dedicated to my beautiful wife, Rebecca,
my inspiration and joy. She believed in me
when all others doubted.

CREDITS

ABOUT THE AUTHOR

 **JOHN PAUL MUELLER** is a freelance author and technical editor. He has writing in his blood, having produced 84 books and more than 300 articles to date. The topics range from networking to artificial intelligence and from database management to heads-down programming. Topics for some of his current books include Windows power optimization, Windows Server 2008 GUI, and Windows Server 2008 Server Core, and he has also written a programmer's guide that discusses the new Office Fluent User Interface (RibbonX). His technical editing skills have helped more than 63 authors refine the content of their manuscripts. John has provided technical editing services to both DataBased Advisor and Coast Compute magazines. He's also contributed articles to the following magazines: *CIO.com*, *DevSource*, *InformIT*, *Informant*, *DevX*, *SQL Server Professional*, *Visual C++ Developer*, *Hard Core Visual Basic*, *asp.netPRO*, *Software Test and Performance*, and *Visual Basic Developer*.

When John isn't working at the computer, he enjoys spending time in his workshop crafting wood projects or making candles. On any given afternoon, you can find him working at a lathe or putting the finishing touches on a bookcase. He also likes making glycerin soap, which comes in handy for gift baskets. You can reach John on the Internet at JMueller@mwt.net. He is also setting up a Web site and blog at http://www.johnmuellerbooks.com/; feel free to look and make suggestions on how he can improve it.

ABOUT THE TECHNICAL EDITOR

RUSS MULLEN has been consulting and programming for more years than he cares to remember. He has tech edited more than 70 books, ghost-written chapters, and co-authored several books.

ACKNOWLEDGMENTS

THANKS TO MY WIFE, REBECCA, for working with me to get this book completed. I really don't know what I would have done without her help in researching and compiling some of the information that appears in this book. She also did a fine job of proofreading most of my rough draft.

Russ Mullen deserves thanks for his technical edit of this book. Russ added greatly to the accuracy and depth of the material that you see here. I appreciated the time that Russ devoted to checking my text, especially the code, for accuracy. As I wrote this book, I also spent a good deal of time bouncing ideas off Russ, which is a valuable aid to any author.

Matt Wagner, my agent, deserves credit for helping me get the contract in the first place and taking care of all the details that most authors don't consider. I always appreciate his assistance. It's good to know that someone wants to help.

A number of people read all or part of this book to help me refine the approach, test the examples, and generally provide input that all readers wish they could have. These unpaid volunteers helped in ways too numerous to mention here. I especially appreciate the efforts of Eva Beattie, Osvaldo Téllez Almirall, and all the others who provided input on this book. I'd like to thank each person by name who wrote me with an idea, but there are simply too many.

Finally, I would like to thank William Bridges, Nancy Rapoport, Kathleen Wisor, and the rest of the editorial and production staff for their assistance in bringing this book to print. It's always nice to work with such a great group of professionals.

CONTENTS

INTRODUCTION

IRONPYTHON IS PROBABLY GOING TO BE ONE OF THE MOST INTERESTING and flexible languages you've ever encountered. If you've never tried a dynamic language, you're really missing something. Dynamic languages make it easy for you to try things on-the-fly, and IronPython is king when it comes to melding the flexibility of both the Python programming language and the functionality of the .NET Framework. You get an amazing array of application development tools with few hindrances to sour the experience. Professional IronPython provides you with a guided tour of this amazing language and makes it possible for you to get started writing applications quickly.

The emphasis of IronPython is fast. You write less code and the code that you do write is easier to understand, making development fast. In the past, using an interpreter meant sluggish application performance, but IronPython is anything but sluggish. Applications you develop using IronPython run quickly because they don't include all of the cumbersome baggage that static languages such as C# and Visual Basic.NET include. *Professional IronPython* helps you understand the benefits of using IronPython and demonstrates techniques to obtain what you want with little fuss and considerable speed.

One of the most amazing parts of IronPython is that it's incredibly easy to add whatever you need to it. IronPython is designed to provide extensive modularity so that you can create extensions to the basic language as dictated by your development needs. Professional IronPython shows you how to create extensions for IronPython that fill in all the gaps you might find.

Do you need multi-platform support for your project? Amazingly, IronPython can provide multi-platform development, despite what you might have heard online. Professional IronPython devotes an entire chapter to the topic of getting your IronPython application onto other platforms such as Linux and the Mac OS X.

Obviously, nothing is perfect. IronPython does have a few blemishes and you'll want to know about them. Professional IronPython doesn't whitewash the problems and try to dress them up as features. This book tackles the issues you'll encounter head on and makes it a lot easier for you to overcome them. For example, you'll discover when you really do need to pair IronPython with a static language to obtain the robust application performance and development environment that you need.

WHO THIS BOOK IS FOR

This book is for the professional developer. While it does include introduction sections, the pace of the introductory material is quite fast and the novice developer will tend to become lost. The book does include all of the beginning IronPython you need such as working with variables and using loops, but this material consumes a relatively small portion of the book. The book assumes that you also have knowledge of the .NET Framework after working with another language such as C# or Visual Basic.NET. The examples do provide complete information on everything you need to include in the source code, so your knowledge of the .NET Framework doesn't have to be extensive, but some knowledge is helpful.

WHAT THIS BOOK COVERS

Professional IronPython begins with an act of discovery. You'll learn how IronPython can help you create better applications in less time and with fewer errors. To keep things balanced, you'll also see where IronPython falls a bit short. The point is to provide a balanced view of what IronPython can do so you don't start a project and experience nasty surprises. As part of this discovery process, you install IronPython on your system and begin building applications with it. The first applications are relatively simple and demonstrate the kinds of things every developer needs to know when starting a new language, such as how to work with structures.

After the introductions are over, the book begins looking at some of the ways in which you can use IronPython to build real applications. You'll discover how to access both the Standard Library and the .NET Framework from IronPython. You'll use your new knowledge to create Windows Forms applications, interact with COM objects, and work at the command line. In fact, you'll even build an ASP.NET application using IronPython.

Next comes some advanced IronPython topics. Everyone needs to know how to work with XML, so that's the first advanced topic you'll tackle. The next advanced topic is the Dynamic Language Runtime (DLR) and you learn what it can do for you. Interestingly enough, you could build your own language using DLR, should you want to do so. The next few chapters discuss how to use IronPython with other .NET languages. First you see how to access IronPython from other languages, and then you discover how to build extensions for IronPython using both C# and Visual Basic.NET.

The last two chapters of the book are possibly the most interesting for someone who has worked with programming languages for a long time. Chapter 18 demonstrates how you can use IronPython to improve your testing process for just about any language. Of course, IronPython works best with .NET languages. Chapter19 discusses techniques for using IronPython on other platforms. The idea of writing an application just once and executing it equally well on Windows, Linux, and the Mac OS X is exciting.

HOW THIS BOOK IS STRUCTURED

This book is structured to discuss IronPython in a progressively complex manner. It doesn't leave you wondering where the basics are — the first few chapters provide a whirlwind tour of the IronPython implementation of the Python language. However, by the end of the book you've discovered some very advanced information indeed. For example, you'll create an IronPython extension that directly accesses the Win32 API. With this in mind, the following list provides you an overview of the book structure so you can find what you want quickly.

> **Part I: Introducing IronPython:** This part of the book begins with an introduction to IronPython. You begin by obtaining and installing the software, using the IronPython console, and then creating your first application. The discussion continues by examining the modules that come with

IronPython and working with some basics such as the standard input, output, and error devices. You also begin creating IronPython functions and performing other simple tasks.

➤ **Part II: Using the IronPython Language:** This part of the book provides a fast-paced tour of the IronPython language. You begin with simple statements, work through loops, examine arrays and collections, and then move on to structures and object. By the time you complete this part of the book, a professional developer will have enough information to write intermediate-level IronPython code.

➤ **Part III: Working with IronPython:** This part of the book begins the process of performing some real work with IronPython. It begins by examining both the Standard Library and the .NET Framework. You discover that it isn't always possible to directly access everything you want, but you can access most items with relative ease. The chapters in this part of the book provide lots of tips and techniques for overcoming difficulties with IronPython. The discussion continues with chapters that examine specific application types: Windows Forms, COM inter-actions, command line applications used for administrative tasks, and ASP.NET applications. This part of the book ends with a complete discussion of debugging techniques — an essential part of using any programming language.

➤ **Part IV: Advanced IronPython Topics:** This part of the book goes beyond basic applications and moves into areas that are a little more exotic. The chapter on XML may not seem very interesting at first, but when you see the ease with which IronPython manipulates XML, you'll really be impressed. The next topic is DLR, which is an exciting technology you can use for all kinds of tasks. Chapter 15 shows how to access your IronPython code from static languages such as C# and Visual Basic.NET. Chapters 16 and 17 show how to access C# and Visual Basic.NET code from IronPython. These three chapters together help you understand that IronPython isn't an isolated language — you really can mix and match it with other languages as needed. Chapter 18 is possibly one of the most exciting chapters because it shows how you can use IronPython to perform application testing. Finally, Chapter 19 describes how you can use IronPython with Mono, a .NET Framework alternative that makes it possible to use your IronPython applications on other platforms.

➤ **Appendices:** This book contains two appendices that contain important information. You can probably skip them if you want, but the information is really helpful in bridging some gaps in IronPython functionality. Appendix A describes the differences between IronPython and CPython, both of which implement the Python language. Appendix B provides infor-mation about using CPython extensions with IronPython. CPython and IronPython don't always work well together, but the information in these appendices can help you overcome any potential problems.

WHAT YOU NEED TO USE THIS BOOK

Theoretically, all you need is a computer with Windows installed on it to work with IronPython. The computer must have a copy of the .NET Framework 3.5 or older installed on it that you can download from http://www.microsoft.com/NET/. Chapter 1 contains complete instructions for downloading and installing your copy of IronPython. You must also have a text editor — even Notepad will do, but it won't be very convenient to use.

If you want to get full use out of this book, however, you must have a copy of Visual Studio.NET 2008 or above. The book examples rely on Visual Studio.NET 2010. You won't be able to work with the examples later in the book unless you have a copy of Visual Studio. In addition, a number of the techniques, such as debugging, require that you have a copy of Visual Studio.NET. Nothing has been tested with the Visual Studio Express Edition products, and there's no guarantee that anything will work with this edition of the product.

CONVENTIONS

To help you get the most from the text and keep track of what's happening, we've used some conventions throughout the book. Typical examples follow:

Notes, tips, hints, tricks, and asides to the current discussion are offset and placed in italics like this.

A warning tells you that something terrible will happen should a particular event occur. For example, if you perform a task incorrectly, you might see data loss.

As for styles in the text:

➤ We *highlight* new terms and important words when we introduce them.

➤ We show keyboard strokes like this: Ctrl+A.

➤ We show filenames, URLs, and code within the text like so: `persistence.properties`.

➤ We show text you should type directly like this: type **Hello** for regular text and type **`MyFile.py`** for code and filenames.

➤ We show text that you should replace with your own values like this: *MyName* for regular text and ***`MyVariable`*** for code and filenames.

➤ We present code in the following way:

```
We use a monofont type with no highlighting for most code examples.
```

SOURCE CODE

As you work through the examples in this book, you may choose either to type in all the code manually or to use the source code files that accompany the book. All of the source code used in this book is available for download at http://www.wrox.com. Once at the site, simply locate the book's title (either by using the Search box or by using one of the title lists) and click the Download Code link on the book's detail page to obtain all the source code for the book.

Because many books have similar titles, you may find it easiest to search by ISBN; this book's ISBN is 978-0-470-54859-2.

Once you download the code, just decompress it with your favorite compression tool. Alternately, you can go to the main Wrox code download page at http://www.wrox.com/dynamic/books/download.aspx to see the code available for this book and all other Wrox books.

ERRATA

We make every effort to ensure that there are no errors in the text or in the code. However, no one is perfect, and mistakes do occur. If you find an error in one of our books, like a spelling mistake or faulty piece of code, we would be very grateful for your feedback. By sending in errata you may save another reader hours of frustration and at the same time you will be helping us provide even higher quality information.

To find the errata page for this book, go to http://www.wrox.com and locate the title using the Search box or one of the title lists. Then, on the Book Search Results page, click the Errata link. On this page you can view all errata that has been submitted for this book and posted by Wrox editors.

A complete book list including links to each book's errata is also available at http://www.wrox.com/misc-pages/booklist.shtml.

If you don't spot "your" error on the Errata page, click the Errata Form link and complete the form to send us the error you have found. We'll check the information and, if appropriate, post a message to the book's errata page and fix the problem in subsequent editions of the book.

P2P.WROX.COM

For author and peer discussion, join the P2P forums at p2p.wrox.com. The forums are a Web-based system for you to post messages relating to Wrox books and related technologies and interact with other readers and technology users. The forums offer a subscription feature to e-mail you topics of interest of your choosing when new posts are made to the forums. Wrox authors, editors, other industry experts, and your fellow readers are present on these forums.

At http://p2p.wrox.com you will find a number of different forums that will help you not only as you read this book, but also as you develop your own applications. To join the forums, just follow these steps:

1.   Go to p2p.wrox.com and click the Register link.

2.   Read the terms of use and click Agree.

3.   Complete the required information to join as well as any optional information you wish to provide, and click Submit.

4.   You will receive an e-mail with information describing how to verify your account and complete the joining process.

You can read messages in the forums without joining P2P but in order to post your own messages, you must join.

Once you join, you can post new messages and respond to messages other users post. You can read messages at any time on the Web. If you would like to have new messages from a particular forum e-mailed to you, click the Subscribe to this Forum icon by the forum name in the forum listing.

For more information about how to use the Wrox P2P, be sure to read the P2P FAQs for answers to questions about how the forum software works as well as many common questions specific to P2P and Wrox books. To read the FAQs, click the FAQ link on any P2P page.

PART I
Introducing IronPython

Discovering IronPython

WHAT'S IN THIS CHAPTER?

> ➤ Understanding why you want to add IronPython to your developer toolbox

> ➤ Obtaining and installing IronPython on your machine

> ➤ Understanding some underlying basics of how IronPython works

> ➤ Using IronPython at the console and within a window

> ➤ Designing and building a simple application

IronPython: It sounds like some kind of metal snake infesting your computer, but it isn't. IronPython is the .NET version of the open source Python language (http://www.python.org/). Python is a dynamic language that can greatly enhance your programming experience, help you create applications in less time, and make the applications you create significantly more responsive to user needs. Of course, you've heard these promises before from other languages. This chapter helps you understand how IronPython delivers on these promises in specific situations. The smart developer soon learns that every language serves specific needs and might not work well in others. So this chapter isn't here to blow smoke at you — once you complete it, you'll understand the strengths and weaknesses of IronPython.

Of course, you'll need to obtain a copy of IronPython before you can use it because Visual Studio doesn't include IronPython as part of the default installation. This chapter helps you get IronPython installed on your system and tells you about some options you may want to install as well.

Once you have IronPython installed, you'll want to know a little about how it works. This chapter won't make you an IronPython guru who's familiar with every nuance of the underlying structural elements, but it will give you a good overview that will make the rest of the book a lot easier to understand. You'll put your new-found knowledge to the test by performing a few tasks at the IronPython console and within the IronPython windowed environment.

Finally, this chapter takes you through the process of creating a simple application. No, this isn't going to be the next great Windows application. It will be a little better than Hello World, but not much. The idea is to get you started doing something useful with IronPython. Don't worry; the examples will become a lot more interesting as the book progresses.

AN OVERVIEW OF IRONPYTHON

It surprises many developers to discover that computer languages are for humans, not for computers. A computer couldn't care less about which language you use, because it's all bits and bytes in the end anyway. Consequently, when you decide to learn another computer language, it really does pay to know what that language will do for you, the developer. Otherwise, there really isn't a point in making the effort.

One phrase you often hear when discussing Python (and by extension, IronPython) is "batteries included." Python has an immense standard library that addresses everything from working with ZIP files to interacting with the file system. You'll discover the details of working with the Standard Library in Chapter 6. For now, it's important to know that the Standard Library has a lot to offer and you may very well be able to build many of your applications without ever thinking about the .NET Framework.

As previously mentioned, IronPython is a .NET version of the Python language. For a .NET developer, using IronPython has the advantage of letting you create extensions using .NET (see Chapters 16 and 17 for details). In addition, you have full access to the .NET Framework (see Chapter 7 for details). You can work with IronPython and other .NET languages that you already know, which means that you can use the right tool for every job. However, IronPython has a few differences from the CPython implementation that everyone else uses (see Appendix A for details), which means that you can occasionally run into some odd compatibility problems when using IronPython. As with most things in life, advantages usually come with a few disadvantages.

You'll see Python appear in many guises when you begin using it. The original implementation of Python is CPython and that's the implementation that most developers target. In fact, you'll often see IronPython compared and contrasted with CPython throughout this book. It's important to remember that all these implementations attempt to achieve the same goal — full support of the Python standard. In most cases, all you really need to worry about is the IronPython implementation, unless you plan to use third-party libraries written for another Python implementation. This book helps you understand the use of CPython extensions in Appendix B.

There are some basic reasons that you want to use IronPython (or Python for that matter). The most important reason is that IronPython is a dynamic language, which means that it performs many tasks during run time, rather than compile time. Using a dynamic language means that your code has advantages of static languages, such as Visual Basic, in that it can more easily adapt to changing environmental conditions. (You'll discover many other dynamic language advantages as the chapter progresses.) Unfortunately, you often pay for runtime flexibility with poorer performance — there's always a tradeoff between flexibility and performance.

> *Performance is a combination of three factors: speed, reliability, and security. When an application has a performance hit, it means a decrease in any of these three factors. When working with IronPython, there is a decrease in speed because the interpreter must compile code at run time, rather than at compile time. This speed decrease is partially offset by an improvement in reliability because IronPython applications are so flexible.*

Dynamic languages provide a number of benefits such as the ability to enter several statements and execute them immediately to obtain feedback. Using a dynamic language also provides easier refactoring and code modification because you don't have to change static definitions throughout your code. It's even possible to call functions you haven't implemented yet and add an implementation later in the code when it's needed. Don't get the idea that dynamic languages are new. In fact, dynamic languages have been around for a very long time. Examples of other dynamic languages include the following:

- ➤ LISP (List Processing)
- ➤ Smalltalk
- ➤ JavaScript
- ➤ PHP
- ➤ Ruby
- ➤ ColdFusion
- ➤ Lua
- ➤ Cobra
- ➤ Groovy

Developers also assign a number of advantages specifically to the Python language (and IronPython's implementation of it). Whether these features truly are advantages to you depends on your perspective and experience. Many people do agree that Python provides these features:

- ➤ Support for the Windows, Linux/Unix, and Mac OS X platforms
- ➤ Managed support using both Java and .NET
- ➤ Considerable object-oriented programming (OOP) functionality that is easy to understand and use
- ➤ The capability to look within the code — .NET developers will know this as a strong form of reflection

➤ An extensive array of standard libraries

➤ Full library support using hierarchical packages (a concept that is already familiar to every .NET developer)

➤ Robust third-party libraries that support just about every need

➤ Support for writing both extensions and modules in both C and C++

➤ Support for writing extensions and modules using third-party solutions for both .NET (IronPython) and Java (Jython)

➤ Modular application development

➤ Error handling through exceptions (another concept familiar to any .NET developer)

➤ High-level dynamic data types

➤ Ease of embedding within applications as a scripting solution

➤ Procedural code that is relatively easy and natural to write

➤ Ease of reading and a clear syntax

All these features translate into increased developer productivity, which is something that dynamic languages as a whole supposedly provide (productivity is one of these issues that is hard to nail down and even harder to prove unless you resort to metrics such as lines of code, which prove useless when comparing languages). In addition to the great features that Python provides, IronPython provides a few of its own. The following list provides a brief overview of these features:

➤ Full access to the .NET Framework

➤ Usability within Silverlight applications

➤ Interactive console with full dynamic compilation provided as part of the product

➤ Accessibility from within a browser (see `http://ironpython.codeplex.com/Wiki/View .aspx?title=SilverlightInteractiveSession` for details)

➤ Full extensibility using the .NET Framework

➤ Complete source code available (see `http://ironpython.codeplex.com/SourceControl/ ListDownloadableCommits.aspx` for details)

One of the negatives of working with IronPython, versus Python (in the form of CPython), is that you lose support for multiple platforms — you only have direct access to Windows. You can get around this problem using Mono (`http://www.mono-project.com/Main_Page`), but it isn't a straightforward fix and many developers will find it cumbersome. (Chapter 19 tells you more about working with Mono — a valuable solution for some Windows versions as well, such as Windows Server 2008 Server Core.) Of course, there isn't any way to get around the lack of Java support — you simply choose one virtual machine or the other. Appendix A lists more IronPython differences from CPython, most of which will cause compatibility and other issues for you.

An interesting use of IronPython is as an application testing tool. In fact, some developers use IronPython exclusively for this purpose. Chapter 18 tells you more about this exciting use of IronPython and demonstrates that using IronPython for this purpose really does make application testing considerably easier.

Don't get the idea that IronPython is going to restrict your use of familiar technologies. You can still create a Windows Forms application (see Chapter 8) and interact with COM (see Chapter 9). It's even possible to create command line (console) applications (see Chapter 10) and work with the Internet (see Chapter 11) just as you always have. What IronPython provides is another way to view problems that you must address using your applications. As with most languages, what you're getting is another tool that lets you create solutions in the least amount of time and with the fewest bugs.

GETTING IRONPYTHON

Before you can use IronPython, you need to get a copy of your own, install it, and check to make sure it works. Theoretically, you might want to obtain the source code and build your own version of IronPython, but most developers simply download the binaries and begin working with IronPython right away. The first three sections that follow tell you what you need to work with IronPython, how to obtain the software, and how to install it. You'll definitely want to read these sections.

The final two sections are completely optional. In fact, you may want to skip them for now and come back to them after you complete more chapters in the book. The first optional section tells you how to build your own copy of IronPython from the source. The second optional section tells you about third-party libraries.

There's a huge base of third-party libraries for IronPython. Generally, you don't need to install any third-party libraries to use this book. Everything you need to work with IronPython is included with the download you get from the CodePlex Web site. The only time you might need to work with third-party libraries is in Part IV. You'll receive specific instructions in the Part IV chapters for any required third-party libraries, so you only need to read "Using Third-Party Libraries" if you plan to work with third-party libraries immediately.

Understanding the IronPython Requirements

As with any software, IronPython has basic system requirements you must meet before you can use it. It turns out that there are actually two versions of IronPython 2.6 — one for the .NET Framework 2.0, 3.0, and 3.5, and a second for the .NET Framework 4.0. Here are the requirements for the .NET Framework 2.0, 3.0, and 3.5 version.

➤ The .NET Framework 2.0, 3.0, and 3.5

➤ (Optional) Visual Studio 2005 or Visual Studio 2008 (your system must meet the prerequisites for this software)

➤ (Optional) .NET Framework 2.0 Software Development Kit (SDK)

You need only the optional requirements if you plan to build IronPython 2.6 from the source code. Here are the requirements for the .NET Framework 4.0 version (again, the optional requirements are there if you want to build IronPython from source code).

➤ The .NET Framework 4.0

➤ (Optional) Visual Studio 2010

Getting the Software

As with most open source software, you have a number of choices when it comes to downloading IronPython. For the sake of your sanity, the best choice when starting with IronPython is to download the binary version of the product from `http://ironpython.codeplex.com/Release/ProjectReleases.aspx?ReleaseId=30315`. You'll see the Microsoft Installer (MSI) link right below the Recommended Download link as IronPython-2.6.msi. If you really must save the few seconds downloading the MSI version, select the IronPython-2.6-Bin.zip link instead.

It's also possible to compile IronPython from the source code. If you want to use this option, select the IronPython-2.6-Src.zip link. You must have a copy of Visual Studio installed on your system to use this option. The "Building the Binaries from Scratch" section of the chapter describes how to build a version from scratch, but this process truly isn't for the IronPython beginner and doesn't serve much of a purpose unless you plan to add your own enhancements.

 Most developers will likely use the standard version of IronPython that works with the .NET Framework 3.5 and earlier. However, you might need some of the new features in the .NET Framework 4.0, such as the C# `dynamic` keyword, which is part of the Dynamic Language Runtime (DLR) (`http://dlr.codeplex.com/`). The section "Understanding the Dynamic Language Runtime" later in this chapter tells you more about this .NET 4.0 feature. You can obtain this version of IronPython at `http://ironpython.codeplex.com/Release/ProjectReleases.aspx?ReleaseId=27320`. The examples in this book will work with either version of IronPython 2.6, except where noted (where I'm demonstrating how to work with the DLR).

Performing the Installation

This section assumes that you've downloaded the MSI file to make life easy for yourself. This procedure works equally well for either version of IronPython 2.6 so you can use it for a DLR install as well. The following instructions help you get IronPython installed on your machine.

1. Double-click the MSI file you downloaded from the CodePlex Web site. You'll see the usual Welcome page — click Next to get past it.

2. Read the licensing agreement, check I Accept the Terms in the License Agreement, and then click Next. You'll see the Custom Setup dialog box shown in Figure 1-1 where you can select the IronPython features you want to install. At a minimum, you must install the Runtime. The Documentation, Standard Library, and Tools features are also strongly recommended. This book assumes that you've installed all the features. However, you might want to install just those features you actually need for a production setup (you might not actually need the samples).

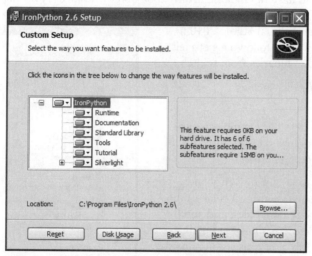

FIGURE 1-1: Choose the features you want to install.

When you perform a DLR installation, you'll see a Do Not NGen Installed Binaries option on the Custom Setup dialog box. Using the Native Image Generator (NGen) can greatly improve application performance, as described at http://msdn.microsoft.com/en-us/magazine/cc163610.aspx. *Earlier versions of IronPython didn't use NGen to build the libraries for you by default. You had to use a special command line to obtain the NGen feature* (msiexec /qn /i "IronPython.msi" NGENDLLS=True). *The default setup for IronPython 2.6 is to use NGen to build the libraries.*

However, using NGen also binds the binaries to the local machine, which may not be what you want when working in a dynamic environment. Consequently, if you plan to use DLR more than you plan to use other IronPython features, you might want to check the Do Not NGen Installed Binaries option.

3. Select the features you want to install. Click Next. You'll see a summary dialog box that simply states you're ready to install IronPython.

4. Click Install. MSI will begin the installation process. At some point, you'll see an installation completion screen.

5. Click Finish. You should be ready to begin working with IronPython at this point.

Building the Binaries from Scratch

You may eventually want to build the IronPython binaries from scratch. The normal reason to perform this task is to create a special version of IronPython that meets specific needs. A company may want to add extensions or special features to IronPython. Because you have the source code, it's acceptable to create a custom version of IronPython for yourself — one that contains any feature set you deem necessary to get your work completed. So have fun molding IronPython and then sharing your modifications with others. In order to perform this task, you must have a copy of Visual Studio (you must have Visual Studio 2010 to build a DLR version of IronPython). The following steps tell you how to build the IronPython 2.6 binaries from scratch.

1. Download the source code file, such as IronPython-2.6-Src.zip.

2. Extract the files into a folder. The example assumes that you extracted the files into the root directory of your hard drive into \IronPython-2.6.

3. Locate the \IronPython-2.6\Src directory and open the IronPython.sln solution using Visual Studio. Visual Studio will load the required files, and you'll see them in Solution Explorer, as shown in Figure 1-2. Figure 1-2 shows that IronPython consists of a number of projects — you must compile the entire solution to obtain a workable group of DLLs.

4. Make any required changes to the source code.

5. Choose Build ⇨ Build Solution. Visual Studio creates the required DLLs, ready for testing.

Using Third-Party Libraries

Python is an extremely flexible language and enjoys strong third-party support. In fact, you can find lists of these libraries in various places on the Internet. Here are a few places to check:

FIGURE 1-2: IronPython consists of multiple projects, so you must compile the entire solution.

➤   http://code.google.com/appengine/docs/python/tools/libraries.html

➤   http://www.amaltas.org/show/third-party-python-libraries-and-frameworks.html

➤   http://dakrauth.com/blog/entry/third-party-python-libraries-interest/

 IronPython is a complex product. If you fail to compile the entire solution every time you make a change, you could end up with an unworkable group of DLLs due to interactions. It's important to build everything so that any changes propagate properly.

You should be able to use some third-party libraries with IronPython. At the time of this writing, you won't actually find any usable third-party libraries. However, you should check `http://www` `.ironpython.info/index.php/Third-Party_Library_Compatibility` from time-to-time to discover whether there are any third-party libraries that do work with IronPython. It's important to note that this list represents only tested libraries — you may find other third-party libraries that do work with the current version of IronPython.

UNDERSTANDING THE DYNAMIC LANGUAGE RUNTIME

IronPython is a dynamic language, yet the Common Language Runtime (CLR) is a static environment. While you can build a compiler that makes it possible to use a dynamic language with CLR, as was done for IronPython 1.0, you'll find that certain functionality is missing because CLR simply doesn't understand dynamic languages. Consequently, Microsoft started the Dynamic Language Runtime (DLR) project (see `http://dlr.codeplex.com/` for additional information). DLR sits on top of CLR and performs a level of interpretation that offers additional functionality for dynamic languages. By relying on DLR, IronPython gains access to the following support:

➤ Shared dynamic type support

➤ Shared hosted model

➤ Quick dynamic code generation

➤ Interaction with other dynamic languages

➤ Improved interaction with static languages such as C# and Visual Basic.NET (see Chapters 15, 16, and 17 for details)

➤ Shared sandbox security model and browse integration

DLR is now part of the .NET Framework 4.0. (In fact, you'll discover the details of this integration in Chapter 14.) Consequently, you can begin accessing these features immediately when using Visual Studio 2010 without having to install any additional support. Microsoft currently supports these languages using DLR:

➤ IronPython

➤ IronRuby

➤ JavaScript (EcmaScript 3.0)

➤ Visual Basic

Silverlight also provides support for DLR and there's even a special SDK for Silverlight DLR. You can discover more about this SDK at `http://silverlight.net/learn/dynamic-languages/`. The relevance of Silverlight support for this book is that you can now use IronPython as part of your Silverlight solution as described in Chapter 11. You can summarize the benefits of using DLR as follows:

➤ Makes it easier to port dynamic languages to the .NET Framework

➤ Lets you include dynamic features in static languages

➤ Creates an environment where sharing of objects and libraries between languages is possible

➤ Makes it possible to perform fast dynamic dispatch and invocation of objects

This section provides a good overview of DLR. You'll discover additional details about DLR as the book progresses. However, if you'd like to delve into some of the architectural details of DLR, check out the article at http://msdn.microsoft.com/library/dd233052.aspx.

USING THE IRONPYTHON CONSOLE

The IronPython console is the best place to begin working with IronPython. You can enter a few statements, test them out, and then work out additional details without too many consequences. In addition, because the console is interactive, you obtain immediate feedback, so you don't have to wait for a compile cycle to discover that something you're doing is completely wrong. In fact, even after you've mastered IronPython, you'll find that you use the console to try things out. Because IronPython is a dynamic language, you can try things without worrying about damaging an application. You can test things quickly using the console and then include them in your application. The following sections describe the IronPython console and how to use it. Expect to see the IronPython console in future chapters.

Opening and Using the Default Console

The IronPython console is an application provided with the default installation. You access it using the Start ➪ Programs ➪ IronPython 2.6 ➪ IronPython Console command. The console, shown in Figure 1-3, looks something like a command prompt, but it isn't.

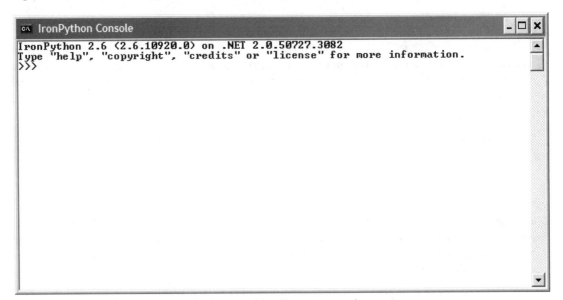

FIGURE 1-3: The IronPython console looks something like a command prompt.

Notice that the top of the window tells you which version of IronPython you're using and which version of the .NET Framework it's running on. This is important information because it helps you understand the IronPython environment and what limitations you have when working with IronPython. Below this first line, you'll see some commands that Microsoft thought you might find useful. The "Getting Help with Any Function" section of the chapter tells you more about the Help command.

To use the console, simply type the commands you want to issue. When you're done, IronPython will execute the commands and output any result you requested. A command need not be a function call or an object instantiation as it is in other languages. For example, type 2 + 2 right now and then press Enter. You'll see the result of this simple command, as shown in Figure 1-4.

```
IronPython Console                                              _ □ ✕
IronPython 2.6 (2.6.10920.0) on .NET 2.0.50727.3603
Type "help", "copyright", "credits" or "license" for more information.
>>> 2 + 2
4
>>>
```

FIGURE 1-4: IronPython is dynamic and the console is interactive.

Whenever you want to end a particular task, such as working with Help, press Enter a second time. The console will take you to the previous level of interaction.

Getting Help with Any Function

You can get help with any function in the console. If you simply type help and press Enter in the console, IronPython tells you how to request interactive help or help about a specific object. To begin interactive help, type help() and press Enter. You'll see the interactive help display shown in Figure 1-5.

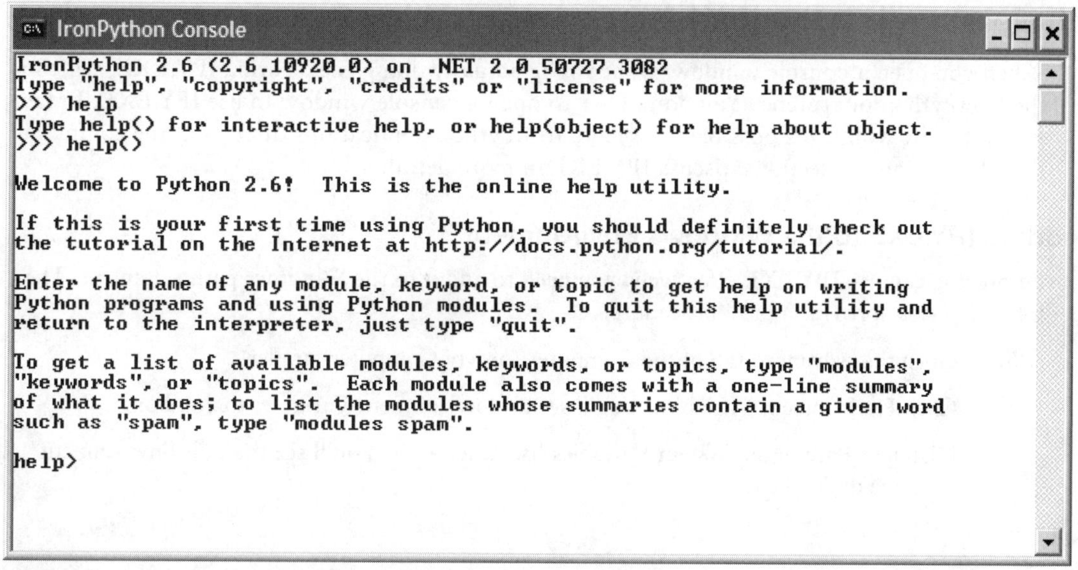

```
IronPython Console                                              _ □ ✕
IronPython 2.6 (2.6.10920.0) on .NET 2.0.50727.3082
Type "help", "copyright", "credits" or "license" for more information.
>>> help
Type help() for interactive help, or help(object) for help about object.
>>> help()

Welcome to Python 2.6!  This is the online help utility.

If this is your first time using Python, you should definitely check out
the tutorial on the Internet at http://docs.python.org/tutorial/.

Enter the name of any module, keyword, or topic to get help on writing
Python programs and using Python modules.  To quit this help utility and
return to the interpreter, just type "quit".

To get a list of available modules, keywords, or topics, type "modules",
"keywords", or "topics".  Each module also comes with a one-line summary
of what it does; to list the modules whose summaries contain a given word
such as "spam", type "modules spam".

help>
```

FIGURE 1-5: Interactive help lets you ask questions about IronPython.

Let's say you have no idea of what you want to find. Console help provides you with a list of words you can type to get general help. These terms are:

➤ Modules

➤ Keywords

➤ Topics

Type any of these terms and press Enter. You'll see a list of additional words you can type, as shown in Figure 1-6 for modules. Using this technique, you can drill down into help and locate anything you want. In fact, it's a good idea to spend some time in help just to see what's available. Even advanced developers can benefit from this approach — I personally follow this approach when I have time to increase my level of knowledge about all of the languages I use.

> *IronPython will constantly refer you to the online help for Python. So you might as well check it out now. You'll find a good Python tutorial at* http://docs.python.org/tutorial/. *While you're at it, there's also a good IronPython-specific tutorial that comes with your installation. Simply choose Start ➪ Programs ➪ IronPython 2.6 ➪ IronPython Tutorial. Although these sources of help are useful, you'll get a much better start working through the examples in the book.*

You might know about the topic you want to find. For example, you might know that you want to print something to screen, but you don't quite know how to use print. In this case, type `help('print')` and press Enter. Figure 1-7 shows the results. You see complete documentation about the `print` keyword.

Understanding the IPY.EXE Command Line Syntax

When you open a console window, what you're actually doing is executing IPY.EXE, which is the IronPython interpreter. You don't have to open a console window to use IPY.EXE. In fact, you normally won't. It's possible to execute IronPython applications directly at the command line. The following sections discuss IPY.EXE in more detail.

Adding IPY.EXE to the Windows Environment

Before you can use IPY.EXE effectively, you need to add it to the Windows path statement. The following steps provide a brief procedure.

1. Open the Advanced tab of the Computer (or My Computer) applet.

2. Click Environment Variables. You'll see an Environment Variables dialog box.

3. Highlight Path in the System Variables list. Click Edit. You'll see the Edit Environment Variable dialog box.

```
IronPython Console                                                    _ □ ×

help> modules

Please wait a moment while I gather a list of all available modules...

BaseHTTPServer        chunk              keyword            select
Bastion               clr                lib2to3            sets
CGIHTTPServer         cmath              linecache          sgmllib
ConfigParser          cmd                locale             sha
Cookie                code               logging            shelve
DocXMLRPCServer       codecs             macpath            shlex
HTMLParser            codeop             macurl2path        shutil
MimeWriter            collections        mailbox            site
Queue                 colorsys           mailcap            smtpd
SimpleHTTPServer      commands           markupbase         smtplib
SimpleXMLRPCServer    compileall         marshal            sndhdr
SocketServer          contextlib         math               socket
StringIO              cookielib          md5                sre_compile
UserDict              copy               mhlib              sre_constants
UserList              copy_reg           mimetools          sre_parse
UserString            ctypes             mimetypes          stat
_LWPCookieJar         datetime           minify             statvfs
_MozillaCookieJar     decimal            modulefinder       string
__builtin__           difflib            multifile          stringold
__future__            dircache           mutex              struct
_abcoll               dis                netrc              sunau
_bytesio              distutils          new                sunaudio
_codecs               doctest            nntplib            symbol
_collections          dumbdbm            nt                 sys
_ctypes               dummy_thread       ntpath             tabnanny
_ctypes_test          dummy_threading    nturl2path         tarfile
_fileio               email              numbers            telnetlib
_functools            encodings          opcode             tempfile
_heapq                errno              operator           textwrap
_locale               exceptions         optparse           this
_md5                  filecmp            os                 thread
_random               fileinput          os2emxpath         threading
_sha                  fnmatch            pdb                time
_sha256               formatter          pickle             timeit
_sha512               fpformat           pickletools        toaiff
_sre                  fractions          pipes              token
_strptime             ftplib             pkgutil            tokenize
_struct               functools          platform           trace
_threading_local      future_builtins    plistlib           traceback
_warnings             gc                 popen2             types
_weakref              genericpath        poplib             unittest
_winreg               getopt             posixfile          urllib
abc                   getpass            posixpath          urllib2
aifc                  gettext            pprint             urlparse
anydbm                glob               profile            user
array                 hashlib            pstats             uu
asynchat              heapq              py_compile         uuid
asyncore              hmac               pyclbr             warnings
atexit                htmlentitydefs     pydoc              wave
audiodev              htmllib            pydoc_topics       weakref
base64                httplib            quopri             whichdb
bdb                   idlelib            random             wsgiref
binascii              ihooks             re                 xdrlib
binhex                imaplib            repr               xml
bisect                imghdr             rexec              xmllib
cPickle               imp                rfc822             xmlrpclib
cStringIO             imputil            rlcompleter        xxsubtype
calendar              inspect            robotparser        zipfile
cgi                   io                 runpy
cgitb                 itertools          sched

Enter any module name to get more help.  Or, type "modules spam" to search
for modules whose descriptions contain the word "spam".

help> _
```

FIGURE 1-6: Drill down into help to find topics of interest.

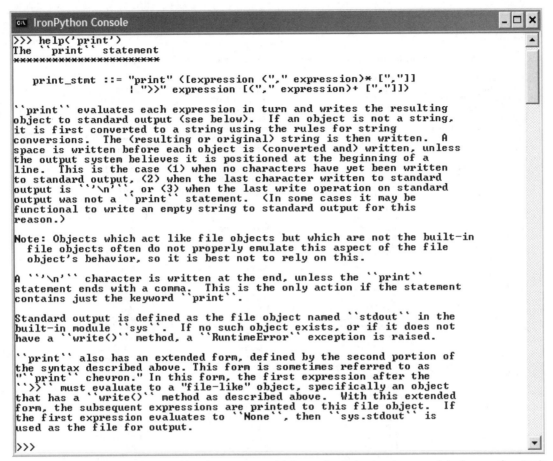

```
IronPython Console                                              _ □ ✕
>>> help('print')
The ``print`` statement
*************************

    print_stmt ::= "print" ([expression ("," expression)* [","]]
                  | ">>" expression [("," expression)+ [","]])

``print`` evaluates each expression in turn and writes the resulting
object to standard output (see below).  If an object is not a string,
it is first converted to a string using the rules for string
conversions.  The (resulting or original) string is then written.  A
space is written before each object is (converted and) written, unless
the output system believes it is positioned at the beginning of a
line.  This is the case (1) when no characters have yet been written
to standard output, (2) when the last character written to standard
output is ``'\n'``, or (3) when the last write operation on standard
output was not a ``print`` statement.  (In some cases it may be
functional to write an empty string to standard output for this
reason.)

Note: Objects which act like file objects but which are not the built-in
  file objects often do not properly emulate this aspect of the file
  object's behavior, so it is best not to rely on this.

A ``'\n'`` character is written at the end, unless the ``print``
statement ends with a comma.  This is the only action if the statement
contains just the keyword ``print``.

Standard output is defined as the file object named ``stdout`` in the
built-in module ``sys``.  If no such object exists, or if it does not
have a ``write()`` method, a ``RuntimeError`` exception is raised.

``print`` also has an extended form, defined by the second portion of
the syntax described above. This form is sometimes referred to as
``print`` chevron." In this form, the first expression after the
``>>`` must evaluate to a "file-like" object, specifically an object
that has a ``write()`` method as described above.  With this extended
form, the subsequent expressions are printed to this file object.  If
the first expression evaluates to ``None``, then ``sys.stdout`` is
used as the file for output.

>>>
```

FIGURE 1-7: The console also provides the means to obtain precise help about any module, keyword, or topic.

4. Select the end of the string that appears in the Variable Value field. Type `;C:\Program Files\IronPython 2.6` and click OK. Make sure you modify this path to match your IronPython configuration.

5. Click OK three times to close the Edit System Variable, Environment Variables, and System Properties dialog boxes. When you open a command prompt, you'll be able to access the IronPython executables.

Executing an Application from the Command Prompt

Normally, you execute an application by typing IPY <Python Filename> and pressing Enter. Give it a try now. Open a command prompt, type CD `\Program Files\IronPython 2.6\Tutorial`, and press Enter. You're in the sample files supplied by IronPython. Type `IPY WFDemo.py` and press Enter. You'll see a window displayed. When you click your mouse in the window, you see the word Hello displayed at each click point, as shown in Figure 1-8. If you look at the command prompt window at this point, you'll see that the mouse cursor is blinking but you can't type anything because the command prompt is waiting for the IronPython interpreter to end. When you click the Close button, the application ends and you can again type something at the command prompt.

Understanding the IPY.EXE Standard Command Line Switches

Sometimes you need to provide IPY.EXE with more information about a particular application. In this case, you can use one of the command line switches shown in the following list to provide IPY.EXE with the required information. It's important to note that the command line switches are case sensitive; -v isn't the same as -V.

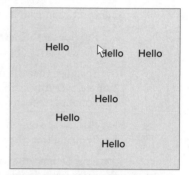

FIGURE 1-8: The WFDemo shows that you can create windowed environments for IronPython applications.

-3: Forces the interpreter to warn about Python 3 compatibility issues in your application.

-c *cmd*: Specifies a command you want to execute. This command line switch must appear last on the line because anything after this command line switch is interpreted as a command you want to execute. For example, if you type ipy -c "print ('Hello')", the interpreter will output the word Hello.

-D: Enables application debugging.

-E: Ignores any environment variables that you specified as part of the Windows environment variable setup or on the command line after you started it. Some applications may not run after you use this command line switch because they won't be able to find modules and other files they need.

-h: Displays a complete list of the command line arguments.

-i: Displays the console after running the script. You can then inspect the results of the script using console commands.

-m *module*: Runs library module as a script.

-O: Tells the interpreter to generate optimized code, which means you can't perform debugging, but the application will run faster.

-OO: Removes all of the doc strings and applies -O optimizations so that the application runs even faster than using the -O command line switch alone.

-Q *arg*: Specifies use of one of several division options. You can use any of these values.

➤   **-Qold** (default): The precision of the output depends on the operators used. For example, if you divide two integers, you get an integer as output.

➤   **-Qwarn:** Outputs warnings about a loss of precision when performing division using integers.

➤   **-Qwarnall:** Outputs warnings about all uses of the classic division operator.

➤   **-Qnew:** The output is always a precise floating point fraction.

-s: Specifies that the interpreter shouldn't add the user site directory to `sys.path`.

-S: Specifies that the interpreter shouldn't imply that it should execute the `import site` command on initialization.

-t: Outputs warnings about inconsistent tab usage, which can lead to code interpretation problems.

-tt: Outputs errors for inconsistent tab usage. Inconsistent tab usage can lead to code interpretation problems, which can result in hard-to-locate bugs.

-u: Provides unbuffered stdout and stderr devices. Typically, the interpreter uses buffering to provide better application performance.

-v: Specifies that the interpreter should provide verbose output, which means that you can see everything going on in the background. You can also obtain this result by using `PYTHONVERBOSE=x` (where x is a True or False environment variable).

-V: Prints the version number and exits. This option is useful when you want to be sure you're using the correct version of IronPython for your application.

-W *arg*: Defines the kind of warning control. Specifying these command line switches tells the interpreter to add the specified warning messages to the output. (Don't worry too much about these warnings — you learn more about them in Chapter 12.) You can use any of these values:

> ➤ **-W*action*:** Actions are one of the following strings: `error` (turns matching warnings into exceptions), `ignore` (never prints matching warnings), `always` (always prints matching warnings), `default` (prints the first occurrence of a warning for each location where the interpreter issues the warning), `module` (prints the first occurrence of a warning for each module where the error occurs), and `once` (prints only the first occurrence of a warning no matter where it appears).

> ➤ **-W*message*:** Messages are Regular Expressions that define which warning messages to match.

> ➤ **-W*category*:** Categories specify the class of the warning message.

> ➤ **-W*module*:** Modules are Regular Expressions that define which module to match.

> ➤ **-W*lineno*:** Line numbers are integer values that specify a line number to match. Using 0 matches all line numbers.

-x: Skips the first line of the source code, which may have special instructions that you don't need for the current session.

 IronPython doesn't support all of the CPython command line switches. Consequently, you may find that a batch file written to execute a CPython application won't work properly with IronPython. For example, IronPython doesn't appear to support the PYTHONHOME environment variable. All IronPython environment variables begin with IRON, so you need to modify batch files to include this first word as part of any environmental variable setup.

Working with the −X: Command Line Switches

In addition to the standard command line switches, you also have access to the −X: command line switches, which configure the IronPython interpreter. The following list describes each of the configuration options:

−X:AutoIndent: Enables auto-indenting in the read-evaluation-print loop (REPL).

−X:ColorfulConsole: Enables ColorfulConsole support.

−X:Debug: Enables application debugging. This option is preferred over the −D command line switch because it's newer and will enjoy a longer support period.

−X:EnableProfiler: Enables profiling support in the compiler, which helps you optimize your applications.

−X:ExceptionDetail: Enables ExceptionDetail mode, which gives you more information about every exception that occurs, making it easier to locate the source of the problem (but filling the screen much faster as well).

−X:Frames: Enables basic `sys._getframe()` support.

−X:FullFrames: Enables `sys._getframe()` with access to local objects and variables.

−X:GCStress: Specifies the garbage collector (GC) stress level. Stressing the GC can point out potential resource problems in your application.

−X:LightweightScopes: Generates optimized scopes that are easier for the GC to collect. Optimizing GC functionality tends to improve the overall performance (both speed and reliability) of your application.

−X:MaxRecursion: Determines the maximum recursion level within the application. Recursion can use a lot of system resources, so controlling the amount of recursion tends to reduce resource usage by applications that rely on recursion. Of course, reducing the recursion levels can also cause application exceptions.

−X:MTA: Runs the application in a multithreaded apartment (MTA).

−X:NoAdaptiveCompilation: Disables the adaptive compilation feature.

−X:PassExceptions: Tells the interpreter not to catch exceptions that are unhandled by script code.

−X:PrivateBinding: Enables binding to private members.

−X:Python30: Enables available Python 3.0 features, such as classic division (where dividing two integers produces an integer result).

−X:ShowClrExceptions: Displays the Common Language Specification (CLS) exception information.

−X:TabCompletion: Enables TabCompletion mode.

−X:Tracing: Enables support for tracing all methods even before the code calls `sys.settrace()`.

Modifying the IPY.EXE Environment Variables

IPY also supports a number of environment variables. The following list describes each of these environment variables.

IRONPYTHONPATH: Specifies the path to search for modules used within an application

IRONPYTHONSTARTUP: Specifies the name and location of the startup module

Exiting the IronPython Interpreter

Eventually, you'll want to leave the console. In order to end your session, simply type exit() and press Enter. As an alternative, you can always press Ctrl+Z and then Enter. The console will close.

USING THE IRONPYTHON WINDOWED ENVIRONMENT

IronPython also provides access to a windowed environment, but you can't access it from the start menu. Instead, you must provide a shortcut to the file you want to run or open a command prompt and start the application manually. The windowed environment simply provides a GUI interface for working with IronPython, but doesn't do anything else for you. You start the windowed environment by using IPYW .EXE. If you type IPYW and press Enter, you see the command line switch help shown in Figure 1-9.

As you can see from Figure 1-9, the windowed environment supports the same command line switches as the character mode command line version. However, you can't use the windowed environment to run the interpreted console environment, which is a shame because many developers would prefer working in the nicer environment. To see that the windowed environment works the same way as the standard console, type IPYW WFDemo.py and press Enter. You'll see the test application shown earlier in Figure 1-8.

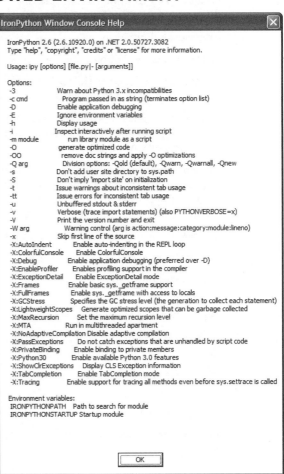

FIGURE 1-9: The windowed version supports the same features as the command line version.

CREATING YOUR FIRST APPLICATION

After all this time, you might have started wondering whether you would get to write any code at all in this chapter. The first application won't be very fancy, but it'll be more than a simple Hello World kind of application. You can use any editor that outputs pure text in this section. Notepad will work just fine. Listing 1-1 shows the code you should type in your editor.

LISTING 1-1: A simple first application that multiplies two numbers

```
def mult(a, b):
     return a * b

print('5 * 10 ='),
print(mult(5, 10))
```

Just five lines, including the blank line between the function and the main code, are all you need for this example. Functions begin with the `def` keyword. You then give the function a name, `mult` in this case, followed by a list of arguments (if any) — a and b for this example.

> *Don't worry too much about the details of the IronPython language just yet. Part II of the book provides you with a good overview of all the language details. As the book progresses, you'll be exposed to additional language details. By the time you reach the end of the book, you'll be working with some relatively complex examples.*

The content of the function is indented with a tab. In this case, the function simply returns the value of multiplying a by b. Except for the indentation requirement, this could easily be a function written in any other language.

The main code section comes next. In this case, the code begins by printing 5 * 10 =. Notice that you enclose the string values in single quotes. The function call ends with an odd-looking comma. This comma tells the interpreter not to add a /n (newline) character after the `print()` call.

At this point, the code calls `print()` a second time, but it calls `mult()` instead of writing text directly. The output of `mult()` is an integer, which IronPython automatically converts to a string for you and then prints out. You'll find that IronPython does a lot of work for you in the background — dynamically (as explained earlier in the chapter).

Save the code you've typed into Notepad as `MyFirst.py`. Make sure you choose All Files in the Save As Type field so that Notepad doesn't add a .txt extension to the output. To execute this example, type `IPY MyFirst.py` at the command line and press Enter. Figure 1-10 shows the output from this quick example.

FIGURE 1-10: The output of the example is a simple equation.

USING IRONPYTHON CONSTRUCTIVELY

This chapter has introduced you to IronPython. You should have a good understanding of why you want to use IronPython and how it differs from other, static .NET languages. Dynamic languages have a special place in your toolbox. They aren't the answer to every need, but they can address specific needs — just as other languages address the needs for which they were built. At the end of the day, the computer doesn't care what language you use — the computer simply cares how that language is translated into the bits and bytes it requires to do something useful. Languages address human needs and it's important to keep that in mind.

Before you do anything else, make sure you get IronPython installed on your system and test the installation out using the examples in this chapter. If you're getting some weird result or nothing at all, you might have a bad installation. Once you know that you do have a good installation, try playing around with the example application in the "Creating Your First Application" section of the chapter. Work with this application as a means of working with the tools discussed in the "Using the IronPython Console" and "Using the IronPython Windowed Environment" sections of the chapter.

At this point, you really don't know too much about the Python language or the IronPython implementation of that language. However, you probably do know something about other .NET languages, and that's a good starting point. Chapter 2 builds on the information you've learned in this chapter and also builds on your personal knowledge of the .NET Framework. In Chapter 2, you begin building knowledge about IronPython so you can see what an interesting language it is and so you can also begin to understand the example in the "Creating Your First Application" section of the chapter. When you get done with Chapter 2, you may want to take another look at the sample application — you'll be surprised to discover that you really do know how the example works.

2

Understanding the IronPython Basics

WHAT'S IN THIS CHAPTER?

➤ Creating your IronPython applications using Visual Studio

➤ Using capitalization and indentation properly

➤ Working with various types of data

➤ Working with the IronPython modules

➤ Using functions in IronPython

➤ Configuring the IronPython environment for maximum productivity

No matter what language you want to learn, you always start with the basics. However, you don't always start with the very basics. Once you know what a loop looks like in one language, you can usually recognize it in other languages as well. That's how this chapter begins the process of working with IronPython. This isn't a comprehensive guide for the rank novice, but rather the kind of guide that someone who has used a .NET language before will appreciate.

Of course, professionals like professional tools. This chapter shows how to forgo the Notepad programming experience to work with Visual Studio to create IronPython applications. You might have already noticed that installing IronPython didn't add any new templates to the New Project dialog box — there isn't any IronPython folder for you to look in.

IronPython is different from most .NET languages in that indentation is an important part of the application code. If you don't indent your code properly, the IronPython interpreter will complain, loudly. As with many programming languages, capitalization is also important when working with IronPython — a variable named MyVariable is completely different from one named myVariable. Of course, you'll also want to know about IronPython data types. You won't find many surprises here, but it's important to review them anyway.

One of the more important features of IronPython is its ability to use external modules. This feature isn't all that different from any .NET language because you're always using code found in other modules. However, you need to know the IronPython method of working with modules because it does differ from what you've done with other .NET languages.

Functions are the basis for modularization in IronPython applications. Yes, you have access to other modularization techniques, too, but for the simple applications that you'll see in these beginning chapters, the function works fine. The IronPython function looks a bit different from functions you create in other languages. In fact, you already saw this difference in the simple example found in Chapter 1.

Finally, this chapter exposes you to the IronPython environment. Normally, the programming language environment is hidden away in configuration files when working with .NET — not so with IronPython. You see the environment up close and personal. You'll also find that you change the environment more often than you do with other languages, so knowing how to change it is important.

All the Visual Studio examples in this book rely on Visual Studio Team System 2010. If you use a different Visual Studio version, the steps may not match precisely and your screenshot will differ slightly. The procedures and techniques will still work, but you may need to modify them slightly for your setup. For example, some versions of Visual Studio have a File ⇨ New Project command (two steps) — Visual Studio Team System 2010 uses a three-step command, File ⇨ New ⇨ Project. The difference is small and easily changed, but you need to be aware of the difference as you work through the book.

USING VISUAL STUDIO TO CREATE IRONPYTHON APPLICATIONS

You might have looked at the New Project dialog box after you installed IronPython, assuming that you'd find a series of new project templates. Unfortunately, you won't find any new templates for IronPython. The current version of the product doesn't include anything you can use directly. Fortunately, you can still create a project for IronPython projects and use Visual Studio to edit and debug it. The following sections take you through a simple configuration scenario and then show the resulting project in action.

Creating the Project

Before you do anything else, you must create a project to hold your IronPython application. The following steps show you how to perform this task.

1.   Open Visual Studio, but don't open any project or template files.

2.   Choose File ⇨ Open ⇨ Project/Solution. You'll see the Open Project dialog box shown in Figure 2-1.

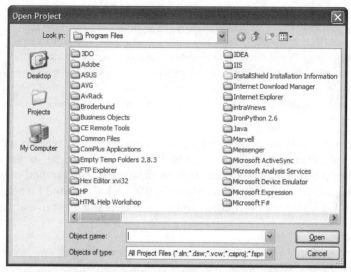

FIGURE 2-1: Use the Open Project dialog box to start the project.

3. Locate and highlight IPY.EXE (normally found in the \Program Files\IronPython 2.6 folder). Click Open. Visual Studio creates a solution based on IPY.EXE, as shown in Figure 2-2. You must still configure this solution.

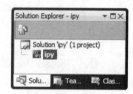

FIGURE 2-2: IPY.EXE becomes the focal point for a new solution.

4. Right-click IPY in Solution Explorer and choose Properties from the context menu. You'll see the General tab of the Properties page shown in Figure 2-3. (Your display may differ slightly from the one shown in Figure 2-3 based on your machine configuration and the Visual Studio 2010 edition you use.) At a minimum, you must change the Arguments and Working Directory fields to match your project.

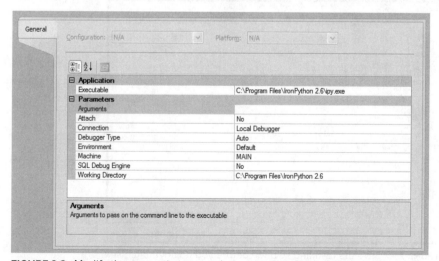

FIGURE 2-3: Modify the properties to match your project requirements.

Command line switches are case sensitive. Using the wrong case can result in unexpected behavior. For example, if you use the -s command line switch in place of the -S command line switch, you'll obtain an unexpected result from the IronPython interpreter. In this case, the interpreter won't add the user site directory to sys.path.

5. Select the Arguments field. Type **-D** *NameOfProject*, where *NameOfProject* is a Python (.py) file. For example, the example project uses MyFirst.py, so you'd type **-D MyFirst.py**. Remember that the -D command line switch turns on debugging. You can find other command line arguments listed in the "Understanding the IPY.EXE Command Line Syntax" section of Chapter 1. Include any other command line switches you want to use in the Arguments field.

 The .py file extension is case sensitive. You must use lowercase for the file extension. For example, IronPython will import a module named MyStuff.py, but it won't import a module named MyStuff.PY. Extensions aren't normally case sensitive, so this IronPython oddity could cause difficult-to-find errors.

6. Select the Working Directory field. Visual Studio will default to using the \Program Files\ IronPython 2.6 directory — a directory that you're unlikely to use to hold your source code files. Change the Working Directory to match your source code directory. Click the ellipses to locate the directory on your hard drive using the Browse for Folder dialog box.

7. Choose File ➪ Save All. You'll see the Save File As dialog box shown in Figure 2-4.

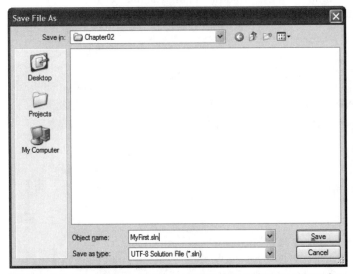

FIGURE 2-4: Save the resulting solution before you do anything else.

8. Locate the folder you want to use to save the project in the Save In field.

9. Type a name for the solution in the Object Name field. Click Save. Visual Studio will save the project to the folder you selected.

Adding Existing Files to the Project

At this point, you have a project without any files in it. Yes, you could run the project and you'd see what you'd expect, but you can't debug the IronPython file or edit it. The following steps tell how to add a file to your project.

1. Right-click the solution entry in Solution Explorer (not the IPY project entry) and choose Add ➪ Exiting Item from the context menu. You'll see the Add Exiting Item dialog box shown in Figure 2-5.

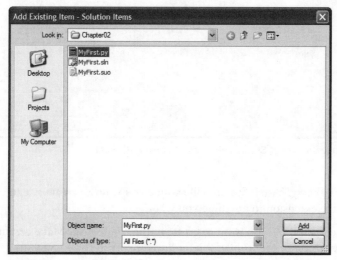

FIGURE 2-5: Add your existing Python files to the project.

FIGURE 2-6: The Solution Items folder holds the Python files you add.

2. Locate the existing file you want to use and click Open. Visual Studio adds a Solution Items folder to Solution Explorer and places the file you selected in the Solution Items folder, as shown in Figure 2-6. In addition, Visual Studio automatically opens the file for you.

Adding New Files to the Project

Once you get used to working with Visual Studio, you may decide to create files from scratch using the Visual Studio IDE. In this case, you need to add blank (new) files to the project. The following steps show you how to perform this task.

1. Right-click the solution entry in Solution Explorer and choose Add ➪ New Item from the context menu. You'll see the Add New Item dialog box shown in Figure 2-7.

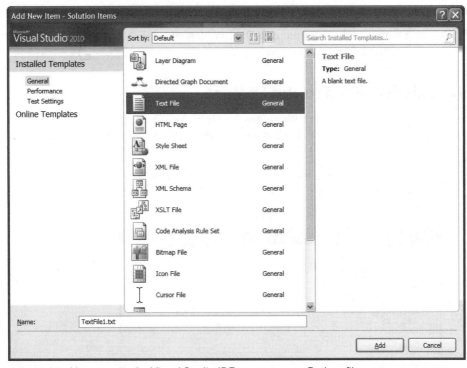

FIGURE 2-7: You can use the Visual Studio IDE to create new Python files.

2. Highlight the Text File entry. Visual Studio will assume you want to create a text (.TXT) file, but you can change the extension to anything you want.

3. Type the name of the Python file you want to create in the Name field. Make certain that your file has a .py extension or the IronPython interpreter may not work with it.

4. Click Add. Visual Studio adds the file to Solution Explorer (similar to the addition shown in Figure 2-6) and automatically opens the file for editing.

IronPython Project Limitations

The project you create using this technique has some serious limitations. Here's a partial list of the things that you won't see in your IronPython project that you'll normally see in other Visual Studio projects.

➤ Color support for keywords or other special text

➤ IntelliSense

➤ New Items dialog support

➤ Immediate window (debugging)

➤ Command window (when working with variables during debugging)

Debugging the Project

After you write your code, you can use the Visual Studio debugger to debug the project. This chapter provides a brief overview of debugging. Chapter 12 discusses debugging in detail. All you really need to worry about now is understanding how the debugger works so that you can use it to trace through sample programs in this and other chapters in the book.

This section assumes you're using the MyFirst.py example found in Chapter 1 and that you've created a project for it. Start by placing a breakpoint on the first line of the application (print('5 * 10 ='),); then place a second breakpoint at the beginning of the function (def mult(a, b):). You can do this by placing your cursor on the line and pressing F9 or choosing Debug ⇨ Toggle Breakpoint. You should see the breakpoint shown in Figure 2-8.

FIGURE 2-8: Visual Studio helps you debug your IronPython applications.

At this point, you can begin debugging your application. The following steps get you started.

1. Press F5 or click Start Debugging to begin debugging your application. Starting the debug process can take a while because Visual Studio has to start a copy of the IronPython interpreter. Visual Studio stops at the function definition. IronPython makes a list of function definitions when it starts the application.

2. Click Step Over. You'll move to the first line of the application. At this point, the debugger begins executing your application code.

3. Click Step Over again. If you look at the command prompt at this point, you'll see that it contains the expected output text, but not the answer, as shown in Figure 2-9. Now, if you clicked Step Over again, you'd see the output from the Mult() function, but you wouldn't actually see the code in Mult() execute. The next step shows how to get inside a function so you can see how it works.

FIGURE 2-9: The console screen will show the results of tasks performed in your application code.

4. Press F5 or click Start Debugging. The application will stop within Mult(). Being able to stop within a function is the reason for setting the second breakpoint at the beginning of this procedure. Now you can use Step Over to execute the lines of code one at a time. Notice the Debug History window. You can select entries in this window to see what the IronPython interpreter has been doing in the background, as shown in Figure 2-10.

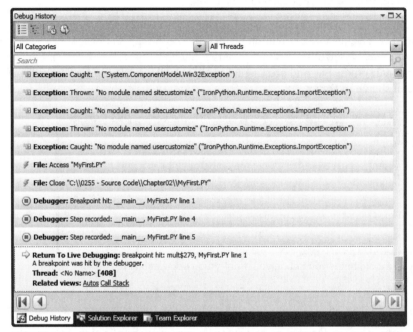

FIGURE 2-10: Use the Debug History window to see what the interpreter is doing in the background.

5. Press F5 or click Start Debugging. The application will end.

Visual Studio does provide you with access to many standard debugging features. For example, you can place variables in the Watch windows and see their values as shown in Figure 2-11. You also have access to the Call Stack and Output windows. The Immediate and Command windows don't work as you might expect them to, so you need to inspect variables and perform other variable-related tasks using the Watch windows.

Name	Value	Type
a	5	object {int}
b	10	object {int}

Watch 2

FIGURE 2-11: The Watch windows provide access to variable information.

UNDERSTANDING THE USE OF INDENTATION AND CAPITALIZATION IN IRONPYTHON

Most application programming languages have rules that help the compiler or interpreter understand what you mean. For example, when working with C, C++, Java, C#, and a number of other languages, you use opening and closing braces to indicate the code that belongs within a structure such as a function or loop. Without these opening and closing braces, the compiler or interpreter for the target language would never be able to understand what you mean — these braces add structure to your application code. Likewise, IronPython relies on rules, indentation and capitalization, to help the interpreter understand your code.

The interpreter does help you with the indentation. The amount you indent a line doesn't seem to matter. Using tabs instead of spaces doesn't seem to matter either, but using tabs will ensure that you don't run into problems seeing the indentation in code properly. Open a copy of IPY to follow along with the discussion in this section. Try the following steps and you'll discover how the interpreter helps you discover when to indent.

1. Type `SomeText = 'Hello'` and press Enter. You'll see that the interpreter adds three greater-than signs (>>>). The >>> is a primary prompt and tells you that you don't need to add any indentation.

2. Type `if SomeText == 'Hello':` and press Enter. Now you'll see that the interpreter adds three dots (. . .) to the next line. The . . . is the secondary prompt. It tells you that you've entered a structure.

3. Type `print SomeText` and press Enter. The interpreter displays an error message like the one shown in Figure 2-12. The interpreter expected an indented block, but you didn't provide any indentation, so the block failed.

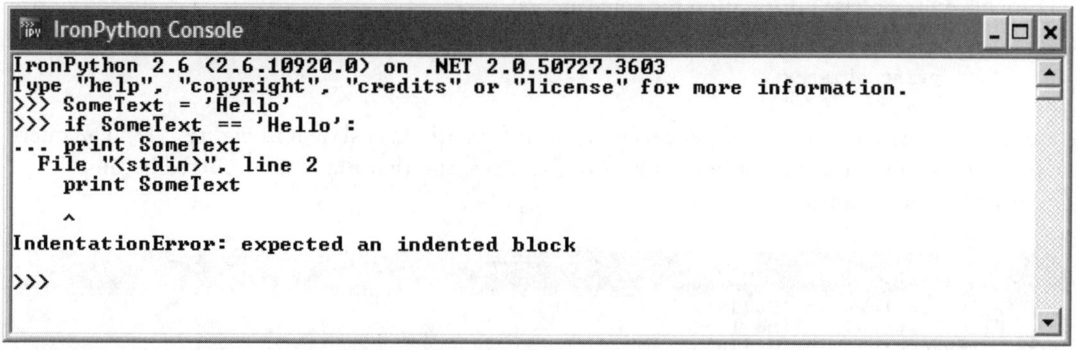

```
IPY  IronPython Console                                           _ □ ×
IronPython 2.6 (2.6.10920.0) on .NET 2.0.50727.3603
Type "help", "copyright", "credits" or "license" for more information.
>>> SomeText = 'Hello'
>>> if SomeText == 'Hello':
... print SomeText
  File "<stdin>", line 2
    print SomeText

    ^
IndentationError: expected an indented block
>>>
```

FIGURE 2-12: Not indenting at a secondary prompt produces an error.

4. Repeat Step 2 again. Press Tab. Type `print SomeText` and press Enter. This time, the entry succeeds, as shown in Figure 2-13. Notice that the interpreter has displayed . . . again so that you can continue the block if desired. In fact, the block continues until you end it by not indenting an entry.

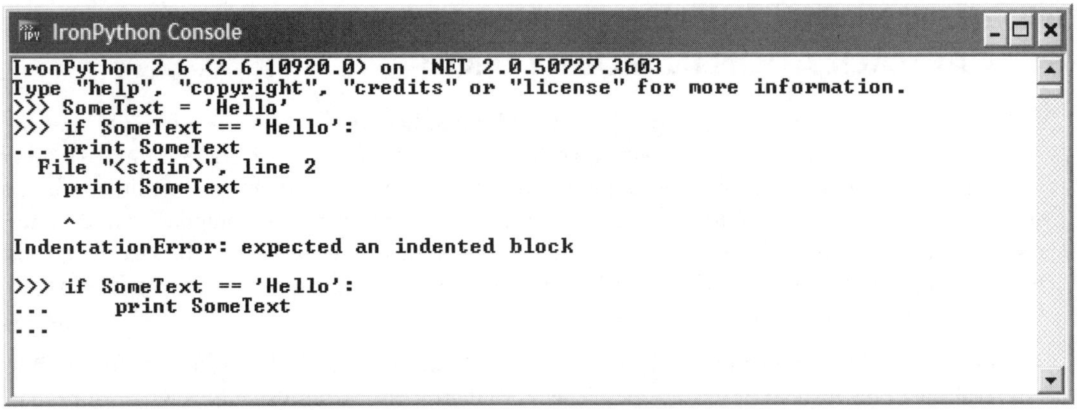

FIGURE 2-13: A properly indented entry succeeds.

5. Press Enter. The interpreter displays the word Hello. The interpreter will keep track of a block until you finish entering the last line of code. It then evaluates the block and performs all of the tasks it contains.

Now that you have the basic idea about indentation, it's time to consider capitalization. IronPython is case sensitive. So, if you type:

```
If SomeText == 'Hello':
```

and press Enter, the code will fail. Figure 2-14 shows that the error information you receive isn't straightforward. All that the interpreter tells you is that the token it received is unexpected (a *token* is a single word that the interpreter parses to discover what you want to do). The interpreter will provide more precise information for some errors. Type:

```
if SomeText == 'Hello':
    print sometext
```

and press Enter. This time you get precise error information, as shown in Figure 2-15. The interpreter tells you that the error lies in line 2 of the block and that the error occurred because SomeText isn't defined.

FIGURE 2-14: Some error messages are ambiguous.

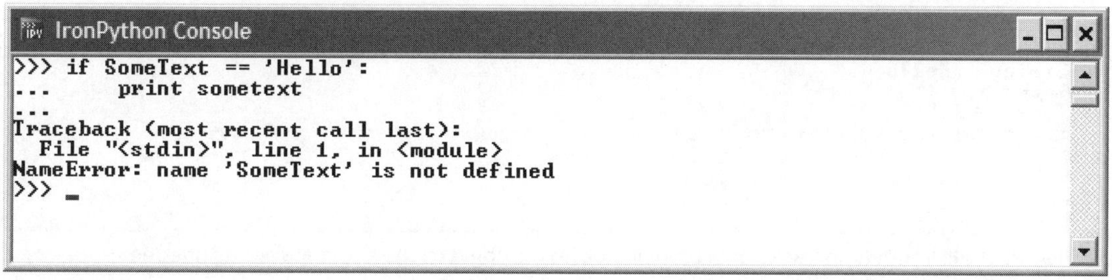

```
IronPython Console                                    _ □ ✕
>>> if SomeText == 'Hello':
...     print sometext
...
Traceback (most recent call last):
  File "<stdin>", line 1, in <module>
NameError: name 'SomeText' is not defined
>>> _
```

FIGURE 2-15: The interpreter can provide precise error information for certain classes of error.

The point of this exercise is that the interpreter will catch indentation and capitalization errors. In some cases, you might scratch your head for a while trying to figure out what went wrong, but the interpreter is accurate about locating such problems for you.

It doesn't matter whether you use tabs or spaces for indentation. Try the example out using spaces instead of a tab. You'll discover that it works just fine. However, using tabs provides uniform spacing that is easier to see when you're reading the code. If you're not careful, you might use one space in one location and four in the next, making it hard to tell when something really is indented.

CONSIDERING DATA TYPES IN IRONPYTHON

You might have noticed an appalling lack of data types in the example so far. When an application needs a string variable, it simply assigns the string to a variable without ever specifying a data type. Likewise, numbers are simply assigned to a variable; it doesn't apparently matter whether the number is an integer or a floating point value. IronPython seemingly doesn't care. For example, the code in Listing 2-1 works just fine.

Available for
download on
Wrox.com

LISTING 2-1: Working with variables of various types

```
String = "Hello"
Integer = 1
Float = 1.5

print "String =", String, "\nInteger =", Integer, "\nFloat =", Float
raw_input('Press any key to continue...')
```

This example shows that you can create a string, integer, or floating point value without actually declaring them. IronPython does track the data type, but it does so in the background, without your knowledge. When you try to print the values, IronPython automatically converts the values in the background for you to standard strings. Figure 2-16 shows the output of this example.

You may also notice that this example makes use of escape characters, the \n in this case. The \n simply tells IronPython to add a newline character to the output. In fact, if you've worked with C, C++, C#, or any of a number of languages that rely on escape codes, you'll find yourself right at home when working with IronPython. Table 2-1 shows the common escape codes that IronPython recognizes.

FIGURE 2-16: IronPython tracks data type and performs conversions automatically as needed.

TABLE 2-1: IronPython Common Escape Codes

ESCAPE CODE	MEANING	EXAMPLE
\'	Single quote (')	'\''
\"	Double quote (")	'\"'
\\	Backslash (\)	'\\'
\a	American Standard Code for Information Interchange (ASCII) Bell (BEL) — produces a beep	'\a'
\b	ASCII Backspace (BS)	'\b'
\f	ASCII Formfeed (FF)	'\f'
\n	ASCII Linefeed (LF)	'\n'
\ooo	Character with octal value ooo. You may provide up to three octal sequences, just as you would when working with C.	'\243' produces the pound monetary symbol
\r	ASCII Carriage Return (CR)	'\r'
\t	ASCII Horizontal Tab (TAB)	'\t'
\uxxxx	Character with 16-bit hexidecimal value xxxx. This escape sequence only works with Unicode characters. You can combine character sequences to obtain a particular complex character.	u'\u00F7' produces the division symbol
\Uxxxxxxxx	Character with 32-bit hex value xxxxxxxx. This escape sequence only works with Unicode characters. Characters outside the Basic Multilingual Plane (BMP) are encoded using a surrogate pair when you compile Python for 16-bit use.	u'\U000000BD' produces ½
\v	ASCII Vertical Tab (VT)	'\v'
\xhh	Character with hex value hh. You must provide precisely two values, as shown in the example.	'\xA2' produces the cent sign

The `raw_input()` function is also new. If you're working in Visual Studio, the console screen appears and disappears so quickly in many cases that you can't see the output of your code. Using the `raw_input()` function as shown simply adds a pause to your code. The string included with the function call provides a prompt. You'll discover more about input and output functionality as the book progresses. For right now, all you really need to know is that you can obtain a value from the console using `raw_input()`.

Don't get the idea that you won't have any access to native data types. It's possible to tell IronPython to react in a certain way to your data. For example, you can use the `str()` and `repr()` functions to interpret a string in multiple ways. In addition, you can specifically convert numbers to a specific type, as shown in Listing 2-2.

LISTING 2-2: Specifying data types

```
# Create a string variable.
String = 'Hello and Goodbye'

# Display using str() and repr()
print 'A string and its representation.'
print 'str()', str(String)
print 'repr()', repr(String)

# Create the numeric variable.
Number = 5.1

# Display the numeric types.
print '\nThe numeric data types.'
print 'int', int(Number)
print 'long', long(Number)
print 'float', float(Number)
print 'complex', complex(Number, 3.5)

# Pause the display
raw_input('Press any key...')
```

This example begins by showing you a comment. Yes, IronPython, like most computer languages, supports comments and you should use them often.

The first part of the code works with a string. When you use the `str()` function, you tell IronPython to take any data within the function, the expression, and convert it to a string. IronPython performs this task for you automatically, but you can use the `str()` function for explicit conversion. The output of the `str()` function is always in human-readable form. The `repr()` function returns a representation of the object you pass to it. In most cases, you use the `repr()` function to create output that the interpreter understands. Figure 2-17 shows the difference in output between the two functions. Notice that `repr()` outputs single quotes so you could pass this information directly to the interpreter.

The second part of the code works with a number. In this case, the number contains floating point data. However, you can convert it directly to an `int` or `long` using the `int()` or `long()` functions. The `float()` function will convert any numeric data into a floating point number and you can even create complex numbers using the `complex()` function. Figure 2-17 shows the output from the numeric conversions as well. IronPython also supports base conversions using the `oct()` and `hex()`

functions. In fact, you can see the entire list of built-in functions at http://docs.python.org/library/functions.html.

```
C:\Program Files\IronPython 2.6\ipy.exe                          _ □ x
A string and its representation.
str() Hello and Goodbye
repr() 'Hello and Goodbye'

The numeric data types.
int 5
long 5
float 5.1
complex (5.1+3.5j)
Press any key...
```

FIGURE 2-17: Use str() or repr() as appropriate to create output for your application.

You'll see a wealth of data types as the book progresses. For example, Chapter 4 discusses arrays and collections, Chapter 5 tells you all about objects, and Chapter 6 begins a discussion of working with the standard library. There are a number of online resources for working with data types as well. The two best sources — the ones used for this book — are at:

➤   http://www.python.org/doc/2.4.4/lib/types.html

➤   http://docs.python.org/library/datatypes.html

EXPLORING THE IRONPYTHON MODULES

In Chapter 1, you used the interpreter to work with IronPython. However, the moment you closed the interpreter, everything you did was gone. Working directly with the interpreter means that your work is temporary, which is fine when you want to experiment, but not a good idea when you want to write longer applications or save your work for posterity. Consequently, in this chapter, you've used Visual Studio to work with Python files that have a .py extension. These files are known as *modules*.

Just like any other programming language, you'll find it worthwhile to place some code in separate files. For example, you might create a math library that contains your favorite math functions. Rather than copy those functions everywhere, you place them in a separate module and then import that module as needed into an application. In order to make this setup work, you must know how to import modules and use them within the application. The following sections discuss modules and how you work with them in IronPython.

Considering Built-in and External Modules

IronPython uses the concept of built-in and external modules. A *built-in module* is one that you can access all the time from within the interpreter. For example, the str() function is part of a built-in module. All the code that the interpreter relies upon to perform basic tasks is part of a library of modules that comes with IronPython. In fact, you can see these modules in the \Program Files\ IronPython 2.6\Lib directory of your installation.

An *external module* is one that you must load separately in order to use. When you create a file of functions you want to use within your application, you must load that module and then provide access to it from within your application. The following sections discuss both built-in and external modules. However, you should consider these sections as an overview because you'll use modules throughout the book.

Working with the Built-in Modules

As previously mentioned, built-in modules are those that come with IronPython. There are actually two levels of built-in modules: those that are available immediately and those that you have to import first. This second group is part of IronPython, but you don't always need them, so the interpreter asks that you import them before using them. The following sections discuss both levels of built-in modules.

Considering the Immediately Available Modules

When you start the IronPython interpreter, you get a few functions immediately. These functions are internal to the interpreter itself. To see these functions, you use the `dir()` function. If you type `dir()` by itself, you see the top-level modules shown in Figure 2-18.

```
IronPython Console                                                 _ □ ×
IronPython 2.6 (2.6.10920.0) on .NET 2.0.50727.3603
Type "help", "copyright", "credits" or "license" for more information.
>>> dir()
['__builtins__', '__doc__', '__name__']
>>>
```

FIGURE 2-18: Use dir() to obtain a list of modules.

The three names, `__builtins__`, `__doc__`, and `__name__`, probably don't tell you very much. (Yes, those are double underscores before and after each module name.) However, all the functions you've used so far in the book appear in these three modules. Type `dir(__builtins__)` and press Enter. Suddenly, you begin seeing function names that you've used before, as shown in Figure 2-19. For example, you'll find the `dir()` function in the list, as well as `raw_input()`. These functions help you create basic applications without importing anything else.

It turns out that `dir()` is an exceptionally helpful function. For example, if you want to discover the methods and attributes that the `raw_input` object supports, then you type `dir(raw_input)`. Go ahead; give it a try right now. You'll find out that `raw_input()` supports additional features such as `__format__` that we'll use later in the book.

You may have noticed that the `__doc__` attribute keeps popping up in the lists that you display. The `__doc__` attribute is also exceptionally important because it provides usage information about the object or function in question. For example, you might want to find out more about `raw_input.__format__()`, so you'd type `print raw_input.__format__.__doc__` and press Enter — the interpreter would display the help information shown in Figure 2-20. In this case, you see that `__format__()` requires an object that requires formatting and a string that tells how to format it.

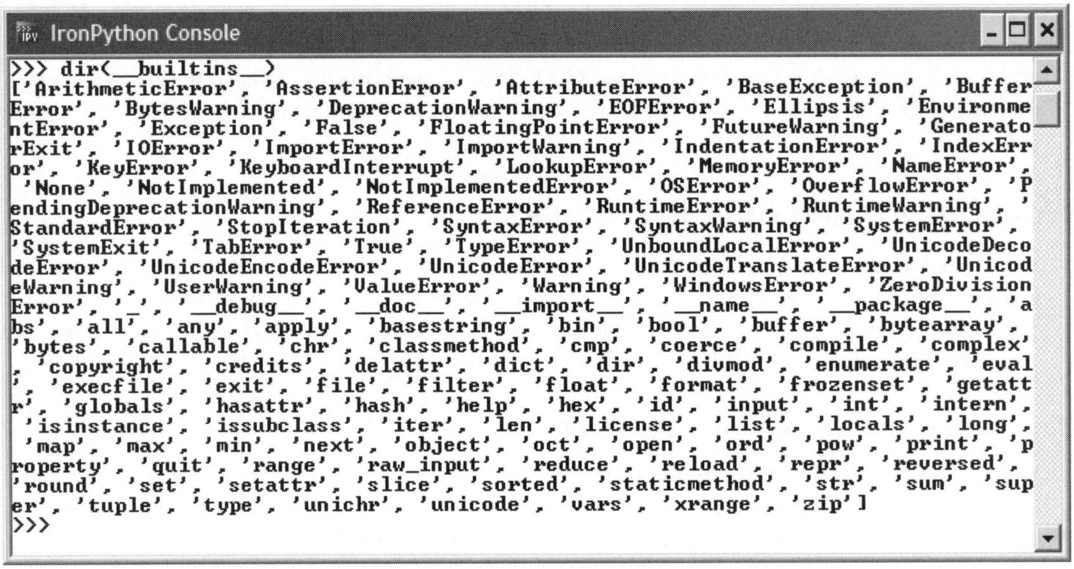

FIGURE 2-19: The __built-ins__ module contains a lot of functions you've already seen.

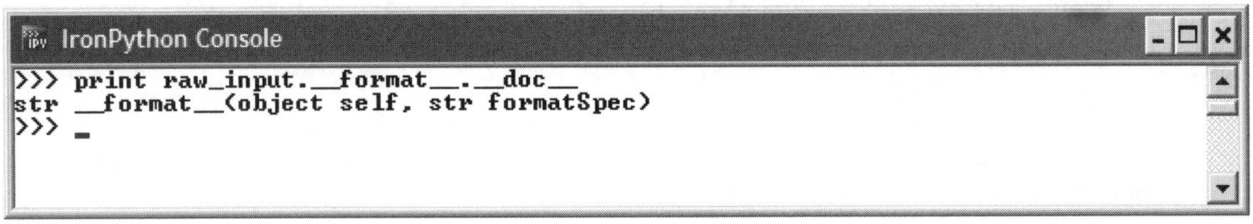

FIGURE 2-20: The __doc__ attribute tells you about the objects and functions IronPython supports.

Using sys.builtin_module_names

The modules loaded with the IronPython interpreter are enough to perform very basic tasks, such as those found so far in the book. However, most applications aren't that simple — you need additional functionality to create something useful. One of the most commonly imported modules is sys. The sys module contains a wealth of extremely useful objects that you'll need to build most complex applications. In order to use the sys module, you simply type `import sys` and press Enter. If you use the `dir()` function at this point, you'll discover that you now have access to the sys module.

The sys module includes an interesting function, `sys.builtin_module_names`. You can use this particular function to obtain a list of all of the modules that are built into the interpreter. These are modules that load as part of the interpreter, instead of as separate files. Try it now and you'll see output similar to that shown in Figure 2-21.

It's important to note that these are module names and not object or function names. These modules appear as part of the executable, rather than as separate files. You'll find them with the IronPython interpreter source code. The `sys.builtin_module_names` function is the only way to obtain this information.

```
IronPython Console                                              - □ ✕
IronPython 2.6 (2.6.10920.0) on .NET 2.0.50727.3603
Type "help", "copyright", "credits" or "license" for more information.
>>> import sys
>>> sys.builtin_module_names
('future_builtins', 'imp', 'sys', '__builtin__', 'exceptions', 'clr', '_locale',
 'cmath', 'socket', '_codecs', 'array', '_winreg', '_weakref', '_warnings', '_sr
e', '_random', '_functools', 'xxsubtype', 'time', 'thread', '_struct', '_heapq',
 '_ctypes_test', '_ctypes', '_sha512', '_sha256', '_sha', 'select', 're', 'opera
tor', 'nt', '_md5', '_fileio', 'math', 'marshal', 'binascii', 'itertools', 'gc',
 'errno', 'datetime', 'cStringIO', 'cPickle', 'copy_reg', '_collections', '_byte
sio')
>>>
```

FIGURE 2-21: Obtain a list of modules you can access using sys.builtin_module_names.

Using External Modules with IronPython

Any application can use external modules. In fact, your IronPython application can have any number of external modules. You can use them as you would any other application. In order to use an external module, you simply import it into the main module. Let's begin this example with a simple external module named MyStuff.py. Listing 2-3 shows the code for this module.

Available for download on Wrox.com

LISTING 2-3: Creating a simple external function

```
# Define a simple function that takes
# two arguments.
def SayHello(msg, name):
    "Displays a hello message -> SayHello(message, user name)"
    print msg, name
    return
```

The SayHello() function is quite simple. All it does is print the message and name onscreen — nothing too complicated. However, it does serve as a useful example of how to work with external modules. Notice the string in the first line. The __doc__ attribute uses this information. After you import the module, you can type print MyStuff.SayHello.__doc__ and press Enter to see this message.

Before you can use SayHello(), you must import it. The main module, External.py, imports the external module as shown in Listing 2-4.

Available for download on Wrox.com

LISTING 2-4: Importing an external module and using it

```
# Import the file
import MyStuff

# Assign the function to a local variable.
```

continues

LISTING 2-4 *(continued)*

```
SayHello = MyStuff.SayHello

# Perform the task.
SayHello('Hello', 'George')

# Pause the display
raw_input('Press any key...')
```

The example begins by importing MyStuff. Placing the external module in the same directory as the rest of the application is the best way to ensure the interpreter can find it. When you plan to use a particular function relatively often, you can assign it to a local variable, as shown in the example. This technique lets you call the function without using the module name, as would normally be required. The code calls `SayHello()` next. It then pauses so you can see the output in Visual Studio. Figure 2-22 shows the results.

FIGURE 2-22: The output shows the result of calling the SayHello() function.

INTERACTING WITH THE IRONPYTHON ENVIRONMENT

At this point, you know how to create basic functions; determine which modules, objects, and functions are available for use; and import external modules as needed. The last major basic task you need to know about is interacting with the IronPython environment. Knowing this information will help you create better applications. The following sections provide an overview of many environmental needs you'll have when using IronPython.

Obtaining Version Information

You may find a need to programmatically process the version information for a particular IronPython installation. Perhaps your application requires a newer version of IronPython. You can obtain this information programmatically using the `sys.version` attribute. The following code shows a simple method for checking the IronPython version.

```
import sys
print sys.version
```

Of course, your concern may revolve around Windows. In this case, you can use `sys.getwindowsversion()` to obtain the information you need. The output is an array containing the following five values:

➤   Major version

➤   Minor version

- ➤ Build

- ➤ Platform

- ➤ String describing installation (such as the current service pack)

Changing sys.path Values

The `sys.path` attribute is an array containing paths to various parts of IronPython. You can use `sys.path` to locate or modify the path for IronPython. For example, if you type `print sys.path[0]` and press Enter, you obtain the path for the currently executing application. The standard list provides these locations:

- ➤ Executing application path (blank if the interpreter can't determine the location)

- ➤ IronPython library directory

- ➤ IronPython DLL directory

- ➤ IronPython executable directory

- ➤ IronPython site-packages directory

The interpreter always searches these paths, looking for any modules you want to import or other resources your application requires. You can add or remove entries as necessary. Chapter 4 tells how to work with arrays.

Obtaining Command Line Arguments

An application can receive command line arguments when it executes and then processes those arguments, just as you would do with any other application. IronPython uses a similar approach to that of C and C++. You use the `sys.argv` array to obtain a list of the arguments passed at the command line. For example, if you type `print sys.argv[0]`, you see the first command line argument passed to the application. The `sys.argv` array is blank when you start the interpreter without specifying a module to execute. You'll see command line processing examples as the book progresses because this is a powerful feature.

 If you're getting the idea that loading the sys module provides all kinds of power for your application, you're right. You can see a complete list of the sys module functions and attributes at `http://docs.python.org/library/sys.html`. *Of course, you'll see additional examples as the book progresses.*

USING IRONPYTHON CONSTRUCTIVELY

This is a chapter of basics. It's the training-wheels chapter of the book because everyone needs to start somewhere. However, this chapter didn't start at the ground floor — I assumed you already know something about programming in general and .NET languages in particular, so this chapter didn't have a lot of handholding in it. Consequently, you learned quite a bit about IronPython, including how to indent and use capitalization, work with data types, use modules, create functions, and control the environment. You'll probably use the information in this chapter so much that you won't need the chapter after a while, but in the meantime keep a bookmark on it so you can refer to it as you progress through the other introductory chapters.

It's time to get a little work done with your IronPython setup. The first step is to get used to working with Visual Studio and IronPython. You won't find any fancy templates to do the work for you, so make sure you practice creating some projects. In addition, put some simple projects together using the techniques described in this chapter. The projects don't have to do anything fancy; all you're trying to do is get the procedure for creating and managing projects down. Try creating a few applications that use functions and exercise the various data types. Have a little fun with the `print()` function!

Chapter 3 builds on what you learned in this chapter. The next step is to work with some structured programming elements such as loops. The pace really is going to pick up, so make sure you spend the time required in each chapter to build your knowledge — otherwise, you're going to get lost pretty quickly. Even so, Chapter 3 is still a basics chapter (as are Chapters 4 and 5).

PART II
Using the IronPython Language

3

Implementing Structured Language Elements

WHAT'S IN THIS CHAPTER?

➤ Creating applications that use multiple statements

➤ Developing applications that select between options

➤ Working with loops in applications

➤ Enumerating data within applications

Up to this point, the sample applications have focused on simple tasks that didn't require much structure. However, real applications solve complex problems that often require decision making and loops. Performing these tasks requires structure within the application. The IronPython interpreter must know where the decision-making process and the loops begin and end. Consequently, you must know how to add structure to your application.

This chapter discusses four levels of structure. First, you'll see how to string a number of statements together in a structured manner. You've already seen some examples of this kind of structure in Chapters 1 and 2, but this chapter goes further. Second, you'll see how to create decision-making structures so that the application can choose between options. Third, you'll discover two looping mechanisms provided by IronPython. And fourth, you'll see how to enumerate data within applications — one of the more important structural techniques.

After you complete this chapter, you might be tempted to ask whether this is all that IronPython provides in the way of structures. It's true that IronPython does provide a few more advanced structural elements not discussed in this chapter, such as the with keyword. However, IronPython doesn't suffer from the complexity of other languages; it really does keep things as simple as they appear in this chapter (and throughout the rest of the book).

STRINGING STATEMENTS TOGETHER

A basic IronPython application begins as a series of statements, as a procedure. These statements perform some task at the command line or within a window, depending on which IronPython interpreter you use. This initial execution path is called the main function, even though there really isn't a function — simply a set of statements.

A lot of people feel uncomfortable with the open feel of IronPython's main function so they create something that looks a bit more like what they're used to using, as shown in Listing 3-1.

LISTING 3-1: Creating an actual main() function

```
import sys

# Create a main() function that everyone can recognize.
def main(argv = None):

    # Obtain the command line arguments.
    if argv is None:
        argv = sys.argv

    # Display the command line arguments.
    for ThisArg in argv:
        print ThisArg

    # Pause after the debug session.
    raw_input('Press any key to continue...')

# Call the main() function.
if __name__ == "__main__":
    main()
```

This code shows a few interesting structural features of IronPython, which is why it's such a good example to start with. The code actually begins with a comparison of __name__ to "__main__". It turns out that __name__ always contains the name of the current function. Using __name__ makes it possible for your application to detect its position in the execution loop.

Most programming languages provide an equivalent of the main() *function described in Listing 3-1. Even C# and Visual Basic have a* main()*-type function that creates the initial form. Whether you actually use a* main() *function in your applications depends upon how you expect other developers to interact with your code. The examples in this book don't rely on a main function for the sake of clarity, but you might want to consider including one when developers are used to working with* main() *as part of their coding experience. Of course, you can call* main() *anything you like to match the programming language that your developers normally use.*

In this case, the application calls main(), the new main function. If you've spent any time writing C or C++ code, this version of main() will look a little familiar. While it lacks argc (the argument count), this main() does have an argv. However, the arguments can change between the time the code starts the application and begins processing main(), so you want to set argv to None (essentially, nothing at all in IronPython), and obtain the command line arguments from sys.argv.

At this point, the code uses a for loop to parse argv and displays its arguments on screen. At a minimum, you get the name of the application. The arguments you see depend on their order on the command line (or in Visual Studio). For example, if you specify -D after the file-name, then you see it as part of the arguments. Figure 3-1 shows an example of what a series of arguments might look like when using a command line of NewMain.py -D -c These are arguments. The code ends by pausing so you can see the output when using the Visual Studio debugger.

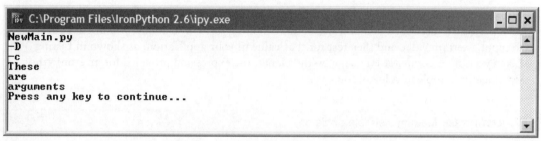

```
C:\Program Files\IronPython 2.6\ipy.exe
NewMain.py
-D
-c
These
are
arguments
Press any key to continue...
```

FIGURE 3-1: Create a main() function and then process the command line arguments in it.

Notice the levels of indentation in this example. The levels of indentation show the structure of the application. Unlike many application development languages, IronPython enforces indentation, with the result that you can see the application structure quite easily.

In IronPython, structure comes in a number of forms, all of which are accessible to you as the developer. Using structure properly makes your applications easier to understand. From the main (and any other) function, you can use the following structural elements:

➤ Import external files

➤ Call other functions

➤ Use decision-making or loop structures

➤ Interact with objects

Chapter 5 demonstrates IronPython objects in detail. For now, you need to consider that IronPython uses many objects that don't appear as objects at first. For example, later in this chapter you'll discover that the common string actually provides a number of methods you can use to modify its content. You'll encounter more objects as the book progresses. For now, focus on the basic structure that IronPython provides so you don't get lost when creating your own applications.

SELECTING BETWEEN OPTIONS

Decision making is an essential part of most applications. IronPython doesn't provide the wide range of decision-making options that other languages do. In fact, you have just one decision-making structure: the `if` statement. Fortunately, the `if` statement takes three forms that meet every possible programming need, even when using the `if` statement isn't quite as elegant as other possibilities, such as `Select...Case`. The following sections describe the three forms of the `if` statement:

➤ `if`

➤ `if...else`

➤ `if...elif...else`

Performing a Simple Decision Using if

The simplest kind of decision is one where you look for a particular value or range of values and then perform a task when you find what you're looking for. For example, you might expect the user to input a certain value and then test for that value in your application, as shown in Listing 3-2. Like every other computer language on the planet, the expression provided for an IronPython `if` statement is a Boolean value of some type.

LISTING 3-2: Making a simple decision

Available for
download on
Wrox.com

```python
# Define an input variable.
Answer = raw_input('Say hello (Y/N)?')

# Check the value of Answer.
if Answer.upper() == 'Y':

    # Perform some tasks based on a positive response.
    print 'You typed:', Answer
    print 'So Hello!'

# Pause after the debug session.
raw_input('Press any key to continue...')
```

The code for this example retrieves some input from the user and reacts to it. You've probably created many applications that do precisely the same thing. In this case, the application uses `raw_input()` to obtain the input from the user. You can see how the prompt looks in Figure 3-2.

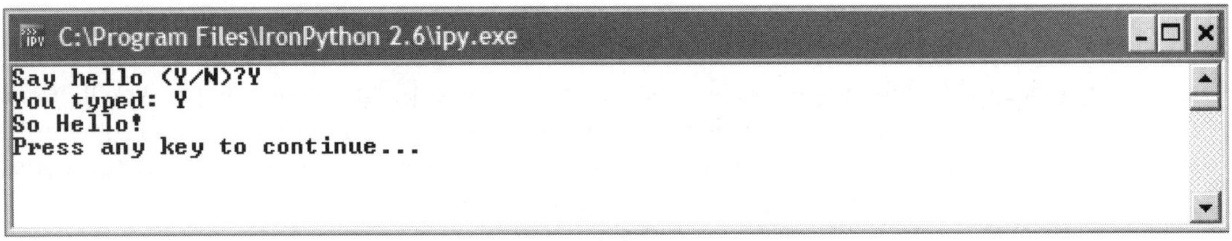

```
 C:\Program Files\IronPython 2.6\ipy.exe
Say hello (Y/N)?Y
You typed: Y
So Hello!
Press any key to continue...
```

FIGURE 3-2: Use the various versions of if to make decisions.

At this point, the code creates the `if` statement. Notice that the `if` statement ends with a colon (:) just as all IronPython statements do. Everything that's indented after the `if` statement is part of the structure. There aren't any opening or closing statements, just the colon and the statements you want to execute (making IronPython one of the least cluttered languages available). Figure 3-2 shows the output from the application when the user provides either a y or Y as input.

> *One of the most common errors that developers who are familiar with other languages make when working with IronPython is to forget to include the colon after a structural element. Unfortunately, the error message doesn't always tell you that the colon is missing — it might point you in some completely different direction. If you get an error message that doesn't make sense, you might want to check for a missing colon in your code. In fact, have someone else look for the missing colon when you can't find it — you'll be amazed at how often a little colon causes you all kinds of woe.*

One of the interesting features of this example is that `Answer` is actually an object. You can't declare it as an object or any data type at all. In fact, the code simply assigns a string to `Answer` and everything happens in the background. You can find a whole list of string methods at `http://docs.python.org/library/stdtypes.html#string-methods`. This book shows how to use a number of these methods. For now, just keep in mind that IronPython tends to hide complexity in ways that other languages don't.

Choosing between Two Options Using if . . . else

Sometimes you need to do more than simply decide to do something based on the output of a Boolean expression — you also need to do something if the expression is false. Most programming languages handle this using some form of `if...else` structure, which is precisely what IronPython does. Listing 3-3 adds to the example shown in Listing 3-2 by doing something when the reader fails to provide the expected input.

LISTING 3-3: Making an either/or decision

```
# Define an input variable.
Answer = raw_input('Say hello (Y/N)?')

# Check the value of Answer.
if Answer.upper() == 'Y':

    # Perform some tasks based on a positive response.
    print 'You typed:', Answer
    print 'So Hello!'
```

continues

LISTING 3-3 *(continued)*

```
# The user must have typed something else.
else:

    # Perform some tasks based on a different response.
    print 'Sorry, you typed:', Answer, 'and not Y.'

# Pause after the debug session.
raw_input('Press any key to continue...')
```

The big thing to notice in this example is that you outdent the `else` clause and follow it with a colon. Every indented statement after the `else` clause is part of the `else` portion of the structure. The output from this example is similar to the output shown in Figure 3-2. The application asks a question and then outputs something based on the response the user provides.

Creating a Decision Tree Using if . . . elif . . . else

Many programming languages provide a special structure to handle complex decisions. IronPython keeps things simple by relying on a special form of the `if` statement, the `if...elif...else` statement. As you might expect, each `elif` clause includes a Boolean expression. In many respects, the `elif` clauses act as the case clauses for the `Select...Case` structure. Of course, you gain some flexibility because the `elif` clause need not match a particular variable. The `else` clause acts like the default clause for the `Select...Case` structure. Listing 3-4 shows how to work with the `elif` clause.

LISTING 3-4: Making complex decisions

```
# Define an input variable.
Answer = raw_input('Say hello (Y/N)?')

# Check the value of Answer.
if Answer.upper() == 'Y':

    # Perform some tasks based on a positive response.
    print 'You typed:', Answer
    print 'So Hello!'

# Check to see if the user entered N
elif Answer.upper() == 'N':

    # Give a reponse for a negative answer.
    print 'Sorry to hear you don\'t want to say hello.'

# The user must have typed something else.
else:

    # Perform some tasks based on a different response.
    print 'You need to type Y or N!'

# Pause after the debug session.
raw_input('Press any key to continue...')
```

As you can see from the code, the `elif` clause looks very much like the `if` clause. The only difference is that the `elif` clause must follow the `if` clause. You can include as many `elif` clauses as required to perform a particular task. The output from this example is similar to that shown in Figure 3-2.

CREATING LOOPS

Computers are far better at repetitive tasks than humans. A computer will perform the same task as long as you want it to. In fact, your computer is currently performing tasks repetitively, even if you didn't start those tasks. For example, you probably have a firewall that's looking for terrifying inputs from outside sources, using some type of repetitive procedure. Applications handle these repetitive tasks using loops. IronPython provides two kinds of loops as described in the following sections:

➤ `for...in`

➤ `while`

Using for . . . in

The `for...in` loop is the best way to process lists of things in most cases. You'll find the `for...in` loop used with both arrays and collections in many situations (rather than the `while` loop, which can appear somewhat clumsy and can perform poorly for list processing). Listing 3-5 shows a `for...in` loop in action.

LISTING 3-5: Looping through data using for...in

```
# Create an array of strings.
MyList = 'Hello', 'Goodbye', 'Red', 'Green'

# Process the array.
for ThisString in MyList:

    # Display the individual values.
    print 'The current value is:', ThisString


# Pause after the debug session.
raw_input('Press any key to continue...')
```

The code begins by creating an array. This is a very simple array, but it demonstrates just how easy IronPython makes certain programming tasks. You don't have to worry about doing anything odd when creating the array. In addition, you'll find that arrays, like strings, come with a wealth of methods. For example, if you want to add a new member to an array, you simply call on the `append()` method to perform the task. The site at `http://docs.python.org/dev/3.0/library/array.html` describes array methods and types in greater detail. You'll see many of these array methods demonstrated in Chapter 4.

After the code creates the array, it uses the `for...in` loop to process it. The interpreter automatically calls the loop code once for each of the values in the array. The individual array values appear in `ThisString`. In this case, the code merely prints out the values of `ThisString`, as shown in Figure 3-3.

```
C:\Program Files\IronPython 2.6\ipy.exe
The current value is: Hello
The current value is: Goodbye
The current value is: Red
The current value is: Green
Press any key to continue...
```

FIGURE 3-3: The for loop is exceptionally efficient at list processing.

The `for...in` loop always has two parts: a target and an expression list. The target can be another expression list, in which case you can nest `for...in` loops to process the target. It's possible to dig down into just about any hierarchy of objects using a `for...in` loop.

Using while

The `while` loop might not be quite as pretty as the `for...in` loop, but it serves an important purpose. The `for...in` loop works with a fixed number of elements. The `while` loop can work with an arbitrary number of elements, or can remain running until told to stop. You use a `while` loop in situations where you don't know how many times a loop will occur during design time. Of course, this means that you must give the `while` loop a positive method of ending, as shown in Listing 3-6.

LISTING 3-6: Looping through data using while

```python
# Create an array of strings.
MyList = 'Hello', 'Goodbye', 'Red', 'Green'

# Define a counter variable.
Counter = 0

# Define the current string.
ThisString = ''

# Process the array.
while ThisString != 'Green':

    # Get the next value.
    ThisString = MyList[Counter]

    # Display the individual values.
    print 'The current value is:', ThisString

    # Update the counter.
    Counter+=1

# Pause after the debug session.
raw_input('Press any key to continue...')
```

This example begins with the same array as shown in Listing 3-5. In order to make the `while` loop work, the code must define `Counter`, which keeps track of the current array element. The code also defines `ThisString`, which holds the current array value. As you can already see, the `while` loop isn't nearly as automatic as the `for...in` loop, but it does provide considerable flexibility.

In this case, the `while` loop continues to run until `ThisString` is equal to `'Green'`, the last value in the array. As always, the `while` statement ends with a colon and every indented statement after it is part of the `while` structure.

The code relies on `Counter` to access the individual array elements. You simply provide Counter as an index into `MyList` using `MyList[Counter]`. The code then prints out the value found in `ThisString`. Finally, the code updates Counter. Notice that IronPython supports the use of the `+=` shortcut. The output from this application appears in Figure 3-4.

FIGURE 3-4: Use the while loop when you need to perform tasks an indeterminate number of times.

You might have noticed that IronPython doesn't appear to support the vast array of loop statement subsets found in other languages. For example, there isn't any version of the `while` statement that tests for the condition after executing the code the first time. In general, this apparent limitation actually makes things considerably easier. You simply need to write your code in such a way as to accommodate the "test first" orientation of the IronPython `while` loop.

PERFORMING ENUMERATIONS

You're going to encounter a lot of enumerations before the book is over because IronPython uses them by the gross. Essentially, enumerating data means to obtain the individual elements from a collection or array and do something with them. One of the more common collections that you'll enumerate is `sys.path`. Listing 3-7 shows a simple example of how this process might work.

LISTING 3-7: Using an enumeration

```
import sys

# Enumerate the path variables.
```

continues

LISTING 3-7 *(continued)*

```
for ThePath in sys.path:
    print ThePath

# Pause after the debug session.
raw_input('Press any key to continue...')
```

As you can see, the for...in loop comes in very handy for enumerating data. Depending on your configuration, you might not see all of the path information shown in Figure 3-5, but your output will look similar. The "Changing sys.path Values" section of Chapter 2 tells you more about each of the elements displayed in Figure 3-5.

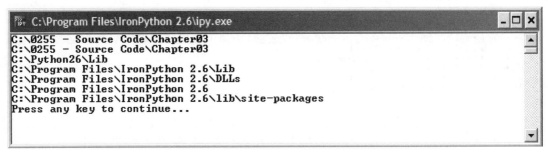

FIGURE 3-5: You can find many uses for enumerations in IronPython.

USING IRONPYTHON CONSTRUCTIVELY

This chapter has demonstrated the essential IronPython structures, including decision making and looping. At first you'll wonder whether you can get the task done with these simple setups. For example, IronPython lacks a Case...Select structure. However, you can duplicate this kind of structure using a simple if...elif...else data structure, so the complication of using Case...Select really isn't necessary. When you think about IronPython, think simple, but elegant.

If you've spent much time programming, you probably don't need a lot of practice creating structures. However, it's important to spend some time reviewing the examples in this chapter because IronPython can really throw a curve at you if you think it works like the other languages you use. Try creating a few applications that have multiple levels to them so that you can see how indentation works within IronPython.

Chapter 4 continues with more IronPython basics. In that chapter, you discover how to work with arrays and collections. IronPython uses a host of arrays internally, so it's important to pay particular attention to that part of the chapter. Just consider the number of times that arrays appeared in Chapter 2 as the output of information. You'll combine the information in Chapter 4 with the information in this chapter to process arrays and collections.

Using Arrays and Collections

➤ Using arrays for simple data storage

➤ Using collections for complex data storage

➤ Importing and using dictionaries for advanced data management

When you think about it, arrays, collections, dictionaries, and other similar storage structures provide a means to manage related items. Yes, you can stick any data in the data structure, but normally, the data elements are going to have some kind of relation. Arrays and other data management structures are like apartment mailboxes, with an individual mailbox to hold each individual data element.

The difference between data storage structures comes in the complexity of the data they can hold and the data management functionality they provide. An array (the term is used generically here to mean any ordered storage mechanism that follows the rules of arrays) is an older, simplistic storage mechanism that still sees plenty of use precisely because it's so simple. If you only need to hold a list of items, there isn't a good reason to use a more complex data storage mechanism.

As applications increased in complexity, developers also encountered data with greater storage needs. Collections and dictionaries are just two of many storage mechanisms designed to meet these needs (and the only two that IronPython supports directly). Collections introduce the idea of enumerated access, while dictionaries provide an easier method than numbering to locate a particular data element. You'll discover that these two storage mechanisms provide other functionality as well.

This chapter examines data storage technology for memory. You'll see how IronPython implements arrays, collections, and dictionaries. The examples will help you better understand how to manage and manipulate objects in memory using IronPython.

WORKING WITH TUPLES, LISTS, AND ARRAYS

Arrays are the backbone of in-memory data storage for most programming languages. At a basic level, an array is simply a sequence of memory entries. These entries normally reside one after another in physical memory and you access them using an index — a numeric value. Arrays have been around about as long as computers have existed. Even early assembler programmers used array-like structures in their programming.

Like every other language, IronPython provides arrays for you to use. However, IronPython has two native structures and several external (imported) structures that can qualify as array-like structures. In fact, unless there's a specific reason to state otherwise, this book will simply use the term *array* to refer to them all. However, it's important to understand that there are subtle differences between these array-like structures, so the following sections discuss the three common array-like structures you'll find in IronPython.

Understanding Tuples, Lists, and Arrays

As with many languages, IronPython has its own set of odd terminology. The array type used in Chapter 3 is more precisely called a *tuple*. Any time you see a list of items separated by commas such as this:

```
MyTuple = 'Hello', 'Goodbye', 'Red', 'Green'
```

the precise terminology for the structure is a `tuple`. IronPython also supports lists natively. Listing 4-1 shows a simple application that creates a `list` and then displays its content. Figure 4-1 shows the output from this example.

LISTING 4-1: Creating and using a list

```
# Define a list
MyList = ['Hello', 'Goodbye', 'Red', 'Green']

# Display each list element.
for TheString in MyList:
    print TheString

# Pause after the debug session.
raw_input('Press any key to continue...')
```

```
C:\Program Files\IronPython 2.6\ipy.exe                                    _ □ ×
Hello
Goodbye
Red
Green
Press any key to continue...
```

FIGURE 4-1: Lists produce the same output as a tuple given the same input.

The main difference between a `tuple` and a `list` is that you can change the content of a `list`, but you can't change the content of a `tuple`. If you create a `tuple` and try to change one of its elements, you get an error message. Listing 4-2 shows what happens when you try to change a `tuple` and a `list`.

LISTING 4-2: Changing tuples and lists

```python
# Create the tuple
MyTuple = 'Red', 'Green', 'Blue', 'Yellow'

# Create the list
MyList = ['Red', 'Green', 'Blue', 'Yellow']

# Attempt to change the tuple, which will result in an error.
try:
    MyTuple[1] = 'Orange'
except TypeError:
    print 'Couldn\'t change the tuple.\n'

# Attempt to change the list.
try:
    MyList[1] = 'Orange'
except TypeError:
    print 'Couldn\'t change the list.\n'

# Verify that the change worked.
print 'Displaying the list content.'
for TheString in MyList:
    print TheString

# Pause after the debug session.
raw_input('Press any key to continue...')
```

The example attempts to change both a `tuple` and a `list`. However, when the example tries to change the `tuple`, it generates an exception, as shown in Figure 4-2. Notice how the code uses a `try...except` structure to catch the exception and display an error message onscreen. The `except` clause can stand alone, but it's better to provide a particular kind of exception, which is `TypeError` in this case. The code does successfully modify the `list` and displays the results in Figure 4-2.

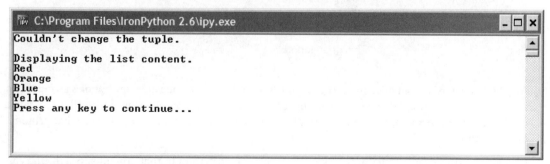

FIGURE 4-2: Lists are mutable; tuples aren't.

`Tuples` and `lists` are more similar than different. For example, it's possible to add elements to a `tuple`, just as you can to a `list`. In fact, except for the fact that `tuples` are *immutable* (not changeable) and lists are *mutable* (you can change them), both structures provide precisely the same features. Both of these structures are also roughly equivalent to arrays in other languages and you can call them arrays without provoking too many odd reactions — at least, not from normal people.

Of course, you're wondering now why Python and IronPython support two array-like structures. `Tuples` come in handy for a few reasons. First, because `tuples` can't change, IronPython can implement them more efficiently, which means that using `tuples` is faster. Second, `tuples` are less susceptible to outside influences such as viruses. Because you can't change the content of a `tuple`, you also can't fill it with things that the application can't use. Third, `tuples` are marginally faster to type.

The object that IronPython uses as an `array` really isn't an `array` in the common sense of the word. It's more along the lines of a byte `array` for most programming languages. However, the IronPython `array` really doesn't fit that description either. Rather, you tell IronPython what kind of sequence you want to store and then provide the storage values. Table 4-1 provides a list of the `array` element types.

TABLE 4-1: IronPython Array Data Types

DESIGNATOR	TYPE	SIZE
'b'	Signed char (byte)	1
'B'	Unsigned char (byte)	1
'c'	Character	1
'd'	Floating point (double)	8
'f'	Floating point (single)	4
'h'	Signed short	2
'H'	Unsigned short	2
'i'	Signed integer	2
'I' (capital eye)	Unsigned integer	2
'l' (lowercase el)	Signed long	4
'L'	Unsigned long	4

As you can see from the table, an `array` in IronPython doesn't include any concept of a string. Strings in IronPython are considered a kind of sequence. To create an `array` of strings in IronPython, you'd need to create an `array` of character arrays. In short, the concept of an `array` is somewhat primitive in IronPython.

`Arrays` also differ from other array-like structures in IronPython in that you must provide a type as part of the `array` definition. Consequently, if you create a character `array`, you can't suddenly decide to use it to store integer values. You must also import the `array` module to use IronPython `arrays`, because `arrays` aren't part of the initial interpreter configuration. Listing 4-3 shows an example of an `array` in use.

LISTING 4-3: Working with an actual array in IronPython

```
import array

# define a local version of array.
array = array.array

# Create a character array and assign it some values.
MyArray = array('c', 'Hello World')

# Display each list element.
for TheCharacter in MyArray:
    print TheCharacter

# Pause after the debug session.
raw_input('Press any key to continue...')
```

The example begins by importing the `array` module and then assigning the `array.array` method to a local variable. You've seen this kind of code before with the `sys` module in previous chapters.

At this point, the code creates a character `array`. Now it may appear that this `array` contains a string, but what it really contains are individual characters. When you output the `array`, you see the individual characters, as shown in Figure 4-3. Consequently, most developers of other languages are going to view the IronPython `array` as a sort of byte `array`.

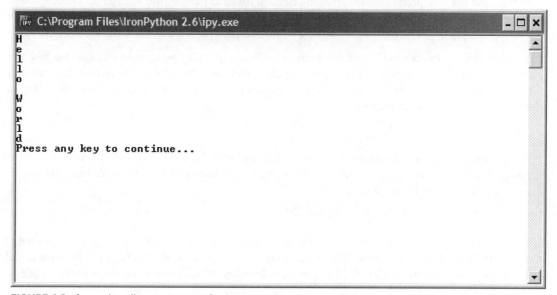

FIGURE 4-3: Arrays handle sequences of values.

After reading this section, you might find yourself a bit confused, especially if you've worked with Visual Basic.NET or C# in the past where `arrays` really are `arrays`. What you'll want most often is a `list` in IronPython and you'll likely use a `tuple` in some situations as well. When you think `array` for IronPython, think about these two kinds of objects. On the other hand, when you really do need to work with individual bits of data, then think about the IronPython `array` because it does work with those individual sequences.

Creating and Accessing Single-Dimension Arrays

Single-dimension arrays are actually a simple list of objects. One item appears after another in memory and you access the items using the numeric value that applies to that particular element. Single-dimension arrays commonly appear in applications because many items fit within the `list` category. You can create arrays in a number of ways. For example, you can create a blank `list` using the following technique

```
MyList = []
```

If you want to fill an array with data as part of the creation process, you can simply provide a list of values. For example, this code creates an array with four values.

```
MyList = [1, 2, 3, 4]
```

You've probably seen these techniques (or similar techniques) in other languages. However, IronPython has a few additional tricks up its sleeve. For example, you can fill an array with a sequence. The following code is perfectly acceptable and fills the array with the path variables.

```
MyList = sys.path
```

In this case, the interpreter creates one array element for each path within `sys.path`. This approach makes it possible to access each path element individually. However, changing an array element won't change `sys.path`. IronPython makes a copy of the content of `sys.path` and places it in `MyList`.

You can also use expressions to fill the array. This is an especially powerful technique because the expression can be any legal Python expression that produces a list of items as output. For example, the following code creates an array with the same list of path items in it, except this code relies on an expression to perform the task.

```
MyList = list('Hello')
```

In this case, `MyList` will contain one element for each letter. However, the expressions can become quite complex — as complex as you need them to generate the array elements. For example, the following code also works just fine.

```
MyList = list(x*x for x in range(10))
```

This bit of code generates the squares of all of the numbers between 0 and 9 — `range()` begins with 0 and ends with 9 as output (see the "Using the range() Function" section of the chapter for more details). The expression need not work with just numeric data either. When you execute the following code

```
MyList = list(x.upper() for x in "abc")
```

MyList fills with the uppercase letters A, B, and C. Consequently, you can fill the array with the product of a method's output. In fact, you can create your own functions to process the input from a `list`, as shown in Listing 4-4.

LISTING 4-4: Creating specialized array input

```
# Define a function to output values for the array.
def ArrayFill(x):

    # Output a value that matches the input.
    if x == 'a':
        return 'Red'
    elif x == 'b':
        return 'Yellow'
    elif x == 'c':
        return 'Blue'
    else:
        return 'Unknown'

# Create the list to process.
AString = 'abcdABCD'

# Create the array.
MyList = list(ArrayFill(x.lower()) for x in AString)

# Print each array element.
for Output in MyList:
    print Output

# Pause after the debug session.
raw_input('Press any key to continue...')
```

The code begins by defining an array to create array elements. This function could be anything you choose. The point is that each call to the function provides a specific output based on the input: Red, Yellow, Blue, or Unknown.

The next step is to define the inputs, which appear in `AString`. Any sequence you want to process works fine.

Now the code creates the array using the complex expression shown in Listing 4-4. The expression loops through each value in `AString` and places it in `x`. The value in `x` is set to lowercase and passed to `ArrayFill()`, which then interprets the value and provides an output. Figure 4-4 shows the output from this example.

IronPython also includes some interesting array access features. For example, if you want to access every other array element, you use the code shown in Listing 4-5.

LISTING 4-5: Accessing specific array elements

```
# Create the array.
```

continues

LISTING 4-5 *(continued)*

```
MyList = [1, 2, 3, 4, 5, 6]

# Access every other element.
for Output in MyList[::2]:
    print Output
```

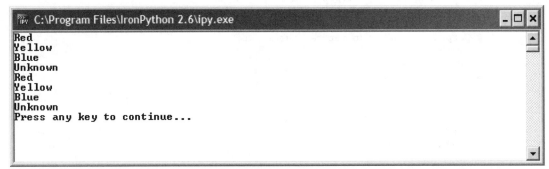

FIGURE 4-4: You can use complex expressions to create arrays.

The output is 1, 3, and 5 for this example. Actually, you can provide more than the step for the output. IronPython provides the means to provide start:stop:step with the colons. For example, if you wanted to start with element 1 instead of element 0, you'd type:

```
for Output in MyList[1::2]:
    print Output
```

This code outputs 2, 4, and 6 based on the previous input. You can control things even more. For example, look at the following code.

```
for Output in MyList[1:4:2]:
    print Output
```

Run this code and you'll see 2 and 4 as output. The code begins with element 1, stops with element 4, and uses a step of 2.

Let's look at one other interesting IronPython array technique. Listing 4-6 shows code that not only shows the array items, but also the index associated with that item.

LISTING 4-6: Looking through array elements

```
# Create the array.
MyList = ['Zero', 'One', 'Two', 'Three', 'Four']

# Display the items and their index.
for index, item in enumerate(MyList):
    print index, item

# Pause after the debug session.
raw_input('Press any key to continue...')
```

In this case, the code begins by creating an array with five strings in it. The `for` loop iterates through the array as normal. However, in this case, the example relies on the `enumerate()` function to obtain the index for the array elements. Consequently, the output consists of two values — the array index and the element value. You can read more about the `enumerate()` function in the "Using the enumerate() Function" section of the chapter. The output from this example appears in Figure 4-5.

```
ipy  C:\Program Files\IronPython 2.6\ipy.exe                        _ □ ✕
0 Zero
1 One
2 Two
3 Three
4 Four
Press any key to continue...
```

FIGURE 4-5: Using functions enables you to extend the output of arrays.

By now you should have gotten the idea that arrays in IronPython are just a bit different from other languages in that they're far more flexible and you can use them for a host of tasks.

Manipulating Single-Dimension Arrays

After you get the data into an array, you'll probably want to manipulate the data in specific ways. For example, you've already discovered that you can change a value in Listing 4-2. However, simply changing values won't be enough. Listing 4-7 shows a number of ways in which you can work with array data (and IronPython provides considerably more methods than those shown in the listing).

Available for
download on
Wrox.com

LISTING 4-7: Manipulating array elements

```
# Define a function for printing.
def Show(type, array):
    print '\n', type
    for String in array:
        print String

# Create the array.
MyList = ['Zero', 'One', 'Two']

# Display the number of elements.
print 'Elements in MyList:',
print len(MyList)

# Add a new element.
MyList.append('Two')
Show('Appended a Value', MyList)

# Add multiple elements.
MyList.extend(['Three', 'Four'])
```

continues

LISTING 4-7 *(continued)*

```
Show('Extended MyList', MyList)

# Display the number of instances of the word 'Two'.
print '\nNumber of instances of Two:',
print MyList.count('Two')

# Remove one of the instances of 'Two' from the array.
MyList.remove('Two')
Show('Removed a Value', MyList)

# Pop the last value in the array.
MyList.pop()
Show('Popped a Value', MyList)

# Delete a value.
del MyList[2]
Show('Deleted a Value', MyList)

# Sort the array.
MyList.sort()
Show('Sorted the List', MyList)

# Reverse the sort order.
MyList.reverse()
Show('Reversed the List', MyList)

# Pause after the debug session.
raw_input('Press any key to continue...')
```

The code begins by defining Show(), a function used to display the array elements and the kind of manipulation performed on the array. This is a simple method to display information from the example without repeating the code. You've already seen this code in a number of examples, so you already know how it works.

Array manipulation falls into two categories. The first is using an external function to perform the task. For example, if you want to obtain the number of array elements, you call on the len() function. Likewise, if you want to delete a specific element or range of elements, you call on the del() function.

The second is using an array method. For example, if you want to add elements to an array, you can either use append() or extend(). The difference between the two is that extend() accepts a sequence, so you can add more than one element in a single call. You also have multiple choices when it comes to removing elements. Of course, you can simply delete elements by number, but you can also use pop() to remove the last element in the array. The remove() method actually deletes an element based on value. If an array contains two elements with the same value, remove() deletes only the first of the two elements. IronPython also makes it easy to sort() and reverse() sort the content of an array. Figure 4-6 shows how these various functions and methods affect the test array.

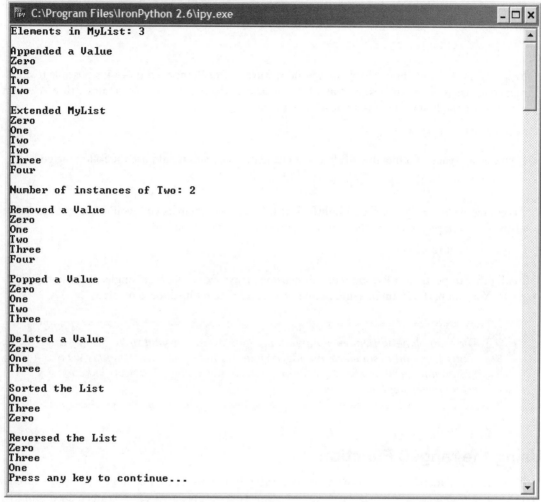

FIGURE 4-6: IronPython makes arrays extremely easy to manipulate using functions and methods.

All these methods (and many others) make it possible to use an array in ways that you might not use arrays in other languages. For example, by combining the append() and pop() methods, you can create a stack. If you want a queue, simply use the append() method and del() function. In short, using a combination of functions and methods enables you to work with arrays in ways that would be difficult in other languages.

Working with Multi-Dimension Arrays

Multi-dimension arrays provide all of the same functionality as a single-dimension array. However, as the name implies, a multi-dimension array has more than one dimension to it. For example, here's a simple multi-dimension array.

```
MyList = [[1, 2], [3, 4]]
```

What you get from this code is a 2 × 2 array. To access a particular element, you use its index as you normally would. For example, to access the value 1, you would use:

```
print MyList[0][0]
```

You may have already figured out the special feature of IronPython arrays — it's possible to create ragged arrays without any problem at all. For example, the following code creates a three-element array where the first element is a two-element array.

```
MyList = [[1, 2], 3, 4]
```

If you want to access a member of that first element, say 2, you would use the following code.

```
print MyList[0][1]
```

Accessing the other elements is straightforward. You access them as you would a single-dimensional array. For example, to access the number 3, you use the following code.

```
print MyList[2]
```

In all other respects, IronPython multi-dimension arrays work like their single-dimension counterparts. You can perform an amazing number of tasks using multi-dimension arrays.

 The example, MultiDimension.py, shows how to use automation to display the contents of both a standard and ragged multi-dimension array. You may want to wait until after you read the following section, "Using the range() Function," before reviewing this example.

Using the range() Function

The `range()` function is one of the more interesting functions when it comes to arrays because you can use it in so many ways. The basic `range()` function outputs a series of numbers beginning with 0 and ending with one less than the number you specify. For example, if you specify `range(10)`, you get the numbers from 0 through 9. Listing 4-8 shows some examples of using the `range()` function.

LISTING 4-8: Using the range() function

```
# Display a simple range.
print('Simple Range:')
for x in range(10):
    print(x),

# Display a specific range.
print('\n\nRange from 5 to 10')
for x in range(5, 11):
    print(x),

# Display the even numbers from 2 through 10.
```

```
print('\n\nEven Numbers 2 Through 10:')
for x in range(2, 11, 2):
    print(x),

# Create an array.
MyList = ['Red', 'Blue', 'Green', 'Yellow']

# Use the range() and len() functions to iterate the array.
print('\n\nIterating an Array')
for Index in range(len(MyList)):
    print MyList[Index]

# Pause after the debug session.
raw_input('\nPress any key to continue...')
```

As previously mentioned, the basic `range()` function outputs numbers starting from 0 through one less than the number you specify. Consequently, if you want to display the range of numbers from 5 through 10, you must actually specify a range of 5 through 11. Notice how you separate a range using a comma. The first number is the starting point and the second is the ending point. You may choose any starting and ending point — even negative numbers.

The `range()` function also supports a step as a third argument. Consequently, you can output the even numbers from 2 through 10 by specifying the correct range and using a step of 2.

Of course, using `range()` by itself has significant limitations. What you really want to do is use `range()` with arrays to make it easier to display the array content. The next part of the example shows how to perform this task. Notice how this example uses the `len()` function to obtain an upper limit for the `range()` function. Figure 4-7 shows the output from this example.

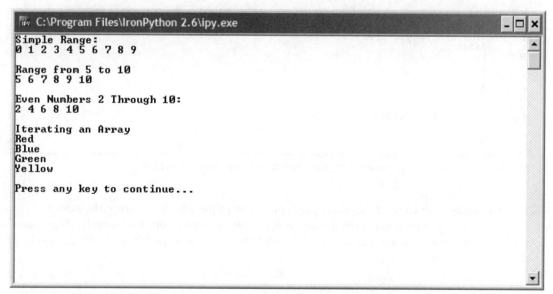

FIGURE 4-7: Use the range() function to generate sequences of numbers for array and other processing.

Now that you know about using `range()` and `len()` together, let's look at an example of ragged array processing. The following code shows how to process a ragged array.

```
# Create a ragged array.
MyList = [[1, 2], 3, 4, [5, 6]]

# Display the array content. In this case, you must place the ragged
# array portion of the example in a try block so that the code
# displays just the first dimension when only one dimension is
# available.
print('\nDisplaying the ragged array.')
print('X Y   Value')
for x in range(len(MyList)):
    try:
        for y in range(len(MyList[x])):
            print x, y, ' ', MyList[x][y]
    except TypeError:
        print x, 'N/A', MyList[x]
```

In this case, you begin with a ragged array that contains the numbers 1 through 6. In order to process this kind of array, you begin with the first array dimension, which will always have either a sub-array or a value. In this case, there are four array elements — two sub-arrays and two values (3 and 4).

Of course, you want the values in those sub-arrays. Consequently, the next step is to place the sub-array processing in a `try...except` block because the processing will fail when the code encounters a value. The moment the code tries to get the length of the sub-array using `len()`, it will fail with a `TypeError`. When the error does occur, the example prints just the first dimension. You can use this pattern for any ragged array you need to process. Figure 4-8 shows the output from this example.

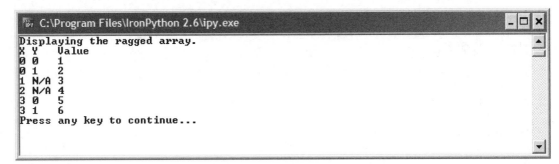

FIGURE 4-8: Ragged arrays are relatively easy to process using range() and len().

When working with IronPython, there are typically multiple ways to perform the same task. Many developers (with good reason) won't process data by exception. Fortunately, there's another way to process a ragged array that doesn't involve the `try...except` block shown earlier. Here's the second method.

```
# Create a ragged array.
MyList = [[1, 2], 3, 4, [5, 6]]

# Display the array content.
```

```
print('\nDisplaying the ragged array.')
print('X Y   Value')
for x in range(len(MyList)):
    if type(MyList[x]).__name__ == 'list':
        for y in range(len(MyList[x])):
            print x, y, ' ', MyList[x][y]
    else:
        print x, 'N/A', MyList[x]
```

In this case, the code simply checks the type of the `MyList` element before it performs any additional processing on it. Notice that this technique relies on the `type()` function, which returns the actual type of the element, and then you obtain the string form of the type using the `__name__` attribute. The results are the same as shown in Figure 4-8.

Processing Arrays Using the break and else Clauses

When you process sequences and arrays using loops, you sometimes need to stop what you're doing. For example, if you find the answer to the question of whether a number is prime or not, you really don't need to continue the loop that was looking for the answer. At this point, you can simply print out the two numbers that result in the target number when multiplied. Then again, you might complete the loop without finding a divisor that can divide equally into the number you're testing, so you need to tell the user that you have, indeed, found a prime number. Listing 4-9 shows one solution to this problem.

LISTING 4-9: Using break and else to process sequences

```
# Create a loop for detecting prime numbers.
for Number in range(1, 10):

    # This loop looks for divisors.
    for Divisor in range(2, Number):

        # If the number can be divided by the divisor evenly.
        if Number % Divisor == 0:

            # Print the values and then exit the loop.
            print Number, '=', Divisor, '*', Number/Divisor
            break
    else:
        # If you can't divide the number by any of the divisors,
        # it's prime.
        print Number, 'is a prime number'

# Pause after the debug session.
raw_input('\nPress any key to continue...')
```

The code begins by looking at the numbers 1 through 9. (Remember that `range()` won't output 10 in this case.) What you have at the beginning of the second loop is a number that you want to examine. You know that you need to check all numbers smaller than the target number to determine whether they divide evenly into the target number. For example, if you were detecting whether 4 is a prime number, you wouldn't try using 5 as a divisor.

The actual detection takes place with the code, `Number % Divisor`. If the output of this calculation is 0, then there isn't any remainder, and you've found the divisor you wanted. At this point, the code outputs the two numbers that will result in the target number when multiplied, such as 4 = 2 * 2. After printing out the result, the inner loop can stop — it's found the divisor you wanted and determined that the number isn't prime.

However, some numbers won't have a divisor because they are prime. In this case, the `else` clause takes over. The `for` loop literally falls through to the `else` clause and performs some other processing when the `for` loop fails. Figure 4-9 shows the output from this example.

```
C:\Program Files\IronPython 2.6\ipy.exe
1 is a prime number
2 is a prime number
3 is a prime number
4 = 2 * 2
5 is a prime number
6 = 2 * 3
7 is a prime number
8 = 2 * 4
9 = 3 * 3

Press any key to continue...
```

FIGURE 4-9: Using break makes it possible to stop loop processing, while else gives an alternative output.

Processing Arrays Using the continue Clause

A loop sometimes finishes the task that it's performing with a particular sequence or array elements, but you want to continue processing with the next element. In this case, you use the `continue` clause rather than the `break` clause of the loop. The `continue` clause will continue with the next loop and bypass the rest of the current loop. Listing 4-10 shows an example of how you can use the `continue` clause to request specific input from the user.

LISTING 4-10: Using continue to process sequences

```
# Define a list of keywords.
Keywords = ['RED', 'YELLOW', 'BLUE']

# Define a variable to detect a correct entry.
IsCorrect = False

# Create a loop to query the user about the keyword.
while not IsCorrect:

    # Ask the user for the keyword.
    Answer = raw_input('Type a keyword: ').upper()

    # Detect a correct keyword.
    if Answer in Keywords:
        print 'Congratulations, you provided the keyword!'
```

```
        IsCorrect = True
        continue

    # Tell the user the answer is incorrect.
    print 'You provided an incorrect keyword'

    # Try again?
    Answer = raw_input('Continue (Y/N)? ').upper()
    if Answer == 'N':
        IsCorrect = True

# Pause after the debug session.
raw_input('\nPress any key to continue...')
```

The code begins by creating a `Keywords` array that contains a list of words the application is seeking. It then creates a variable, `IsCorrect`, to track the correctness of the user input and a `while` loop to keep asking for input until the user either gives up or provides a correct term.

The next step is to get some input. The example uses `raw_input()` to obtain the information. Notice the use of `upper()` to change the case of the input text (so the user can input it without worrying about case sensitivity).

At this point, the code checks the input. If `Answer` is in `Keywords` (in other words, if the word in `Answer` matches one of the words in `Keywords`), then the loop prints a congratulatory message and loops without processing the rest of the information. Because `IsCorrect` is now `True`, the loop ends.

When the user doesn't provide good input, the loop continues. The code outputs an error response and asks the user about continuing. When the user enters N, the loop ends; otherwise, the loop continues. Figure 4-10 shows example output from this application.

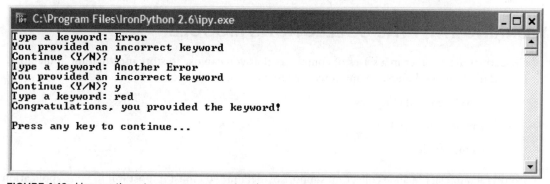

FIGURE 4-10: Use continue to resume processing the next element.

Using the enumerate() Function

Newer versions of Python and IronPython include the `enumerate()` function, which makes it easier to enumerate values in a sequence or array. Instead of using the `range(len(MyList))` code, you can simplify things by using `enumerate(MyList)` instead. The output is two values: an index for the current element and the element value. Listing 4-11 shows the final version of the code for parsing a ragged array. It's helpful to compare this version to the other versions in this chapter.

LISTING 4-11: Enumerating a ragged array

```
# Create a ragged array.
MyList = [[1, 2], 3, 4, [5, 6]]

# Display the array content.
print('Displaying the ragged array.')
print('X Y   Value')
for x, value in enumerate(MyList):
    if type(value).__name__ == 'list':
        for y, subvalue in enumerate(value):
            print x, y, ' ', subvalue
    else:
        print x, 'N/A', value

# Pause after the debug session.
raw_input('\nPress any key to continue...')
```

The output of this code is the same as that shown in Figure 4-8, but the code itself is easier to under-stand than either example in the "Using the range() Function" section of the chapter. When you use the enumerate() function, you don't have to calculate so many items — there's less guesswork. Notice that the first for loop already has the index and associated value for the first array level. The inner loop performs less work to get the secondary array level as well.

The only negative about using enumerate() is the same negative associated with any new function — you won't find it in older versions of Python or IronPython. Consequently, you could encounter com-patibility issues when using this, or any, new function. Make sure you look at your platform before you use the enumerate() function in your code.

WORKING WITH THE COLLECTIONS MODULE

Collections are another in a series of containers that you can use to store information in memory. For IronPython developers, the main reasons to use collections are:

➤   Developmental efficiency

➤   Application speed

➤   Design flexiblity

IronPython doesn't include collection support by default; you must import it into your application through the collections module. The collections module comes with a number of collection objects. If you're using the latest version of IronPython, you gain access to these collection features:

➤   deque (data type)

➤   defaultdict (data type)

➤   namedtuple() (data type factory function)

For the most part, collections really are just replacements for the default IronPython storage con-tainers such as list. In many cases, you see collections used to support specialized storage classes — something not discussed in this chapter. To give you an example of how the objects in the containers module work, this section discusses the deque, which has the following methods associated with it.

➤ **append()**: Appends a new item to the right side of the deque.

➤ **appendleft()**: Appends a new item to the left side of the deque.

➤ **clear()**: Removes all of the elements from the deque and leaves the length at 0.

➤ **extend()**: Adds elements to the right side of the deque using an iterable argument, such as a sequence.

➤ **extendleft()**: Adds elements to the left side of the deque using an iterable argument, such as a sequence. Adding items to the left side of the deque reverses the order of the elements in the iterable argument. For example, if you have a list that contains ['a', 'b', 'c'], this method will add them in the order ['c', 'b', 'a'].

➤ **pop()**: Removes an item from the right side of the deque and returns it as output to the caller. If the deque is empty, this call will raise an IndexError.

➤ **popleft()**: Removes an item from the left side of the deque and returns it as output to the caller. If the deque is empty, this call will raise an IndexError.

➤ **remove()**: Removes the first occurrence of an item, starting from the left side of the deque. If the deque doesn't contain the requested value, this method raises a ValueError.

➤ **rotate()**: Rotates the elements in the deque to the right the number of steps specified. If the supplied value is negative, the method rotates the deque elements the number of steps requested to the left.

Now that you have a basic idea of what a deque can do, it's time to take a look at one in action. Listing 4-12 shows a basic deque example.

LISTING 4-12: Interacting with a deque

Available for
download on
Wrox.com

```
# Define a function for printing.
def Show(type, array):
    print type
    for String in array:
        print String

# Import just the deque feature of the collections module.
from collections import deque

# Create the deque.
Numbers = deque(['Red', 'Yellow', 'Blue'])
Show('Original Deque', Numbers)

# Add a value to the deque.
Numbers.append('Orange')
```

continues

LISTING 4-12 *(continued)*

```
Show('\nAppend Orange to the Right', Numbers)

# Add a value to the left side of the deque.
Numbers.appendleft('Green')
Show('\nAppend Green to the Left', Numbers)

# Remove a value.
Numbers.remove('Yellow')
Show('\nRemoved Yellow', Numbers)

# Pop a value.
Popped = Numbers.pop()
print '\nPopped:', Popped

# Rotate the deque.
Numbers.rotate(2)
Show('\nRotated 2 to the Right', Numbers)

# Pause after the debug session.
raw_input('Press any key to continue...')
```

This example begins with a slightly modified version of the Show() function provided in Listing 4-7. Essentially, using this function saves a little of the coding time the developer requires to display the output onscreen.

A deque is more flexible than the built-in structures because you can work with both the right and left side of the deque. In this case, the code appends a value to the right and then to the left.

As with the built-in structures, you can remove, delete, or pop values from the deque. Unlike the built-in structures, you can also pop values from the left, which means you can create a number of interesting structure types. For example, you could create a rotating queue. Of course, you don't even have to worry about popping values if you want to rotate values — simply use rotate() as shown in the example. Figure 4-11 shows the output from this example.

USING DICTIONARIES

Dictionaries take a different approach to storing information. Every other structure covered in this chapter uses some type of numeric index — a dictionary relies on a key. Using a key does increase the memory footprint of a dictionary so you don't want to use a dictionary all the time, even though the quick access of a key may seem quite attractive. The key does make it possible to access elements considerably faster. Listing 4-13 shows a dictionary in use.

LISTING 4-13: Accessing data using a dictionary

```
# Create the dictionary.
PeopleColors = {'George':'Red', 'Ann':'Purple', 'Sam':'Yellow'}

# Randomly access a value.
```

```
print 'The color George likes best is', PeopleColors['George']

# Add a new person and color.
PeopleColors['Nancy'] = 'Blue'

# Verify that the new person was added.
if PeopleColors.has_key('Nancy'):
    print 'Added Nancy with color', PeopleColors['Nancy']

# Iterate through all of the values.
print '\nHere are the colors people like:'
for Key, Value in PeopleColors.iteritems():
    print Key, 'likes', Value

# Pause after the debug session.
raw_input('Press any key to continue...')
```

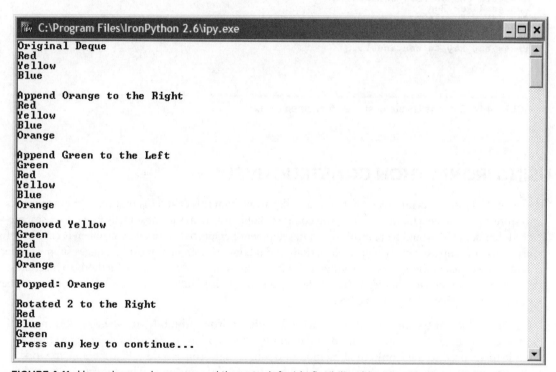

```
C:\Program Files\IronPython 2.6\ipy.exe

Original Deque
Red
Yellow
Blue

Append Orange to the Right
Red
Yellow
Blue
Orange

Append Green to the Left
Green
Red
Yellow
Blue
Orange

Removed Yellow
Green
Red
Blue
Orange

Popped: Orange

Rotated 2 to the Right
Red
Blue
Green
Press any key to continue...
```

FIGURE 4-11: Use a deque when you need the extra left-side flexibility this structure can provide.

Creating a dictionary is different from other sorts of storage types. Notice that you enclose all of the values in curly braces ({}). The key appears first and the value second. You separate key from value using a colon (:). The key is normally a string, but the value can be anything. The example could just as easily have used numbers.

Accessing a particular dictionary element is different, too. You don't need to know an index number — you simply need to know the value you want. In this case, the example shows the color that George likes best. The code doesn't need to know that George appears first in the dictionary (he actually doesn't, but more about that in a moment).

Adding new members to a dictionary is easy. You simply provide a new key and assign a value to it, as shown in the code. If you want to verify that a particular key appears in the dictionary, simply use the has_key() method. It's important to remember that dictionaries use methods different from those of other storage techniques. For example, there's no append() method when working with a dictionary. Interestingly enough, a dictionary does provide the pop() method.

Iterating through a dictionary (listing its content) is also a bit different. You still use a for loop to perform the task. However, notice that you use the iteritems() method to obtain a list of key/value pairs from the dictionary. Figure 4-12 shows the output from this example.

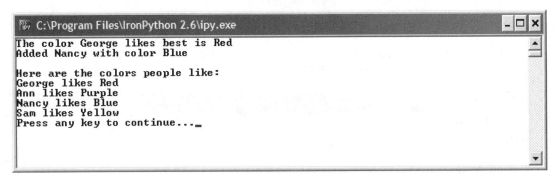

FIGURE 4-12: Dictionaries are best used for named data.

USING IRONPYTHON CONSTRUCTIVELY

One of the most important facts that you can take away from this chapter is that there are many ways to store and manage data in memory. You could probably use arrays for absolutely every data storage need, but doing so would be painful from a development perspective. Not every problem is easy to solve using just an array, so you also need collections and dictionaries. In fact, most languages support other data storage mechanisms — only IronPython could successfully use these three methods to meet most needs. As mentioned in Chapter 1, IronPython tends to simplify things and so far you've seen a number of examples of that strategy in the book.

It's time to look at the memory storage methodologies in IronPython. If you've been working with another language for a long time (and I'm assuming that you have), it's probably going to take a while to get used to the IronPython method of doing things. You should take time now to work through the examples in the chapter and then create a few of your own. The question you need to ask is how the data storage structures in IronPython relate to those used in the language you already know. In many cases, making this comparison can help you become productive considerably faster. In addition, this exercise will firmly implant the IronPython methodology in your brain.

Chapter 5 is the last of the basics chapters in the book. In this case, you discover how to interact with objects. This means looking at objects that IronPython already provides, as well as creating new objects of your own. Up to this point, you could probably look at IronPython as you would any other scripting language. However, Chapter 5 starts to show you some of the impressive capabilities that IronPython provides. Of course, Chapter 5 will build on what you've learned so far — all the basics in Chapters 1 through 4 will come into play as you begin working with objects.

5

Interacting with Structures and Objects

WHAT'S IN THIS CHAPTER?

➤ Using native IronPython objects

➤ Creating your own classes and objects

Most developers work with structures and objects today because structures and objects focus on data, rather than on the procedure for modifying the data. Structures and objects are also extremely flexible when compared to procedures. In fact, if you've been programming for any time at all, you probably wouldn't be without structures and objects as part of your programmer toolbox.

Like all modern languages, IronPython provides the means for working with both structures and objects. In fact, a surprising number of the IronPython features you've already worked with are objects. For example, when you work with a string, you have access to a number of methods for manipulating the string. The "Performing a Simple Decision Using if" section of Chapter 3 is the first place in the book where you work with a string as an object, but it won't be the last. Because IronPython hides so many objects from view through sheer simplicity, the first section of this chapter discusses common IronPython objects and how to work with them.

Providing objects in IronPython wouldn't be very helpful if you couldn't create new objects of your own. After all, objects help you model the real world and make sense out of it from within an application. IronPython lets you create your own classes, derive objects from the classes, and use the objects with the same ease as built-in objects. The third section of the chapter fills you in on all the details of working with objects in IronPython. If you're used to working with other languages, you'll want to pay close attention to IronPython object differences because there are a few tricks that you'll want to know before you begin creating your own objects.

WORKING WITH EXISTING OBJECTS

In many respects, most of what you work with in IronPython is some sort of object. When working with most languages, you have a vision of data types as being just that — data only. You assign a number to a variable and see that the variable has some kind of presence on the stack as simply a number. However, in IronPython, a variable holding a number is a lot more than simply a number — the variable is actually an object with callable methods and properties that tell you more about the variable. For example, try assigning a number to a variable (say i in this case), and then call i.__sizeof__(). You'll discover that you get back the size of the variable in memory. With this bit of information in mind, it's time to discover what other objects lurk beneath the surface of the supposed simplicity that IronPython provides. The following sections tell you more about the existing objects in IronPython.

Discovering IronPython Objects

IronPython objects are everywhere, just waiting for you to discover them. Let's take a closer look at the number example in the introduction to this section. Go ahead and open a copy of the IronPython interpreter, type int = 5, and press Enter. Now type dir(int) and press Enter. That's right, you can treat int as an object in IronPython. You'll see the information shown in Figure 5-1. All these methods and properties apply to int because int is an object, not just a variable as you might suppose when using other languages.

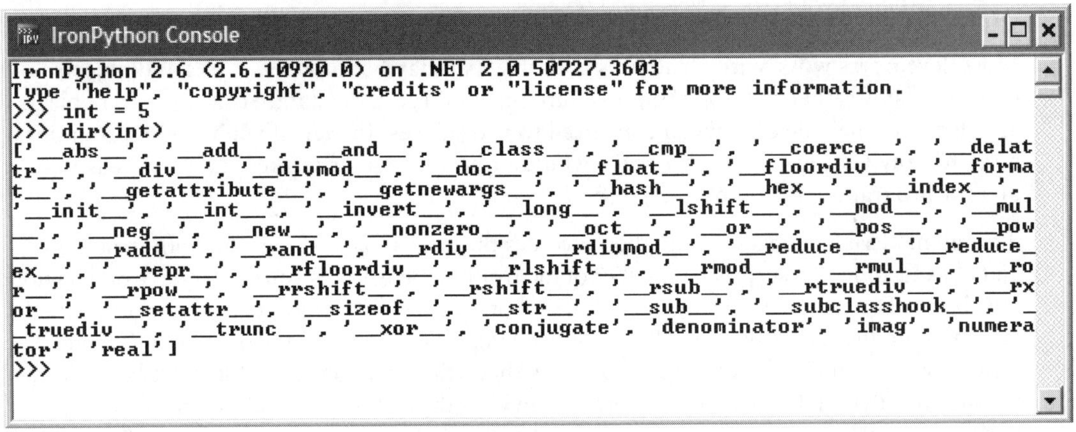

```
IronPython 2.6 (2.6.10920.0) on .NET 2.0.50727.3603
Type "help", "copyright", "credits" or "license" for more information.
>>> int = 5
>>> dir(int)
['__abs__', '__add__', '__and__', '__class__', '__cmp__', '__coerce__', '__delat
tr__', '__div__', '__divmod__', '__doc__', '__float__', '__floordiv__', '__forma
t__', '__getattribute__', '__getnewargs__', '__hash__', '__hex__', '__index__',
'__init__', '__int__', '__invert__', '__long__', '__lshift__', '__mod__', '__mul
__', '__neg__', '__new__', '__nonzero__', '__oct__', '__or__', '__pos__', '__pow
__', '__radd__', '__rand__', '__rdiv__', '__rdivmod__', '__reduce__', '__reduce_
ex__', '__repr__', '__rfloordiv__', '__rlshift__', '__rmod__', '__rmul__', '__ro
r__', '__rpow__', '__rrshift__', '__rshift__', '__rsub__', '__rtruediv__', '__rx
or__', '__setattr__', '__sizeof__', '__str__', '__sub__', '__subclasshook__', '__
_truediv__', '__trunc__', '__xor__', 'conjugate', 'denominator', 'imag', 'numera
tor', 'real']
>>>
```

FIGURE 5-1: Objects lurk everywhere in IronPython.

In fact, you may have noticed in previous chapters that it appears that everything in IronPython is an object. It's true; everything you use in IronPython is an object, so always remember to use the dir() function to display the things you can do with the objects you use. The following sections describe a few of the more common IronPython objects and how to work with them. Don't worry — you'll see a lot more objects before you complete the book. These sections are simply here to whet your appetite for more objects later.

To obtain help on a particular object while working in the interpreter, use the object's type as the starting point. For example, if you want to obtain help on the count() *method for the* str *type, you'd type* help(str.count) *and press Enter. The interpreter will display the required information for the string type.*

Working with String Objects

Strings are one of the first objects many people use. You write that first "Hello World" application and marvel when the words appear on screen. In fact, strings are the mainstay of many applications. Without strings you can't provide prompts to the user or ask for input. Sure, you may not do any heavy lifting with strings, but every application out there requires strings to work properly. The following sections discuss the IronPython string object in more detail.

TYPING VARIABLES WITH TYPE()

One of the problems you can encounter when working with an application is thinking a variable is of one type when it's actually something else. Each of the object types in IronPython has something different to offer, so it's important not to confuse one type with another. Chapter 4 demonstrated one potential type problem in working with ragged arrays — you never know whether you'll receive a list or a value. Consequently, you must check the type (or provide error trapping) before you make any assumptions. In order to perform a check, always use the __name__ attribute for comparison purposes like this:

```
MyVar = 'Hello'
if type(MyVar).__name__ == 'str':
    print 'MyVar is a string'
```

As with most things in IronPython, there are multiple ways to perform this task. You don't have to use the type() function. Use the __class__ attribute as shown here instead:

```
MyVar = 'Hello'
if MyVar.__class__.__name__ == 'str':
    print 'MyVar is a string'
```

The result is the same. Theoretically, using __class__ provides a performance boost. However, that performance boost, if any, is quite small, so you should use the approach that works best with your typing skills.

Performing Standard Tasks with Strings

You've already seen a few of the things you can do with strings in previous chapters. This chapter takes a little more organized look at the methods and properties associated with strings. The following list provides an overview of the most common tasks you can perform.

➤ **center(int width[, Char fillchar])**: Centers the string within the space defined by `width`. The default is to use spaces to pad the left and right side of the string to center it. However, you can specify another character by specifying the optional `fillchar`. For example, if you want to center a string named MyString in a 40-character area using the * as a fill character, you'd type `MyString.center(40, '*')`.

➤ **int count(str ssub, [int start[, int end]])**: Counts the number of instances of a substring, `ssub`, within a string. The substring can be one or more letters that you want to find within the string. You may optionally provide a starting point, `start`, and an ending point, `end`, for the count. For example, if you want to count the number of ls found in MyString, you'd type `MyString.count('l', 0, len(MyString))`.

➤ **decode([object encoding[, str errors]])**: Decodes an encoded string. Even though `encoding` is optional, you must provide a value in order to decode the string. You can find a list of standard encodings at `http://www.python.org/doc/2.5.2/lib/standard-encodings.html`. The errors argument defines how `decode()` treats errors, with a default value of `strict`. You can find a list of error strings at `http://www.python.org/doc/2.5.2/lib/codec-base-classes.html`. For example, you might have a Unix-to-Unix Encode (uuencode) string named EncodeString that you want to decode into plain text. To convert the string, you'd type `EncodeString.decode('uu_codec')`.

➤ **encode([object encoding[, str errors]])**: Encodes a string to another format. You have the same options as when decoding a string (see the `decode()` entry in this list). For example, you might want to encode a string using uuencode. To perform this task, you'd type `EncodeString = MyString.encode('uu_codec')`. After the call, `EncodeString` would contain the uuencoded string.

➤ **endswith(object suffix[, int start[, int end]])**: Determines whether the string ends with a particular letter or substring, `suffix`. You may optionally provide a starting point, `start`, and ending point, `end`, in the string. When using an end value, `endswith()` checks the designated endpoint, rather than the actual end of the string. For example, if you want to determine whether there's a l at position 4 (an end point of 3 since the string count begins with 0), you'd type `MyString.endswith('l', 0, 3)`.

➤ **expandtabs([int tabsize])**: Expands the tabs within a string using spaces. You may optionally provide the number of spaces to use for each tab using `tabsize`. For example, if you want to expand the tabs in a string to four spaces, you'd type `MyString.expandtabs(4)`.

➤ **find(str sub[, int start[, int end]]) or find(str sub, object start, object end)**: Locates the substring, `sub`, within the string and outputs an integer value defining the first occurrence of the substring. You can optionally add a starting, `start`, and ending, `end`, value to change the location that the method searches within the string (the default is to search the entire string). In this case, the starting and ending value need not be an integer value, but can be an object that defines the starting and ending point instead. For example, if you want to search for the first occurrence of l within a string, you'd type `MyString.find('l')`. This method returns a value of –1 when the string doesn't contain the search value.

➤ `format(*args[, *kwargs])`: Formats the string using a template (see the "Formatting String Output" section for details). The `args` argument contains positional information and `kwargs` contains a keyword argument.

➤ `index(str sub[, int start[, int end]])` or `index(str sub, object start, object end)`: Performs precisely the same task as `find()`. However, instead of returning –1 when a value isn't found, `index()` raises a `ValueError` instead.

➤ `isalnum()`, `isalpha()`, `isdecimal()`, `isdigit()`, `islower()`, `isnumeric()`, `isspace()`, `istitle()`, `isunicode()`, and `isupper()`: Detects the state of the string and returns True when the specified condition exists. For example, `isalnum()` returns True when a string contains some combination of letters and numbers. The string must contain at least one letter, but need not necessarily contain any numbers. The `isalpha()` method, on the other hand, only returns True when the string contains only letters, and `isnumeric()` returns True when the string contains only numbers.

➤ `join(list sequence)` or `join(object sequence)`: Appends a string to a list or a sequence. This method joins each member of the sequence to the source string. For example, if the source string contains ABC and you join 123 to it, you obtain '1ABC2ABC3' as output. To obtain this output, you'd type `MyString.join('123')`. As an alternative, you could type `MyString.join(['1', '2', '3'])` to obtain the same output using a list.

➤ `ljust(int width[, Char fillchar])`: Left-justifies the string to a length specified by `width` by padding the left end with the specified number of characters. You can optionally specify a fill character other than the default of a space by providing `fillchar`. For example, if you want to left-justify a string to 40 spaces and fill the spaces with an *, you'd type `MyString.ljust(40, '*')`.

➤ `lower()`: Returns the lowercase version of the string.

➤ `lstrip([str chars])`: Removes white space from the beginning of a string by default. You may also provide a `chars` value as input. In this case, the method removes that character from the beginning of the string when it exists. For example, to remove the leading spaces from a string, you'd type `MyString.lstrip()`.

➤ `partition(str sep)`: Divides the string into three parts based on the value of `sep`. The first part contains the piece of the string before `sep`, the second part contains `sep`, and the third part contains the piece of the string after `sep`. For example, to split a string at the first space, you'd type `MyString.partition(' ')`.

➤ `replace(object old, object new[, int maxsplit])`: Replaces the occurrences of `old` with `new` in the target string. You may provide an optional number of replacements to make by defining `maxsplit`. For example, if you want to replace the spaces in a string with the newline escape code, you'd type `MyString.replace(' ', '/n')`.

➤ `rfind()`: Performs the same task as `find()`, except that this method searches from the right end of the string, rather than the left. See the `find()` entry in the list for details.

➤ **rindex():** Performs the same task as `index()`, except that this method indexes from the right end of the string, rather than the left. See the `index()` entry in the list for details.

➤ **rjust():** Performs the same task as `ljust()`, except that this method right-justifies the string, rather than left-justifying it. See the `ljust()` entry in the list for details.

➤ **rpartition():** Performs the same task as `partition()`, except that this method partitions the right side of the string, rather than the left side. See the `partition()` entry in the list for details.

➤ **rsplit():** Performs the same task as `split()`, except that this method begins at the right side of the string, rather than the left. See the `split()` entry in the list for details.

➤ **rstrip():** Performs the same task as `lstrip()`, except that this method begins at the right side of the string, rather than the left. See the `lstrip` entry in the list for details.

➤ **split(str sep[, int maxsplit]):** Divides the string into a list using `sep` as the point of division. You may provide an optional number of replacements to make by defining `maxsplit`. For example, if you want to divide a string into individual words, you'd type `MyString.split(' ')`.

➤ **splitlines([bool keepends]):** Breaks a string apart by lines. The output is a list of lines within the string. Normally, the output doesn't include the newline character. However, you can keep the newline character by setting `keepends` to `True`. For example, to break a string part into individual lines, you'd type `MyString.splitlines()`.

➤ **startswith():** Performs the same task as `endswith()`, except that this method works with the beginning of the string, rather than the end of the string. See the `endswith()` entry in the list for details.

➤ **strip():** Performs the same task as `lstrip()`, except that this method removes spaces (or other characters) from both ends of the string, rather than just the left. See the `lstrip()` entry in the list for details.

➤ **swapcase():** Sets all of the lowercase characters to uppercase and all of the uppercase characters to lowercase. For example, if you begin with 'Hello World', you'd receive 'hELLO wORLD' as output if you typed `MyString.swapcase()`.

➤ **title():** Returns a title-cased version of a string where the first letter of each word is capitalized and all other letters are lowercase. For example, if you begin with 'helLo wORLD', you'd receive 'Hello World' as output if you typed `MyString.title()`.

➤ **translate(str table, [str deletechars])** or `translate(dict table)`: Replaces the characters in a string with the equivalents specified by `table`. The `table` argument is 256 characters long and you can create it using the `MakeTrans()` function found in the string module. (Remember to use `from string import maketrans` to make accessing the function easy.) For example, if you want to replace the first 16 lowercase letters with hexadecimal equivalents, you'd type `MyString.translate(maketrans('abcdefghijklmnop', '0123456789ABCDEF'))`. Using this code as a starting point, 'Hello World' becomes 'H4BBE WErB3'.

➤ **upper():** Returns the uppercase version of the string.

➤ `zfill(int width)`: Returns a string that has zeros placed on the left side to pad the string to the length specified by width. For example, if you typed `MyString.zfill(40)`, you'd receive a string that is 40 characters long with as many zeros on the left side as required to produce the required length.

Formatting String Output

String formatting can become quite complex in Python and IronPython. However, if you start with the basics, you'll find that you can usually figure out the complex elements without too much trouble. A basic format string contains one or more fields. A *field* is simply some text that appears within curly braces that you replace with a value. In fact, if you've worked with any .NET language, you've already used fields. Here's a simple sentence that contains a field.

```
MyString = 'Hello {0}'
```

Of course, you won't want to print this string directly onscreen. Instead, you'll want to replace `{0}` with some other value. In order to do this, you can use the `format()` method as shown here.

```
MyString.format('George')
```

The interpreter replaces the `{0}` with the name `George`. Consequently, you see 'Hello George' as output from these two lines of code. You have a number of options when working with replaceable variables in a string. The following list shows just a few of the options:

➤ **`MyString = 'Hello {0}'`**: Provides a simple replacement from a list of input arguments. The input arguments must appear in the order required in the string.

➤ **`MyString = 'Hello {0[name]}'`**: Provides a replacement from a dictionary. The corresponding `format()` method input is `MyString.format({'name':'George'})`. Of course, you can provide additional field information if your dictionary contains arrays for each of the elements. In this case, you specify the element you want to use like this: `MyString = 'Hello {0[names][0]}'`. The resulting `format()` method input is `MyString.format({'names':['George', 'Amy']})`. The advantage of this method is that the input arguments can appear in any order.

➤ **`MyString = 'The paths are {0.path}'`**: Provides a means of accessing an attribute within an object. The corresponding `format()` method input is `MyString.format(sys)`. If you want to access a specific path, simply include the element specifier like this: `MyString = 'The path is {0.path[0]}'`. The advantage of this technique is that you can access properties within objects without first placing the property value in a variable.

A formatting string can contain as many variables as needed to provide complete information to the user. For example, you can add a second argument like this.

```
MyString = 'Hello {0} from {1}'
```

When you call the `format()` method, you now need to add some more information. The `format()` method input for this string might look like this.

```
MyString.format('George', 'London')
```

In many cases, you need to provide input that doesn't translate into a string. For example, you might need to provide integer input for some strings. The interpreter won't automatically perform a conversion in this case so you need to perform the task manually. The conversion symbol is the exclamation mark (!) and the most common conversion is string (s). You can also call the repr() conversion function by using r in place of s. Here's an example of a conversion:

```
MyString = '{0!s} + {1!s} = {2!s}'
MyString.format(1, 2, 1+2)
```

In this case, you get an output of '1 + 2 = 3'. Notice that this example places the math directly in the format string. You could place the output of a function there as well.

So far, the examples haven't done much formatting — they have simply replaced field values with information found in other sources. The format operator is the colon (:) and you can combine it with the conversion operator if you want. To see how this works, think about displaying the previous example in hexadecimal format. In that case, your code might look like this:

```
MyString = '{0:X} + {1:X} = {2:X}'
MyString.format(10, 20, 10+20)
```

The output from this code is in hexadecimal format — you'd see 'A + 14 = 1E'. Of course, you might want all the values to take up the same space. In this case, you can tell the interpreter to add some space to the output using the following string:

```
MyString = '{0:0=4X} + {1:0=4X} = {2:0=4X}'
```

This string outputs numbers with zeros as padding. The padding appears after any sign information. In addition, each of the entries is four digits long. Consequently, the output now looks like this: '000A + 0014 = 001E'. The formatting has specific entries, all of which are options. It looks like this:

```
[[fill]align][sign][#][0][width][.precision][type]
```

Fill characters determine what appears as part of the padding the interpreter uses when you specify a width, and the field value doesn't fill the entire space. The default padding is the space, but you can specify any character other than the closing brace, which would end the formatting definition. When you specify a fill character, such as the 0 used in the previous example, you must also use one of the alignment characters found in Table 5-1.

TABLE 5-1: String Formatting Alignment Options

OPTION	MEANING
'<'	Sets the field to use left alignment, which is the default.
'>'	Sets the field to use right alignment.
'='	Adds the padding after the sign (if any), but before any digits. You've already seen the effect of this alignment option earlier in this chapter. The interpreter recognizes this alignment only when working with numeric types.
'^'	Centers the field information within the available space.

The use of signs in the output comes next. For example, you can choose to have all positive numbers begin with a plus sign (+) so there's no confusion about their positive value. Table 5-2 shows the sign formatting options you can use.

TABLE 5-2: String Formatting Sign Options

OPTION	MEANING
'+'	Adds a sign for both positive and negative numbers.
'-'	Adds a sign only for negative numbers. This is the default behavior.
Spacebar space	Adds a leading space for positive numbers and a minus sign for negative numbers. Using this option lets you align numbers in tables that contain both positive and negative numbers.

The pound sign (#), which is called by a host of names, such as octothorp and number sign, tells the interpreter to add a letter after numeric values to show their base — b for binary, o for octal, or x for hexadecimal (decimal values never have the letter added). For example, if you change the previous formatting string to include the # like this:

```
MyString = '{0:0=#6X} + {1:0=#6X} = {2:0=#6X}'
```

the output changes to include the correct base designation. You'll see '0X000A + 0X0014 = 0X001E' as the output.

The width and precision entries come next. If you precede the width value with a 0, then the interpreter will pad the numeric values with zeros. The precision entry tells the interpreter how many decimal places to use for the output.

The final formatting you can request is the output type. In this case, you must decide in advance what kind of value that the field will accept — integers use different type designations than floating point and decimal types. Table 5-3 shows the types you can use for integer input, while Table 5-4 shows the types for floating point and decimal.

TABLE 5-3: Integer Formatting Types

OPTION	MEANING
'b'	Outputs the number as a base 2 (binary) value.
'c'	Converts the integer value to a Unicode character prior to printing. The acceptable value range is from 0 to 255. The output shows printable characters up to 126 (the tilde, ~).
'd'	Outputs the number as a base 10 (decimal) value. This is the default output.
'o'	Outputs the number as a base 8 (octal) value.

continues

TABLE 5-3 *(continued)*

OPTION	MEANING
'x'	Outputs the number as a base 16 (hexadecimal) value. The interpreter uses lowercase characters for any value above 9 and also for the base indicator.
'X'	Outputs the number as a base 16 (hexadecimal) value. The interpreter uses uppercase characters for any value above 9 and also for the base indicator.
'n'	Outputs the number as a base 10 (decimal) value. However, this setting uses the user's locale setting for separator characters. For example, many countries use the comma for the decimal point instead of a period.

TABLE 5-4: Floating Point and Decimal Formatting Types

OPTION	MEANING
'e'	Outputs the number in exponent (scientific notation) form, using the letter 'e' (lowercase) to indicate the exponent.
'E'	Outputs the number in exponent (scientific notation) form, using the letter 'E' (uppercase) to indicate the exponent.
'f' or 'F'	Outputs the number in fixed-point format.
'g'	Outputs the number in a general format. The presentation depends on the numeric magnitude. Smaller numbers appear in fixed-point format, while larger numbers appear in scientific notation.
	The rules for determining whether a number appears in either fixed-point or scientific notation are relatively complex, but are based on the size and precision of the number. If a number would require too many zeros (due to being too large or too small) to present as fixed point, the interpreter automatically chooses scientific notation. No matter how the interpreter presents the number, it removes insignificant trailing zeros. In addition, the interpreter removes the decimal point if there aren't any digits following it.
	The interpreter also presents positive infinity as inf, negative infinity as -inf, positive zero as 0, negative zero as -0, and Not-a-Number (NaN) as nan. You can read more about these special value representations at `http://steve.hollasch.net/cgindex/coding/ieeefloat.html`.
'G'	Outputs the number in general format using the same requirements as the 'g' type. The difference is that this type uses an uppercase 'E' for scientific notation. Both representations of infinity and NaN appear in uppercase as well.
'n'	Outputs the number in general format using the same requirements as the 'g' type. This type differs because it relies on the user's current locale settings to insert the appropriate number separator characters.
'%'	Outputs the number as a percentage by multiplying the number by 100 and appending a percent sign.

Working with Numeric Objects

Numeric objects include a number of methods that make working with them easier. It's important to realize that some of the methods that apply to strings also apply to numbers. For example, you can access the __format__() method when working with a number. In addition, you can easily turn a number into a string using the __str__() method. Some string-oriented methods actually revolve around numbers, such as the format typing described in Tables 5-3 and 5-4. In short, don't think that numbers are limited to number-specific methods. The following sections consider the kinds of things you can do with numbers.

Considering Numeric Type Differences

IronPython generally splits numbers between integers and floats (decimals are included with floats). The two numeric presentations are handled differently by the interpreter and even have different representations at the hardware level, so it's no surprise that there are differences you must consider when working with a number. However, as when working with strings, you can cause numbers to cross the divide. An integer can appear as a float using the __float__() method. Likewise, you can use __int__() or __trunc__() methods.

Numeric types have some similarities. For example, both integers and floats support the __abs__() method, which returns the absolute value of the number. In some cases, you have to look for the similarities. For example, floats provide a hex() method that performs the same task as __hex__() does for integers.

Integers have a few interesting methods that floats can't support because of their memory representation. For example, you can use the __and__() method to "and" the value of the variable with another integer (where "anding" 5 and 4 would result in an output of 4, and "anding" 5 and 7 would result in an output of 5). In fact, here's a list of methods that appear for integers that don't appear for floats (you'll notice that most of them have something to do with bit-level manipulation):

- ➤ __and__
- ➤ __cmp__
- ➤ __hex__
- ➤ __index__
- ➤ __invert__
- ➤ __lshift__
- ➤ __oct__
- ➤ __or__
- ➤ __rand__
- ➤ __rlshift__
- ➤ __ror__
- ➤ __rrshift__
- ➤ __rshift__

➤ __rxor__

➤ __xor__

➤ denominator

➤ numerator

Floats, likewise, have a few methods that apply only to them. Most of these methods deal with performing comparisons. For example, you need a special method to determine that two floats are equal to each other (the __eq__() method). The following list shows these methods:

➤ __eq__

➤ __ge__

➤ __getformat__

➤ __gt__

➤ __le__

➤ __lt__

➤ __ne__

➤ __setformat__

➤ as_integer_ratio

➤ fromhex

➤ hex

➤ is_integer

Performing Standard Tasks with Numbers

Now that you have a better idea of how numbers compare, it's time to look at some specific methods. This section describes some of the more common methods used with numbers. You'll see a good many of the other methods demonstrated as the book progresses.

➤ **as_integer_ratio()** (float only): Displays a tuple showing the integer ratio used to produce the float. For example, if the float value is 5.5, then this method outputs (11L, 2L). To use this method type MyFloat.as_integer_ratio().

➤ **conjugate()**: Returns the conjugate of a complex number or the identity value of a real number. You can read more about conjugation at http://en.wikipedia.org/wiki/Complex_conjugate.

➤ **fromhex(str input)** (float only): Outputs the decimal equivalent of a hexadecimal number input as a string. For example, to determine the decimal value of the hexadecimal number A5, you'd type MyFloat.fromhex('A5'). In this case, the output is 165.

➤ **hex()** (float) or **__hex__()** (integer): Outputs the hexadecimal value of the float or integer. For example, to find the hexadecimal value of MyInt, you'd type MyInt.__hex__().

➤ **imag:** Contains the imaginary part of a complex number. To use this attribute you'd type `MyComplex.imag`.

➤ **is_integer()** (float only): Determines whether the content of a floating point number is an integer in value. When using this method, a value of 5.0 would return `True`, while a value of 5.1 would return `False`. To use this method, you'd type `MyFloat.is_integer()`.

➤ **real:** Contains the real part of a complex number. To use this attribute you'd type `MyComplex.real`.

 The `int.denominator` *and* `int.numerator` *attributes are in place for support of rational numbers. You can read more about this support at* `http://www.python.org/dev/peps/pep-0239/`.

Working with Boolean Objects

Boolean objects provide access to truth values about other objects and their relationships. Many objects have Boolean methods built in. For example, when working with a float, you can use the equality methods `__eq__()`, `__ge__()`, `__gt__()`, `__le__()`, `__lt__()`, and `__ne__()` to determine relationships between values. In fact, Boolean objects also include these equality methods and you might find them useful at times for comparing the truth value of two Boolean objects.

For the most part, Boolean objects have little in the way of other methods that you need when creating a typical IronPython application. For example, you could use the `__long__()` method to convert the Boolean to long integer, but that really wouldn't accomplish much for most developers. About the only other method that you really need to know about is `__format__()`, which is explained in the "Formatting String Output" section of the chapter.

CREATING NEW OBJECTS

Although IronPython has a wealth of built-in objects, you eventually need to create your own objects for an application of any complexity. If you've worked with other languages and scratched your head over some of the requirements for creating a class, you'll find that IronPython is a welcome change. Creating and using custom classes in IronPython is amazingly easy. The following sections tell you how to create a basic class and then show how to use it. Don't worry about the simplicity of this example; you'll have plenty of opportunity to create more complex classes later in the book.

Defining the IronPython Class

An IronPython class can have both attributes (properties) and methods, just as any class in any other language can have. However, IronPython classes have a few quirks as well. Listing 5-1 shows an example of a simple IronPython class.

You've probably worked with a language that has both structures and classes. The structures serve as a means to tightly pack information and possibly add some information to it. Using structures in other languages usually incurs a performance benefit at a cost of some flexibility. IronPython also has structures, but these structures work differently from other languages. An IronPython structure is more like a marshaling mechanism used for binary protocols and some types of networking, and you probably won't use it very often. Consequently, this book concentrates on objects. If you do need a structure-like construct for your application, most experts recommend using dictionaries or field-only class constructs in IronPython. You can read more about IronPython structures at `http://docs.python.org/library/struct.html`*.*

LISTING 5-1: Defining a simple class

```
class MyGreetings:

    # Greeting name variable.
    Name = 'Sammy'

    # Provides a hello greeting.
    def SayHello(self):
        print 'Hello there', self.Name, '!'

    # Provides a goodbye message.
    def SayGoodbye(self):
        print 'See you later', self.Name, '!'
```

The class description starts out with the word `class`, as you might expect, and the name of the class. If you plan to inherit from another class, you enclose its name in parentheses behind the class name like this:

```
class MyGreetings(sys):
```

In this case, the `MyGreetings` class would inherit from the `sys` class. A class definition ends with a colon, just like every other structure in IronPython. You use indentation, as normal, to signify the end of the class.

Attributes are simply variables that you declare as part of the class. As you can see, you normally define a default value for attributes. An attribute can be of any type.

You might have noticed that Name *doesn't include anything other than the variable name and its value. IronPython doesn't support the concept of data hiding — it isn't possible to declare attributes and methods as private. More than a few people have discussed the topic online, but the general consensus is that IronPython knows what you're doing and will let you shoot yourself in the foot if you really want to do so.*

Methods are simply a different kind of function in IronPython. You define them within the class as you might expect. A method uses `def` as the starting point, followed by the method name. Notice that both methods, `SayHello()` and `SayGoodbye()`, have an input variable named `self`. When you create an instance of a class, the interpreter automatically creates the `self` variable for that instance. The `self` variable contains all of the data associated with that instance, such as `Name` in this case. As you discover in the "Using Custom Objects in IronPython" section, you don't actually assign any value to `self`, the interpreter does it for you.

As shown in the method code, you can use any of the data that `self` provides. In this case, the code accesses `self.Name` to obtain the name you assigned to the `Name` attribute (or the default, if you haven't). If you were to try to access `Name` directly, the interpreter would display an error message.

Using Custom Objects in IronPython

At this point, you have a shiny new class named `MyGreetings`. Normally, you won't place the class and the code that uses it in the same file, so the example places the test code in `TestFirstClass.py`. Consequently, the first thing the example does is import `MyGreetings` from `FirstClass`, as shown in Listing 5-2.

LISTING 5-2: Testing the simple class

```
from FirstClass import MyGreetings

# Create an instance of the class.
TestIt = MyGreetings()

# Set the Name attribute.
TestIt.Name = 'George'

# Call the two methods.
TestIt.SayHello()
TestIt.SayGoodbye()

# Pause after the debug session.
raw_input('Press any key to continue...')
```

At this point, the code creates an instance of `MyGreetings` and places it in `TestIt`. Notice that the call to `MyGreetings` doesn't require any data. If you want to request data from the caller during instantiation, you must provide an `__init__()` method in your class declaration. Otherwise, the interpreter provides a default declaration for you that creates the desired object.

The code changes the value of `Name` by assigning a new value to it. Notice that you assign the new value to `TestIt.Name`, just as you would in any other language.

Next, the code calls the two methods, `SayHello()` and `SayGoodbye()`. Notice that the method calls don't require any input, and IronPython would complain if you tried to provide it. Remember that the interpreter provides `self` in the background. Figure 5-2 shows the output from this application.

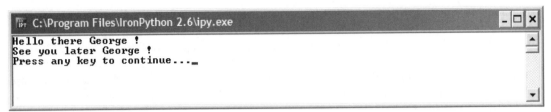

FIGURE 5-2: The simple class outputs the expected information.

Adding Documentation

It's important to add documentation to your class as soon as possible — preferably while you're typing the code. Many IronPython developers work in the interpreter to create applications faster and rely on the help() function or __doc__ attribute to understand what a method does with considerably less effort than finding the documentation.

Adding documentation to your class is straightforward. You simply add strings immediately after the class or method definition. A string that documents your class is called a *docstring*. IronPython doesn't recognize docstrings that appear in places other than class and method declarations. For example, if you place a docstring after an attribute, it won't appear when you use the help() function or __doc__ attribute. However, third-party tools often pick up these additional docstrings and place them in any documentation they output. Listing 5-3 shows the example class with docstrings in place.

LISTING 5-3: Adding documentation to a class

```
class MyGreetings:
    """Contains a list of messages that you want to send to the user.
    Make sure you assign a value to Name before using any of the
     greetings so the message is customize for that user."""

    # Greeting name variable.
    Name = 'Sammy'
    """Provides the user's name."""

    # Provides a hello greeting.
    def SayHello(self):
        """Outputs an interesting greeting to the user."""
        print 'Hello there', self.Name, '!'

    # Provides a goodbye message.
    def SayGoodbye(self):
        """Outputs a goodbye message to the user."""
        print 'See you later', self.Name, '!'
```

Docstrings can consume one or more lines. The standard convention is to place docstrings within triple quotes as shown in the listing. You can find a number of other docstring conventions at http://www.python.org/dev/peps/pep-0257/.

After you create your docstrings, start the IronPython interpreter and load your class. You can try the docstrings out using either the `help()` function or `__doc__` attribute. Figure 5-3 shows the docstring output for the example class.

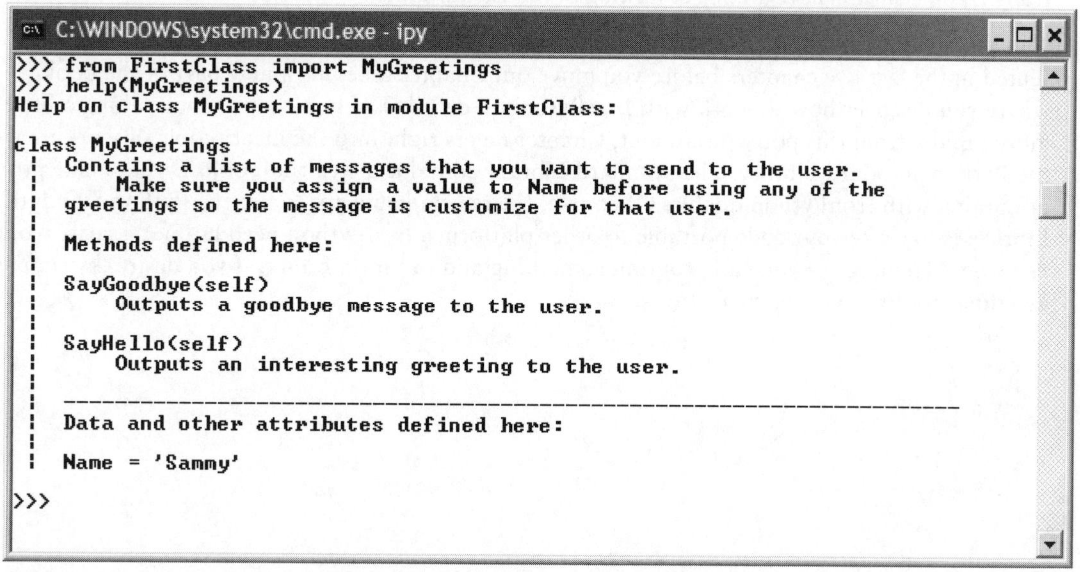

```
C:\WINDOWS\system32\cmd.exe - ipy
>>> from FirstClass import MyGreetings
>>> help(MyGreetings)
Help on class MyGreetings in module FirstClass:

class MyGreetings
 |  Contains a list of messages that you want to send to the user.
 |      Make sure you assign a value to Name before using any of the
 |  greetings so the message is customize for that user.
 |
 |  Methods defined here:
 |
 |  SayGoodbye(self)
 |      Outputs a goodbye message to the user.
 |
 |  SayHello(self)
 |      Outputs an interesting greeting to the user.
 |
 |  ----------------------------------------------------------------
 |
 |  Data and other attributes defined here:
 |
 |  Name = 'Sammy'
>>>
```

FIGURE 5-3: Docstrings add greatly to the usability of your application.

Self-documenting your application is great, but some people will prefer some sort of HTML documentation. Don't worry; you can get a tool to handle this requirement as well. PythonDoc (`http://effbot.org/zone/pythondoc.htm`) provides the same type of functionality that JavaDoc does. It's akin to generating the documentation you need when you compile your application in Visual Studio. PythonDoc locates all of the comments in your code and uses them to create HTML documentation that others can use when working with your classes.

USING IRONPYTHON CONSTRUCTIVELY

This chapter has helped you discover the objects lurking beneath the surface in IronPython. These objects provide a surprising number of features that simply occur automatically. In fact, IronPython makes objects look surprisingly simple. Of course, you won't be happy using just the objects that IronPython provides, so this chapter also demonstrates how to create structures and objects of your own. The key thing to take from this chapter is not to make structures and objects too hard in IronPython — think simple. Otherwise, you'll end up doing a lot more work than you really need to do to make use of objects. More important, your objects might not actually work as you intend if you make them too complex (to look like objects you create in other languages).

By now, you should have some interesting ideas for creating objects of your own. Try creating some structures and objects in IronPython. In fact, try creating some of both structures and objects to ensure you understand the difference between the two. Take time to work with enough objects that you understand how they differ from those you create in other languages.

You can play around with searching for objects in IronPython. Use the techniques in this chapter to locate potential objects and then look them up in the IronPython help. Don't cheat now — look for the objects first and then study about them in the documentation. You'll be amazed at how many IronPython elements have an object lurking in the background.

This is the last basic chapter of the book. It's important that you understand the concepts presented in the last five chapters before you move on. Chapter 6 begins a new part of the book where you discover how to work with IronPython in detail. The book topics move along a little more rapidly from this point on. In fact, Chapter 6 gets right into the meaty topic of working with the Python Standard Library. The Standard Library contains a wealth of objects that make programming with IronPython doable. Of course, the reason you want to use the Python Standard Library is to make your code portable to other platforms. IronPython need not necessarily work as its own language — you can program something and run it on Linux, if you desire, by simply avoiding IronPython-specific features.

PART III
Working with IronPython

Using the Python Standard Library

WHAT'S IN THIS CHAPTER?

➤ Understanding what the Standard Library can do for you

➤ Getting a copy of the Standard Library for your system

➤ Using the Standard Library from within IronPython

➤ Working with the Standard Library

The Python Standard Library is the centerpiece of any IronPython you want to create of any complexity. If you want to ensure that your IronPython application will run on other platforms using other Python interpreters, then you need to stick with the functionality that the Standard Library provides and avoid the temptation to use .NET features (see Chapter 7 for details) in your application. Of course, the first thing you'll want to do is discover what the Standard Library can do for you — perhaps it contains everything you need and falling back on .NET won't be a problem.

Interestingly enough, IronPython does ship with a version of the Standard Library that's been tuned for maximum compatibility with IronPython. Of course, the problem word in that previous sentence is "tuned." If you want to ensure maximum compatibility outside the IronPython environment, you must download a copy of the Python Standard Library, install it on your machine, and use it in place of the IronPython equivalent. It's also important to know that the IronPython version of the Standard Library isn't complete. You won't have all the functionality that other Python developers have unless you use the Python Standard Library.

Whichever version of the Standard Library you use, you'll need to import modules into your application before you can use them. This chapter provides a few tricks and techniques you can use to make accessing the modules easier. It'll also explain how IronPython locates the modules so you don't spend a lot of time trying to figure out why a particular module is seemingly inaccessible.

Finally, in this chapter, you'll spend some time working with the Standard Library. You'll also spend a considerable amount of time exploring parts of the Standard Library as the book progresses because you need it for everything from working from files to parsing XML. The examples in this chapter are meant to whet your appetite and demonstrate a few of the more interesting things you can do with the Standard Library. Make sure you take some time to play with the Standard Library on your own, too. You'll be amazed at what you can accomplish after reading this chapter!

CONSIDERING THE STANDARD LIBRARY FEATURES

The Standard Library comes with a number of features not found in IronPython. Of course, there are all those missing modules. If you look in \Python26\Lib you'll find that the Python Standard Library contains 256 modules in the main library directory, while IronPython has only 186. (Table 6-1 shows a complete list of the missing modules — each module contains a header telling you about the task it performs.) In addition, the Python library contains 20 subdirectories, while IronPython has only 11. In short, the IronPython version of the Standard Library has a lot to offer; the Python version of the Standard Library has more. Here's a list of the missing directories:

➤ **bsddb:** Provides access to the Berkeley database library. This element is deprecated and will disappear in Python 3.0, but you can still use it today. See http://docs.python.org/library/bsddb.html for details.

➤ **compiler:** Contains elements that help you analyze your code. This element is deprecated and will disappear in Python 3.0, but you can still use it today. See http://docs.python.org/library/compiler.html for details.

➤ **curses:** Provides the means to handle character-cell displays. See http://docs.python.org/library/curses.html for details.

➤ **hotshot:** Gives you a high-performance logging profiler. See http://docs.python.org/library/hotshot.html for details.

➤ **json:** Implements the JavaScript Object Notation (JSON) encoder and decoder used as a light-weight data exchange format. See http://docs.python.org/library/json.html for details.

➤ **msilib:** Reads and writes Microsoft Installer (MSI) files. The Microsoft Installer Library (MSILib) is an essential library for Windows systems where you need to work with .MSI files often. See http://docs.python.org/library/msilib.html for details.

➤ **multiprocessing:** Helps you create multi-processing applications. This is an exciting new addition for Python 2.6. See http://docs.python.org/library/multiprocessing.html for details.

➤ **sqlite3:** Provides access to the SQLite database library. See http://docs.python.org/library/sqlite3.html for details. You can learn more about the SQLite database at http://www.sqlite.org/.

➤ **test:** Contains a complete test package for the Python Standard Library. If you make any changes to the Standard Library to meet your specific needs, you want to perform regression testing to ensure the changes don't introduce incompatibilities. See http://docs.python.org/library/test.html for details.

Standard Library files that have a .pyc extension are Python-compiled files that contain byte code. You can't read them, but they're always accompanied by a .py file that you can read. The .pyc files are useful because they execute faster than the .py files because the interpreter doesn't have to turn them into byte code first.

TABLE 6-1: Standard Library Modules Missing from IronPython

__future__.pyc	_abcoll.pyc	abc.pyc	ast.py
BaseHTTPServer.pyc	bdb.pyc	bisect.pyc	code.pyc
codecs.pyc	codeop.pyc	collections.pyc	ConfigParser.pyc
copy.pyc	copy_reg.py	copy_reg.pyc	cProfile.py
csv.py	dbhash.py	dis.pyc	fnmatch.pyc
functools.pyc	genericpath.pyc	getopt.pyc	gzip.py
heapq.pyc	inspect.pyc	keyword.pyc	linecache.pyc
locale.pyc	mimetools.pyc	ntpath.pyc	opcode.pyc
os.pyc	pkgutil.pyc	pty.py	pydoc.pyc
Queue.pyc	random.pyc	re.py	re.pyc
repr.pyc	rfc822.pyc	shlex.pyc	site.pyc
socket.py	socket.pyc	SocketServer.pyc	sre.py
sre_compile.pyc	sre_constants.pyc	sre_parse.pyc	ssl.py
stat.pyc	string.pyc	stringprep.py	struct.pyc
subprocess.py	subprocess.pyc	symtable.py	tabnanny.pyc
tempfile.pyc	threading.pyc	token.pyc	tokenize.pyc
traceback.pyc	tty.py	types.pyc	UserDict.pyc
warnings.pyc	webbrowser.py	webbrowser.pyc	

Getting all of the modules found in the original Python Standard Library would be reason enough to download, install, and use it. However, the Python Standard Library provides a number of additional features in the form of help files and utilities. Although you can't use the utilities to perform .NET-specific work, you can use them to ensure your code is truly compatible with Python, which is a big deal if you plan to use your application on other platforms. With this in mind, here's a list of the additional help files and utilities provided with the Python Standard Library. (You can read more about them in the "Using the Standard Library Features" section of the chapter.)

➤ **IDLE (Integrated DeveLopment Environment):** A graphical user interface to work with Python code. In many respects, this is a much nicer interface than the command line version of the IronPython interpreter. Most important, you can save your work, which means that you can possibly use IDLE as an alternative to Visual Studio if desired. Of course, IDLE doesn't know anything about working with the .NET Framework and you can't use it to write multi-language applications.

➤ **Module Docs:** An HTML-formatted help file that provides complete documentation of the various Python Standard Library modules. Interestingly enough, you can use this help file with IronPython without modification because this is the documentation that IronPython's Standard Library is written to support. For the most part, this help file is brief and not very detailed, but it's good when you need a quick reference.

➤ **Python (command line):** An application that works precisely like the IronPython command line. In fact, you'd be hard pressed to tell the two apart. The only reason you'd want to use the Python command line is to test the cross-platform compatibility of a module you write. Otherwise, you'll want to use the IronPython command line to ensure your code runs properly with IronPython.

➤ **Python Manuals:** This is the detailed help file you probably wanted with IronPython, but didn't receive. You'll definitely want to spend some time looking around this help file and discovering new things about the Python language.

Now that you have a better idea of what the Python Standard Library provides, you need to consider how you'll use it or whether you want to use it at all. Just how the Python Standard Library affects your organization and you depends on your goals. For the most part, you'll use these tools when you want to write pure Python applications or applications that rely heavily on Python (versus the mixed language applications found later in this book). It's important to remember that IronPython has a lot to offer that Python doesn't, so you need to decide which route your organization will take before you make a commitment to pure Python by using the Python Standard Library.

OBTAINING AND INSTALLING THE PYTHON STANDARD LIBRARY

You can obtain the Python Standard Library from a number of sources, but the best place to go is directly to the Python Web site at `http://www.python.org/download/`. Download the Python 2.6.4 Windows installer version of the product (about 14.2 MB). IronPython won't currently work with the newer 3.1.1 version of Python (nor will many third-party libraries). After you complete the download, you'll have a file named `python-2.6.4.msi`. The following steps tell how to install the product on your machine.

1. Right-click the file and choose Install from the context menu. You'll see a Welcome page like the one shown in Figure 6-1 that asks whether you want to install Python for all users or just for your own needs. Notice that you can't perform a personal installation on Windows Vista — it really doesn't work.

2. Choose an installation option (either will work for the book) and click Next. The installer will ask where you want to install Python. In most cases, the installer will choose `C:\Python26\`, which works out well for using the Standard Library from IronPython. As an alternative, you

could install Python in a directory below the IronPython directory, but the default usually works fine.

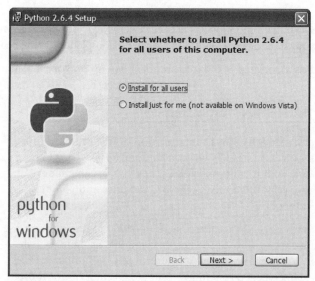

FIGURE 6-1: Tell the installer whether you want a personal install or one for everyone.

3. Choose an installation location and click Next. You'll see the Customize Python 2.6.4 dialog box shown in Figure 6-2. Notice the Register Extensions entry. If you let the installer make this change, Python, not IronPython, will be the default installation.

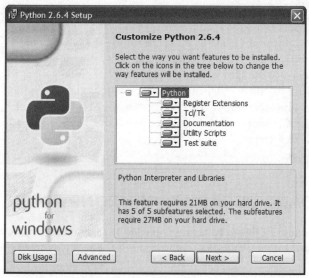

FIGURE 6-2: Customize the Python installation to meet your needs.

4. Click the down arrow in the Register Extensions option and choose Entire Feature Will Be Unavailable from the menu. You can choose to keep all of the remaining features if desired (highly recommended).

5. Configure any of the other installation options as needed. Click Next. You'll see a status dialog box as Python installs to your hard drive. Eventually, you see a completion dialog box.

6. Click Finish. Python (and its associated Standard Library) is set up on your machine.

C MODULES IN THE PYTHON STANDARD LIBRARY

One of the reasons that IronPython installs a tuned version of the Standard Library is that the full Standard Library has modules written in C included with it. These modules generally won't work with IronPython. As Python has become more advanced, the developers have removed many of these C modules and you may eventually find that they're all gone.

Of course, you might find that you really do need that C module because nothing else will work. In this case, you can try to gain access to the C module using IronClad (http://code.google.com/p/ironclad/). You won't always have complete success using IronClad, but it does help considerably, and you should give it a try for those stubborn modules.

Another potential fix is getting a pure Python version of the module you need from PyPy (http://codespeak.net/pypy/dist/pypy/doc/). In many cases, the PyPy solution is actually a little more compatible than other solutions because it does rely on pure Python code to provide access to the module you want. A potential disadvantage of this solution is that the pure Python alternatives will tend to run slower than the C modules they replace.

Finally, there's the IronPython Community Edition (also known as FePy) (http://fepy.sourceforge.net/). This group has created solutions for the C modules based on the .NET Framework. From an IronPython perspective, this solution is probably the most compatible option. However, in using the .NET Framework, you potentially give up some cross-platform independence. Fortunately, the IronPython Community Edition also has information on using its version of IronPython with Mono (http://mono-project.com/Main_Page), which lets .NET applications run on both Linux and Macintosh systems.

ACCESSING THE STANDARD LIBRARY FROM IRONPYTHON

Before you can use the Python Standard Library to create applications, you must provide a means for IronPython to find the Standard Library so it can import modules. You have three options for performing this task.

➤ Create an environment variable named IRONPYTHONPATH and provide the path to the Standard Library through it. The "Understanding the IPY.EXE Command Line Syntax" section of Chapter 1 tells you how to work with environment variables. This option is machine-specific, but it does work.

➤ Manually add the path to the import search path (discussed later in this section). The advantage of this method is that the import requirements move with the application. However, if the user has their copy of the Standard Library in a different location (or doesn't have the Standard Library installed at all), the change can break your application.

➤ Add the path to `site.py`, which is located in the `\Program Files\IronPython 2.6\Lib` directory of your machine. The interpreter loads this file every time it starts, so you can be sure that everyone using the IronPython interpreter on your machine will have the required access. As with the `IRONPYTHONPATH` environment variable, this solution works on the current machine only.

Manually Adding the Import Search Path

In order to manually add the import search path, you need to add code to every application created. The code isn't long or hard to understand, but you must add it to every application that requires the Standard Library or the application won't be able to access it. Here's an example of the code you need.

```
import sys
sys.path.append('C:\Python26\Lib')
```

In this case, my copy of the Standard Library is located in `C:\Python26\Lib`, which is the default setup. You need to change this value to match your system. After you make the change, you can verify that it's correct by using the following code.

```
print sys.path[len(sys.path)-1]
```

All that this code does is display the last path added to `sys.path`. If you see the appropriate path, you know you're ready to go.

Modifying the Site.py File

It's less convenient to modify the `Site.py` file than it is to use the other two techniques, but you're also sure that every application will see the path addition when you modify `Site.py`. Of course, if you reinstall IronPython, it will overwrite your `Site.py`, and you'll need to remember to make the change again. As previously mentioned, the `Site.py` file is located in the `\Program Files\ IronPython 2.6\Lib` directory of your machine. Open this file with your editor and add the following code to the top of the file:

```
import sys
sys.path.append('C:\Python26\Lib')
```

Make sure you change `C:\Python26\Lib` to match the location of the Standard Library on your machine. This example uses the default location. After you save the file, restart the interpreter and you should see the path added to the `sys.path` attribute.

An interesting side effect of using the Site.py file is that the Standard Library path will appear before the IronPython paths, which means that the Python Standard Library receives preferential treatment. Remember that you can always tell the interpreter not to load the Site.py file by using the –S command line switch (see the section "Understanding the IPY.EXE Command Line Syntax" in Chapter 1 for details).

USING THE STANDARD LIBRARY FEATURES

The Standard Library provides a lot of features that you don't get with IronPython. Many of these features you can use while developing IronPython applications. The following sections describe how to use each of the features. In addition, you'll see how to use the Standard Library to create an application. Before you use this section, you must install the Python Standard Library and determine how you plan to access it from IronPython. Because the Python command line console is essentially the same as the IronPython command line console, you won't find it in the sections that follow.

Using the Module Documentation

The module documentation provides terse information about each of the modules provided in the Standard Library. However, the information you receive is normally enough to use the module. To start this feature, choose Start ➪ Programs ➪ Python 2.6 ➪ Module Docs. You'll see the pydoc dialog box shown in Figure 6-3. This dialog box already has a search term entered into it.

When you enter a search term and press Enter, Module Docs searches the documentation to locate all of the matching entries. To use a particular search result, highlight its entry in the list and click Go To Selected. Your browser will open and show a search topic similar to the one shown in Figure 6-4.

You might want to do a little exploring, rather than enter a specific search term. In this case, click Open Browser on the pydoc dialog box to go to the top-level Module Docs page shown in Figure 6-5. Simply click the links to drill down to the search topic you want.

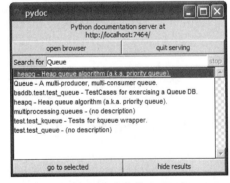

FIGURE 6-3: Use Module Docs to discover specifics about Python modules.

After you find all of the information you want, click Quit Serving on the pydoc dialog box. Module Docs will shut down. Because Module Docs runs on an internal Web server, you'll want to shut Module Docs down when your search is complete to save processing cycles.

Using the Python Manuals

The Python Manuals are a full-fledged compiled help module, which is the same kind of help you've been using in Windows for just about every other application you own. To access this feature, choose Start ➪ Programs ➪ Python 2.6 ➪ Python Manuals. You'll see the Python 2.6.4 Documentation window shown in Figure 6-6.

As you can see, the Python Manual relies on a standard help file. You can search it, look through the table of contents, click links, and do everything else you'd do with a standard help file.

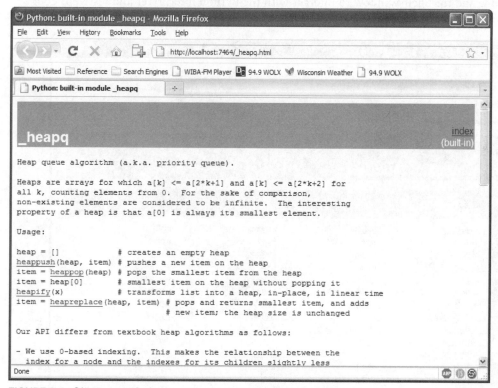

FIGURE 6-4: Obtain specific help on the module for which you searched.

One potential issue with using the Python Manuals is that the help is Python-specific. This help file will contain information that won't apply to IronPython in some cases because IronPython doesn't precisely implement the full Python feature set. Consequently, you need to test any help you receive before you accept it as completely useful.

Working with IDLE

IDLE is the IDE that IronPython should have shipped with because it lets you perform all kinds of interesting tasks using Python. To access this feature, choose Start ➪ Programs ➪ Python 2.6 ➪ IDLE (Python GUI). You'll see a window similar to the one shown in Figure 6-7.

The window opens immediately with a fully functional interpreter by default. The interpreter is called the *Shell Window*. For example, in Figure 6-7, if you type 2 + 2 and press Enter, you'll see the answer 4 on the next line. However, it's the next feature that you'll like best. When you type a method, such as help, you see an IntelliSense-like help feature, as shown in the figure.

IDLE also has a full-fledged editor, called the *Editor Window.* The Editor Window contains all of the editing features that you'd expect in any IDE. You use the Editor Window to edit your code and the Shell Window to interact with the Python interpreter and test your code using the debugger.

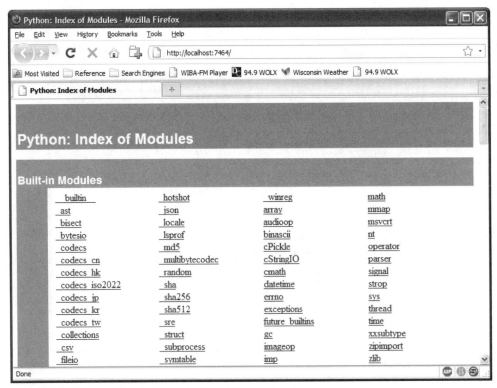

FIGURE 6-5: Browse Module Docs starting at the top-level page.

Of course, IDLE has a lot more to offer you, including a full-fledged debugger and a number of editing tools. Most important, you can open and save files quite easily using IDLE. You can even track down modules by exploring the paths accessible using sys.path. The following sections tell you considerably more about this interesting IDE.

Configuring IDLE

IDLE has a number of configuration options that you can set. These options make it possible to customize IDLE to an extent. For example, you can choose a theme for coloring the editor, if desired. Choose Options ⇨ Configure IDLE to display the dialog box shown in Figure 6-8.

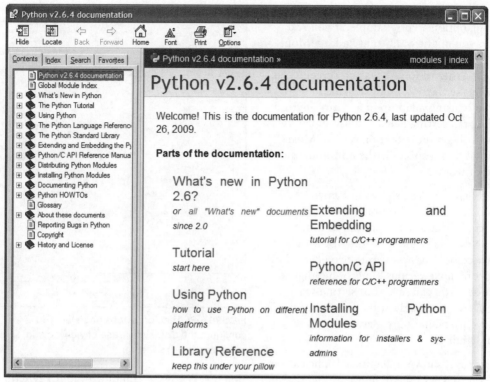

FIGURE 6-6: The Python Manual relies on a standard help file to provide detailed information about Python.

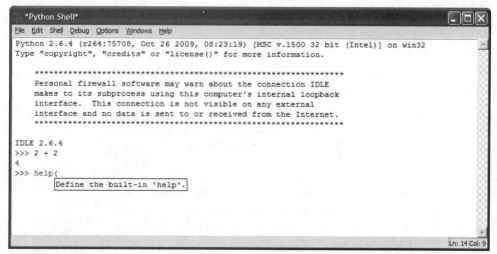

FIGURE 6-7: IDLE is a nice development environment for working with Python.

The Font/Tabs page contains a number of interesting options. For example, if you're a bit older, you might want to use a larger font than the default or even a font that offers serifs to make it easier to follow text on screen. You can also make the text bold, which can help when you're using a laptop in a sunny environment. The tab setting helps you use indentation, but still get more text on screen. Most people find that 3 spaces is the minimum indentation that works.

The Highlighting page, shown in Figure 6-9, helps you adjust the coloration used to display certain kinds of code and application features. This is an especially useful feature for people who have color blindness because you can adjust the colors to make various kinds of highlights easier to see. You can save your settings as a theme. In fact, you might want to have special themes for particular purposes, such as low ambient lighting.

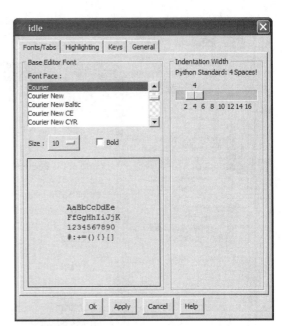

FIGURE 6-8: The Fonts/Tabs page lets you configure the display for ease of viewing and optimize the tab spacing.

The Keys page, shown in Figure 6-10, helps you set the control keys used to move around the application quickly. IDLE comes with four key setups as a default.

➤ IDLE Classic Mac

➤ IDLE Classic OS/X

➤ IDLE Classic Unix

➤ IDLE Classic Windows

Of course, you can always create your own key setups and save them. Some people (such as those who are left-handed) might find that the default key setups don't work for them.

The General page, shown in Figure 6-11, lets you set general application settings. For example, you can tell IDLE what to do during certain events such as startup and before you run your application. You can also control the initial size of the IDLE window and the encoding used for the text.

For some reason, IDLE lacks a command to start the editor from within the shell. The editor, however, has a command to start the shell. Consequently, you want to configure IDLE to start with the editor open by choosing the Open Edit Window as the At Startup option.

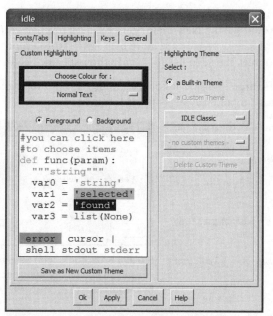

FIGURE 6-9: Modify the highlighting to make application features easier to use.

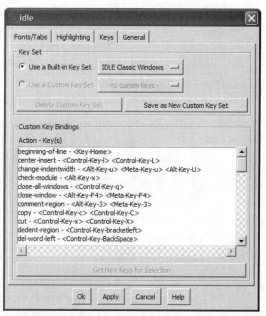

FIGURE 6-10: Modify key setups to make IDLE faster and easier to work with.

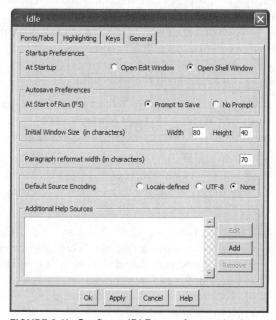

FIGURE 6-11: Configure IDLE to perform tasks the way you feel most comfortable.

The item of special interest on the General page is the Additional Help Sources list at the bottom of the page. To add a new help source, click Add. You'll see the New Help Source dialog box shown in Figure 6-12. Notice that you can use either a local help source or a remote help URL. IronPython developers have good reason to add other help sources they can use for IronPython-specific needs.

IronPython doesn't provide a lot of specific help sources, but it does provide some. The following list provides some suggestions of URLs you might want to add to your copy of IDLE.

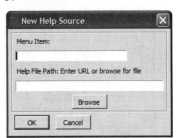

FIGURE 6-12: IronPython developers should add IronPython-specific help sources.

➤ **Differences between IronPython 2.0.x and CPython 2.5.2:** `http://ironpython.codeplex.com/ wikipage?title=IPy2.0.xCPyDifferences`

➤ **IronPython Readme:** `/Program Files/IronPython 2.6/ Readme.html`

➤ **IronPython Tutorial:** `/Program Files/IronPython 2.6/ Tutorial/Tutorial.htm`

➤ **IronPython Samples:** `http://ironpython.codeplex.com/ wikipage?title=Samples`

➤ **More Information About IronPython:** `http://ironpython .codeplex.com/wikipage?title=More Information`

Performing an Interactive Edit

To use IDLE as an editor, you simply begin entering commands in the Shell Window. If you have IDLE configured to open the Editor Window first, choose Run ⇨ Python Shell to open the Shell Window. The interpreter will tell you the result of each command you enter, so you know immediately whether the command will work. After you've completed the task you want to perform, choose File ⇨ Save and save the file. At this point, IDLE will save everything you typed, some of which isn't useful for an application, so you need to edit the code.

If you haven't already configured IDLE to open the Editor Window first, do so now. Choose Options ⇨ Configure IDLE, select Open Edit Window in the At Startup section on the General tab, and click OK. Choose File ⇨ New Window. IDLE will open an Editor Window that you can use to edit the code you just created interactively.

In the Editor Window, choose File ⇨ Open. You'll see an Open dialog box like the one shown in Figure 6-13. Select the file you just saved and click Open. IDLE opens the file you saved from your interpreter section.

Figure 6-14 shows a short example of an interpreter session saved as a file. As you can see, you need to perform a number of edits, such as removing the initial startup information. Modify the file just as you would using any other editor and save the result. The Edit menu contains a full list of editing tools, including the familiar Cut, Copy, and Paste commands, as well as a Find command. It even includes a command to go directly to a specific line in the file, Edit ⇨ Go To Line, which comes in handy for dealing with interpreter error messages.

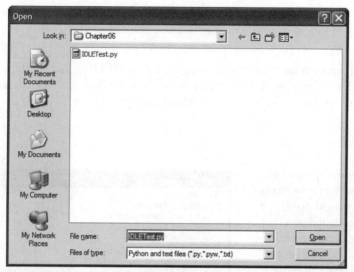

FIGURE 6-13: Open the file you created and saved using the interpreter.

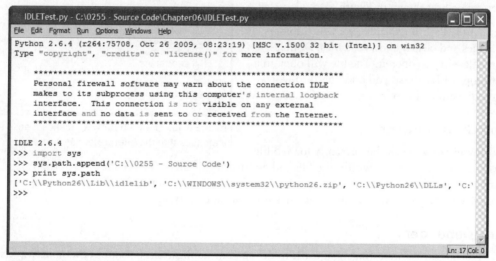

FIGURE 6-14: Editing interpreter sessions can be messy, but you know the result will work.

In this case, you can cut the text shown in Figure 6-14 down to three simple lines.

```
import sys
sys.path.append('C:\\0255 - Source Code\\Chapter06')
print sys.path
```

After you make the changes, you can always reload the file into the interpreter and debug it or work with it in other ways. For example, if you want to run the application, press F5 or choose Run ➪ Run Module.

Of course, you can always build an application from scratch using the Editor Window. You get the same IntelliSense-type help as you do when using the interpreter in the Shell Window. Unfortunately, when using the Editor Window directly, you don't get instant feedback, but you do benefit from not having to edit the result.

Using the Path Browser

IDLE provides more than one way to locate a file you want to edit. One of these methods is to display a dialog box that contains a hierarchical display of the current `sys.path` content. You drill down through the list to find the file you want to work with. Not only does this technique make it easy to find what you want, but it also tells you that the interpreter can see the file. To use this feature, choose File ➪ Path Browser. You'll see the Path Browser dialog box shown in Figure 6-15.

Notice that the Path Browser shows which folders are packages and clearly shows the files. Double-click any file entry to open it. The file will open in a separate copy of IDLE, so you don't need to worry about modifications to your current session.

FIGURE 6-15: The Path Browser makes it easy to locate files that the interpreter can see.

Using the Class Browser

Class Browser works with the currently loaded file. It helps you see the elements within the file and go directly to them. To see the class setup for your application, choose File ➪ Class Browser. You'll see a dialog similar to the one shown in Figure 6-16, except that it contains specifics for your application.

Using the Debugger

The IDLE debugger is interesting. You use it to debug your application, but not in the same way as you would within Visual Studio.

In order to make the debugger useful, choose Run ➪ Python Shell in the Editor Window. IDLE starts a copy of the Shell Window. In the Shell Window, choose Debug ➪ Debugger. You'll see the strange Debug Control dialog box shown in Figure 6-17 open. At this point, you're ready to debug your application.

FIGURE 6-16: Browsing by class makes it easy to navigate your application.

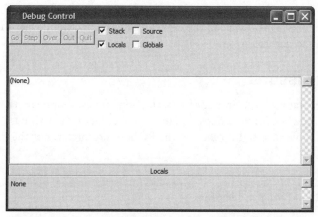

FIGURE 6-17: Start the Debug Control before you start the application.

To start debugging the application, choose Run ⇨ Run Module or press F5 in the Editor Window (not the Shell Window). IDLE actually picks the Shell Window that you opened earlier and stops execution immediately so you can see what's happening with your application, as shown in Figure 6-18.

At this point, you can click Step within the Debug Control to go to the next line of execution, Over to skip over a line of execution (the commands still execute, but you won't see them), or Out to move out of a function or method. If you click Go, the application will continue to execute without debugging support. Clicking Quit ends the application.

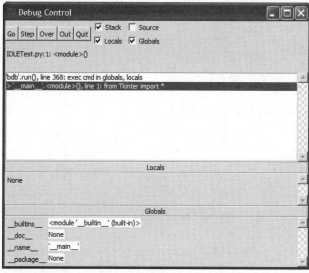

FIGURE 6-18: Running the module automatically fills the Debug Control with information.

The IDLE debugger has no concept of breakpoints. You have no immediate window for entering commands or watch windows to track expressions. Even so, the debugger does work well, even if it does take a while for the .NET developer to get used to it.

Looking for Standard Library Issues

It's important to exercise care when working with the Standard Library. Sometimes, it appears that IronPython provides support for a feature when it really doesn't. For example, Listing 6-1 shows an application that runs fine within IDLE because IDLE relies on the Python interpreter, not the IronPython interpreter.

LISTING 6-1: An example of a Standard Library application

```
from Tkinter import *
import aboutDialog

# Represents the main window of an application.
root = Tk()

class TestIDLE:
    "Defines a basic test of IDLE"

    def ShowAbout(self):
        "Display the IDLE About dialog box"
        aboutDialog.AboutDialog(root, 'About')

        # Make sure you destroy the window when you get done with it.
        root.destroy()

def SayHello():
    "A very basic function in Python"
    print 'Hello'

# Set the path to include the application directory.
import sys
sys.path.append('C:\\0255 - Source Code\\Chapter06')
print sys.path

# Call SayHello()
SayHello()

# Display the IDLE About dialog box.
MyAbout = TestIDLE()
MyAbout.ShowAbout()
```

This is an interesting example because it displays the IDLE About dialog box. When you run this example, the code begins by doing something simple — it modifies the path to point to the example directory and then it displays a simple hello message to the user.

The problem occurs with the second part of the example. The process is relatively straightforward. The TestIDLE class contains a method called ShowAbout(). ShowAbout() creates a window and then displays the IDLE About dialog box in it. The code then destroys the window it created and ends.

When you try to run this example using IronPython by typing IPY IDLETest.py at the command prompt and pressing Enter, the first message you see says that IronPython knows nothing about a Tkinter module, which provides access to the windowing environment provided by Tk. You can read all about Tkinter at http://www.pythonware.com/library/tkinter/introduction/. The bottom line is that Tkinter is a windowing environment that many Python developers use, so you're going to run into it when working with IronPython.

At this point, you notice that IronPython does indeed include support for Tkinter in the \Program Files\IronPython 2.6\Lib\lib-tk folder. So you add this directory to your IRONPYTHONPATH environment variable by typing Set IRONPYTHONPATH=%IRONPYTHONPATH %;C:\Program Files\IronPython 2.6\Lib\lib-tk and pressing Enter. This command adds the required directory to your application environment, so you type IPY IDLETest.py again and press Enter. Now you see an error message, "ImportError: No module named _tkinter."

Unfortunately, you'll never find a _tkinter module in the IronPython folders. You'll find it in the \Python26\DLLs directory as _tkinter.pyd and in the \Python26\libs directory as _tkinter .lib. The alarms should be going off in your head at this moment. Python implements Tkinter as a C library, which means that IronPython doesn't support it, despite the fact that IronPython includes the required Tkinter.py file. The point of this whole exercise is that you're going to run into some very popular Python features that simply won't work in IronPython because they require C support (despite the fact that it appears that IronPython does support it). Your only choice (in most cases) is to avoid using the module or rely on straight Python instead. Happily, some developers are working on the Tkinter problem. You can read about one such solution at http://www.voidspace.org .uk/ironpython/cpython_extensions.shtml.

 Whenever you have a question about IronPython support for a particular Python feature, check the not-supported-module-list at http://ironpython .codeplex.com/wikipage?title=List of Standard Library components not included in the MSI.

USING IRONPYTHON CONSTRUCTIVELY

This chapter has given you insights into the Standard Library. The Standard Library is a necessary ingredient for any IronPython application, even if you plan to use the .NET Framework extensively. However, by using the Standard Library alone, you can create applications that will work well on other platforms. Unlike many other languages that Microsoft supports, the applications you build in IronPython really are for the rest of the world too — at least, as long as you abide by a few rules.

It's time to explore! Nothing will get you more involved with IronPython than exploring the Standard Library to determine what it can do for you. Go ahead; try out a few experimental applications. Better yet, use one of the IronPython features that make experimentation so easy. Start up a copy of the interpreter and try things out one line at a time. It won't take long for you to understand just how huge the Standard Library is. Don't forget the lessons learned in Chapter 5 — use `dir()`, `__doc__`, and `help()` to drill down into the Standard Library.

You're working with IronPython, not Python. One of the advantages of working with IronPython is that you have options other than the Standard Library available to you. You might decide that you really do need to build a Windows Forms application using .NET code instead of the more standard Python interfaces. Chapter 7 gets you started working with the .NET Framework. Because most of you already have some .NET experience, you'll probably find that working with the .NET Framework in IronPython is pretty easy once you get the basics down. Even so, IronPython lets you work with both the Standard Library and the .NET Framework — use the tool that works best for your particular needs.

7

Accessing the .NET Framework

WHAT'S IN THIS CHAPTER?

➤ Gaining access to the .NET Framework from IronPython

➤ Working with .NET data types in your application

➤ Using .NET classes within your application

➤ Creating applications that use generics

Chapter 6 emphasized the Python portion of IronPython. As you learned in that chapter, IronPython doesn't quite provide full Python capability, but it comes very close. In this chapter, you discover the .NET capabilities of IronPython. In this case, you'll see that IronPython has its own take on the .NET Framework but that it does provide you with full access.

Of course, before you can work with the .NET Framework in IronPython, you need to know how to import the assemblies. It turns out that you have several levels of import capability that you can use to work with assemblies in different ways. In most cases, you'll perform a standard import and use the .NET assemblies much as you would any other IronPython class.

The .NET Framework provides strict data typing and a wider range of data types than Python does. You need to know how to use these data types within IronPython in order to write applications that make full use of the .NET Framework. The second section of this chapter addresses this need.

Once you know about the data types, you can begin working with classes. This chapter provides you with an overview of the process. You get more details as the book progresses. However, this chapter is important because it explains basics you absolutely must know in order to move on to more advanced examples in the book.

Finally, this chapter looks at one of the more interesting uses of the .NET Framework with IronPython — generics. The use of generics with IronPython can greatly improve your ability to create flexible applications that can work with a wide range of data types. Eventually, you'll begin using generics with a number of examples in the book, but for now you should focus on understanding the technique used to work with generics.

IMPORTING THE .NET FRAMEWORK ASSEMBLIES

Importing an assembly into IronPython isn't much different from importing a Python module. In fact, you use about the same code. The primary difference is that you can't import some .NET assemblies directly into IronPython, just as you can't import them directly into any .NET language. Instead, you must first create a reference to the .NET assembly and then import it. For anyone who has worked with .NET languages in the past, nothing will have changed from the normal procedure they follow.

> *One odd thing about IronPython is that it's case sensitive even when it comes to .NET Framework assemblies. As a consequence, importing* system.math *won't work but importing* System.Math *will. Because many developers aren't used to thinking about the case of .NET Framework assemblies, you might be caught off guard when an application fails for some unknown reason. One issue always to consider is whether you've capitalized the assembly name incorrectly.*

Performing a Standard Import

As with Python modules, you can perform a standard import of a .NET assembly. For example, you might want to import the .NET Framework's `System` assembly. In this case, you type

```
import System
```

and press Enter. If you want to see what the System assembly contains, type

```
dir(System)
```

and press Enter. Figure 7-1 shows typical results from importing the `System` assembly.

Now, let's say that you want to create a `UInt32` variable, just like a `UInt32` that you'd create in any other .NET language. Simply type something like `MyVar = System.UInt32(5)`. Of course, you can use any variable within the range that fits within a `UInt32`. If you don't provide a value by typing `MyVar = System.UInt32()` the .NET Framework automatically assigns the variable a value of 0. You can read more about .NET data types in the section "Using .NET Data Types" later in this chapter.

However, let's take a look at `MyVar`. If you type `MyVar` by itself, you see that it's an object that has a value of 5, as shown in Figure 7-2. Type `dir(MyVar)` and you see that `MyVar` contains many of the same methods as a standard Python integer. For example, you still have access to the absolute value function, `__abs__()`, and comparison method, `__eq__()`. In addition to these standard methods, you also have access to .NET-specific functions such as `Parse()` and `ToChar()`.

```
>>> import System
>>> dir(System)
['AccessViolationException', 'Action', 'ActivationContext', 'Activator', 'AppDom
ain', 'AppDomainInitializer', 'AppDomainManager', 'AppDomainManagerInitializatio
nOptions', 'AppDomainSetup', 'AppDomainUnloadedException', 'ApplicationException
', 'ApplicationId', 'ApplicationIdentity', 'ArgIterator', 'ArgumentException', '
ArgumentNullException', 'ArgumentOutOfRangeException', 'ArithmeticException', 'A
rray', 'ArraySegment', 'ArrayTypeMismatchException', 'AssemblyLoadEventArgs', 'A
ssemblyLoadEventHandler', 'AsyncCallback', 'Attribute', 'AttributeTargets', 'Att
ributeUsageAttribute', 'BadImageFormatException', 'Base64FormattingOptions', 'Bi
tConverter', 'Boolean', 'Buffer', 'Byte', 'CLSCompliantAttribute', 'CannotUnload
AppDomainException', 'Char', 'CharEnumerator', 'CodeDom', 'Collections', 'Compar
ison', 'ComponentModel', 'Configuration', 'Console', 'ConsoleCancelEventArgs', '
ConsoleCancelEventHandler', 'ConsoleColor', 'ConsoleKey', 'ConsoleKeyInfo', 'Con
soleModifiers', 'ConsoleSpecialKey', 'ContextBoundObject', 'ContextMarshalExcept
ion', 'ContextStaticAttribute', 'Convert', 'Converter', 'CrossAppDomainDelegate'
, 'DBNull', 'DataMisalignedException', 'DateTime', 'DateTimeKind', 'DateTimeOffs
et', 'DayOfWeek', 'Decimal', 'Delegate', 'Deployment', 'Diagnostics', 'DivideByZ
eroException', 'DllNotFoundException', 'Double', 'DuplicateWaitObjectException',
'EntryPointNotFoundException', 'Enum', 'Environment', 'EnvironmentVariableTarge
t', 'EventArgs', 'EventHandler', 'Exception', 'ExecutionEngineException', 'Field
AccessException', 'FileStyleUriParser', 'FlagsAttribute', 'FormatException', 'Ft
pStyleUriParser', 'GC', 'GCCollectionMode', 'GenericUriParser', 'GenericUriParse
rOptions', 'Globalization', 'GopherStyleUriParser', 'Guid', 'HttpStyleUriParser'
, 'IAppDomainSetup', 'IAsyncResult', 'ICloneable', 'IComparable', 'IConvertible'
, 'ICustomFormatter', 'IDisposable', 'IEquatable', 'IFormatProvider', 'IFormatta
ble', 'IO', 'IServiceProvider', 'IndexOutOfRangeException', 'InsufficientMemoryE
xception', 'Int16', 'Int32', 'Int64', 'IntPtr', 'InvalidCastException', 'Invalid
OperationException', 'InvalidProgramException', 'LdapStyleUriParser', 'LoaderOpt
imization', 'LoaderOptimizationAttribute', 'LocalDataStoreSlot', 'MTAThreadAttri
bute', 'MarshalByRefObject', 'Math', 'Media', 'MemberAccessException', 'MethodAc
cessException', 'MidpointRounding', 'MissingFieldException', 'MissingMemberExcep
tion', 'MissingMethodException', 'ModuleHandle', 'MulticastDelegate', 'Multicast
NotSupportedException', 'Net', 'NetPipeStyleUriParser', 'NetTcpStyleUriParser',
'NewStyleUriParser', 'NonSerializedAttribute', 'NotFiniteNumberException', 'Not
ImplementedException', 'NotSupportedException', 'NullReferenceException', 'Nulla
ble', 'Object', 'ObjectDisposedException', 'ObsoleteAttribute', 'OperatingSystem
', 'OperationCanceledException', 'OutOfMemoryException', 'OverflowException', 'P
aramArrayAttribute', 'PlatformID', 'PlatformNotSupportedException', 'Predicate',
'Random', 'RankException', 'Reflection', 'ResolveEventArgs', 'ResolveEventHandl
er', 'Resources', 'Runtime', 'RuntimeArgumentHandle', 'RuntimeFieldHandle', 'Run
timeMethodHandle', 'RuntimeTypeHandle', 'SByte', 'STAThreadAttribute', 'Security
', 'SerializableAttribute', 'Single', 'StackOverflowException', 'String', 'Strin
gComparer', 'StringComparison', 'StringSplitOptions', 'SystemException', 'Text',
'ThreadStaticAttribute', 'Threading', 'TimeSpan', 'TimeZone', 'TimeoutException
', 'Timers', 'Type', 'TypeCode', 'TypeInitializationException', 'TypeLoadExcepti
on', 'TypeUnloadedException', 'TypedReference', 'UInt16', 'UInt32', 'UInt64', 'U
IntPtr', 'UnauthorizedAccessException', 'UnhandledExceptionEventArgs', 'Unhandle
dExceptionEventHandler', 'Uri', 'UriBuilder', 'UriComponents', 'UriFormat', 'Uri
FormatException', 'UriHostNameType', 'UriIdnScope', 'UriKind', 'UriParser', 'Uri
Partial', 'UriTypeConverter', 'ValueType', 'Version', 'Void', 'WeakReference', '
Web', '_AppDomain']
>>>
```

FIGURE 7-1: Performing a standard import places the System assembly where you'd expect.

When you import an assembly using the standard approach, some code can become long and cumbersome. For example, if you want to change the console foreground color, you must type the following:

```
System.Console.ForegroundColor = System.ConsoleColor.Blue
```

Notice that you must use the correct enumeration when specifying the color, or the change won't occur. This code really does work — give it a try and then print the current console foreground color, as shown in Figure 7-3 (the screenshot in this book shows only shades of gray, but you'll see color on your display). The console color changes to whatever value you specify without creating a variable first because `System.Console.ForegroundColor` is a property.

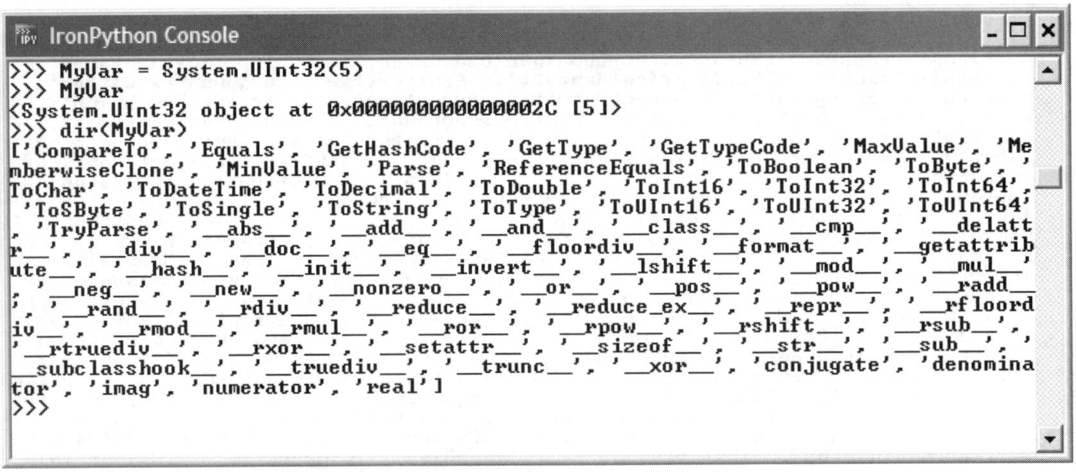

FIGURE 7-2: Creating a .NET object provides a mix of Python and .NET methods.

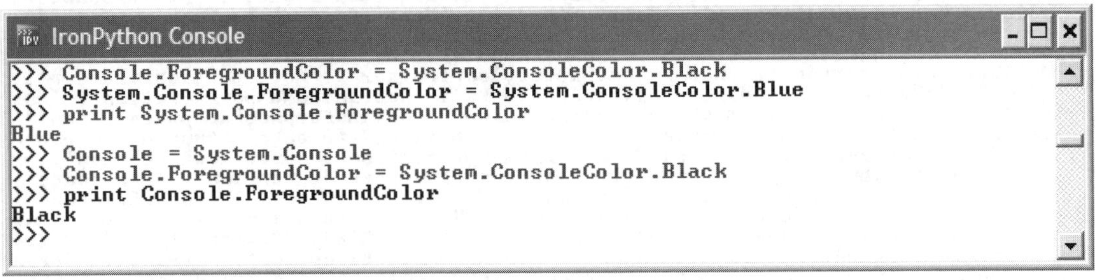

FIGURE 7-3: Using the standard import can become a little cumbersome.

As with Python modules, you can get around the problem by assigning a particular object to a variable. For example, if you type `Console = System.Console`, then you can shorten the code a little, as shown in Figure 7-3. The bottom line is that using a standard import with .NET isn't much different from using it with Python modules. The only real difference is that you use a different name.

Importing an Assembly into the Global Namespace

Sometimes you need to have an entire assembly available at a global level. Using variables to bring part of the assembly up to the right level won't work. In this case, you rely on a different import strategy than used in the section "Performing a Standard Import" earlier in this chapter. You've already seen this technique before as applied to Python modules, but now you'll see how it applies to .NET assemblies. Simply use the `from AssemblyName import Assembly | *` format used for Python modules. For example, if you want to import the `System` assembly into the global namespace, you type

```
from System import *
```

The asterisk (*) means that you import everything in the System assembly at the global namespace level. Figure 7-4 shows what happens when you use the dir() function to see the global namespace.

FIGURE 7-4: You can import an entire assembly into the global namespace.

If you want a specific class within the System assembly imported at the global namespace level, you simply specify the name of the class as you would when working with Python. For example, if you want to work with the Console class, then you'd type

```
from System import Console
```

Some developers will be tempted to import everything they need into the global namespace. While this strategy works fine for a .NET application created in a language such as C#, it doesn't always work well in IronPython because of the way the Python language works. For example, Figure 7-4 shows an example of the problems that can occur. Imagine importing four or five assemblies into the global namespace and then using the dir() *function to display a list of classes, methods, enumerations, or other .NET features you want to use. The list would be so large as to make any search pointless. Import only what you need into the global namespace.*

You can extend individual imports by separating classes, enumerations, or other assembly members with commas. For example, if you want to import both the Console class and the ConsoleColor enumeration into the global namespace, you type

```
from System import Console, ConsoleColor
```

If you use the dir() function to see the result, you see output similar to Figure 7-5. Importing only what you need keeps clutter down, makes your application run faster, and reduces potential security issues. In this case, you can reduce the foreground color-changing code shown in the "Performing a Standard Import" section to

```
Console.ForegroundColor = ConsoleColor.Blue
```

```
IronPython Console                                          _ □ x
IronPython 2.6 (2.6.10920.0) on .NET 2.0.50727.3603
Type "help", "copyright", "credits" or "license" for more information.
>>> from System import Console, ConsoleColor
>>> dir()
['Console', 'ConsoleColor', '__builtins__', '__doc__', '__name__']
>>> Console.ForegroundColor = ConsoleColor.Blue
>>> print Console.ForegroundColor
Blue
>>>
```

FIGURE 7-5: Importing into the global namespace reduces the size and complexity of your code.

Configuring the Console for .NET Help

Believe it or not, the help() function works fine with .NET assemblies. However, Microsoft designed the assembly help for a much larger display area. If you type help(ConsoleColor) and press Enter, the help output is so long that you can't see even a small portion of it. In fact, you won't actually see the help you need because it appears at the beginning of the help listing.

The console window has a buffer associated with it. When you type a command and the interpreter presents output, the buffer accepts all the output up to the size of the buffer. At that point, all the old information drops off the end into the bit bucket and you never see it again. The standard buffer size is 300 lines, which seems like it would be enough, but it isn't nearly enough for the .NET help. What you really need for .NET help is about 3,000 lines. Use these steps to change the buffer size.

1. Click the system menu in the upper-left corner of the console window and choose Properties from the context menu. You see the IronPython Console Properties dialog box.

2. Select the Layout tab. You see the information shown in Figure 7-6.

3. Change the Height property in the Screen Buffer Size area to 3000. This means that the screen buffer can now hold up the 3,000 lines of output. However, it also means that the screen buffer consumes ten times more memory, which means you won't want to make this change to a console window unless you need the extra space.

4. Click OK. You see the Apply Properties To Shortcut dialog box shown in Figure 7-7. If you plan to work with .NET very often, you'll definitely want to choose "Modify Shortcut that Started this Window" so that you don't have to make the change every time.

5. Select one of the configuration change options and then click OK. Windows makes the change you requested.

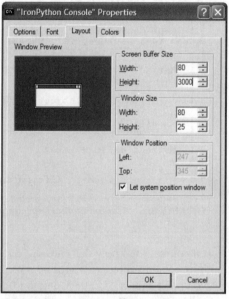

FIGURE 7-6: Modify the buffer to hold more lines of information.

At this point, you need to try out the `help()` function. Try typing

```
help(ConsoleColor)
```

and press Enter. You'll see that the display takes a second or so to return. At this point, you can scroll through the massive help display to find the information you need. Figure 7-8 shows typical output.

FIGURE 7-7: Choose a configuration change option that matches your .NET usage habits.

Creating a Reference to .NET Assemblies

Not every .NET assembly is available to IronPython by default, even if that assembly appears in the Global Assembly Cache (GAC). As with any other .NET language, you sometimes need to reference .NET assemblies in order to import and use them. For example, try typing

```
from System.Xml import *
```

and press Enter. You get an error message as output stating the following:

```
from System.Xml import *
Traceback (most recent call last):
  File "<stdin>", line 1, in <module>
ImportError: No module named Xml
```

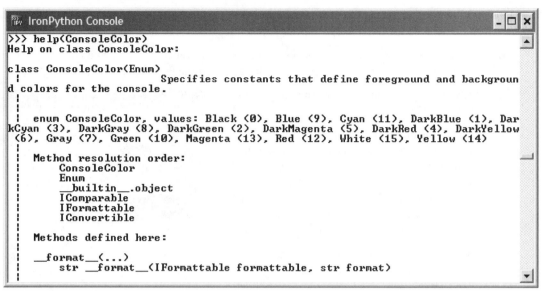

FIGURE 7-8: The screen buffer is now large enough to hold the help information you need.

Of course, you know that the System.Xml assembly does exist. This error message tells you that you have to add a reference to the System.Xml assembly before you can use it. In order to add a reference, you must import the clr (Common Language Runtime) module. You can then use one of the five following methods to import the assembly.

➤ **clr.AddReference(*AssemblyObjectOrFilename*):** Adds a reference to the .NET assembly by passing an assembly object directly or by specifying the assembly filename. (You can provide either a partial or full filename.) This is a generic sort of assembly reference addition because you don't have control over which assembly version IronPython loads. You can use this method when you're experimenting and really don't care about which version of the .NET assembly you get. This is also a good method to use when you're not sure which version of the assembly the user has installed on his or her machine but do know that all versions of the .NET Framework include the functionality you require.

➤ **clr.AddReferenceToFile(*AssemblyFilename[, AssemblyFilename...]*):** Adds a reference to the .NET assembly by passing a filename. You may supply multiple filenames to load multiple assemblies. IronPython looks for the assembly using the sys.path attribute. Consequently, you can partially control which version of the assembly you get by controlling the sys.path attribute. However, if more than one assembly has the correct filename, IronPython doesn't guarantee which version of the assembly will load. You can use the clr.AddReferenceByName() method to better control which version of the assembly loads.

➤ **clr.AddReferenceToFileAndPath(*AssemblyPathAndFilename[, AssemblyPathAndFilename ...]*):** Performs about the same task as the clr .AddReferenceToFile() method. However, in this case, you must provide an absolute path to the assembly you want to load, which means that you have better control over which assembly version loads. This method automatically adds the assembly path to sys.path for you.

➤ **clr.AddReferenceByName(*AssemblyName*, Version=*VersionNumber*, Culture= *CultureIdentifier*|neutral, PublicKeyToken=*TokenValue*):** Adds an assembly reference based on assembly specifics normally found in the GAC. You must supply values that fully define the assembly. For example, to import the .NET Framework 2.0 version of the System. Xml assembly, you would supply: `'System.Xml, Version=2.0.0.0, Culture=neutral, PublicKeyToken=b77a5c561934e089'`.

➤ **clr.AddReferenceByPartialName(*PartialAssemblyName*):** Adds a reference to the .NET assembly by passing a partial name that IronPython looks up in the GAC. This method doesn't assure that you obtain any particular version of the assembly you need. You can use the `clr.AddReferenceByName()` method to better control which version of the assembly loads.

Now that you have a better idea of how to add a reference, let's try importing the System.Xml assembly. The following steps help you get the assembly referenced and imported into IronPython.

1. Type `import sys`

   and press Enter. This step makes the `sys` module accessible.

2. Type `sys.path.append('C:\\WINDOWS\\Microsoft.NET\\Framework\\v2.0.50727')` and press Enter. In order to add a reference to an assembly, you must provide its location as part of `sys.path`. You may need to change the drive and directory to match your system.

 If you provide the wrong .NET Framework location, you can use the `sys` `.path.remove()` *method to remove it from the list. For example, if you want to remove the .NET Framework 2.0 path, you type* `sys.path.remove('C:\\ WINDOWS\\Microsoft.NET\\Framework\\v2.0.50727')` *and press Enter.*

3. Type `import clr` and press Enter. This step makes the `clr` module accessible, which has the various assembly reference methods described earlier.

4. Type `clr.AddReference('System.Xml.DLL')` and press Enter. IronPython now has a reference to the assembly file it needs, but the assembly isn't imported yet. If you receive an IO Error message, it means that IronPython couldn't find the assembly you requested in the location provided as part of `sys.path`.

5. Type `import System.Xml` and press Enter. The `System.Xml` assembly is now available for use. It's time to test to verify that the assembly is available.

6. Type `dir(System.Xml)` and press Enter. You should see the content of the `System.Xml` assembly, as shown in Figure 7-9.

This technique works with any .NET assembly, not just those found in the GAC. If you have a custom .NET assembly you want to use in your application, this technique lets you access it with ease. Make sure you use the right technique for the kind of assembly you want to import. If version number is important, then make sure you use the `clr.AddReferenceByName()` method.

```
IronPython Console                                                    _ □ ×
>>> dir(System.Xml)
['ConformanceLevel', 'EntityHandling', 'Formatting', 'IHasXmlNode', 'IXmlLineInf
o', 'IXmlNamespaceResolver', 'NameTable', 'NewLineHandling', 'ReadState', 'Schem
a', 'Serialization', 'ValidationType', 'WhitespaceHandling', 'WriteState', 'XPat
h', 'XmlAttribute', 'XmlAttributeCollection', 'XmlCDataSection', 'XmlCharacterDa
ta', 'XmlComment', 'XmlConvert', 'XmlDateTimeSerializationMode', 'XmlDeclaration
', 'XmlDocument', 'XmlDocumentFragment', 'XmlDocumentType', 'XmlElement', 'XmlEn
tity', 'XmlEntityReference', 'XmlException', 'XmlImplementation', 'XmlLinkedNode
', 'XmlNameTable', 'XmlNamedNodeMap', 'XmlNamespaceManager', 'XmlNamespaceScope'
, 'XmlNode', 'XmlNodeChangedAction', 'XmlNodeChangedEventArgs', 'XmlNodeChangedE
ventHandler', 'XmlNodeList', 'XmlNodeOrder', 'XmlNodeReader', 'XmlNodeType', 'Xm
lNotation', 'XmlOutputMethod', 'XmlParserContext', 'XmlProcessingInstruction', '
XmlQualifiedName', 'XmlReader', 'XmlReaderSettings', 'XmlResolver', 'XmlSecureRe
solver', 'XmlSignificantWhitespace', 'XmlSpace', 'XmlText', 'XmlTextReader', 'Xm
lTextWriter', 'XmlTokenizedType', 'XmlUrlResolver', 'XmlValidatingReader', 'XmlW
hitespace', 'XmlWriter', 'XmlWriterSettings', 'Xsl']
>>> _
```

FIGURE 7-9: Verify that you can access the System.Xml assembly.

If you import a module or assembly by mistake, you can unload it in the same way as you remove variables you no longer need, by typing del <NameOfModuleOrAssembly>. *For example, if you want to get rid of the* System.Xml *assembly after using it, type* del System *and press Enter. The module or assembly you want to remove must appear in the* dir() *list. In this case, when you type* dir() *after importing* System.Xml, *you see* System, *not* System.Xml *in the* dir() *list, so you must* del System, *not* del System.Xml. *Never set an assembly or module reference to* None *(as you would for clearing a variable) because the reference will remain, but none of the content will exist, causing hard to find errors in your application.*

USING .NET DATA TYPES

When you work with .NET in IronPython, you have full access to every type that .NET supports. However, you don't always create these types as you would in another language. For example, when working with C# or Visual Basic, you simply declare a variable of a certain type and then make an assignment to it. When working in IronPython, you must remember that making an assignment creates a Python type, not a .NET type. For example, let's suppose you create a UInt32 variable and then make an assignment to it. Figure 7-10 shows the sequence of events that will occur.

As you can see, when you initially create the variable, IronPython recognizes it as a UInt32. In fact, even the type() function knows that this is a UInt32. When the code makes a simple assignment, however, notice that IronPython changes the type to a simple int. A check using type() shows that the data type has indeed changed. In order to change the value of a UInt32, you must make another assignment using the UInt32() constructor.

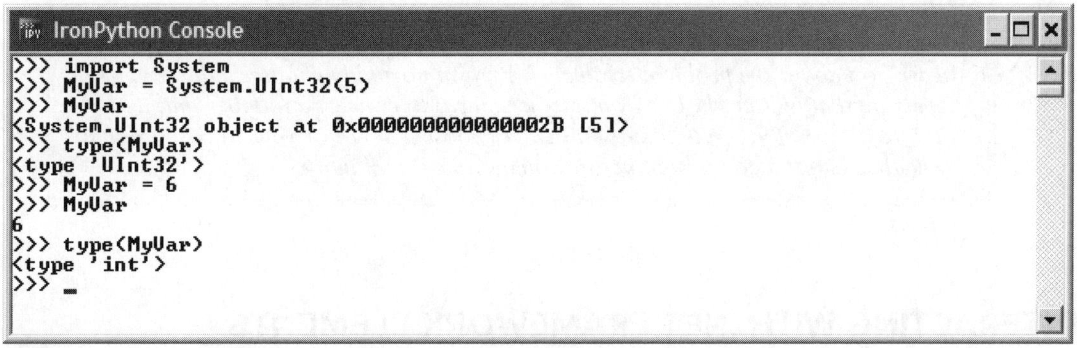

FIGURE 7-10: .NET and Python variables don't mix very well in most cases.

You can easily convert Python variables to their .NET counterparts in many cases. For example, you can use the following code to create a Python variable and then use it to create a .NET variable.

```
PVar = 5
NetVar = System.UInt32(PVar)
```

In some cases, you'll find that a direct conversion won't work for any of a number of reasons. For example, you might find that converting Python numeric variables won't work in some cases because .NET is expecting a string. In this case, you can try the `clr.Convert()` method. Here's an example of using `clr.Convert()` to produce the same results as the previous example. (Remember that you must type `import clr` before you can use it.)

```
NetVar2 = clr.Convert(PVar, System.UInt32)
```

The first argument contains the Python variable. The second argument contains the .NET data type you want as output. Of course, you must ensure you have imported the .NET assembly that contains the desired output type because the call will fail otherwise. In fact, any time `clr.Convert()` fails to convert the data, you get a `TypeError`.

Of course, before you can convert anything, you need to know the best type to use for the conversion. For example, you run the `type()` function against a Python variable to obtain the type information, but don't know the equivalent .NET type. In this case, you can use `clr.GetClrType()` to obtain the closest .NET equivalent, as shown here.

```
# Produces System.Int32 as output.
clr.GetClrType(int)

# Produces System.String as output.
clr.GetClrType(str)
```

The `clr.GetPythonType()` method obtains the Python equivalent of .NET data types. For example, if you type `clr.GetPythonType(System.Int32)`, you get `int` as output. Of course, you'll want to know how to convert your .NET data into a Python equivalent. In this case, you simply rely on the Python functions you use to create variables of specific types. For example, the following code converts a .NET `UInt32` into a Python `long`.

```
MyVar = long(NetVar)
```

Some .NET to Python conversions will result in data loss and Python won't warn you about the problem. However, Python normally chooses a data type override that will work. For example, if you try to convert a number that won't fit into an int, *Python will automatically choose a* long *for you. Make sure that you always test a conversion before you assume it will work.*

INTERACTING WITH .NET FRAMEWORK ELEMENTS

Now that you know how to get a .NET assembly loaded into IronPython, it's time to consider where to go next. Of course, it's not going to be possible to cover every potential destination in a single chapter of a book. However, the following sections provide some basics you can use to get started. For example, most developers need to know a little about the assemblies they have loaded, such as the version number. The following sections also show how to work with static methods and objects created from .NET classes. The final section provides a quick example that shows how to obtain a list of files and directories found in the root directory of your system. All these examples work together to help you get an idea of how .NET works within IronPython.

Obtaining Assembly Information

Developers will want to obtain information about the assemblies they load into IronPython. Part of the problem is going to be that you won't see a list of these assemblies in Solution Explorer because Visual Studio doesn't provide direct support for IronPython. Consequently, the application itself will need to have some level of assembly management support built into it. With this in mind, Listing 7-1 shows you how to perform some basic tasks with assemblies.

LISTING 7-1: Interacting with assemblies

Available for
download on
Wrox.com

```
# Add the .NET Framework 2.0 to the path.
import sys
sys.path.append('C:\\WINDOWS\\Microsoft.NET\\Framework\\v2.0.50727')

# Make clr accessible.
import clr

# Import the System assembly.
import System

# Add a reference for System.Xml and import it.
clr.AddReference('System.Xml.DLL')
import System.Xml

# Display a list of available assemblies.
print 'List of Assemblies:'
for ThisRef in clr.References:
```

```
    print ThisRef

# Access a specific assembly and display more information about it.
ThisRef = clr.References[2]
print '\nFull Name of System.Xml:'
print ThisRef.FullName

# Display the referenced assemblies.
print '\nReferenced Assemblies:'
for Reference in ThisRef.GetReferencedAssemblies():
    print Reference.ToString()

# Display the assembly attributes.
print '\nAttributes:'
for AnAttribute in ThisRef.GetCustomAttributes(type(ThisRef)):
    print AnAttribute.ToString()

# Pause after the debug session.
raw_input('Press any key to continue...')
```

The code begins by importing sys and adding the .NET Framework 2.0 path to sys.path. Adding just the path you need tends to reduce the risk of importing the wrong assembly. Even so, you want to verify that you're using the right assembly, especially when the code is running on another system.

The next step is to import clr. This module provides the features required to interact with the assemblies. The next few lines of code import System and System.Xml so that you can see a number of assemblies in IronPython. Notice that the System.Xml import requires use of the clr.AddReference() method.

At this point, the example obtains the list of loaded assemblies from the clr.References property and displays them onscreen using a for loop. Figure 7-11 shows the list of assemblies for this example. Notice that the first assembly is mscorlib, which always loads.

You can drill down into an assembly as far as you want. The example continues by working with the System.Xml assembly. As a first step, the code displays the full name of the assembly. Using string manipulation, you can obtain the assembly name, version, culture, and public key token.

When creating an installation program, you often need to know the list of referenced assemblies. The next portion of application code shows how to perform this task using the ThisRef .GetReferencedAssemblies() method. The output includes the same four pieces of information as the assembly information, so you know precisely which assemblies to include with your application.

Some developers also want to know about attributes assigned to an assembly. The ThisRef .GetCustomAttributes(type(ThisRef)) method call obtains this information. You must provide the type of the assembly you want to interact with. Notice that the example uses the Python type() function, rather than a .NET equivalent. In some situations, you mix .NET and Python code to obtain a desired result. The code shows how to use a loop to obtain the list of attributes. Most assemblies include a wealth of attributes (some inherited). A developer might need to know some of these attributes, such as System.Security.Permissions.SecurityPermissionAttribute (which provides security information about the assembly), to create a functional application.

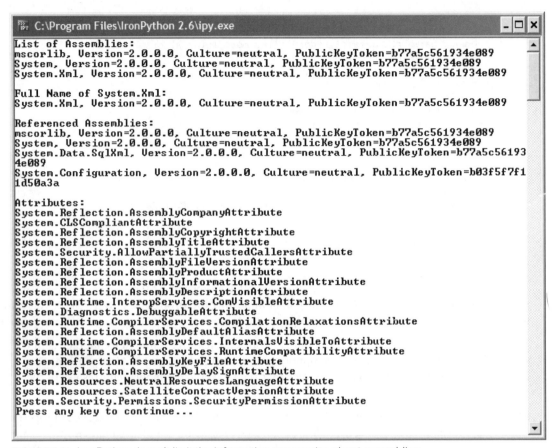

FIGURE 7-11: IronPython doesn't limit the information you receive about assemblies.

Working with the attributes can prove a little tricky because they each contain different values. When working with the `AssemblyCompanyAttribute`, for example, you can access the `Company` property that contains the name of the company that created the attribute. Of course, nothing differs from any other .NET language in this case. You need to know precisely which attributes you want to query and the properties within those attributes that contain the values you need in order to interact with attributes successfully.

Making Static Method Calls

Many of the tasks you perform using .NET require use of static methods. Static methods work the same in IronPython as they do in any .NET language. Listing 7-2 shows some static method calls that work with the current date and time. The techniques shown work with any static method.

LISTING 7-2: Performing tasks using static methods

```python
# Add the .NET Framework 2.0 to the path.
import sys
sys.path.append('C:\\WINDOWS\\Microsoft.NET\\Framework\\v2.0.50727')

# Make clr accessible.
import clr

# Import the System assembly.
import System

# Get the system date and time.
CurrDateTime = System.DateTime.Now

# Display the date and time in a number of formats.
print 'Short date and time:'
print System.DateTime.Now.ToShortDateString(),
print System.DateTime.Now.ToShortTimeString()

print '\nLong date and time:'
print CurrDateTime.ToLongDateString(),
print CurrDateTime.ToLongTimeString()

# Display a few statistics.
print '\n Date Statistics:'
print 'Days in Month:',
print CurrDateTime.DaysInMonth(CurrDateTime.Year, CurrDateTime.Month)
print 'Daylight Savings?', CurrDateTime.IsDaylightSavingTime()
print 'Leap Year?',
print CurrDateTime.IsLeapYear(CurrDateTime.Year)

# Manipulate the date.
print '\nAdding a Day, Month, and Year:'
CurrDateTime = CurrDateTime.AddDays(1)
CurrDateTime = CurrDateTime.AddMonths(1)
CurrDateTime = CurrDateTime.AddYears(1)
print CurrDateTime.ToLongDateString()

# Pause after the debug session.
raw_input('Press any key to continue...')
```

The code begins by adding the required sys.path entry and importing the necessary modules and assemblies. It then creates a variable named CurrDateTime, which is only in place for convenience. The code sets CurrDateTime to reference System.DateTime.Now. You can do the same thing without relying on the variable.

The first outputs are the short and long date and time. Notice that the short date and time rely on System.DateTime.Now, while the long date and time rely on CurrDateTime. In both cases, the code calls on static methods to output the date and time in a specific format using ToShortDateString(), ToShortTimeString(), ToLongDateString(), and ToLongTimeString(). Figure 7-12 shows the output from these calls.

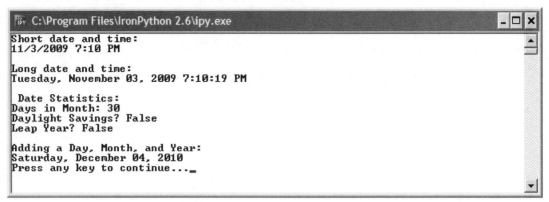

FIGURE 7-12: Static methods enable you to perform tasks without creating objects.

As with any date and time example, you can output statistics for the date and time in question. The example shows how to determine the number of days in the month, whether daylight savings time is in effect, and whether this is a leap year. Notice that some of these calls also require that you provide property values to obtain the output. You could just as easily replace `CurrDateTime` with `System.DateTime.Now` for the properties.

You do need a variable to hold date and time manipulations. The method calls are still static, but when you add date or time values, you need a place to store the result. The final portion of the example shows how you'd perform this task. The output is one day, one month, and one year later than the current date.

Creating .NET Objects

The .NET Framework provides access to a lot of objects and following chapters will explore many of them. However, one of the objects that developers need to know about first is the exception. The .NET code you run will generate exceptions at times, and Python does provide support for them as long as you have some idea of what to expect. In fact, you can even create and catch .NET exceptions in your IronPython code, as shown in Listing 7-3.

LISTING 7-3: Catching and handling .NET exceptions

```python
# Add the .NET Framework 2.0 to the path.
import sys
sys.path.append('C:\\WINDOWS\\Microsoft.NET\\Framework\\v2.0.50727')

# Make clr accessible.
import clr

# Import the System assembly.
import System

# Create an exception.
```

```
    ThisException = System.OperationCanceledException('The User Said No!')

    # Ask the user a question.
    try:
        Answer = raw_input('Do you want to continue? (Y/N)')

        # Check the response.
        if Answer.upper() == 'Y':
            print 'Great!'
        else:
            raise(ThisException)

    except SystemError as (SysErr):
        print '\nMessage:', SysErr.message
        print '\nClass:', SysErr.clsException.GetType()
        print '\nClass, Message, and Stack Trace:', SysErr.clsException

    # Pause after the debug session.
    raw_input('Press any key to continue...')
```

The example starts out as most do in the chapter by making the appropriate references and import-ing the correct modules and assemblies. The first bit of code creates an exception, `ThisException`, by calling the `System.OperationCanceledException()` constructor. You can embed previous exceptions in the current exception by using the correct constructor, but the example uses just one level to keep things simple.

The code then asks the user a simple question. If the user answers N, the code raises an excep-tion and then catches it as a `SystemError`. Notice that this exception handler provides a means of accessing the error through `SysErr`. The easiest way to obtain the error message is through the `SysErr.message`.

Of course, you'll probably want more information. All of the .NET errors will appear as the `SystemError` type. Consequently, you need to consider how to detect the proper error class in your IronPython code. The `SysErr.clsException.GetType()` provides the answer. You can also display a complex message by displaying the `SysErr.clsException` attribute. Figure 7-13 shows the output from this example.

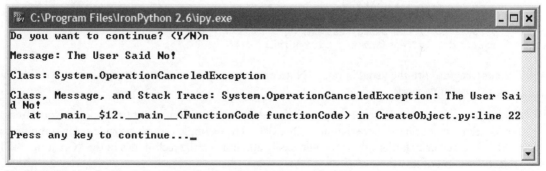

FIGURE 7-13: Use SysErr.clsException.GetType () to obtain an error class.

Creating the Directory Example

You'll probably find that you need access to the user's hard drive at some point. IronPython does provide the functionality that Python provides for working with drives, directories, and folders, but many developers will find using the .NET functionality easier — especially if that's what they normally rely upon. Listing 7-4 shows a very simple example of gaining access to directories and files. Once you gain this access, you can perform any task that you'd normally perform with a directory or file. The rest of `System.IO` works amazingly like what you'd expect from any .NET language.

LISTING 7-4: Obtaining access to directories and files

```python
# Add the .NET Framework 2.0 to the path.
import sys
sys.path.append('C:\\WINDOWS\\Microsoft.NET\\Framework\\v2.0.50727')

# Make clr accessible.
import clr

# Import the required assemblies.
import System
import System.IO

# Get the starting directory.
Start = raw_input('Type a starting directory (such as C:\\)')

# Create the DirectoryInfo object.
MyDir = System.IO.DirectoryInfo(Start)

# Display a list of subdirectories.
print 'Subdirectories:'
for EachDir in MyDir.GetDirectories():
    print EachDir, '\t',

# Display a list of files.
print '\n\nFiles:'
for EachFile in MyDir.GetFiles():
    print EachFile, '\t',

# Pause after the debug session.
raw_input('\nPress any key to continue...')
```

The code begins with the usual imports. Notice that you must import the `System.IO` assembly to make this example work.

At this point, the code asks the user to provide a drive specification as a starting point. You can type any location on your hard drive that actually exists. The example doesn't provide error-trapping code for the sake of clarity (although, you could easily add it using the techniques in the "Creating .NET Objects" section of this chapter).

Now that the code has a drive specification to use, it creates a `System.IO.DirectoryInfo()` object, `MyDir`, just as you would when using a .NET language. The code uses `MyDir` to access the list of directories using `MyDir.GetDirectories()` and a list of files using `MyDir.GetFiles()`. In this case, the code simply prints out the result, but you could go on to process the directories and files. Figure 7-14 shows typical output from this example (of course, the actual directory and filenames will match your system).

```
C:\Program Files\IronPython 2.6\ipy.exe                                    _ □ ×
Type a starting directory (such as C:\)C:\
Subdirectories:
$AVG8.VAULT$        $RECYCLE.BIN       0153 - Source Code        0174 - Source Code
 0184 - Source Code         0188 - Source Code       0195 - Source Code        0217 -
Source Code        0247 - Source Code         0248 - Source Code        0249 - Source C
ode        0252 - Source Code        0253 - Source Code        0255 - Source Code
 0256 - Source Code        BIBLEU              Boot      Config.Msi          Countdown
 Documents and Settings            Email    Excel Data        Games      GrabAPicture
 IDEACOURSE        Inetpub         MSOCache              My Pictures      My Web Site
 My Web Site Project        Personal          Program Files    Python26          RECYCLE
R        Reference          Registry          Search Engines           SQL Data
 SQLAnywhere        System Volume Information          Temp      Time Check 2004
 Time Check 2005        Time Check 2006           Time Check 2007         Time Ch
eck 2008            TODAY      TypingBuddy      Win      WINDOWS

Files:
AUTOEXEC.BAT        boot.ini          bootmgr            BOOTSECT.BAK     CAD.LOG
 CHCKSTAT.BAT       Check Time Status 2.pif            Check Time Status.pif     CONFIG.
SYS        Countdown.exe     Countdown.exe.config       DBASE.LOG            GrabAPicture.ex
e        IO.SYS          Log Off 2.pif      Log Off.pif        Log On 2.PIF        Log On.
PIF        LOGOFF.BAT        LOGON.BAT          MAINT.LOG        MSDOS.SYS           NTDETEC
T.COM        ntldr      OTHER.LOG          pagefile.sys      PROGRAM.LOG        Read Time Statu
s 2.PIF        Read Time Status.PIF        READ.BAT          SPRDSHT.LOG        Test.BA
T        TIME.ICO          TRAX.EXE          TRAXSTAT.EXE      TypingBuddy.exe
 updatedatfix.log          Weekly Backup for Main Systems.nbt          WORDP.LOG

Press any key to continue...
```

FIGURE 7-14: A list of directories and subdirectories is in the C:\ folder.

WORKING WITH GENERICS

Generic classes are exceptionally easy to work with in IronPython, which is a good feature to have because the .NET Framework includes a lot of generic classes. Listing 7-5 starts with a simple `List`, but the technique shown in this listing works with every other generic class that .NET provides.

LISTING 7-5: Using .NET generics

```python
# Add the .NET Framework 2.0 to the path.
import sys
sys.path.append('C:\\WINDOWS\\Microsoft.NET\\Framework\\v2.0.50727')

# Make clr accessible.
import clr

# Import the required assemblies.
import System
```

continues

LISTING 7-5 *(continued)*

```
import System.Collections.Generic

# Create an integer list.
MyList = System.Collections.Generic.List[int]()

# Add items to the list.
MyList.Add(1)
MyList.Add(2)
MyList.Add(3)

# Enumerate the list.
print 'Initial List'
for I in MyList:
    print I,

# Add a range of numbers.
MyList.AddRange(range(5))

# Enumerate the updated list.
print '\n\nList With Range Added'
for I in MyList:
    print I,

# Remove a value that's no longer needed.
MyList.Remove(4)

# Display the results.
print '\n\nList With 4 Removed'
for I in MyList:
    print I,

# Remove a range of items.
MyList.RemoveRange(1, 2)

# Display the results.
print '\n\nRemoved Items 1 and 2'
for I in MyList:
    print I,

# Pause after the debug session.
raw_input('\nPress any key to continue...')
```

The code begins with the usual imports. Notice that you must import System.Collections.Generic to make this example work. If you were going to work quite a bit with this namespace, you'd want to import it into the global namespace because typing the longer namespace would prove time consuming and error prone. Fortunately, you use it only once in this example, to create MyList, which is an int List. Notice that the data type of List appears within square brackets and that the example uses a Python data type. You could just as easily use a .NET data type.

At this point, the code makes some additions to `MyList` using the `Add()` method. Most .NET developers have used this technique since they first started working with their .NET language of choice, so there aren't any surprises here. The initial output appears in Figure 7-15.

```
C:\Program Files\IronPython 2.6\ipy.exe                              _ □ ×
Initial List
1 2 3

List With Range Added
1 2 3 0 1 2 3 4

List With 4 Removed
1 2 3 0 1 2 3

Removed Items 1 and 2
1 0 1 2 3
Press any key to continue...
```

FIGURE 7-15: You can use generics to interact with a list.

The next addition might surprise you a little. The code uses the `AddRange()` method to add a range of numbers supplied by the `range()` function. This is another example where you can easily mix .NET and Python code without any problems. Figure 7-15 shows that `MyList` now contains both the initial additions and the range of numbers.

You can also remove values from `MyList`. The first example uses `Remove()` to remove a specific value. The `RemoveRange()` method removes a range of the entries by position. Both removals appear in Figure 7-15 so you can see their effect.

Like many of the techniques described in this chapter, `List` has a lot more to offer. Make sure you perform a `dir(MyList)` to see other tasks you can perform with the `List` generic class. For example, you might want to see the results of using `Reverse()` or `Sort()` on `MyList`. Have some fun with this example because discovering what generics can add to IronPython is important.

USING IRONPYTHON CONSTRUCTIVELY

This chapter provides you with an introduction to working with the .NET Framework in IronPython. Access to the .NET Framework is a huge advantage that IronPython possesses that you won't find with any other version of Python. This advantage limits you to the Windows environment in most cases, unless you use a subset of the .NET Framework that also works with Mono (http://www.mono-project.com/Main_Page). If you can find a way to work with just the subset, your applications will also work without problem on both Mac and Linux so you get the best of both worlds — full access to Python and full access to the .NET Framework in one language. Amazing!

You've probably spent a good deal of time working with the .NET Framework when using other languages. However, IronPython has specific needs and requirements when working with the .NET Framework. It's a good idea to spend some time working through examples of your own with IronPython before you move on to the next chapter. Try converting a few of your simpler applications from the language you currently use to IronPython. The exercise will help you understand the IronPython differences and may help you understand where IronPython can help with your current application development needs.

This chapter is about .NET Framework basics. In Chapter 8 you move beyond basics to a specific kind of application — the Windows Forms application. The examples in Chapter 8 help you understand how you can use IronPython to create a standard desktop application with a full GUI, something that most developers will need to know in order to use IronPython fully in their application development environment. It's important to keep the basics in mind, however, as you move from this chapter to the graphical examples in Chapter 8.

8

Creating Windows Forms Applications

WHAT'S IN THIS CHAPTER?

➤ Creating a form design without using the Visual Designer

➤ Building a Windows Forms application

➤ Using events and delegates in IronPython

Most of the applications you've worked with in the book so far rely on a character-mode interface. Of course, character-mode is just fine when you're dealing with utilities or example applications, but most users want a GUI. The idea of typing commands at the command prompt is so foreign to most of today's users that you'd never get them all trained to use your application.

Fortunately, you can create a number of graphical application types using IronPython. Unfortunately, many of the graphical programming tools available to Python developers won't work with IronPython because IronPython lacks support for C-style libraries. This is a situation where you really do need Windows Forms support to provide what the user needs in the way of an application.

The problem for the IronPython developer is that IronPython isn't integrated into Visual Studio. Consequently, you won't have Visual Designer support in a pure IronPython environment. (Chapters 16 and 17 show how to overcome this problem by using either C# or Visual Basic.NET to produce the user interface.) This chapter discusses some ways in which you can produce a great interface without using the Visual Designer.

A graphical interface naturally implies writing code that responds to events (*handlers*) and providing the code required to produce an event (*delegates*). When the user clicks a button, something needs to happen in your application. This chapter addresses the requirements for working with both handlers and delegates. You'll discover the techniques used to create event handlers that act just like those created in other languages.

The final section of this chapter puts everything you've discovered into practice. You'll build a Windows Forms application. The application isn't designed to do anything too complex — the main purpose of the example is to show you how to put all of the component parts together so that you end up with a working application. You'll discover how to perform more complex processing as the book progresses.

WORKING WITHOUT A VISUAL DESIGNER

Tools are a good thing because they help you perform tasks faster and more accurately. However, tools aren't indispensible. You use a tool when it's available to gain the benefits it provides, but a good developer can get by without the tools. The Visual Designer found in Visual Studio is simply a tool, nothing more. It doesn't perform any sort of magic or suddenly make your application do things that it couldn't in the past. In fact, you can dispense with the Visual Designer when creating any application using Visual Studio. Developers simply use the Visual Designer because it performs its task so admirably.

Unfortunately, tools can also hide the work they perform. The Visual Designer does a lot of work in the background that most developers could figure out given time but most developers don't bother to learn. Consequently, when approaching a Windows Forms application for IronPython, you might find that you have to develop some new skills to get the window to display at all. Let's hope that IronPython will eventually become integrated with the Visual Studio IDE enough that you won't have to create your Windows Forms interface by hand. In the meantime, the following sections describe what the Visual Designer does in a little more detail and then tell you what you need to know to work without it.

Understanding How the Visual Designer Works

The Visual Designer is nothing more than a code writer. When you place a new control on the form, the Visual Designer writes the code to create the control in the form when the application executes. Sizing and other property changes are merely coding additions to the form code. When you're done, you end up with a class that defines a form using code — code that you didn't write.

The class that Visual Designer creates appears in a separate file so that the Windows Form code doesn't interfere with code you write. For example, if you create a form named frmMain.CS, the designer code appears in frmMain.Designer.CS. When you open the frmMain.Designer.CS file, you see code such as that shown in Figure 8-1.

The code in Figure 8-1 shows that the form has two buttons (btnOK and btnCancel) and a label (label1) defined. You then see the code used to define the properties for each control. For example, the btnOK.DialogResult property is set to System.Windows.Forms.DialogResult.OK. There isn't anything mysterious about this code — you've probably written similar code yourself, so you can easily do it now.

Understanding the Elements of a Window

Before you tackle an IronPython Windows Forms application, it's a good idea to spend a little time looking at simple examples in languages you know. If you don't have a simple example to review, check out CSharpExample, which is provided with the book's source code. The frmMain.Designer.CS file is the best place to start.

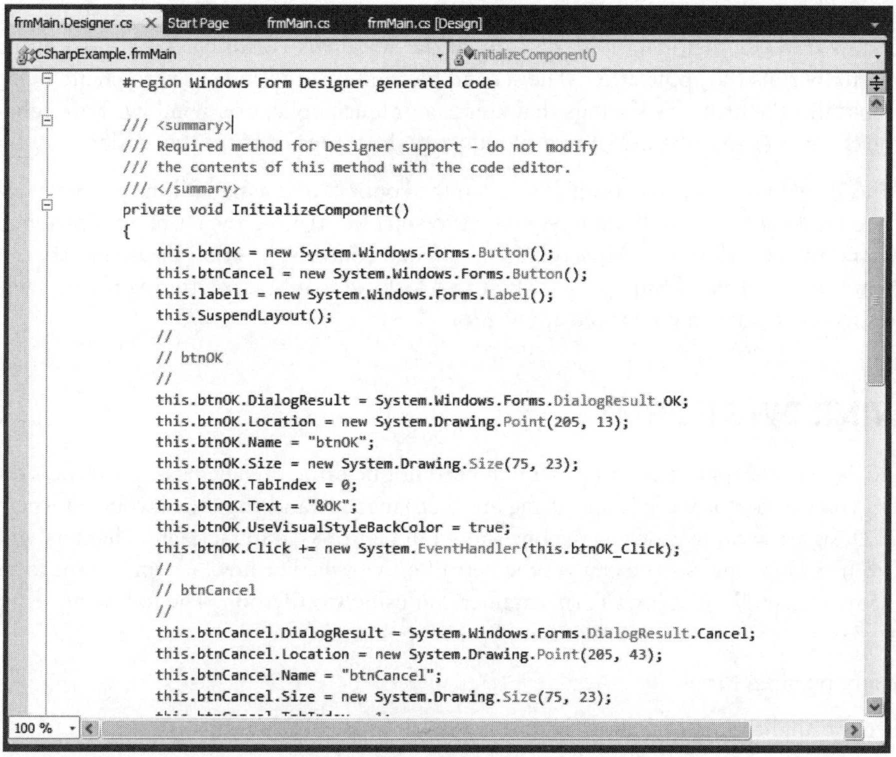

FIGURE 8-1: The Visual Designer writes the code used to create a form.

All Windows Forms applications inherit from `System.Windows.Forms.Form`. This class provides the basic window, which is configurable for a variety of needs. All of the properties you see in the Visual Designer are also available programmatically. For example, if you want to create a dialog box, you simply change the `FormBorderStyle` property.

Inside the window are controls. It's important to realize that even if controls appear within another control, you define them as part of the window. Now, you might add the control to another control, but eventually, the host control is added to the window or it isn't displayed.

Emulating the Visual Designer Results

When working with IronPython, you become the Visual Designer. It helps if you have a familiarity with what the Visual Designer does so that you can emulate its output and produce an application faster.

There are certain features the Visual Designer needs that you don't need to consider when working with IronPython. For example, you don't need to include a call to `SuspendLayout()` or `ResumeLayout()`, which prevent multiple `Layout` events when using the Visual Designer. You also don't need to include any of the designer variables or the `Dispose()` method.

It helps to create two files when building a Windows Forms application. The first file contains the client application — the code that instantiates a copy of the Windows Forms class, provides event handlers, and actually runs the application. The second file contains the code used to create the form. This file contains the property settings that create a unique application window. Throughout this chapter, you'll discover that the use of two files does make things considerably easier.

When you use the Visual Designer, you probably set up the controls and assign all the property values in one step. When working with IronPython, you want to start by creating the client application and a basic window and then try the code. After this step, you add controls, position them, and try the application again. Only after you complete these first two tasks do you start cluttering the files with the property settings that define a completed application.

DEFINING WINDOWS FORMS

Creating a Windows Forms application from scratch need not be difficult. The basic problem is one of layout. Often, you can perform the layout using another language and copy the layout information from the Visual Designer window (such as the one shown in Figure 8-1). In fact, later chapters will show you how to mix languages so you can get the best of all worlds. For now, it's important to see how you'd implement a simple Windows Forms application using IronPython. The following sections describe the five basic steps in creating a Windows Forms application:

1. Define any required forms.

2. Initialize the application, including the forms.

3. Add event handlers for control events.

4. Perform useful work when an event occurs.

5. Run the application by starting the main form.

Creating the Window Code

Every Windows Forms application begins with one or more windows. You define the code used to create the window, starting with the window itself. As previously explained, creating a class that inherits from the `System.Windows.Forms.Form` class is enough to create the window, but then you need to add controls to the window to define the interface. The following sections describe how to create a basic control structure for a window and then how to enhance that structure to make life easier for the user.

Creating the Basic Control Structure

It's helpful to lay out your controls and give them the visual appearance that you expect before doing anything else. The example is relatively simple — it includes two buttons and a static label containing a message. The first button displays a message, while the second ends the application. Listing 8-1 shows the code required to create the interface for this example.

LISTING 8-1: Designing the form and controls

```python
# Set up the path to the .NET Framework.
import sys
sys.path.append('C:\\WINDOWS\\Microsoft.NET\\Framework\\v2.0.50727')

# Make clr accessible.
import clr

# Add any required references.
clr.AddReference('System.Windows.Forms.DLL')
clr.AddReference('System.Drawing.DLL')

# Import the .NET assemblies.
import System
import System.Windows.Forms
import System.Drawing.Point

class frmMain(System.Windows.Forms.Form):

    # This function performs all of the required initialization.
    def InitializeComponent(self):

        # Configure btnOK
        self.btnOK = System.Windows.Forms.Button()
        self.btnOK.Text = "&OK"
        self.btnOK.Location = System.Drawing.Point(263, 13)

        # Configure btnCancel
        self.btnCancel = System.Windows.Forms.Button()
        self.btnCancel.Text = "&Cancel"
        self.btnCancel.Location = System.Drawing.Point(263, 43)

        # Configure lblMessage
        self.lblMessage = System.Windows.Forms.Label()
        self.lblMessage.Text = 'This is a sample label.'
        self.lblMessage.Location = System.Drawing.Point(13, 13)
        self.lblMessage.Size = System.Drawing.Size(120, 13)

        # Configure the form.
        self.Text = 'Simple Python Windows Forms Example'
        self.ClientSize = System.Drawing.Size(350, 200)

        # Add the controls to the form.
        self.Controls.Add(self.btnOK)
        self.Controls.Add(self.btnCancel)
        self.Controls.Add(self.lblMessage)
```

The code begins by adding the .NET Framework path to sys.path. It then uses clr.AddReference()
to add references for both System.Windows.Forms.DLL and System.Drawing.DLL. Finally, the code
imports a number of .NET assemblies. The example uses individual import statements for each assembly. Theoretically, you can combine all the imports into a single import statement, but most developers
find using individual import statements is a lot more readable and easy to maintain.

The next step is to create the window class, `frmMain`, which inherits from `System.Windows.Forms`
`.Form`. It's important to remember that this class is simply a blueprint, as all classes are, and that
your application can create as many instances of it as required. This is the reason that every element
in the code is prefaced with `self`, which refers to the current instance.

You can perform the configuration tasks found in
`InitializeComponent()` in any order. Most developers
like to create the controls first, followed by the client area,
as shown in Listing 8-1. However, you must add the controls to the window after you configure them, or the controls will appear partially configured onscreen (and make
for a difficult debugging chore). For this reason, the code
calls on `self.Controls.Add()` last to add the controls to
the window. Figure 8-2 shows the output from the example
based on the configuration criteria in Listing 8-1.

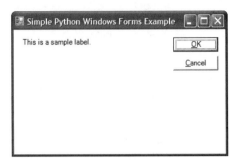

FIGURE 8-2: The form created by this
example is simple but works for demonstration purposes.

It's easy to get lost while configuring the controls, especially if you have multiple control levels to consider (such
as when using container controls). Most controls require
five configuration steps and you want to perform them in
this order to ensure you accomplish them all:

1. Instantiate the control.

2. Set the control's output text, if any.

3. Set the control's position on the window (starting from the upper-left corner).

4. (Optional) Set the control's size when the default size won't work.

5. (Optional) Add control enhancements, such as the tooltips discussed in the section "Making
   the Application Easier to Use," which follows.

Making the Application Easier to Use

One interesting point about using IronPython to create a Windows Forms application is that it tends
to reduce the number of unnecessary bells and whistles. However, don't make your application so
Spartan that the user spends a lot of head-scratching time trying to figure out how to use it. You
have to create a balance between the amount of code you must write and the needs of the user.

An easy addition is the use of speed keys. Simply type an ampersand (&) in front of the letter you
want to use for a speed key. When the user presses Alt+<Speed Key Letter>, the application selects
the associated control. Providing speed keys is incredibly easy, yet has a big impact on user productivity and also makes it possible for users who can't work with a mouse to use your application. The
sample application described in Listing 8-1 already has this feature.

When users rely on the keyboard instead of the mouse, they also want to select the controls in order —
from left to right and from top to bottom (unless your language has a different natural order for reading
text). In some cases, this means changing the `TabIndex` property. The form defaults to the tab order
provided by the order in which the controls appear in the code. Careful placement of the controls often
negates the need to change the `TabIndex` property.

Windows can also have default actions. The two most common default actions occur when you press Enter (default acceptance) and Escape (default cancel). Providing controls for these two features helps users move quickly through a form and can speed processing of wizards. Here's the code you use to provide default actions for the example application.

```
self.AcceptButton = self.btnOK
self.CancelButton = self.btnCancel
```

 You must configure the controls for a form before you configure any default actions. The control must exist before you make the assignment to either self .AcceptButton *or* self.CancelButton. *Otherwise, you receive an ambiguous error message when you run the application that will prove difficult to debug.*

Another useful enhancement that doesn't require a lot of work is the ToolTip component. Using tooltips makes it easier for the user to figure out how an application works. These bits of mini-help are quite useful and they provide all that many users need to become proficient quickly. Tooltips also make it easy for someone who hasn't used the application for a while to get back up to speed quickly. Tooltips also provide input to screen readers (commonly used by those with special visual needs) so that the screen reader can tell the user the control's purpose. Here's the code used to add ToolTip to the window.

```
# Add a tooltip control.
self.Tips = System.Windows.Forms.ToolTip()
```

You don't add the ToolTip component to the window itself using self.Controls.Add() because ToolTip lacks a visual interface. The ToolTip component sits in the background and waits for a visual control to require its services. The following code shows how to add a ToolTip to individual controls.

```
self.Tips.SetToolTip(self.btnOK, 'Displays an interesting message.')
```

The SetToolTip() method of the ToolTip adds a tooltip to the control specified by the first argument. The message appears as the second argument. Figure 8-3 shows a typical example of a tooltip created using this technique.

Visual Studio provides a wealth of additional enhancements that usually won't require a lot of implementation time, but can make a big difference to the user. The best way to determine how to add these enhancements is to add them to a C# or Visual Basic.NET application and then view the Visual Designer file. For example, you might want to add information to the AccessibleDescription, AccessibleName, and AccessibleRole

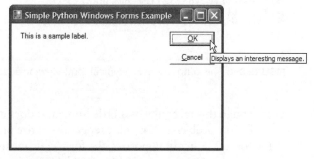

FIGURE 8-3: Adding tooltips is easy and helps most users considerably.

properties when your application will see even moderate use by those with special physical needs. Obviously, you don't add precisely the same code to your IronPython application that the Visual Designer adds to the C# or Visual Basic.NET application, but the Visual Designer file provides enough insight to make the transition to IronPython work with relative ease.

Performing Quick Form Tests

You'll want to see your form from time to time, before you've written the rest of the application code. Fortunately, you're using IronPython, so you have the interpreter at your disposal. The following steps outline a quick way to see what your form looks like.

1. Start the interpreter (`IPY.EXE`) in the directory that contains the form code.

2. Type `from frmMain import *` and press Enter. This step imports the form into the interpreter for testing.

3. Type `TestForm = frmMain()` and press Enter. This step instantiates a copy of `frmMain` that you'll use for testing.

4. Type `TestForm.InitializeComponent()` and press Enter. In this step, you execute the code used to create and configure the controls within the form.

5. Type `TestForm.ShowDialog()` and press Enter. At this point, you see the dialog box appear onscreen, just as you'd normally see it when executed from the application. However, you see just the dialog box and its controls. The dialog box is pretty much non-functional because you don't have any event handlers in place.

6. After you finish viewing the dialog box, click Cancel or the close button. This act closes the dialog box. You'll see a dialog result value as part of the output, as shown in Figure 8-4.

```
C:\WINDOWS\system32\cmd.exe - IPY

C:\0255 - Source Code\Chapter08>IPY
IronPython 2.6 (2.6.10920.0) on .NET 2.0.50727.3603
Type "help", "copyright", "credits" or "license" for more information.
>>> from frmMain import *
>>> TestForm = frmMain()
>>> TestForm.InitializeComponent()
>>> TestForm.ShowDialog()
System.Windows.Forms.DialogResult.Cancel
>>>
```

FIGURE 8-4: This output shows a typical form-viewing session in the interpreter.

Even though this technique is a little limited, it does give you a view of your form so that you can easily fix any problems. You must repeat the entire process every time you want to test changes to the form. The act of importing the form code means that you won't see any changes within the interpreter until you import the form code again. In short, if you make changes and don't see them during testing, it's probably because you didn't exit the interpreter and start over.

Initializing the Application

After you've created a form and tested its functionality, you can begin to create an application that uses the form. The first step in this process is to initialize the application as shown in Listing 8-2. You might think that adding all of the .NET assembly imports is unnecessary given that the form code already has them, but it turns out that you really do need to include the imports or the code won't work.

> **LISTING 8-2: Starting the application**
>
> ```
> # Set up the path to the .NET Framework.
> import sys
> sys.path.append('C:\\WINDOWS\\Microsoft.NET\\Framework\\v2.0.50727')
>
> # Make clr accessible.
> import clr
>
> # Add any required references.
> clr.AddReference('System.Windows.Forms.DLL')
>
> # Import the .NET assemblies.
> import System
> import System.Windows.Forms
>
> # import the form.
> from frmMain import *
>
> # Define the Windows Form and the elements of this specific instance.
> TestForm = frmMain()
> TestForm.InitializeComponent()
> ```

This part of the example shows all the required startup code. It begins by adding the path and making all the required imports, as usual. The code ends by creating `TestForm`, the object used to interact with the `frmMain` instance. A common error developers make is that they don't call `TestForm.InitializeComponent()`. When this problem occurs, the form won't look as expected — it may not appear at all. In fact, sometimes the IronPython interpreter will simply freeze, requiring you to force a restart.

Providing Handlers for the Control Events

After the form initialization is complete, you have access to a form object and could display it using `ShowDialog()`. However, the form object still won't perform any useful work because you don't have any event handlers in place. You might be used to working with other .NET languages, where double-clicking the control on the form or double-clicking one of the event entries in the Properties window performs all the configuration for you. However, when working with IronPython, you must perform these steps manually. Here is the code used to assign an event handler to a particular control event.

```
# Always add event handlers after defining the Windows Form.
TestForm.btnOK.Click += btnOK_Click
TestForm.btnCancel.Click += btnCancel_Click
```

Notice that you must drill down into the form in order to access the controls. Consequently, you must provide the full path to the event, such as `TestForm.btnOK.Click`. IronPython lets you use the += operator to add an event handler to the `Click` event. If you want to remove the event handler, all you need to use is the -= operator instead. Assigning the event handler is as easy as providing the method name as shown in the code.

IronPython events can have more than one handler, as you'll see in the section "Developing Your Own Events." As with any OOP language, you simply keep adding event handlers with the correct signature (a combination of the right return type and input arguments). Unlike most OOP languages, IronPython tends to make things very simple and you could actually find this approach detrimental because there are times where the interpreter will output odd messages instead of telling you that the event handler won't work for the event to which you assigned it.

Performing Some Useful Work as the Result of User Input

The Windows Forms application now has a form object and methods assigned to some of the events. Of course, this means you need to provide the event handlers required to do the work. Event handlers can come in a number of forms. When working with Windows Forms controls, you may never even need the arguments that IronPython passes. The following code shows the event handlers used for this example.

```
# Define the event handlers.
def btnOK_Click(*args):

    # Display a message showing we arrived.
    System.Windows.Forms.MessageBox.Show('Hello!')

def btnCancel_Click(*args):

    # Close the application.
    TestForm.Close()
```

The code is a standard IronPython function. However, notice that the arguments have an asterisk (*) in front of them. Essentially, this means that all the arguments passed to the event handler end up in a sequence. In this case, that means you'll end up with a list of event arguments. For a button handler, you obtain two arguments:

➤ Sender

➤ Mouse arguments

Let's say for a minute that the user has clicked OK. Then the sender argument would contain

```
System.Windows.Forms.Button, Text: &OK
```

and the mouse arguments would contain the following (in a single line, rather than the multiple lines shown in the book):

```
<System.Windows.Forms.MouseEventArgs object at 0x000000000000002B
 [System.Windows.Forms.MouseEventArgs]>
```

Sometimes you need to access the event arguments. In this case, you could easily rewrite this event handler as shown here:

```
def btnOK_Click(Sender, MArgs):

    # Display a message showing we arrived.
    SenderText = 'Text: ' + Sender.Text
    MouseText = '\nButton: ' + MArgs.Button.ToString()
    MousePosit = '\nX/Y: ' + MArgs.X.ToString() + '/' + MArgs.Y.ToString()
    System.Windows.Forms.MessageBox.Show(SenderText + MouseText + MousePosit)
```

When you run this code, you see more of the information that the event handler receives. It turns out that `Sender` is actually a `System.Windows.Forms.Button` object and you can perform any task you'd normally perform with that object. Likewise, `MArgs` is a `System.Windows.Forms.MouseEventArgs` object. The example code shows only a few of the items you receive. Figure 8-5 shows the output when you click OK using this alternate event handler.

Figure 8-5 shows that the button `Text` property is `&OK`. You can read more about the `Button` class at `http://msdn.microsoft.com/library/system.windows .forms.button.aspx`. The user clicked the left mouse button, and the X/Y position shows the mouse pointer location within the control. You can read more about the `MouseEventArgs` class at `http://msdn.microsoft.com/library/system.windows .forms.mouseeventargs.aspx`.

FIGURE 8-5: Event handlers receive a number of pieces of information from .NET.

> The IronPython environment won't always provide a default value for some class properties. In many cases, the Visual Designer provides these defaults in the background. If you don't define a property, such as `Name`, then you won't see this property defined for the object sent to the event handler.

Running the Application

The window is complete. A user can now see the window displayed, interact with it, and expect some type of output from the application. However, one more task remains. The application that's running now is an IronPython interpreted application, not a .NET Windows Forms application. In order to get a true Windows Forms application, you must perform one more step as shown in the following code.

```
# Run the application.
System.Windows.Forms.Application.Run(TestForm)
```

This code exists in your C# and Visual Basic.NET applications as well. However, you normally find it hidden in the `Program.CS` or `Program.VB` file (along with a lot of other code that you won't need for this example). All that this code says is that the Common Language Runtime (CLR) should execute the .NET application using `TestForm` as a starting point.

When you run the default version of the application, you see a dialog box like the one shown previously in Figure 8-1. Clicking OK displays a simple message like the one shown in Figure 8-6. Clicking Cancel will close the dialog box, much as you might expect. Congratulations! You've just created a simple Windows Forms application using IronPython — an example that will help you create more complex Windows Forms applications in the future.

FIGURE 8-6: Clicking OK displays a familiar message box.

INTERACTING WITH PREDEFINED AND CUSTOM EVENTS

Being able to define, create, and respond to events is a major part of working in a windowed environment. Even when a .NET developer isn't working in a windowed environment, the use of events and delegates is an important part of creating responsive applications. Whenever an event occurs, the application must be able to respond to it, no matter what the source of the event might be (including Windows messages, such as a shutdown warning). The following sections discuss events and delegates.

Handling Events Using Existing Classes

The .NET Framework includes a host of controls and components that you find useful in IronPython. For example, one of the more interesting (and useful) components is `Timer`. The `Timer` component lets you set an interval for automatic events. All you need to do is set the interval between event ticks. You've probably used this component before, but working in IronPython introduces a few twists. Listing 8-3 shows the form code for this example.

Available for download on Wrox.com

LISTING 8-3: Creating a form containing a component

```python
# This function performs all of the required initialization.
def InitializeComponent(self):

    # Configure the form.
    self.ClientSize = System.Drawing.Size(350, 200)
    self.Text = 'Using a Timer Example'

    # Configure btnStart
    self.btnStart = System.Windows.Forms.Button()
    self.btnStart.Text = "&Start"
    self.btnStart.Location = System.Drawing.Point(263, 13)

    # Configure btnQuit
    self.btnQuit = System.Windows.Forms.Button()
    self.btnQuit.Text = "&Quit"
    self.btnQuit.Location = System.Drawing.Point(263, 43)
```

```
# Configure lblTime
self.lblTime = System.Windows.Forms.Label()
self.lblTime.Text = System.DateTime.Now.ToLongTimeString()
self.lblTime.Location = System.Drawing.Point(13, 13)
self.lblTime.Size = System.Drawing.Size(120, 13)

# Configure objTimer
self.objTimer = System.Windows.Forms.Timer()
self.objTimer.Interval = 1000

# Add the controls to the form.
self.Controls.Add(self.btnStart)
self.Controls.Add(self.btnQuit)
self.Controls.Add(self.lblTime)
```

Quite a bit of this form code should look familiar from Listing 8-1. However, lblTime is set to show the long time format (using ToLongTimeString()) based on the application starting time. You can use any value desired for control properties as long as you perform the required conversions. In this case, the code calls System.DateTime.Now.ToLongTimeString() to obtain the correct string value.

Notice that the code doesn't add objTimer to the form using self.Controls.Add(). As with all components, objTimer waits in the background for a control to call on it for services. However, unlike the ToolTip component used in the section "Making the Application Easier to Use," you must configure a Timer component as part of the form code. This example sets the objTimer interval to 1 second (1,000 ms). Figure 8-7 shows the initial presentation of the dialog box.

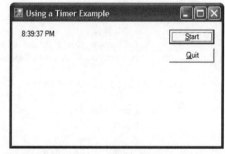

FIGURE 8-7: The started application shows the current long time format.

The initial form shown in Figure 8-7 appears quite useful, but the time doesn't update. In order to make the time update, you must provide an event handler for the objTimer.Tick event. Listing 8-4 shows the code required to create the form, display it onscreen, and then handle the various events required to make this application work.

LISTING 8-4: Handling timer events in a form

```
# Set up the path to the .NET Framework.
import sys
sys.path.append('C:\\WINDOWS\\Microsoft.NET\\Framework\\v2.0.50727')

# Make clr accessible.
import clr

# Add any required references.
clr.AddReference('System.Windows.Forms.DLL')

# Import the .NET assemblies.
```

continues

LISTING 8-4 *(continued)*

```
import System
import System.Windows.Forms

# import the form.
from frmUseTimer import *

# Define the event handlers.
def btnStart_Click(*args):

    # Check the button status.
    if TestForm.btnStart.Text == '&Start':

        # Start the timer.
        TestForm.objTimer.Start()

        # Change the button text.
        TestForm.btnStart.Text = '&Stop'

    else:

        # Start the timer.
        TestForm.objTimer.Stop()

        # Change the button text.
        TestForm.btnStart.Text = '&Start'

def btnQuit_Click(*args):

    # Close the application.
    TestForm.Close()

def objTimer_Tick(*args):

    # Handle the timer tick.
    TestForm.lblTime.Text = System.DateTime.Now.ToLongTimeString()

# Define the Windows Form and the elements of this specific instance.
TestForm = frmMain()
TestForm.InitializeComponent()

# Always add event handlers after defining the Windows Form.
TestForm.btnStart.Click += btnStart_Click
TestForm.btnQuit.Click += btnQuit_Click
TestForm.objTimer.Tick += objTimer_Tick

# Run the application.
System.Windows.Forms.Application.Run(TestForm)
```

This example begins as any Windows Forms application does, by providing access to the .NET Framework directory and then importing the required assemblies after adding any required references. The `btnStart_Click()` event handler doesn't just display a simple message this time. When the user clicks Start, the code checks the current `TestForm.btnStart.Text` value. When this value is `&Start`, the code calls `TestForm.objTimer.Start()`, which starts the timer and changes the `TestForm.btnStart.Text` value to `&Stop`. When the value is `&Stop`, the opposite sequence of events occurs. Figure 8-8 shows the dialog box with the timer started.

Starting `objTimer` causes the component to begin emitting `Tick` events. The `objTimer_Tick()` handles these `Tick` events by updating the `TestForm.lblTime.Text` with the latest time. Notice that even though you don't add `objTimer` to the window, you must still add the event handler to the event using `TestForm.objTimer.Tick += objTimer_Tick`. In fact, you'll often find that components require you to handle a number of events because events are the main form of communication for components (versus controls, which rely on their interface elements for interaction and use events only to register control changes so you can act on them).

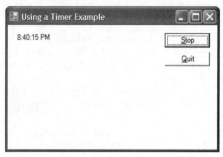

FIGURE 8-8: The Timer component updates the time shown in this example.

Developing Your Own Events

It's true that the .NET Framework comes with more events than you'll probably use in an entire lifetime. However, it's also true that IronPython developers simply can't see every need (and even if they did, it just wouldn't pay to create a general event that only two people would ever use). Consequently, you'll eventually need to create your own events to handle those situations that don't neatly fit within someone else's pigeonhole. The following sections show how to create a simple custom event that you can use as a model for creating events of your own.

Creating the Event Class

An event class defines the custom event. Of course, you have to also write code to implement and respond to the custom event, but let's focus on the definition first. The most basic event class must include four activities:

➤ An initialization that defines a container for holding a list of event handlers

➤ A method for adding new event handlers

➤ A method for removing old event handlers

➤ A method that calls the event handlers in turn whenever an external source invokes (fires) the event

You can always add more items to your event handler, but a basic event handler must include these four items. With this in mind, Listing 8-5 shows a basic event definition. You might be surprised at how little code you need to perform this task.

LISTING 8-5: Defining a simple event class

```python
class MyEvent:

    # Create the initial HandlerList.
    def __init__(self):
        self.HandlerList = set()

    # Add new handlers to the list.
    def Add(self, NewHandler):
        self.HandlerList.add(NewHandler)

    # Remove existing handlers from the list.
    def Remove(self, OldHandler):
        try:
            self.HandlerList.remove(OldHandler)
        except KeyError:
            pass

    # Invoke the handler.
    def Fire(self, Msg):

        # Call each of the handlers in the list.
        for self.Handler in self.HandlerList:
            self.Handler(Msg)
```

The code begins with __init__(), which IronPython calls automatically anytime someone creates an event of this type. The only purpose of __init__() is to create a container for storing event handler references. You can use any container you want, but the example relies on a set() because this particular container works very well as a means of storing event handlers. The initialization code creates an empty set() that you'll later fill with event handler references.

There are many different ways to create a delegate using IronPython — this chapter shows one of the more basic techniques you can use. However, you might find that this technique doesn't work for your particular need. It's always a good idea to look at what other people are doing with Python and IronPython. For example, there's another example of an event system at http://www.valuedlessons.com/2008/04/events-in-python.html. *In this case, the author wanted to create a lightweight event system that mimicked C#. Another, more ambitious example is at* http://code.activestate.com/recipes/410686/. *Don't forget the* pyevent.py *class provided with the IronPython tutorial (it does work). The point is that you don't want to give up on events in IronPython. If what you want doesn't exist now, you can probably create it without too much trouble.*

The Add() method simply adds a reference to the event handler passed as one of the arguments. In this case, the code uses the self.HandlerList.add() method to perform the task.

Likewise, `Remove()` takes the requested event handler reference out of the container using the `self.HandlerList.remove()` method. Because someone could pass an invalid reference, the code must perform this task within a `try...except` block, capturing the `KeyError` exception as needed. The `pass` keyword tells IronPython not to do anything about the exception. Normally, you'd provide some type of error handling code.

Invoking (firing) the event is the responsibility of the `Fire()` method. This event accepts a message, `Msg`, and does something with it. Precisely what happens with `Msg` is up to the event handler. All the event knows is that it must accept a `Msg` object and pass it along to the event handler. As you can see, the code calls each event handler reference in turn and passes the `Msg` to it. In short, the event handler must have the proper signature (set of input arguments) to handle the event correctly.

> *It's important to realize that event handlers may not receive calls in the order in which you add them to the event. Consequently, you should never create event handlers that depend on a specific order of calling.*

Devising an Event Class Test Form

Now that you have a new event, you'll want to do something with it. Listing 8-6 shows code used to create the form for this example.

LISTING 8-6: Creating an event class test form

```python
# Set up the path to the .NET Framework.
import sys
sys.path.append('C:\\WINDOWS\\Microsoft.NET\\Framework\\v2.0.50727')

# Make clr accessible.
import clr

# Add any required references.
clr.AddReference('System.Windows.Forms.DLL')
clr.AddReference('System.Drawing.DLL')

# Import the .NET assemblies.
import System
import System.Windows.Forms
import System.Drawing.Point

class frmMain(System.Windows.Forms.Form):

    # This function performs all of the required initialization.
    def InitializeComponent(self):

        # Configure the form.
        self.ClientSize = System.Drawing.Size(350, 200)
        self.Text = 'Creating an Event Example'
```

continues

LISTING 8-6 *(continued)*

```
# Configure btnFireEvent
self.btnFireEvent = System.Windows.Forms.Button()
self.btnFireEvent.Text = "&Fire Event"
self.btnFireEvent.Location = System.Drawing.Point(263, 13)

# Configure btnQuit
self.btnQuit = System.Windows.Forms.Button()
self.btnQuit.Text = "&Quit"
self.btnQuit.Location = System.Drawing.Point(263, 43)

# Add the controls to the form.
self.Controls.Add(self.btnFireEvent)
self.Controls.Add(self.btnQuit)
```

 It's generally a good practice to keep the event, form, and operational code separate. Doing so will make the application easier to debug later. This example actually uses three separate files, even though it's a very simple example. Make sure you follow this principle when creating events of your own.

As you can see, this form is a very simple version of the other forms used so far in this chapter. All it does is provide access to two buttons: one to fire the event and the other to close the form. Figure 8-9 shows the output from this code.

Running the Code

It's time to try out the new event and its associated test form. Listing 8-7 shows the code required for this part of the example.

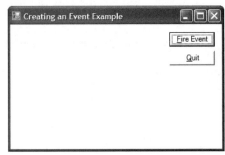

FIGURE 8-9: A simple form used to test the custom event and associated handler.

LISTING 8-7: Testing the event class

```
# Set up the path to the .NET Framework.
import sys
sys.path.append('C:\\WINDOWS\\Microsoft.NET\\Framework\\v2.0.50727')

# Make clr accessible.
import clr

# Add any required references.
clr.AddReference('System.Windows.Forms.DLL')
```

```
# Import the .NET assemblies.
import System
import System.Windows.Forms

# import the form.
from frmCreateEvent import *

# import the NewEventClass.
from NewEventClass import *

# Create the event handler.
def HandleMsg(Msg):
    System.Windows.Forms.MessageBox.Show(Msg)

# Define the event and add the handler to it.
ThisEvent = MyEvent()
ThisEvent.Add(HandleMsg)

# Define the event handlers.
def btnFireEvent_Click(*args):

    # Fire the event.
    ThisEvent.Fire('Hello World')

def btnQuit_Click(*args):

    # Close the application.
    TestForm.Close()

# Define the Windows Form and the elements of this specific instance.
TestForm = frmMain()
TestForm.InitializeComponent()

# Always add event handlers after defining the Windows Form.
TestForm.btnFireEvent.Click += btnFireEvent_Click
TestForm.btnQuit.Click += btnQuit_Click

# Run the application.
System.Windows.Forms.Application.Run(TestForm)
```

The code begins like many of the other examples in this chapter — it makes the proper additions to sys.path, creates references to .NET assemblies, and then imports them. Make sure you import all the classes required to make your event work. In this case, the code imports both frmCreateEvent and NewEventClass.

The next step is to define an event handler for the new event. This event handler takes a simple approach. It accepts Msg from Fire() and displays it using a simple message box similar to the one shown in Figure 8-6 (the message is slightly different, but the idea is the same).

Now that there's an event handler, HandleMsg(), to use, it's time to assign it to the event. The code creates a new event, ThisEvent, and assigns HandleMsg() as an event handler to it. In many respects, this approach is no different from using a delegate in a .NET language such as C# or Visual Basic .NET. The techniques are a bit different, but the basic concept is the same.

Whenever the user clicks Fire Event, the code calls `btnFireEvent_Click()` because this is the event handler assigned to the `btnFireEvent.Click` event. The code inside `btnFireEvent_Click()` simply calls `ThisEvent.Fire()` with a message of Hello World. At this point, the event calls `HandleMsg()` to display the message using a standard message box.

WHY NOT USE DELEGATES?

When you write an application using a language such as C# or Visual Basic.NET, you usually rely on delegates to create custom events. Using a delegate is simple and well understood. You can see examples all over the place, but check out the example at `http://www.akadia.com/services/dotnet_delegates_and_events.html` for a good overview.

Theoretically, there must be a way to use delegates with IronPython too, but the process would be extremely difficult and error prone for a number of reasons. The fact is that IronPython simply doesn't provide good support for delegates, so using the other techniques described in this chapter simply works better.

However, it's interesting to view one particular issue when considering delegates in IronPython. You must provide a method that's compatible with delegates in order to use delegates. As part of the preparation for this chapter, I played around with delegates for a while and found that you simply can't obtain the method information in a way that delegates will understand. To see this for yourself, try this code:

```
import System

class MyClass:
    def MyMsgDisplay(self, Msg, Title):
        print Msg, Title

for Methods in System.Type.GetMethods(type(MyClass)):
    print Methods
```

When you run this code, you'll begin to understand something interesting about IronPython. The output from this example does include methods such as `__new__()`, `ToString()`, and `__repr__()`, but nowhere will you see `MyMsgDisplay()`. It turns out that `MyMsgDisplay()` is implemented as part of the IronPython run time, so it looks like this (even though the code appears on two lines in the book, you must type it as a single line in your code):

```
System.Object Call(IronPython.Runtime.CodeContext, System.Object[])
```

All that code is the little `MyMsgDisplay()` method. What you're seeing is the method that marshals information to the IronPython run time. For example, `IronPython.Runtime.CodeContext` is actually `self`. The `System.Object[]` array is a collection of two objects, `Msg` and `Title`, sent to `MyMsgDisplay()`. Unless something changes drastically, you won't ever be able to use delegates in IronPython.

USING IRONPYTHON CONSTRUCTIVELY

This chapter has demonstrated basic principles for creating a Windows Forms application using IronPython. Admittedly, the process isn't as easy as it could be because you lack Visual Designer support. In fact, some developers will do better by creating the user interface using C# or Visual Basic.NET. However, this chapter does demonstrate that the technique is useful and that you can make IronPython work quite well in a graphical environment.

Before you leave this chapter, spend some time enhancing the sample application. You might want to try out some additional controls or work with other events. For example, you might want to think about how you'd create an event handler that reacts to a right-click on the form. Try adding a context menu that the user can use to configure the form in some way. The point of this chapter is that you can create a GUI with IronPython and it's a nice-looking GUI, but that you'll have to do a little extra work to make the techniques viable.

Chapter 9 explores a new topic — the Component Object Model (COM). Microsoft has used COM for a very long time to make it possible to execute code found in other executables on a machine. You might think that COM is outdated; however, even .NET developers need to rely on COM sometimes to accomplish specific tasks. In fact, it shouldn't surprise you to discover that the code base for COM is far larger than the one for .NET and still growing. Learning how to work with COM from within IronPython is a particularly important task.

Interacting with COM Objects

WHAT'S IN THIS CHAPTER?

➤ Accessing COM components from IronPython

➤ Deciding on a COM binding technique

➤ Designing an Interop DLL

➤ Using Activator.CreateInstance() for late binding

➤ Using Marshal.GetActiveObject() for late binding

The Component Object Model (COM) has been around for a very long time in terms of computer technology. Of course, the predecessor of COM is Object Linking and Embedding (OLE), which is still found all over the place. COM spawned a few technologies of its own, such as Distributed COM (DCOM), used for connecting to objects over a network connection, and COM+, which is used to implement objects in a service-like environment. COM-like technologies even appear on other platforms in the form of technologies such as Common Object Request Broker Architecture (CORBA) and Java/Remote Method Invocation (Java/RMI). You can see these technologies compared at http://my.execpc.com/~gopalan/misc/compare.html (among many other places). It isn't too surprising, then, that you really do need to know how to interact with COM using IronPython. Otherwise, you'd miss out on a huge installed code base.

One chapter can't possibly cover many years' worth of technology. In fact, entire books can't cover the topic any longer — not that any users in their right minds would try. This chapter does provide a basic overview of how to work with COM using IronPython. It contains topics that most of you will find helpful and that will lead you to other discoveries of the beauties of working with COM and IronPython. The chapter starts at the beginning by trying to build on knowledge you already have about working with COM.

An important issue to decide before you begin your project is the kind of binding you should use. This chapter discusses both early and late binding issues. It then shows how to access COM components using several different techniques — two of which rely on late binding `Activator` `.CreateInstance()` and `Marshal.GetActiveObject()`. In short, you can access COM components in numerous ways, and this chapter discusses a few of the more popular techniques that the .NET developer is likely to know about.

AN OVERVIEW OF COM ACCESS DIFFERENCES WITH PYTHON

COM access is an area where IronPython and Python take completely different approaches. In fact, it's safe to say that any Python code you want to use definitely won't work in IronPython. Python developers normally rely on a library such as Python for Windows Extensions (`http://sourceforge.net/` `projects/pywin32/`). This is a library originally created by Mark Hammond (`http://starship` `.python.net/crew/mhammond/win32/`) that includes not only the COM support but also a really nice Python editor. You can see a basic example of using this library to access COM at `http://www` `.boddie.org.uk/python/COM.html`. Even if you download the required library and try to follow the tutorial, you won't get past step 1. The tutorial works fine with standard Python, but doesn't work at all with IronPython.

> *It's important to remember that IronPython is a constantly moving target. The developers who support IronPython constantly come out with new features and functionality, as do the third parties that support it. You may find at some point that there's a COM interoperability solution that does work for both Python and IronPython. The solution doesn't exist today, but there's always hope for tomorrow. If you do encounter such a solution, please be sure to contact me at* `JMueller@mwt.net`.

Fortunately, IronPython developers aren't left out in the cold. COM support is built right into IronPython in the form of the .NET Framework. An IronPython developer uses the same techniques as a C# or a Visual Basic.NET developer uses to access COM — at least at a code level.

When you work with COM in Visual Studio in either a C# or Visual Basic.NET project, the IDE does a lot of the work for you. If you want to use a COM component in your application, you right-click References in Solution Explorer and choose Add Reference from the context menu. At this point, you see the Add Reference dialog box where you choose the COM tab shown in Figure 9-1.

When you highlight an item, such as the Windows Media Player, and click OK, the IDE adds the COM component to the References folder of Solution Explorer, as shown in Figure 9-2. The IDE writes code for you in the background that adds the COM component and makes it accessible. You'll find this code in the .CSProj file and it looks something like this:

```
<COMReference Include="MediaPlayer">
  <Guid>{22D6F304-B0F6-11D0-94AB-0080C74C7E95}</Guid>
  <VersionMajor>1</VersionMajor>
  <VersionMinor>0</VersionMinor>
  <Lcid>0</Lcid>
  <WrapperTool>tlbimp</WrapperTool>
```

```
<Isolated>False</Isolated>
<EmbedInteropTypes>True</EmbedInteropTypes>
</COMReference>
```

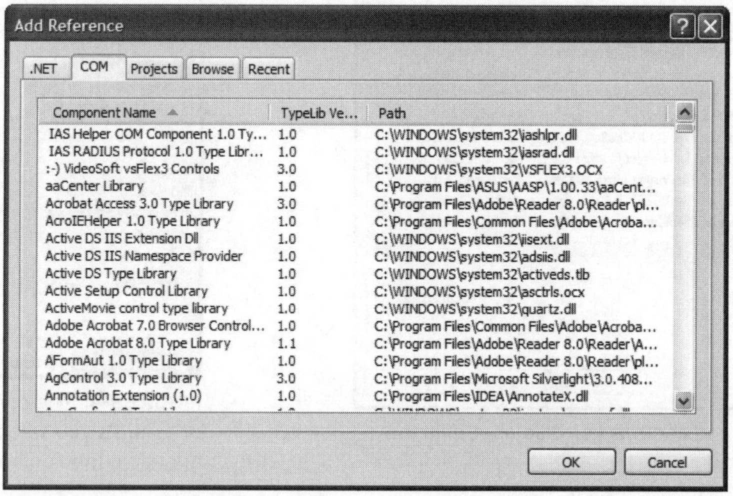

FIGURE 9-1: The Add Reference dialog box provides you with a list of COM components you can use.

In addition, the IDE creates `Interop.MediaPlayer.DLL`, which resides in the project's `obj\x86\Debug` or `obj\x86\Release` folder. This interoperability (interop for short) assembly makes it easy for you to access the COM component features.

Of course, if the COM component you want to use is actually a control, you right-click the Toolbox instead and select Choose Items from the context menu. The COM Components tab looks much like the one shown in Figure 9-3.

In this case, check the controls you want to use and click OK. Again, the IDE does some work for you in the background to make the control accessible and usable. For example, it creates the same interop assembly as it would for a reference. You'll see the control in the Toolbox, as shown in Figure 9-4.

FIGURE 9-2: Any reference you add appears in the References folder of Solution Explorer.

The tasks that the IDE performs for you as part of adding a reference or Toolbox item when working with C# or Visual Basic.NET are manual tasks when working with IronPython. As you might imagine, all of this manual labor makes IronPython harder to use with COM than when you work with Python. While a Python developer simply imports a module and then writes a little specialized code, you're saddled with creating interop assemblies and jumping through coding hoops.

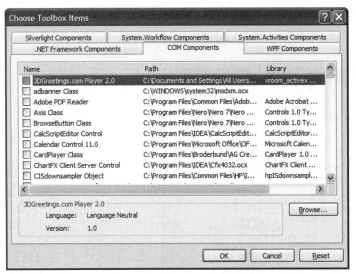

FIGURE 9-3: COM components and controls can also appear in the Choose Toolbox Items dialog box.

FIGURE 9-4: The control or controls you selected appear in the Toolbox.

You do get something for the extra work, though. IronPython provides considerably more flexibility than Python does and you can use IronPython in more places. For example, you might find it hard to access Word directly in Python. The bottom line is that IronPython and Python are incompatible when it comes to COM support, so you can't use all the online Python sources of information you normally rely on when performing a new task.

CHOOSING A BINDING TECHNIQUE

Before you can use a COM component, you must *bind* to it (create a connection to it). The act of binding gives you access to an instance of the component. You use binding to work with COM because, in actuality, you're taking over another application. For example, you can use COM to create a copy of Word, do some work with it, save the resulting file, and then close Word — all without user interaction. A mistake that many developers make is thinking of COM as just another sort of class, but it works differently and you need to think about it differently. For the purposes of working with COM in IronPython, the act of binding properly is one of the more important issues. The following sections describe binding in further detail.

Understanding Early and Late Binding

When you work with a class, you create an instance of the class, set the resulting object's properties, and then use methods to perform a particular task. COM lets you perform essentially the same set of steps in a process called *early binding*. When you work with early binding, you define how to access the COM object during design time. In order to do this, you instantiate an object based on the COM class.

These sections provide an extremely simplified view of COM. You can easily become mired in all kinds of details when working with COM because COM has been around for so long. For example, COM supports multiple interface types, which in turn determines the kind of binding you can perform. This chapter looks at just the information you need to work with COM from IronPython. If you want a better overview of COM, check the site at `http://msdn.microsoft.com/library/ms809980.aspx`. *In fact, you can find an entire list of COM topics at* `http://msdn.microsoft.com/library/ms877981.aspx`.

The COM approach relies on a technique called a virtual table (vtable) — essentially a list of interfaces that you can access, with `IUnknown` as the interface that's common to all COM components. Your application gains access to the `IUnknown` interface and then calls the `queryinterface()` method to obtain a list of other interfaces that the component supports (you can read more about this method at `http://msdn.microsoft.com/library/ms682521.aspx`). Using this approach means that your application can understand a component without really knowing anything about it at the outset.

It's also possible to tell COM to create an instance of an object after the application is already running. This kind of access is called *late binding* because you bind after the application starts. In order to support late binding, a COM component must support the `IDispatch` interface. This interface lets you create the object using `CreateObject()`. Visual Basic was the first language product to rely on late binding. You can read more about `IDispatch` at `http://msdn.microsoft.com/library/ms221608.aspx`.

Late binding also offers the opportunity to gain access to a running copy of a COM component. For example, if the system currently has a copy of Excel running, you can access that copy, rather than create a new Excel object. In this case, you use `GetObject()` instead of `CreateObject()` to work with the object. If you call `GetObject()` where there isn't any copy of the component already executing, you get an error message — Windows doesn't automatically start a new copy of the application for you.

If a COM component supports both the vtable and `IDispatch` technologies, then it has a dual interface that works with any current application language. Most COM components today are dual interface because adding both technologies is relatively easy and developers want to provide the greatest exposure for their components. However, it's always a good idea to consider the kind of binding that your component supports. You can read more about dual interfaces at `http://msdn.microsoft.com/library/ekfyh289.aspx`.

Using Early Binding

As previously mentioned, using early binding means creating a reference to the COM component and then using that reference to interact with the component. IronPython doesn't support the standard methods of early binding that you might have used in other languages. What you do instead is create an interoperability DLL and then import that DLL into your application. The "Defining an Interop

DLL" section of the chapter describes this process in considerably more detail. Early binding provides the following benefits:

➤ **Faster execution:** Generally, your application will execute faster if you use early binding because you rely on compiled code for the interop assembly. However, you won't get the large benefits in speed that you see when working with C# or Visual Basic.NET because IronPython itself is interpreted.

➤ **Easier debugging:** In most cases, using early binding reduces the complexity of your application, making it easier to debug. In addition, because much of the access code for the COM component resides in the interop assembly, you won't have to worry about debugging it.

➤ **Fuller component access:** Even though both early and late binding provide access to the component interfaces, trying to work through those interfaces in IronPython is hard. Using early binding provides you with tools that you can use to explore the interop assembly, and therefore discover more about the component before you use it.

➤ **Better access to enumerations and constants:** Using early binding provides you with access to features that you might not be able to access when using late binding. In some cases, IronPython will actually hide features such as enumerations or constants when using late binding.

Using Late Binding

When using late binding, you create a connection to the COM component at run time by creating a new object or reusing a running object. Some developers prefer this kind of access because it's less error prone than early binding where you might not know about runtime issues during design time. Here are some other reasons that you might use late binding.

➤ **More connectivity options:** You can use late binding to create a connection to a new instance of a COM component (see the "Performing Late Binding Using Activator.CreateInstance()" section of this chapter) or a running instance of the COM component (see the "Performing Late Binding Using Marshal.GetActiveObject()" section of the chapter).

➤ **Fewer modules:** When you use late binding, you don't need an interop assembly for each of the COM components you want to use, which decreases the size and complexity of your application.

➤ **Better version independence:** Late binding relies on registry entries to make the connection. Consequently, when Windows looks up the string you use to specify the application, it looks for any application that satisfies that string. If you specify the Microsoft Excel 9.0 Object Library COM component (Office 2000 specific), Windows will substitute any newer version of Office on the system for the component you requested.

➤ **Fewer potential compatibility issues:** Some environments don't work well with interop assemblies. For example, you might be using IronPython within a Web-based application. In this case, the client machine would already have to have the interop assembly, too, and it probably doesn't. In this case, using late binding allows your application to continue working when early binding would fail.

DEFINING AN INTEROP DLL

Before you can do much with COM, you need to provide some means for .NET (managed code) and the component (native code) to talk. The wrapper code that marshals data from one environment to another, and that translates calls from one language to the other, is an interoperability (interop) assembly, which always appears as a DLL. Fortunately, you don't have to write this code by hand because the task is somewhat mundane. Microsoft was able to automate the process required to create an interop DLL.

Of course, Microsoft couldn't make the decision straightforward or simple. You use different utilities for controls and components. The Type Library Import (TLbImp) utility produces a DLL suitable for component work, while the ActiveX Import (AxImp) utility produces a pair of DLLs suitable for control work. In many cases, the decision is easy — a COM component that supports a visual interface should use AxImp. However, some COM components, such as Windows Media Player (WMP.DLL) are useful as either controls or components. The example in this chapter uses the control form because that's the way you'll use Windows Media Player most often, but it's important to make the decision. The following sections describe how to use both the TLbImp and AxImp utilities.

Accessing the Visual Studio .NET Utilities

You want to create an interop assembly in the folder that you'll use for your sample application. However, you also need access to the .NET utilities. The best way to gain this access is to open a Visual Studio command prompt by choosing Start ➪ Programs ➪ Microsoft Visual Studio 2010 ➪ Visual Studio Tools ➪ Visual Studio Command Prompt (2010). If you're working with Vista or Windows 7, right-click the Visual Studio Command Prompt (2010) entry and choose Run As Administrator from the context menu to ensure you have the rights required to use the utilities. Windows will open a command prompt that provides the required access to the .NET utilities.

Understanding the Type Library Import Utility

Remember that you always use Type Library Import (TLbImp) for components, not for controls. Before you can use TLbImp, you need to know a bit more about it. Here's the command line syntax for the tool:

```
TlbImp TypeLibName [Options]
```

The TypeLibName argument is simply the filename of the COM component that you want to use to create an interop assembly. A COM component can have a number of file extensions, but the most common extensions are .DLL, .EXE, and .OCX.

The TypeLibName argument can specify a resource identifier when the library contains more than one resource. Simply follow the filename with a backslash and the resource number. For example, the command line TlbImp MyModule .DLL\1 *would create an output assembly that contains only resource 1 in the* MyModule.DLL *file.*

You can also include one or more options that modify the behavior of TLbImp. The following list describes these options.

➤ **/out:*FileName*:** Provides the name of the file you want to produce as output. If you don't provide this argument, the default is to add `Lib` to the end of the filename for the type library. For example, `WMP.DLL` becomes `WMPLib.DLL`.

➤ **/namespace:*Namespace*:** Defines the namespace of the classes within the interop assembly. The default is to add `Lib` to the filename of the type library. For example, if the file has a name of `WMP.DLL`, the namespace is `WMPLib`.

➤ **/asmversion:*Version*:** Specifies the file version number of the output assembly. This information appears on the Version tab of the file Properties dialog box shown in Figure 9-5. The default version number is 1.0.0.0.

> *You must specify a version number using dotted syntax. The four version number elements are: major version, minor version, build number, and revision number. For example, 1.2.3.4 would specify a major version number of 1, minor version number of 2, a build number of 3, and a revision number of 4.*

➤ **/reference:*FileName*:** Determines the name of the assembly that TLbImp uses to resolve references. There's no default value. You may use this command line switch as many times as needed to provide a complete list of assemblies.

➤ **/tlbreference:*FileName*:** Determines the name of the type library that TLbImp uses to resolve references. There's no default value. You may use this command line switch as many times as needed to provide a complete list of assemblies.

➤ **/publickey:*FileName*:** Specifies the name of a file containing a strong name public key used to sign the assembly. There's no default value.

➤ **/keyfile:*FileName*:** Specifies the name of a file containing a strong name key pair used to sign the assembly. There's no default value.

➤ **/keycontainer:*FileName*:** Specifies the name of a key container containing a strong name key pair used to sign the assembly. There's no default value.

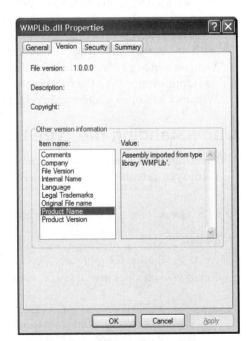

FIGURE 9-5: Include version information for the assembly so others know about it.

➤ **/delaysign:** Sets the assembly to force a delay in signing. Use this option when you want to use the assembly for experimentation only.

➤ **/product:** *Product*: Defines the name of the product that contains this assembly. This information appears on the Version tab of the file Properties dialog box shown in Figure 9-5. The default is to say that the assembly is imported from a specific type library.

➤ **/productversion:** *Version*: Defines the product version number of the output assembly. This information appears on the Version tab of the file Properties dialog box shown in Figure 9-5. The default version number is 1.0.0.0.

➤ **/company:** *Company*: Defines the name of the company that produced the output assembly. This information appears on the Version tab of the file Properties dialog box shown in Figure 9-5. There's no default value.

➤ **/copyright:** *Copyright*: Defines the copyright information that applies to the output assembly. This information appears on the Version tab of the file Properties dialog box shown in Figure 9-5. There's no default value.

➤ **/trademark:** *Trademark*: Defines the trademark and registered trademark information that applies to the output assembly. This information appears on the Version tab of the file Properties dialog box shown in Figure 9-5. There's no default value.

➤ **/unsafe:** Creates an output assembly that lacks runtime security checks. Using this option will make the assembly execute faster and reduce its size. However, you shouldn't use this option for production systems because it does reduce the security features that the assembly would normally possess.

➤ **/noclassmembers:** Creates an output assembly that has classes, but the classes have no members.

➤ **/nologo:** Prevents the TLbImp utility from displaying a logo when it starts execution. This option is useful when performing batch processing.

➤ **/silent:** Prevents the TLbImp utility from displaying any output, except error information. This option is useful when performing batch processing.

➤ **/silence:** *WarningNumber*: Prevents the TLbImp utility from displaying output for the specified warning number. This option is useful when an assembly contains a number of warnings that you already know about and you want to see only the warnings that you don't know about. You can't use this option with the /silent command line switch.

➤ **/verbose:** Tells the TLbImp utility to display every available piece of information about the process used to create the output assembly. This option is useful when you need to verify the assembly before placing it in a production environment or when you suspect a subtle error is causing application problems (or you're simply curious).

➤ **/primary:** Creates a Primary Interop Assembly (PIO). A COM component may use only one PIO and you must sign the PIO (use the /publickey, /keyfile, or /keycontainer switches to sign the assembly). See http://msdn.microsoft.com/library/aax7sdch.aspx for additional information.

➤ **/sysarray:** Specifies that the assembly should use SAFEARRAY in place of the standard System.Array.

➤ **/machine:*MachineType***: Creates an assembly for the specified machine type. The valid inputs for this command line switch are:

   ➤ X86

   ➤ X64

   ➤ Itanium

   ➤ Agnostic

➤ **/transform:*TransformName***: Performs the specified transformations on the assembly. You may use any of these values as a transformation.

   ➤ **SerializableValueClasses:** Forces TLbImp to mark all of the classes as serializable.

   ➤ **DispRet:** Applies the `[out, retval]` attribute to methods that have a dispatch-only interface.

➤ **/strictref:** Forces TLbImp to use only the assemblies that you specify using the `/reference` command line switch, along with PIAs, to produce the output assembly, even if the source file contains other references. The output assembly might not work properly when you use this option.

➤ **/strictref:nopia:** Forces TLbImp to use only the assemblies that you specify using the `/reference` command line switch to produce the output assembly, even if the source file contains other references. This command line switch ignores PIAs. The output assembly might not work properly when you use this option.

➤ **/VariantBoolFieldToBool:** Converts all `VARIANT_BOOL` fields in structures to `bool`.

➤ **/?** or **/help:** Displays a help message containing a list of command line options for the version of TLbImp that you're using.

Understanding the ActiveX Import Utility

The example in this chapter relies on the ActiveX Import (AxImp) utility because it produces the files you need to create a control (with a visual interface) rather than a component. When you use this utility, you obtain two files as output. The first contains the same information you receive when using the TLbImp utility. The second, the one with the Ax prefix, contains the code for a control. Before you can use AxImp, you need to know a bit more about it. Here's the command line syntax for the tool:

```
AxImp OcxName [Options]
```

The `OcxName` argument is simply the filename of the COM component that you want to use to create a control version of an interop assembly. A COM component can have a number of file extensions, but the most common extensions are `.DLL`, `.EXE`, and `.OCX`. It's uncommon for an OLE Control eXtension (OCX), a COM component with a visual interface, to have a `.EXE` file extension.

You can also include one or more options that modify the behavior of AxImp. The following list describes these options.

➤ **/out:*FileName*:** Provides the name of the ActiveX library file you want to produce as output. If you don't provide this argument, the default is to add `Lib` to the end of the filename for the type library. For example, `WMP.DLL` becomes `WMPLib.DLL` and `AxWMPLib.DLL`. Using this command line switch changes the name of the `AxWMPLib.DLL` file. For example, if you type `AxImp WMP .DLL /out:WMPOut.DLL` and press Enter, the utility now outputs `WMPLib.DLL` and `WMPOut.DLL`.

➤ **/publickey:*FileName*:** Specifies the name of a file containing a strong name public key used to sign the assembly. There's no default value.

➤ **/keyfile:*FileName*:** Specifies the name of a file containing a strong name key pair used to sign the assembly. There's no default value.

➤ **/keycontainer:*FileName*:** Specifies the name of a key container containing a strong name key pair used to sign the assembly. There's no default value.

➤ **/delaysign:** Sets the assembly to force a delay in signing. Use this option when you want to use the assembly for experimentation only.

➤ **/source:** Generates the C# source code for a Windows Forms wrapper. You don't need to use this option when working in IronPython because the code doesn't show how to use the wrapper — it simply shows the wrapper code itself.

➤ **/rcw:*FileName*:** Specifies an assembly to use for Runtime Callable Wrapper (RCW) rather than generating a new one. In most cases, you want to generate a new RCW when working with IronPython.

➤ **/nologo:** Prevents the AxImp utility from displaying a logo when it starts execution. This option is useful when performing batch processing.

➤ **/silent:** Prevents the AxImp utility from displaying any output, except error information. This option is useful when performing batch processing.

➤ **/verbose:** Tells the AxImp utility to display every available piece of information about the process used to create the output assembly. This option is useful when you need to verify the assembly before placing it in a production environment or when you suspect a subtle error is causing application problems (or you're simply curious).

➤ **/?** or **/help:** Displays a help message containing a list of command line options for the version of AxImp that you're using.

Creating the Windows Media Player Interop DLL

Now that you have an idea of how to use the AxImp utility, it's time to see the utility in action. The following command line creates an interop assembly for the Windows Media Player.

```
AxImp %SystemRoot%\System32\WMP.DLL
```

This command line switch doesn't specify any options. It does include `%SystemRoot%`, which points to the Windows directory on your machine (making it possible to use the command line on more than one system, even if those systems have slightly different configurations). When you execute this command line, you see the AxImp utility logo. After a few minutes work, you'll see one or more warning or error messages if the AxImp utility encounters problems. Eventually, you see a success message, as shown in Figure 9-6.

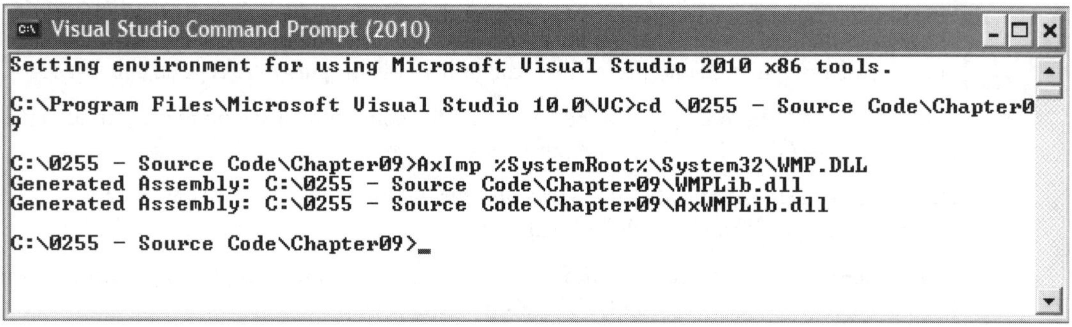

```
Visual Studio Command Prompt (2010)
Setting environment for using Microsoft Visual Studio 2010 x86 tools.

C:\Program Files\Microsoft Visual Studio 10.0\VC>cd \0255 - Source Code\Chapter0
9

C:\0255 - Source Code\Chapter09>AxImp %SystemRoot%\System32\WMP.DLL
Generated Assembly: C:\0255 - Source Code\Chapter09\WMPLib.dll
Generated Assembly: C:\0255 - Source Code\Chapter09\AxWMPLib.dll

C:\0255 - Source Code\Chapter09>_
```

FIGURE 9-6: The AxImp tells you that it has generated the two DLLs needed for a control.

Exploring the Windows Media Player Interop DLL

When working with imported Python modules, you use the `dir()` function to see what those modules contain. In fact, you often use `dir()` when working with .NET assemblies as well, even though you have the MSDN documentation at hand. Theoretically, you can also use `dir()` when working with imported COM components as well, but things turn quite messy when you do. The "Using the Windows Media Player Interop DLL" section of this chapter describes how to import and use an interop assembly, but for now, let's just look at WMPLib.DLL using `dir()`. Figure 9-7 shows typical results.

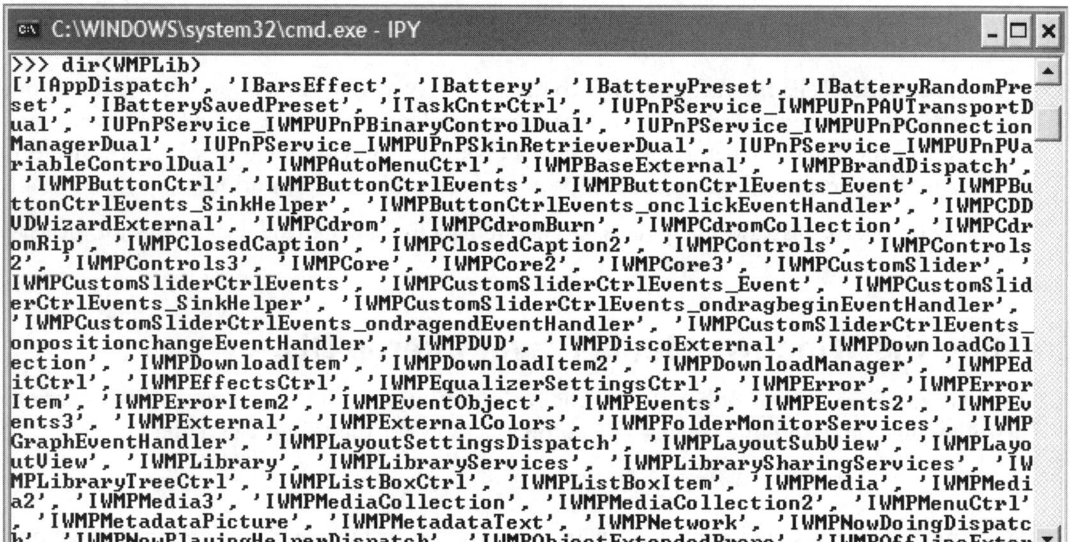

```
C:\WINDOWS\system32\cmd.exe - IPY
>>> dir(WMPLib)
['IAppDispatch', 'IBarsEffect', 'IBattery', 'IBatteryPreset', 'IBatteryRandomPre
set', 'IBatterySavedPreset', 'ITaskCntrCtrl', 'IUPnPService_IWMPUPnPAVTransportD
ual', 'IUPnPService_IWMPUPnPBinaryControlDual', 'IUPnPService_IWMPUPnPConnection
ManagerDual', 'IUPnPService_IWMPUPnPSkinRetrieverDual', 'IUPnPService_IWMPUPnPVa
riableControlDual', 'IWMPAutoMenuCtrl', 'IWMPBaseExternal', 'IWMPBrandDispatch',
 'IWMPButtonCtrl', 'IWMPButtonCtrlEvents', 'IWMPButtonCtrlEvents_Event', 'IWMPBu
ttonCtrlEvents_SinkHelper', 'IWMPButtonCtrlEvents_onclickEventHandler', 'IWMPCDD
VDWizardExternal', 'IWMPCdrom', 'IWMPCdromBurn', 'IWMPCdromCollection', 'IWMPCdr
omRip', 'IWMPClosedCaption', 'IWMPClosedCaption2', 'IWMPControls', 'IWMPControls
2', 'IWMPControls3', 'IWMPCore', 'IWMPCore2', 'IWMPCore3', 'IWMPCustomSlider', '
IWMPCustomSliderCtrlEvents', 'IWMPCustomSliderCtrlEvents_Event', 'IWMPCustomSlid
erCtrlEvents_SinkHelper', 'IWMPCustomSliderCtrlEvents_ondragbeginEventHandler',
'IWMPCustomSliderCtrlEvents_ondragendEventHandler', 'IWMPCustomSliderCtrlEvents_
onpositionchangeEventHandler', 'IWMPDVD', 'IWMPDiscoExternal', 'IWMPDownloadColl
ection', 'IWMPDownloadItem', 'IWMPDownloadItem2', 'IWMPDownloadManager', 'IWMPEd
itCtrl', 'IWMPEffectsCtrl', 'IWMPEqualizerSettingsCtrl', 'IWMPError', 'IWMPError
Item', 'IWMPErrorItem2', 'IWMPEventObject', 'IWMPEvents', 'IWMPEvents2', 'IWMPEv
ents3', 'IWMPExternal', 'IWMPExternalColors', 'IWMPFolderMonitorServices', 'IWMP
GraphEventHandler', 'IWMPLayoutSettingsDispatch', 'IWMPLayoutSubView', 'IWMPLayo
utView', 'IWMPLibrary', 'IWMPLibraryServices', 'IWMPLibrarySharingServices', 'IW
MPLibraryTreeCtrl', 'IWMPListBoxCtrl', 'IWMPListBoxItem', 'IWMPMedia', 'IWMPMedi
a2', 'IWMPMedia3', 'IWMPMediaCollection', 'IWMPMediaCollection2', 'IWMPMenuCtrl'
, 'IWMPMetadataPicture', 'IWMPMetadataText', 'IWMPNetwork', 'IWMPNowDoingDispatc
h', 'IWMPNowPlayingHelperDispatch', 'IWMPObjectExtendedProps', 'IWMPOfflineExter
```

FIGURE 9-7: Using dir() won't work well with interop assemblies in many cases.

The list goes on and on. Unfortunately, this is only the top level. You still need to drill down into the interop assembly, so things can become confusing and complex. Figuring out what you want to use is nearly impossible. Making things worse is the fact that any documentation you obtain for the interop assembly probably won't work because the documentation will take the COM perspective of working with the classes and you need the IronPython perspective. Using dir() won't be very helpful in this situation.

Fortunately, you have another alternative in the form of the Intermediate Language Disassembler (ILDasm) utility. This utility looks into the interop assembly and creates a graphic picture of it for you. Using this utility, you can easily drill down into the interop assembly and, with the help of the COM documentation, normally figure out how to work with the COM component — even complex COM components such as the Windows Media Player.

To gain access to ILDasm, you use the same process you use for TLbImp to create a Visual Studio Command Prompt. At the command prompt, type ILDasm WMPLib.DLL and press Enter (see more of the command line options in the "Using the ILDasm Command Line" section of the chapter). The ILDasm utility will start and show entries similar to those shown in Figure 9-8.

ILDasm is an important tool for the IronPython developer who wants to work with COM. With this in mind, the following sections provide a good overview of ILDasm and many of its usage details. Most important, these sections describe how to delve into the innermost parts of any interop assembly.

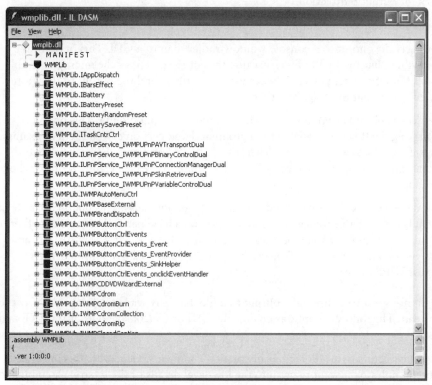

FIGURE 9-8: Use ILDASM to explore WMPLib.DLL.

Using the ILDasm Command Line

The ILDasm utility usually works fine when you run it and provide the filename of the interop assembly you want to view. However, sometimes an interop assembly is so complex that you really do want to optimize the ILDasm view. Consequently, you use command line options to change the way ILDasm works. ILDasm has the following command line syntax.

```
ildasm [options] <file_name> [options]
```

> *Even though this section shows the full name of all the command line switches, you can use just the first three letters. For example, you can abbreviate /BYTES as /BYT. In addition, ILDasm accepts both the dash (-) and slash (/) as command line switch prefixes, so /BYTES and -BYTES work equally well.*

The options can appear either before or after the filename. You can divide the options into those that affect output redirection (sending the output to a location other than the display) and those that change the way the file/console output appears. ILDasm further divides the file/console options into those that work with EXE and DLL files, and those that work with EXE, DLL, OBJ, and LIB files. Here are the options for output redirection.

➤ **/OUT=*Filename*:** Redirects the output to the specified file rather than to a GUI.

➤ **/TEXT:** Redirects the output to a console window rather than to a GUI. This option isn't very useful for anything but the smallest files because the entire content of the interop assembly simply scrolls by. Of course, you can always use a pipe (|) to send the output to the More utility to view the output one page at a time.

➤ **/HTML:** Creates the file in HTML format (valid with the /OUT option only). This option is handy for making the ILDasm available for a group of developers on a Web site. For example, if you type ILDasm /OUT=WMPLib.HTML /HTML WMPLib.DLL and press Enter, you obtain WMPLib.HTML. The resulting file is huge — 7.53 MB for WMPLib.HTML. Figure 9-9 shows how this file will appear.

➤ **/RTF:** Creates the file in RTF format (valid with the /OUT option only). This option is handy for making the ILDasm available for a group of developers on a local network using an application such as Word. For example, if you type ILDasm /OUT=WMPLib.RTF /RTF WMPLib.DLL and press Enter, you obtain WMPLib.RTF. The resulting file is huge — 5.2 MB for WMPLib.RTF, and may cause Word to freeze.

Of course, you might not want to redirect the output to a file, but may want to change the way the console appears instead. The following options change the GUI or file/console output for EXE and DLL files only.

➤ **/BYTES:** Displays actual bytes (in hex) as instruction comments. Generally, this information isn't useful unless you want to get into the low-level details of the interop assembly. For example, you might see a series of hex bytes such as // SIG: 20 01 01 08, which won't be helpful to most developers. (In this case, you're looking at the signature for the WMPLib .IAppDispatch.adjustLeft() method.)

FIGURE 9-9: HTML output is useful for viewing ILDasm output in a browser.

➤ **/RAWEH:** Shows the exception handling clauses in raw form. This isn't a useful command line switch for interop assemblies because interop assemblies don't require exception handlers in most cases.

➤ **/TOKENS:** Displays the metadata tokens of classes and members as comments in the source code, as shown in Figure 9-10 for the WMPLib.IAppDispatch.adjustLeft() method. For example, the metadata token for mscorlib is /*23000001*/. Most developers won't require this information.

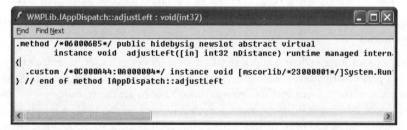

FIGURE 9-10: The metadata tokens appear as comments beside the coded text.

➤ **/SOURCE:** Shows the original source lines as comments when available. Unfortunately, when working with an interop assembly, there aren't any original source lines to show, so you won't need to use this command line switch.

➤ **/LINENUM:** Shows the original source code line numbers as comments when available. Again, when working with an interop assembly, there aren't any original source code line numbers to show so you won't need to use this command line switch.

➤ **/VISIBILITY=Vis[+Vis...]:** Outputs only the items with specified visibility. The valid inputs for this argument are:

  ➤ **PUB:** Public

  ➤ **PRI:** Private

  ➤ **FAM:** Family

  ➤ **ASM:** Assembly

  ➤ **FAA:** Family and assembly

  ➤ **FOA:** Family or assembly

  ➤ **PSC:** Private scope

➤ **/PUBONLY:** Outputs only the items with public visibility (same as /VIS=PUB).

➤ **/QUOTEALLNAMES:** Places single quotes around all names. For example, instead of seeing mscorlib, you'd see 'mscorlib'. In some cases, using this approach makes it easier to see or find specific names in the code.

➤ **/NOCA:** Suppresses the output of custom attributes.

➤ **/CAVERBAL:** Displays all of the Custom Attribute (CA) blobs in verbal form. The default setting outputs the CA blobs in binary form. Using this command line switch can make the code more readable, but also makes it more verbose (larger).

➤ **/NOBAR:** Tells ILDasm not to display the progress bar as it redirects the interop assembly output to another location (such as a file).

ILDasm includes a number of command line switches that affect file and console output only. The following command line switches work for EXE and DLL files.

➤ **/UTF8:** Forces ILDasm to use UTF-8 encoding for output in place of the default ANSI encoding.

➤ **/UNICODE:** Forces ILDasm to use Unicode encoding for output in place of the default ANSI encoding.

➤ **/NOIL:** Suppresses Intermediate Language (IL) assembler code output. Unfortunately, this option isn't particularly useful because it creates a file that contains just the disassembly comments, not any of the class or method information. You do get the resource (.RES) file containing the resource information for the interop assembly (such as the version number). To use this command line switch, you must include redirection such as ILDasm /OUT=WMPLib.HTML / HTML /NOIL WMPLib.DLL to produce WMPLib.HTML as output.

➤ **/FORWARD:** Forces ILDasm to use forward class declaration. In some cases, this command line switch can reduce the size of the disassembly.

➤ **/TYPELIST:** Outputs a full list of types. Using this command line switch can help preserve type ordering.

➤ **/HEADERS:** Outputs the file header information in the output.

➤ **/ITEM=*Class*[::Method[(*Signature*)]]:** Disassembles only the specified item. Using this command line switch can greatly reduce the confusion of looking over an entire interop assembly.

➤ **/STATS:** Provides statistical information about the image. The statistics appear at the beginning of the file in comments. Here's a small segment of the statistics you might see (telling you about the use of space in the file).

```
// File size           : 331776
// PE header size       : 4096 (496 used)    ( 1.23%)
// PE additional info   : 1015               ( 0.31%)
// Num.of PE sections   : 3
// CLR header size      : 72                 ( 0.02%)
// CLR meta-data size   : 256668             (77.36%)
// CLR additional info  : 0                  ( 0.00%)
// CLR method headers   : 9086               ( 2.74%)
// Managed code         : 51182              (15.43%)
// Data                 : 8192               ( 2.47%)
// Unaccounted          : 1465               ( 0.44%)
```

➤ **/CLASSLIST:** Outputs a list of the classes defined in the module. The class list appears as a series of comments at the beginning of the file. Here's an example of the class list output for WMPLib.DLL (a very small part of it, reformatted to fit within the book).

```
// Classes defined in this module:
//~~~~~~~~~~~~~~~~~~~~~~~~~~~~~~~~~~~~~~~~~~~~~~~~~~~~~~~~~~~~~~~~~~~~~~~~~~~
// Interface IWMPEvents              (public) (abstract) (auto) (ansi) (import)
// Class WMPPlaylistChangeEventType  (public) (auto) (ansi) (sealed)
// Interface IWMPEvents2             (public) (abstract) (auto) (ansi) (import)
// Interface IWMPSyncDevice          (public) (abstract) (auto) (ansi) (import)
// Class WMPDeviceStatus             (public) (auto) (ansi) (sealed)
// Class WMPSyncState                (public) (auto) (ansi) (sealed)
// Interface IWMPEvents3             (public) (abstract) (auto) (ansi) (import)
// Interface IWMPCdromRip            (public) (abstract) (auto) (ansi) (import)
```

➤ **/ALL:** Performs the combination of the /HEADER, /BYTES, /STATS, /CLASSLIST, and /TOKENS command line switches.

This set of command line switches also affects just file and console output. However, you can use them for EXE, DLL, OBJ, and LIB files.

➤ **/METADATA[=*Specifier*]:** Shows the interop assembly metadata for the elements defined by *Specifier*. Here are the values you can use for Specifier.

➤ **MDHEADER:** MetaData header information and sizes

➤ **HEX:** More data in hex as well as words

➤ **CSV:** Record counts and heap sizes

➤ **UNREX:** Unresolved externals

➤ **SCHEMA:** MetaData header and schema information

➤ **RAW:** Raw MetaData tables

➤ **HEAPS:** Raw heaps

➤ **VALIDATE:** MetaData consistency validation

The final set of command line switches affects file and console output for LIB files only.

➤ **/OBJECTFILE=*Obj_Filename*:** Shows the MetaData of a single object file in library.

Working with ILDasm Symbols

When working with ILDasm, you see a number of special symbols. Unfortunately, the utility often leaves you wondering what the symbols mean. Here are some of the most common symbols you encounter when working with COM components.

Interface: Represents an interface with which you can interact.

Private Class: Represents an abstract or sealed class in most cases.

Enumeration: Contains a list of enumerated items you use to provide values for method calls and other tasks.

Attribute: Provides access to the attributes that describe a COM component. Common attributes and attribute containers include:

➤ Manifest (and its associated attributes)

➤ Extends (defines a class that the class extends)

➤ Implements (defines an interface that the class implements)

➤ ClassInterface (see http://msdn.microsoft.com/library/system .runtime.interopservices.classinterfaceattribute.aspx for details)

➤ GuidAttribute (see http://msdn.microsoft.com/library/system .runtime.interopservices.guidattribute.aspx for details)

➤ TypeLibTypeAttribute (see http://msdn.microsoft.com/library/ system.runtime.interopservices.typelibtypeattribute.aspx for details)

➤ InterfaceTypeAttribute (see http://msdn.microsoft.com/library/ system.runtime.interopservices.interfacetypeattribute.aspx for details)

Method: Describes a method that you can use within an interface or private class.

Property: Describes a property that you can use within an interface or private class.

Variable: Defines a variable of some type within an interface or private class. The variable could be an interface, such as IConnectionPoint, or an array, such as ArrayList, or anything else that the developer wanted to include.

Event: Specifies an event that occurs within the interface or private class.

Exploring ILDasm entries

It's important to remember that interop assemblies simply provide a reference to the actual code found in the COM component. Even so, you can use ILDasm to find out all kinds of interesting information about the component. At the top level, you can see a list of all of the interfaces, classes, and enumerations, as shown in Figure 9-8. The next level is to drill down into specific methods and properties, as shown in Figure 9-11.

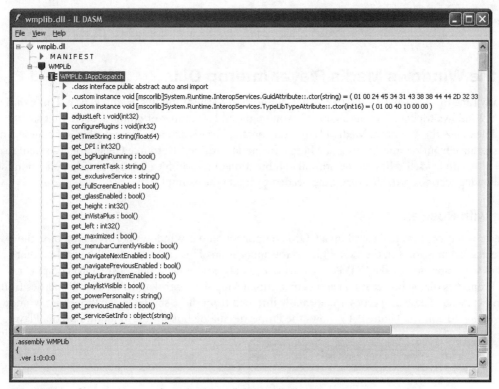

FIGURE 9-11: Opening an interface displays all the methods it contains.

The information shown in this figure is actually the most valuable information that ILDasm provides because you can use it to discover the names of methods and properties you want to use in your application. In addition, these entries often provide clues about where to look for additional information in the vendor help files. Sometimes these help files are a little disorganized and you might not understand how methods are related until you see this visual presentation of them.

It's possible to explore the interop assembly at one more level. Double-click any of the methods, properties, or attributes and you'll see a dialog box like the one shown in Figure 9-12. The amount of information you receive may seem paltry at first. However, look closer and you'll discover that this display often tells you about calling requirements. For example, you can discover the data types you need to rely on to work with the COM component (something that COM documentation can't tell you because the vendor doesn't know that you're using the component from .NET).

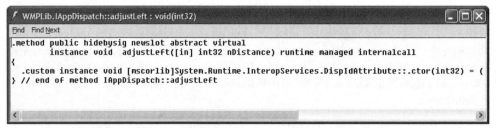

FIGURE 9-12: Discover the calling requirements for methods by reviewing the methods' underlying code.

Using the Windows Media Player Interop DLL

It's finally time to use early binding to create a connection to the Windows Media Player. This example uses the Windows Media Player as a control. You might find a number of online sources that say it's impossible to use the Windows Media Player as a control, but it's actually quite doable. Of course, you need assistance from yet another one of Microsoft's handy utilities, Resource Generator (ResGen) to do it. The example itself relies on the normal combination of a form file and associated application file. The following sections provide everything needed to create the example.

Working with ResGen

Whenever you drop a control based on a COM component onto a Windows Forms dialog box, the IDE creates an entry for it in the .RESX file for the application. This entry contains binary data that describes the properties for the COM component. You may not know it, but most COM components have a Properties dialog box that you access by right-clicking the control and choosing Properties from the context menu. These properties are normally different from those shown in the Properties window for the managed control. Figure 9-13 shows the Properties dialog box for the Windows Media Player.

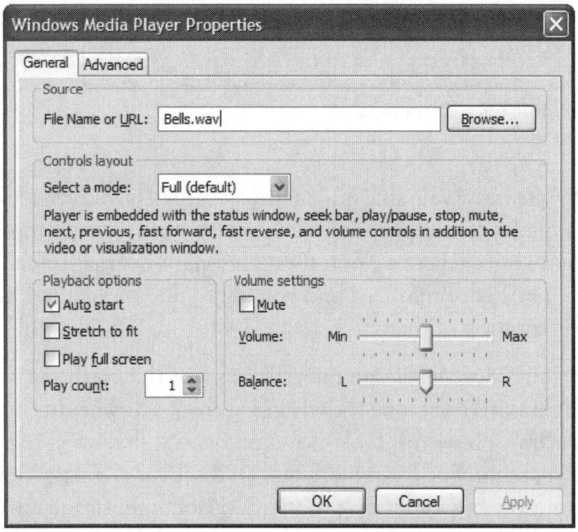

FIGURE 9-13: The COM component has properties that differ from the managed control.

It's essential to remember that the managed control is separate from the COM component in a Windows Forms application. The COM component properties appear in a separate location and the managed environment works with them differently. If you look in the .RESX file, you see something like this:

```
<data name="MP.OcxState" mimetype="application/x-microsoft.net.object.binary.base64">
  <value>
      AAEAAAD/////AQAAAAAAAAMAgAAAFdTeXN0ZW0uV2luZG93cy5Gb3JtcywgVmVyc2lvbj00LjAuMC4w
      LCBDdWx0dXJlPW5ldXRyYWwsIFB1YmxpY0tleVRva2VuPWI3N2E1YzU2MTkzNGUwODkFAQAAACFTeXN0
      ZW0uV2luZG93cy5Gb3Jtcy5BeEhvc3QrU3RhdGUBAAAABERhdGEHAgIAAAAJAwAAAA8DAAAAywAAAAIB
      AAAAQAAAAAAAAAAAAALYAAAAwAACAAUAAAQgBlAGwAbABzAC4AdwBhAHYAAAFAAAAAAAAPA/
      AwAAAAAABQAAAAAAAAgAAgAAAAAwABAAAACwD//wMAAAAAAsA//8IAAIAAAAAAMAMgAAAAsA
      AAAIAAoAAABmAHUAbABBsAAAACwAAAAsAAAALAP//CwD//wsAAAAIAAIAAAAAAgAAgAAAAAACAACAAAA
      AAAIAAIAAAAAAsAAAAuHgAAfhsAAAs=
  </value>
</data>
```

This binary data contains the information needed to configure the COM aspects of the component. When the application creates the form, the binary data is added to the component using the OcxState property like this:

```
this.MP.OcxState =
    ((System.Windows.Forms.AxHost.State)(resources.GetObject("MP.OcxState")));
```

Because of the managed code/COM component duality of a Windows Forms application, you can't simply embed the COM component into an IronPython application using techniques such as the one shown at http://msdn.microsoft.com/library/dd564350.aspx. You must provide the binary data to the COM component using the OcxState property. Unfortunately, IronPython developers have an added twist to consider. The C# code shown previously won't work because you don't have access to a ComponentResourceManager for the IronPython form. Instead, you must read the resource from disk using code like this (note the code will appear on a single line in the source code file, even though it appears on multiple lines in the book):

```
self.resources = System.ComponentModel.ComponentResourceManager.
    CreateFileBasedResourceManager(
        'frmUseWMP', 'C:/0255 - Source Code/Chapter09', None)
```

Now, here's where the tricky part begins (you might have thought we were there already, but we weren't). The CreateFileBasedResourceManager() method doesn't support .RESX files. Instead, it supports .RESOURCES files. The ResGen utility can create .RESOURCES files. You might be tempted to think that you can duplicate the binary data from the .RESX file using .TXT files as suggested by the ResGen documentation. Unfortunately, .TXT files can only help you create string data in .RESOURCES files.

So your first step is to create a Windows Forms application, add the component to it, perform any required COM component configuration (no need to perform the managed part), save the result, and then take the resulting .RESX file for your IronPython application. You can then use ResGen to create the .RESOURCES file using a command line like this:

```
ResGen frmUseWMP.RESX
```

ResGen outputs a .RESOURCES file you can use within your application. Of course, like every Microsoft utility, ResGen offers a little more than simple conversion. Here's the command line syntax for ResGen:

```
ResGen inputFile.ext [outputFile.ext] [/str:lang[,namespace[,class[,file]]]]
ResGen [options] /compile inputFile1.ext[,outputFile1.resources] [...]
```

Here are the options you can use.

➤ **/compile:** Performs a bulk conversion of files from one format to another format. Typically, you use this feature with a response file where you provide a list of files to convert.

➤ **/str:language[, namespace[, classname[, filename]]]:** Defines a strongly typed resource class using the specified programming language that relies on Code Document Object Model (CodeDOM) (see http://msdn.microsoft.com/library/y2k85ax6.aspx for details). To ensure that the strongly typed resource class works properly, the name of your output file, without the .RESOURCES extension, must match the [namespace.]classname of your strongly typed resource class. You may need to rename your output file before using it or embedding it into an assembly.

➤ **/useSourcePath:** Specifies that ResGen uses each source file's directory as the current directory for resolving relative file paths.

➤ **/publicClass:** Creates the strongly typed resource class as a public class. You must use this command line switch with the /str command line switch.

➤ **/r:assembly:** Tells ResGen to load types from the assemblies that you specify. A .RESX file automatically uses newer assembly types when you specify this command line switch. You can't form the .RESX file to rely on older assembly types.

➤ **/define:A[,B]:** Provides a means for performing optional conversions specified by #ifdef structures within a .RESTEXT (text) file.

➤ **@file:** Specifies the name of a response file to use for additional command line options. You can only provide one response file for any given session.

Creating the Media Player Form Code

As normal, the example relies on two files to hold the form and the client code. Because we're using a COM component for this example, the form requires a number of special configuration steps. Listing 9-1 shows the form code.

LISTING 9-1: Creating a Windows Forms application with a COM component

```
# Set up the path to the .NET Framework.
import sys
sys.path.append('C:\\WINDOWS\\Microsoft.NET\\Framework\\v2.0.50727')

# Make clr accessible.
import clr

# Add any required references.
```

```
clr.AddReference('System.Windows.Forms.DLL')
clr.AddReference('System.Drawing.DLL')
clr.AddReference('AxWMPLib.DLL')

# Import the .NET assemblies.
import System
import System.Windows.Forms
import System.Drawing.Point
import AxWMPLib

class frmUseWMP(System.Windows.Forms.Form):

    # This function performs all of the required initialization.
    def InitializeComponent(self):

        # Create a Component Resource Manager
        self.resources = System.ComponentModel.ComponentResourceManager.
          CreateFileBasedResourceManager(
              'frmUseWMP', 'C:/0255 - Source Code/Chapter09', None)

        # Configure Windows Media Player
        self.MP = AxWMPLib.AxWindowsMediaPlayer()
        self.MP.Dock = System.Windows.Forms.DockStyle.Fill
        self.MP.Enabled = True
        self.MP.Location = System.Drawing.Point(0, 0)
        self.MP.Name = "MP"
        self.MP.Size = System.Drawing.Size(292, 266)
        self.MP.OcxState = self.resources.GetObject("MP.OcxState")

        # Configure the form.
        self.ClientSize = System.Drawing.Size(350, 200)
        self.Text = 'Simple Windows Media Player Example'

        # Add the controls to the form.
        self.Controls.Add(self.MP)
```

The code begins with the normal steps of adding the .NET Framework path, making clr accessible, importing the required DLLs, and importing the required assemblies. Notice that the example uses the AxWMPLib.DLL file and AxWMPLib assembly. Remember that the Ax versions of the files provide wrapping around the ActiveX controls to make them usable as a managed control.

The code begins by creating a ComponentResourceManager from a file, using the CreateFileBasedResourceManager() method. Normally, a managed application would create the ComponentResourceManager directly from the data stored as part of the form. This is a special step for IronPython that could cause you grief later if you forget about it.

Even though Listing 9-1 shows the CreateFileBasedResourceManager() *method call on multiple lines, it appears on a single line in the actual source code. The IronPython call won't work if you place it on multiple lines because IronPython lacks a line continuation character (or methodology).*

Media Player (MP) configuration comes next. You must instantiate the control from the `AxWMPLib` `.AxWindowsMediaPlayer()` constructor, rather than using the COM component constructor. The Ax constructor provides a wrapper with additional features you need within the Windows Forms environment. Like most controls, you need to specify control position and size on the form. However, because of the nature of the Windows Media Player, you want it to fill the client area of the form, so you set the `Dock` property to `System.Windows.Forms.DockStyle.Fill`.

The one configuration item that you must perform correctly is setting the COM component values using the `MP.OcxState` property. The `ComponentResourceManager`, `resources`, contains this value. You simply set the `MP.OcxState` property to `resources.GetObject("MP.OcxState")` — this technique is also different from what you'd use in a C# or Visual Basic.NET application. The rest of the form code isn't anything special — you've seen it in all of the Windows Forms examples so far.

Creating the Media Player Application Code

Some COM components require a lot of tinkering by the host application, despite being self-contained for the most part. However, the Windows Media Player is an exception to the rule. Normally, you want to tinker with it as little as possible to meet your programming requirements. In some cases, you won't want to tinker at all, as shown in Listing 9-2.

LISTING 9-2: Interacting with the COM component

```
# Set up the path to the .NET Framework.
import sys
sys.path.append('C:\\WINDOWS\\Microsoft.NET\\Framework\\v2.0.50727')

# Make clr accessible.
import clr

# Add any required references.
clr.AddReference('System.Windows.Forms.DLL')

# Import the .NET assemblies.
import System
import System.Windows.Forms

# import the form.
from frmUseWMP import *

# Define the Windows Form and the elements of this specific instance.
WMPForm = frmUseWMP()
WMPForm.InitializeComponent()

# Run the application.
System.Windows.Forms.Application.Run(WMPForm)
```

This code does the minimum possible for a Windows Forms application. It contains no event handlers or anything of that nature. In fact, the code simply displays the forms. Believe it or not, the actual settings for the application appear as part of the .RESOURCES file. What you see when you run this application appears in Figure 9-14.

This is a fully functional Windows Media Player. You can adjust the volume, set the starting position, pause the play, or do anything else you normally do with the Windows Media Player. It's even possible to right-click the Windows Media Player to see the standard context menu. The context menu contains options to do things like slow the play time, see properties, and change options. Play with the example a bit to see just how fully functional it is.

FIGURE 9-14: The example application shows a form with Windows Media Player on it.

A QUICK VIEW OF THE WINDOWS MEDIA PLAYER COMPONENT FORM

You may encounter times when you really don't want to display the Windows Media Player as a control — you simply want it to work in the background. In this case, you can use the Windows Media Player as a component. The following code snippet shows the fastest way to perform this task in IronPython (the sys.path.append() call should appear on a single line, even though it appears on two lines in the book). (You can find the entire source in the MPComponent example supplied with the book's source code.)

```
# Set up the path to the .NET Framework.
import sys
sys.path.append(
    'C:\\WINDOWS\\Microsoft.NET\\Framework\\v2.0.50727')

# Make clr accessible.
import clr

# Add any required references.
clr.AddReference('System.Windows.Forms.DLL')
clr.AddReference('WMPLib.DLL')

# Import the .NET assemblies.
import System
import System.Windows.Forms
import WMPLib

# import the form.
from frmMPComponent import *

# Define the event handlers.
 def btnPlay_Click(*args):

   # Create the Media Player object.
```

(continues)

(continued)

```
        MP = WMPLib.WindowsMediaPlayerClass()

        # Assign the media player event.
        MP.MediaError += PlayerError

        # Assign a sound to the Media Player.
        MP.URL = "Bells.WAV"

        # Play the sound.
        MP.controls.play()
```

Notice that you start by adding a reference to `WMPLib.DLL` and importing `WMPLib` into IronPython, rather than using the Ax versions. The next step appears in the `btnPlay_Click()` event handler. After the code imports the required support, it instantiates an object (`MP`) of the `WindowsMediaPlayerClass`, not `WindowsMediaPlayer` (an interface) as many of the Microsoft examples show.

Now you can perform various tasks with the resulting component. The example is simple. All it does is assign a filename to the `URL` property, and then call on `controls.play()` to play the file. You can find additional information on using this technique at `http://msdn.microsoft.com/library/dd562692.aspx`.

PERFORMING LATE BINDING USING ACTIVATOR.CREATEINSTANCE()

The `Activator.CreateInstance()` method is one of the more powerful ways to work with objects of all kinds. In fact, this particular method can give your IronPython applications the same kind of support as the Windows scripting engines CScript and WScript.

When working with the `Activator.CreateInstance()` method, you describe the type of object you want to create. The object can be anything. In fact, if you look through the HKEY_CLASSES_ ROOT hive of the registry, you'll find a number of objects to try on your system.

The example in this section does something a bit mundane, but also interesting — it demonstrates how to interact with the `Shell` objects. You can get a description of the `Shell` objects at `http://msdn.microsoft.com/library/bb774122.aspx`. The main reason to look at the Shell objects is that every Windows machine has them and they're pretty useful for detecting user preferences. Listing 9-3 shows the code used for this example.

LISTING 9-3: Working with Shell objects

```
# We only need the System assembly for this example.
from System import Activator, Type

# Import the time module to help with a pause.
import time
```

```
# Constants used for Shell settings.
from ShellSettings import *

# Create the Shell object.
ShObj = Activator.CreateInstance(Type.GetTypeFromProgID('Shell.Application'))

# Toggle the Desktop.
raw_input('Press Enter to show and then hide the Desktop')
ShObj.ToggleDesktop()
time.sleep(2)
ShObj.ToggleDesktop()

# Show some of the settings.
print '\nThe user wants to show file extensions:',
print ShObj.GetSetting(SSF_SHOWEXTENSIONS)
print 'The user wants to see system files:',
print ShObj.GetSetting(SSF_SHOWSYSFILES)
print 'The user also wants to see operating system files:',
print ShObj.GetSetting(SSF_SHOWSUPERHIDDEN)

# Check Explorer policies.
print '\nThe NoDriveTypeAutoRun policies are:'

# Obtain the bit values. These values are:
# 0 Unknown drives
# 1 No root directory
# 2 Removable drives (Floppy, ZIP)
# 3 Hard disk drives
# 4 Network drives
# 5 CD-ROM drives
# 6 RAM disk drives
# 7 Reserved
MyBits = ShObj.ExplorerPolicy('NoDriveTypeAutoRun')

# Display the results.
if MyBits.__and__(0x01) == 0x01:
    print('\tAutorun Disabled for Unknown Drives')
else:
    print('\tAutorun Enabled for Unknown Drives')
if MyBits.__and__(0x02) == 0x02:
    print('\tAutorun Disabled for No Root Directory')
else:
    print('\tAutorun Enabled for No Root Drives')
if MyBits.__and__(0x04) == 0x04:
    print('\tAutorun Disabled for Removable (Floppy/ZIP) Drives')
else:
    print('\tAutorun Enabled for Removable (Floppy/ZIP) Drives')
if MyBits.__and__(0x08) == 0x08:
    print('\tAutorun Disabled for Hard Disk Drives')
else:
    print('\tAutorun Enabled for Hard Disk Drives')
if MyBits.__and__(0x10) == 0x10:
    print('\tAutorun Disabled for Network Drives')
else:
    print('\tAutorun Enabled for Network Drives')
```

continues

LISTING 9-3 *(continued)*

```
if MyBits.__and__(0x20) == 0x20:
    print('\tAutorun Disabled for CD-ROM Drives')
else:
    print('\tAutorun Enabled for CD-ROM Drives')
if MyBits.__and__(0x40) == 0x40:
    print('\tAutorun Disabled for RAM Disk Drives')
else:
    print('\tAutorun Enabled for RAM Disk Drives')

# Pause after the debug session.
raw_input('Press any key to continue...')
```

This example starts by showing a different kind of `import` call. In this case, the `import` retrieves only the `Activator` and `Type` classes from the `System` assembly. Using this approach reduces environmental clutter. In addition, using this technique reduces the memory requirements for your application and could mean the application runs faster. The example also imports the `time` module.

The first step in this application can seem a little complicated so it pays to break it down into two pieces. First, you must get the type of a particular object by using its identifier within the registry with the `Type.GetTypeFromProgID()` method. As previously mentioned, the object used in this example is `Shell.Application`. After the code obtains the type, it can create an instance of the object using `Activator.CreateInstance()`.

The `Shell.Application` object, `ShObj`, provides several interesting methods and this example works with three of them. The first method, `ToggleDesktop()`, provides the same service as clicking the Show Desktop icon in the Quick Launch toolbar. Calling `ToggleDesktop()` the first time shows the desktop, while the second call restores the application windows to their former appearance. Notice the call to `time.sleep(2)`, which provides a 2-second pause between the two calls.

The second method, `GetSetting()`, accepts a constant value as input. Listing 9-4 shows common settings you can query using `GetSetting()`. The example shows the results of three queries about Windows Explorer settings for file display. You can see these results (as well as the results for the third method) in Figure 9-15.

Available for download on Wrox.com

LISTING 9-4: Queryable information for GetSetting()

```
SSF_SHOWALLOBJECTS = 0x00000001
SSF_SHOWEXTENSIONS = 0x00000002
SSF_HIDDENFILEEXTS = 0x00000004
SSF_SERVERADMINUI = 0x00000004
SSF_SHOWCOMPCOLOR = 0x00000008
SSF_SORTCOLUMNS = 0x00000010
SSF_SHOWSYSFILES = 0x00000020
SSF_DOUBLECLICKINWEBVIEW = 0x00000080
SSF_SHOWATTRIBCOL = 0x00000100
SSF_DESKTOPHTML = 0x00000200
SSF_WIN95CLASSIC = 0x00000400
SSF_DONTPRETTYPATH = 0x00000800
SSF_SHOWINFOTIP = 0x00002000
```

```
SSF_MAPNETDRVBUTTON = 0x00001000
SSF_NOCONFIRMRECYCLE = 0x00008000
SSF_HIDEICONS = 0x00004000
SSF_FILTER = 0x00010000
SSF_WEBVIEW = 0x00020000
SSF_SHOWSUPERHIDDEN = 0x00040000
SSF_SEPPROCESS = 0x00080000
SSF_NONETCRAWLING = 0x00100000
SSF_STARTPANELON = 0x00200000
SSF_SHOWSTARTPAGE = 0x00400000
```

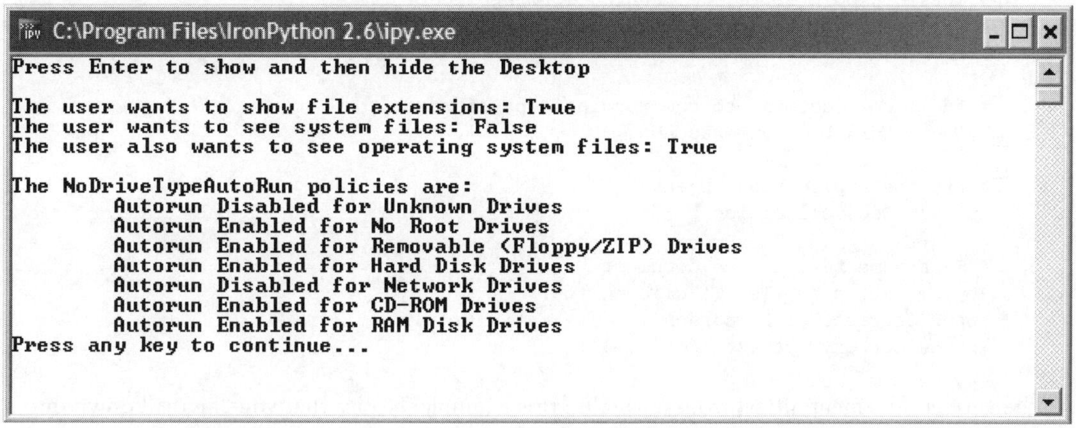

```
C:\Program Files\IronPython 2.6\ipy.exe

Press Enter to show and then hide the Desktop

The user wants to show file extensions: True
The user wants to see system files: False
The user also wants to see operating system files: True

The NoDriveTypeAutoRun policies are:
        Autorun Disabled for Unknown Drives
        Autorun Enabled for No Root Drives
        Autorun Enabled for Removable (Floppy/ZIP) Drives
        Autorun Enabled for Hard Disk Drives
        Autorun Disabled for Network Drives
        Autorun Enabled for CD-ROM Drives
        Autorun Enabled for RAM Disk Drives
Press any key to continue...
```

FIGURE 9-15: The shell objects provide access to all sorts of useful information.

The third method, `ExplorerPolicy()`, is a registry-based query that relies on bit positions to define a value. You find these values in the `HKEY_CURRENT_USER\Software\Microsoft\Windows\CurrentVersion\Policies\Explorer` registry key. The two most common policies are `NoDriveAutorun` and `NoDriveTypeAutoRun`. When working with the `NoDriveAutorun` policy, Windows enables or disables autorun on a drive letter basis where bit 0 is drive A and bit 25 is drive Z. Listing 9-3 shows how to work with the bits for the `NoDriveTypeAutoRun` policy, while Figure 9-15 shows the results for the host machine.

You can find a number of other examples of this kind of late binding for IronPython on the Internet. For example, you can see a Word late binding example at `http://www.ironpython.info/index.php/Extremely_Late_Binding`. This particular example would possibly be the next step for many developers in working with `Activator.CreateInstance()`. The important thing to remember is that this method is extremely flexible and that you need to think of the impossible, as well as the possible, when using it.

PERFORMING LATE BINDING USING MARSHAL.GETACTIVEOBJECT()

Sometimes you need to interact with an application that's already running. In this case, you don't want to create a new object; you want to gain access to an existing object. The technique used to perform this type of late binding is to call `Marshal.GetActiveObject()` with the type of object you want to access. Typically, you use this technique with application objects, such as a running copy of Word. Listing 9-5 shows an example of how to use `Marshal.GetActiveObject()` to gain access to a running Word application.

LISTING 9-5: Working with a running copy of Word

```
# Import only the required classes from System.
from System.Runtime.InteropServices import Marshal

# Obtain a pointer to the running Word application.
# Word must be running or this call will fail.
WordObj = Marshal.GetActiveObject('Word.Application')

# Add a new document to the running copy of Word.
MyDoc = WordObj.Documents.Add()

# Get the Application object.
App = MyDoc.Application

# Type some text in the document.
App.Selection.TypeText('Hello World')
App.Selection.TypeParagraph()
App.Selection.TypeText('Goodbye!')
```

The `import` statement differs from normal in this example. Notice that you can drill down into the namespace or class you want, and then import just the class you need. In this case, the example requires only the `Marshal` class from `System.Runtime.InteropServices`.

The first step is to get the running application. You must have a copy of Word running for this step to work; otherwise, you get an error. The call to `Marshal.GetActiveObject()` with `Word.Application` returns a Word object, `WordObj`. This object is the same object you get when working with Visual Basic for Applications (VBA). In fact, if you can do it with VBA, you can do it with IronPython.

After gaining access to Word, the application adds a new document using `WordObj.Documents.Add()`. It then creates an `Application` object, `App`. Using the `App.Selection.TypeText()` method, the application types some text into Word, as shown in Figure 9-16. Of course, you can perform any task required — the example does something simple for demonstration purposes.

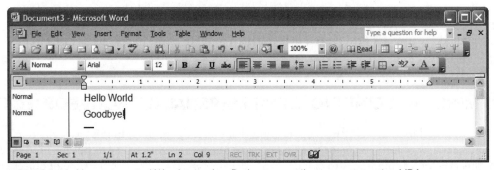

FIGURE 9-16: You can control Word using IronPython as easily as you can using VBA.

USING IRONPYTHON CONSTRUCTIVELY

This chapter has demonstrated techniques for working with COM in your applications. Direct COM access has a lot of benefits so it really does pay to discover how to make COM work from IronPython. Remember that there's no one best way to work with COM, simply the way that works best in a particular situation.

Your organization probably has a lot of COM code sitting around. COM appears not only in custom applications, but as part of Windows, server applications, desktop applications, services, and in many other coded forms on all of the machines on your network. One of the things you should do now is identify the critical applications that you might need to access from IronPython and then decide on a strategy to access them. You might not need to access these applications any time soon, but the exercise of thinking through the process of accessing them is helpful in seeing how IronPython works with COM. The time you spend now will pay dividends later.

Chapter 10 goes back to the command line. However, Chapter 10 doesn't go to the command line to perform common tasks. Many administrators prefer to use the command line to perform tasks because it's fast and efficient. In addition, the command line lends itself to automation that would be difficult to implement in a GUI. Microsoft has even recognized the role of the command line in management tasks and has placed a new emphasis on it. When working with Windows Server 2008 Server Core, you have only a command line with which to work, which means that command line tools have taken on a new significance in that environment. Of course, you can take what you've learned in this chapter to build powerful applications using a command line interface. It's also possible to mix the command line and GUI environments (and many applications do just that).

10

Using IronPython for Administration Tasks

WHAT'S IN THIS CHAPTER?

➤ Developing command line utilities

➤ Using and configuring the command line environment

➤ Using IronPython to script other command line applications

➤ Outputting status information from the command line

Administration occurs at many levels and for many different tasks. For example, many administrators today rely on graphical tools to accomplish tasks manually. As you saw in Chapters 8 and 9, you can use IronPython to create graphical applications. However, where IronPython excels is at the command line. You can create IronPython applications to perform a host of tasks at the command line quite quickly and with less effort than using many other languages. In addition, IronPython works well as a batch processor — a special kind of application that executes a list of commands normally found in a file.

Of course, some people feel the command line is dead — that no one uses it any longer. The converse is true. Many administrators have soured on the time-consuming nature of graphical utilities and now prefer the functionality provided by command line utilities, especially those designed to work in batch files. Microsoft is actually introducing a number of new applications that rely on the command line, such as latest versions of Exchange Server. In addition, Windows Server 2008 Server Core lacks a graphical environment (strictly speaking) and relies on the administrator's knowledge of command line tools for management tasks. In short, the command line is alive and well.

You have a number of options available to provide input to command line applications. The one that comes to mind immediately is to provide an interactive environment. However, you can also let the user enter data using command line switches (as shown by the many utilities described so far in the book) or through environment variables. This chapter concentrates on the latter two techniques, but shows all three to some extent. (Theoretically, you have a fourth option in forcing the application to gather information from an external source such as a database, but this chapter doesn't discuss that option because most command line applications don't use it.)

The user also expects your application to provide output as appropriate. As with data input, command line applications have three major options for outputting data. The common method is to display the output directly on the console screen. However, the user might not be looking at the console screen, so you need alternatives. The two most common alternatives are to use log files on disk or to add entries to the Windows event log. This chapter discusses all three techniques because they're all important.

UNDERSTANDING THE COMMAND LINE

The command line is a text-based environment that some users never even see. You type a command and the computer follows it — nothing could be simpler. In fact, early PCs relied on the command line exclusively (even earlier systems didn't even have a console and instead relied on punched tape, magnetic tape, punched cards, or other means for input, but let's not go that far back). Some people are amazed at the number of commands that they can enter at the command line and the usefulness of those commands even today. A few administrators still live at the command line because they're used to working with it. The following sections give you a better understanding of the command line and how it functions.

Newer versions of Windows (such as Vista and Windows 7) display a command prompt with reduced privileges as a security precaution. Many command line utilities require administrator privileges to work properly. To open an administrator command prompt when working with a newer version of Windows, right-click the Command Prompt icon in the Start menu and choose Run As Administrator from the context menu. You may have to provide a password to complete the command. When the command prompt opens, you have full administrator privileges, which let you execute any of the command line applications.

Understanding the Need for Command Line Applications

Many administrators today work with graphical tools. However, the graphical tools sometimes have problems — perhaps they're slow or they don't offer a flexible means of accomplishing a task. For this reason, good administrators also know how to work at the command line. A command line application can accomplish with one well-constructed command what a graphical application may require hundreds of mouse clicks to do — for example, the FindStr utility that lets you find any string in any file. Using FindStr is significantly faster than any Windows graphical search application and always provides completely accurate results. In addition, there's that option of searching any file — many search applications skip executables and other binary files. Give it a try right now. Open a command prompt, change directories to the root directory (CD \), and type FindStr /M /S "*Your Name*" and press Enter. You'll find every file on the hard drive that contains your name.

In some cases, the administrator must work at the command line. If you've taken a look at Windows Server 2008 Server Core edition, you know that it doesn't include much in the way of a graphical interface. In fact, this version of Windows immediately opens a command processor when you start it. There's no desktop, no icons, nothing that looks even remotely like a graphical interface. In fact, many graphical applications simply don't work in Server Core because it lacks the required DLLs. When faced with this environment, you must know how to use command line applications.

 You see the terms "application," "utility," and "command" used throughout this chapter. An application can refer to any executable code. A utility is a specialized kind of application that performs low-level tasks and includes automation support. Utilities aren't part of the command processor (the application that provides the command line interface) — they exist as separate files. A command is a utility that resides within the command processor. For example, the Dir *command is a command because it exists as part of* CMD.EXE; *you won't find a separate* Dir.EXE *residing somewhere on the hard drive.*

Don't get the idea that command line applications are a panacea for every application ailment or every administrator need. Command line applications share some common issues that prompted the development of graphical applications in the first place. Here are the issues you should consider when creating a command line application of your own:

➤ Isn't intuitive or easy to learn.

➤ Requires the user to learn arcane input arguments.

➤ Relies on the user to open a separate command prompt.

➤ Is error prone.

➤ Output results can simply disappear when starting the application without opening a separate command prompt.

Of course, you wouldn't even be reading this chapter if command line applications didn't also provide some benefits. In fact, command line applications are the only answer for certain application needs. Here are the benefits of using a command line application.

➤ Fast, no GUI to slow things down

➤ Efficient, single command versus multiple mouse clicks

➤ Usable in automation, such as batch files

➤ Less development time, no GUI code to write

➤ Invisible when executed in the background

Command line applications can have other benefits. For example, a properly written, general command line application can execute just fine on more than one platform. Even if you use .NET-specific functionality, there's a very good chance that you can use an alternative, such as

Mono (`http://www.mono-project.com/Main_Page`), to run your application on other platforms. Adding a GUI always complicates matters and makes your application less easy to move.

Reading Data from the Command Line

You have a multitude of options when working with data from the command line. Precisely which method you use depends on what you're trying to achieve. If you merely want to see what the command line contains, you should use the Python approach because it's fast and easy. However, Python doesn't provide the widest range of command line processing features — it tends to focus on Unix methodologies. If you want additional flexibility in working with the command line options, you might use the .NET approach instead. The following sections describe both techniques.

Using the Python Method

Most programming languages provide some means of reading input from the command line and Python is no exception. As an IronPython developer, you also have full access to the Python method of working with the command line. While you're experimenting, you may simply want to read the command line arguments. Listing 10-1 shows how to perform this task.

LISTING 10-1: Displaying the command line arguments

Available for
download on
Wrox.com

```
# Perform the required imports.
import sys

# Obtain the number of command line arguments.
print 'The command line has', len(sys.argv), 'arguments.\n'

# List the command line arguments.
for arg in sys.argv:
    print arg

# Pause after the debug session.
raw_input('\nPress any key to continue...')
```

Developers who have worked with C or C++ know that the `main()` function can include the `argc` (argument count) and `argv` (argument vector — a type of array) arguments. Python includes the `argv` argument as part of the `sys` module. To obtain the `argc` argument, you use the `len(sys.argv)` function call. The example relies on a simple `for` loop to display each of the arguments, as shown in Figure 10-1.

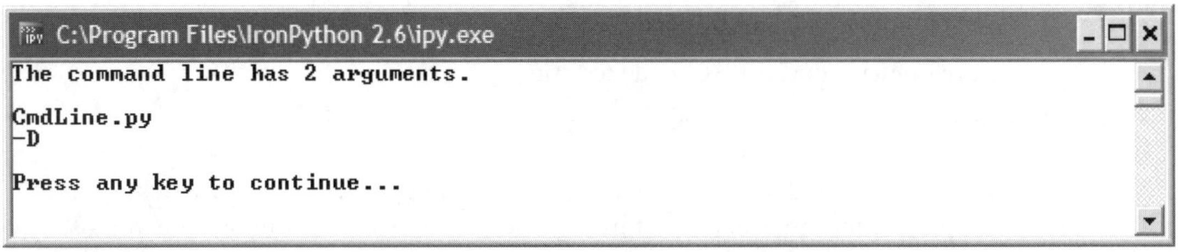

```
C:\Program Files\IronPython 2.6\ipy.exe                          _ □ ×
The command line has 2 arguments.

CmdLine.py
-D

Press any key to continue...
```

FIGURE 10-1: Python makes it easy to list the command line arguments.

Of course, you'll want to expand beyond simply listing the command line arguments into doing something with them. Listing 10-2 shows an example of how you could parse command line arguments for the typical Windows user.

LISTING 10-2: Using the Python approach to parse command line arguments

```python
# Perform the required imports.
import sys
import getopt

# Obtain the command line arguments.
def main(argv):
    try:
        # Obtain the options and arguments.
        opts, args = getopt.getopt(argv, 'Dh?g:s', ['help', 'Greet=', 'Hello'])

        # Parse the command line options.
        for opt, arg in opts:

            # Display help when requested.
            if opt in ('-h', '-?', '--help'):
                usage()
                sys.exit()

            # Tell the user we're in debug mode.
            if opt in ('-D'):
                print 'Application in Debug mode.'

            # Display a user greeting.
            if opt in ('-g', '--Greet'):
                print 'Good to see you', arg.strip(':')

            # Say hello to the user.
            if opt in ('-s', '--Hello'):
                print 'Hello!'

        # Parse the command line arguments.
        for arg in args:

            # Display help when requested.
            if arg.upper() in ('/?', '/HELP'):
                usage()
                sys.exit()

            # Tell the user we're in Debug mode.
            elif arg in ('/D'):
                print 'Application in Debug mode.'

            # Display a user greeting.
            elif '/GREET' in arg.upper() or '/G' in arg.upper():
                print 'Good to see you', arg.split(':')[1]

            # Say hello to the user.
```

continues

LISTING 10-2 *(continued)*

```
            elif arg.upper() in ('/S', '/HELLO'):
                print 'Hello!'

            # User has provided bad input.
            else:
                raise getopt.GetoptError('Error in input.', arg)

    # The user supplied command line contains illegal arguments.
    except getopt.GetoptError:

        # Display the usage information.
        usage()

        # exit with an error code.
        sys.exit(2)

# Call main() with only the relevant arguments.
if __name__ == "__main__":
    main(sys.argv[1:])

# Pause after the debug session.
raw_input('\nPress any key to continue...')
```

This example actually begins at the bottom of the listing with an `if` statement:

```
if __name__ == "__main__":
    main(sys.argv[1:])
```

Many of your IronPython applications will use this technique to pass just the command line arguments to the `main()` function. As shown in Figure 10-1, the first command line argument is the name of the script and you don't want to attempt processing it.

Python assumes that everyone works with Linux or some other form of Unix. Consequently, it only supports the short dash (–) directly for command line options. An *option* is an input that you can parse without too much trouble because Python does most of the work for you. Options use a single dash for a single letter (short option) or a double dash for phrases (long option). Anything that doesn't begin with a dash, such as something that begins with a slash (/) is an *argument*. Unfortunately, most of your Windows users will be familiar with arguments, not options, so your application should process both.

The code begins by separating options and arguments that you've defined. The `getopt.getopt()` method requires three arguments:

➤   The list of options and arguments to process

➤   A list of short options

➤   A list of long options

In this example, `argv` contains the list of options and arguments contained in the command line, except for the script name. Each option and argument is separated by a space in the original string.

The list of short options is `'Dh?g:s'`. Notice that you don't include a dash between each of the options — Python includes them for you automatically. Each of the entries is a different command line switch, except for the colon. So, this application accepts –D, –h, –?, –g:, and –s as command line switches. The command line switches are case sensitive. The colon after –g signifies that the user must also provide a value as part of the command line switch.

The list of long options includes `['help', 'Greet=', 'Hello']`. Notice that you don't include the double dash at the beginning of each long option. As with the short versions of the command line switch, these command line switches are case sensitive. The command line switches for this example are:

- ➤ **–D:** Debug mode
- ➤ **–h, –?, and ––help:** Help
- ➤ **–g:Username and ––Greet:*Username*:** Greeting that includes the user's name
- ➤ **–s and ––Hello:** Says hello to the user without using a name

At this point, the code can begin processing `opts` and `args`. In both cases, the code relies on a `for` loop to perform the task. However, notice that `opts` relies on two arguments, `opt` and `arg`, while `args` relies on a single argument `arg`. That's because `opts` and `args` are stored differently. The `opts` version of –g:John appears as `[('-g', ':John')]`, while the `args` version appears as `['/g:John']`. Notice that `opts` automatically separates the command line switch from the value for you.

Processing `opts` takes the same course in every case. The code uses an `if` statement such as `if opt in ('-h', '-?', '--help')` to determine whether the string appears in `opt`. In most cases, the code simply prints out a value for this example. The help routine calls on `usage()`, which is explained in the "Providing Command Line Help" section of the chapter. Calling `sys.exit()` automatically ends the application. If the application detects any command line options that don't appear in your list of command line options to process, it raises the `getopt.GetoptError()` exception. Standard practice for Python applications is to display usage information using `usage()` and then exit with an error code (of 2 in this case by calling `sys.exit(2)`).

Now look at the `args` processing and you see something different. Python doesn't provide nearly as much automation in this case. In addition, your user will likely expect / command line switches to behave like those for most Windows applications (case insensitive). The example handles this issue by using a different `if` statement, such as `if arg.upper() in ('/?', '/HELP')`. Notice that the options use a slash, not a dash.

Argument processing relies on a single `if` statement, rather than individual `if` statements. Consequently, the second through the last command line switches actually rely on an `elif` clause. Python won't automatically detect errors in / command line switches. Therefore, your code also requires an else clause that raises the `getopt.GetoptError()` event manually.

Remember that arguments are single strings, not command line switch and value pairs. You need some method to split the command line switch from the value. The code handles this case using `elif '/GREET' in arg.upper()` or `'/G' in arg.upper()` where it compares each command line switch individually. In addition, it relies on `arg.split(':')[1]` to display the value. The argument processing routine shows that you can accommodate both Linux and Windows users quite easily with your application.

It's time to test the example. Figure 10-2 shows the output of using `IPY CmdLine2`
`.py −D −s −g:John /Hello /g:John`.

```
C:\Program Files\IronPython 2.6\ipy.exe                              _ □ ✕
Application in Debug mode.
Hello!
Good to see you John
Hello!
Good to see you John

Press any key to continue...
```

FIGURE 10-2: An IronPython application can accommodate both − and / command line switches.

Using the .NET Method

The .NET method of working with command line arguments is similar to the Python method, but
there are distinct differences. When you design your application, you should use one technique of
parsing the command line or the other because mixing the two will almost certainly result in application errors. Listing 10-3 shows a simple example of the .NET method.

LISTING 10-3: Using the .NET approach to list command line arguments

```
# Perform the required imports.
import System

# Obtain the number of command line arguments.
print 'The command line has',
print len(System.Environment.GetCommandLineArgs()),
print 'arguments.\n'

# List the command line arguments.
for arg in System.Environment.GetCommandLineArgs():
   print arg

# Pause after the debug session.
raw_input('\nPress any key to continue...')
```

This example also relies on `len()` to obtain the number of command line arguments contained in
`System.Environment.GetCommandLineArgs()`. As before, the code relies on a `for` loop to process
the command line arguments. You might expect that the results would also be the same, but look at
Figure 10-3 and compare it to Figure 10-1. Notice that the .NET method outputs not only the script
name, but also the name of the script processor and its location on the hard drive. Using the .NET
method can have benefits if you need to verify the location of `IPY.EXE` on the user's system.

It's time to see how you might parse a command line using the .NET method. Many of the techniques are similar, but there are significant differences because .NET lacks any concept of options
versus arguments. In short, you use a single technique to process both in .NET. Listing 10-4 shows
how to parse a command line using the .NET method.

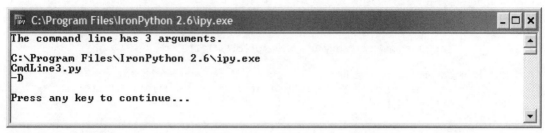

FIGURE 10-3: The .NET method produces different results than the Python method.

LISTING 10-4: Using the .NET approach to parse command line arguments

```python
# Perform the required imports.
from System import ArgumentException, Array, String
from System.Environment import GetCommandLineArgs
import sys

print '.NET Version Output\n'

try:
    # Obtain the number of command line arguments.
    Size = GetCommandLineArgs().Count

    # Check the number of arguments.
    if Size < 3:

        # Raise an exception if there aren't any arguments.
        raise ArgumentException('Invalid Argument', arg)

    else:
        # Create an array that has just command line arguments in it.
        Arguments = Array.CreateInstance(String, Size - 2)
        Array.Copy(GetCommandLineArgs(), 2, Arguments, 0, Size - 2)

    # Parse the command line options.
    for arg in Arguments:

        # Display help when requested.
        if arg in ('-h', '-?', '/?', '--help') or arg.upper() in ('/H', '/HELP'):
            usage()
            sys.exit()

        # Tell the user we're in Debug mode.
        elif arg in ('-D', '/D'):
            print 'Application in Debug mode.'

        # Display a user greeting.
        elif '-g' in arg or '--Greet' in arg or '/G' in arg.upper() or
            '/GREET' in arg.upper():
```

continues

LISTING 10-4 *(continued)*

```
        print 'Good to see you', arg.split(':')[1]

    # Say hello to the user.
    elif arg in ('-s', '--Hello') or arg.upper() in ('/S', '/HELLO'):
        print 'Hello!'

    else:
        raise ArgumentException('Invalid Argument', arg)

except ArgumentException:
    usage()
    sys.exit(2)

# Pause after the debug session.
raw_input('\nPress any key to continue...')
```

The .NET implementation is a little simpler than the Python implementation — at least if you want to use both kinds of command line switches. This example begins by importing the required .NET assemblies. The example also relies on `sys` to provide the `exit()` function.

The code begins by checking the number of arguments. When using .NET parsing, you must have at least three command line arguments to receive any input. The example uses the `ArgumentException()` method to raise an exception should the user not provide any inputs.

In the IronPython example, the code uses a special technique to get rid of the script name. The .NET method also gets rid of the application name and the script name. In this case, the code creates a new array, `Arguments`, to hold the command line arguments. You must make `Arguments` large enough to hold all of the command line arguments, so the code uses the `Array.CreateInstance()` method to create an `Array` object with two fewer elements than the original array provided by `GetCommandLineArgs()`. The `Array.CreateInstance()` method requires two inputs: the array data type and the array length. The `Array.Copy()` method moves just the command line arguments to `Arguments`. The `Array.Copy()` method requires five inputs: source array, source array starting element, destination array, destination array starting element, and the number of elements to copy.

At this point, the code can begin parsing the input arguments. Notice that unlike the Python method, you can parse all the permutations in a single line of code using the .NET method. The example provides the same processing as the Python method example, so that you can compare the two techniques. As with the Python method, the .NET method raises an exception when the user doesn't provide correct input. The result is that the example displays usage instructions for the application. Figure 10-4 shows the output from this example.

 The Listing 10-4 code line `elif '-g' in arg or '--Greet' in arg or '/G' in arg.upper() or '/GREET' in arg.upper():` *appears on one line in the example application, even though it appears on multiple lines in this book due to space considerations. Remember that IronPython lacks any form of line continuation character. All your code must appear on a single line.*

FIGURE 10-4: Parsing arguments produces the same results in .NET as it does with Python.

Providing Command Line Help

Your command line application won't have a user interface — just a command. While some people can figure out graphical applications by pointing here and clicking there, figuring out a command line application without help is nearly impossible. The methods used to understand an undocumented command line application are exotic and usually require advanced debugging techniques, time spent in the registry, lots of research online, and more than a little luck. If you seriously expect someone to use your command line application, you must provide help.

Unlike a graphical application, you won't need tons of text and screenshots to document most command line applications. All you really need is a little text that's organized in a certain manner. Most command line applications use the same help format, which makes them easier to understand and use. However, not all command line applications provide all the help they really need. In order to provide your command line application with superior help, you need to consider the five following elements:

➤ Application description

➤ Application calling syntax

➤ Command line switch summary and description

➤ Usage examples

➤ (Optional) Other elements

The following sections describe all these elements and help you understand why they're important. Of course, every command line application is different, so you'll want to customize the suggestions in the following sections to meet your particular needs. The point is, you must provide the user with help of some kind.

Creating an Application Description

Many of the command line applications you see lack this essential feature. You ask for help and the application provides you with syntax and a quick overview of the command line switches. At the outset, you have little idea of what the application actually does and how the developer envisioned your using it. After a little experimentation, you might still be confused and have a damaged system as well.

An application description doesn't have to be long. In fact, you can make it a single sentence. If you can't describe your command line application in a single sentence, it might actually be too big — characteristically, command line applications are small and agile. Of course, there are exceptions and you may very well need an entire paragraph to describe your application. The big mistake is writing a huge tome. Most people using your application have worked with computers for a long time, so a shorter description normally works fine.

As a minimum, your application description should include the application name so the user can look for additional information online. The description should tell the user what the application does and why you created it. These three elements can fit quite easily in a single sentence as you see in the "Showing Usage Examples" section of this chapter.

Describing the Application Calling Syntax

Applications have a *calling syntax* — a protocol used to interact with the application. Unfortunately, you won't have access to any formatting when writing your application help screen. Developers have come up with some methods to show certain elements over the years and you should use these methods for your command line syntax. Consider the following command line:

```
MyApp <Filename> [-S] [-s] [-D [-U[:<Name>]]] [-X | -Y | -Z | <Delta>] [-?]
```

Believe it or not, all these strange looking symbols do have a meaning and you need to consider them for your application. Any item that appears in square brackets ([]), such as [-S], is optional. The user doesn't need to provide it to use the application.

Anything that appears in angle brackets (<>), such as *<Filename>*, is a variable. The user replaces this value with some other value. Normally, you provide a descriptive name for the variable. For example, when you see *<Filename>*, you know that you need to provide the name of a file. In this case, *<Filename>* isn't optional — the user must provide it unless asking for help. It's understood that requesting help, normally -? or /?, doesn't require any other input.

Command line switches within other command line switches are dependent on that command line switch. For example, you can use -D alone. However, if you want to use –U, you must also provide –D. In this case, –U is dependent on –D. Notice that you can use –U alone or you can include a *<Name>* variable with it. When you use the *<Name>* variable, the command line switch sequence must appear as -D -U:<Name>.

Sometimes a command line switch is mutually exclusive with other command line switches or even variables. For example, the [-X | -Y | -Z | *<Delta>*] sequence says that you can provide -X or –Y or –Z or *<Delta>*, but you can't provide more than one of them.

Most Windows command line applications are case insensitive. However, there are notable exceptions to this rule. If you find that you must make your application case sensitive, be sure to use the correct case for the command line syntax. For example, –S isn't the same as –s for this application and the command line syntax shows that. You should also note that the application is case sensitive in other areas of your help screen because some users won't notice the difference in case.

Some developers will simply use [Options] *for the command line syntax if you can use any of the command line switches at any time, or simply ignore them completely. There isn't anything wrong with this approach, especially when your application defaults to showing the help screen when the user doesn't provide any command line switches. However, make absolutely certain that your application truly doesn't have a unique calling syntax before you use this approach.*

Documenting the Command Line Switches

No matter how simple or complex the application, you need to document every command line switch. Most application writers use anywhere from one to three sentences to document the command line switch unless it's truly complex. The command line switch documentation should focus on the purpose of the command line switch. Save any examples you want to provide for the usage examples portion of the help screen.

You must document every command line switch or the user won't know it exists. Placing alternative command line switches together is a good idea because it reduces the complexity of the help screen. The order in which you place the command line switches depends on the purpose and complexity of your application. However, most developers use one of the following ordering techniques:

➤ **Alphabetical:** Useful for longer lists of command line switches because alphabetical order can make it easier to find a particular command line switch in the list.

➤ **Syntactical:** Developers especially like to see the command line switches in syntactical order. After viewing the syntax, the developer can find the associated command line switch description quickly.

➤ **Order of potential usage:** Placing the command line switches in order of popularity means that the user doesn't have to search the entire list to find a particular command line switch description. This approach is less useful on long or complex lists because you really don't know how the user will work with the application.

➤ **Order of required use:** In some cases, an application requires that a user place the command line switches in a particular order. For example, when creating a storyboard effect with a command line application, you want the user to know which command line switch to use first.

Some command line switch lists become quite long. In this case, you might want to group like command line switches together and place them in groups on the help screen. For example, you might have a set of command line switches that affects input and another that affects output. You could create two groups, one for each task, on your help screen to make finding a particular command line switch easier.

Showing Usage Examples

Most users won't really understand your command line application unless you provide some usage examples. A usage example should show the command line and its result — if you do this, then you get that as output. Precisely how you put the examples together depends on your application and its intended audience. An application designed for advanced users can probably get by with fewer examples, while a complex application requires more examples. The usage examples should be non-trivial. You should try to show common ways in which you expect the user to work with your application.

Putting Everything Together

Now that you have a basic understanding of the required help screen elements, it's time to look at an example. Listing 10-5 shows a typical `usage()` function. It displays help information to users who need it, using simple `print()` statements.

LISTING 10-5: Creating a help screen for your application

```python
# Create a usage() function.
def usage():
    print 'Welcome to the command line example.'
    print 'This application shows basic command line argument reading.'
    print '\nUsage:'
    print '\tIPY CmdLine2.py [Options]'
    print '\nOptions:'
    print '\t-D: Places application in debug mode.'
    print '\t-h or -? or --help: Displays this help message.'
    print '\t-g:<Name> or --Greet:<Name>: Displays a simple greeting.'
    print '\t-s or --Hello: Displays a simple hello message.'
    print '\nExamples:'
    print '\tIPY CmdLine2.py -s outputs Hello!'
    print '\tIPY CmdLine2.py -g:John outputs Good to see you John'
    print '\tYou can use either the - or / as command line switches.'
    print '\tFor example, IPY CmdLine2.py /s outputs Hello!'
```

Notice the use of formatting in the code. The code places section titles at the left and an extra space below the previous section. Section content is indented so it appears as part of the section. Figure 10-5 shows the output from this code. Even though this help screen is quite simple, it provides everything needed for someone to use the example application to test command line switches.

Including Other Elements

Some command line application help screens become enormous and hard to use. In fact, some of Microsoft's own utilities have help that's several layers deep. Just try drilling into the Net utility sometime and you'll discover just how cumbersome the help can become. Of course, you do want to document everything for the user. As an alternative, some command line application developers will provide an overview as part of the application, and then include a URL for detailed material online. It's not a perfect solution because you can't always count on the user having an Internet connection, but it does work most of the time.

You don't have to stop with simple information redirection as part of your help. Some utilities include a phone number (just in case the user really is lacking that Internet connection). E-mail addresses aren't unusual, and some developers get creative in providing other helpful tips. It's also important to take ownership of your application by including a company or developer name. If copyright is important, then you should provide a copyright notice as well. The thing is to make it easy for someone to identify your command line application without cluttering up the help screens too much.

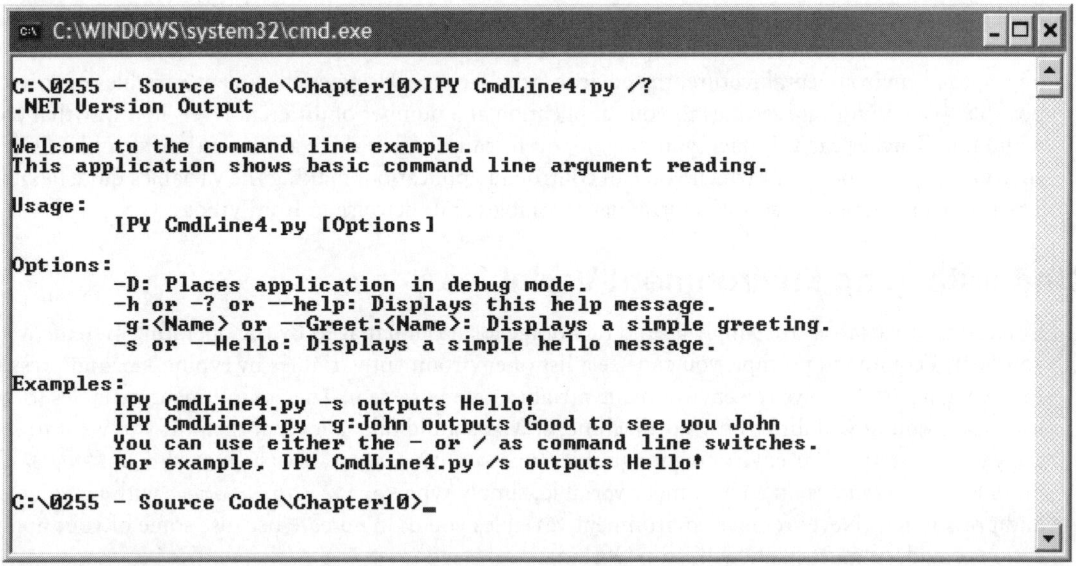

```
C:\WINDOWS\system32\cmd.exe                                      _ □ ✕

C:\0255 - Source Code\Chapter10>IPY CmdLine4.py /?
.NET Version Output

Welcome to the command line example.
This application shows basic command line argument reading.

Usage:
        IPY CmdLine4.py [Options]

Options:
        -D: Places application in debug mode.
        -h or -? or --help: Displays this help message.
        -g:<Name> or --Greet:<Name>: Displays a simple greeting.
        -s or --Hello: Displays a simple hello message.

Examples:
        IPY CmdLine4.py -s outputs Hello!
        IPY CmdLine4.py -g:John outputs Good to see you John
        You can use either the - or / as command line switches.
        For example, IPY CmdLine4.py /s outputs Hello!

C:\0255 - Source Code\Chapter10>_
```

FIGURE 10-5: The application help screen is simple, but helpful.

To break the help screens up, you might want to include layered help. Typing MyApp /? might display an overview, while MyApp /MySwitch /? provides detailed information. Microsoft uses this approach with several of its utilities. If you use layered help, make sure you mention it on the overview help screen, or most users will think that the overview is all they get in the way of useful information.

Special settings require a section as well. For example, IPY.EXE provides access to some application features through environment variables. These environment variables appear in a separate section of the help screen.

Applications that could damage application data or the system as a whole in some way require warnings. Too few command line applications provide warnings, so command line applications have gotten a reputation for being dangerous — only experts need apply. The fact is that many of these applications would be quite easy to use with the proper warning information. However, don't go too far in protecting the user by providing messages that request the user confirm a particular task. Using confirmations would reduce the ability of developers to use the command line applications for batch processing and automation needs.

Given that your application might inadvertently damage something when the user misuses it, you might also want to include fixes and workarounds as part of your help. Unfortunately, it's the nature of command line utilities that the actions they perform are one-way — once done, you can't undo them.

INTERACTING WITH THE ENVIRONMENT

The application environment consists of a number of elements. Of course, you need to consider whether the application uses a character mode interface or a graphical interface. The platform on which the application runs is also a consideration. Depending on the application's purpose, you may need to consider background task management as part of the picture. Most developers understand that these elements, and more, affect the operation of the application. However, some developers miss out on a special environmental feature, the environment variable. Using environment variables makes it possible to communicate settings to your application at a number of different levels in a way that command line switches can't. In fact, you may not even realize it, but there are several different levels of environment variables with which you can control an application, making the variables quite flexible. The following sections describe environment variables and their use in IronPython.

Understanding Environment Variables

Environment variables are simply a kind of storage location managed by the operating system. When you open a command prompt, you can see a list of environment variables by typing Set and pressing Enter. Figure 10-6 shows the environment variables on my system. The environment variables (or at least their values) will differ on your machine, so you should take a look at them. If you want to see the value of a particular environment variable, type Set *VariableName* (such as Set USERNAME) and press Enter. To remove an environment variable, simply type Set *VariableName=* (with no value) and press Enter. (Never remove environment variables you didn't create because some of your applications could, or more likely will, stop working.)

```
C:\WINDOWS\system32\cmd.exe

C:\0255 - Source Code\Chapter10>Set
ALLUSERSPROFILE=C:\Documents and Settings\All Users
APPDATA=C:\Documents and Settings\John\Application Data
CLIENTNAME=Console
CommonProgramFiles=C:\Program Files\Common Files
COMPUTERNAME=MAIN
ComSpec=C:\WINDOWS\system32\cmd.exe
FP_NO_HOST_CHECK=NO
HOMEDRIVE=C:
HOMEPATH=\Documents and Settings\John
IRONPYTHONPATH=C:\Python26\Lib
LOGONSERVER=\\MAIN
NUMBER_OF_PROCESSORS=1
OS=Windows_NT
Path=C:\WINDOWS\system32;C:\WINDOWS;C:\WINDOWS\System32\Wbem;C:\Program Files\Mi
crosoft SQL Server\100\Tools\Binn\;C:\Program Files\Microsoft SQL Server\100\DTS
\Binn\;C:\Program Files\Microsoft SQL Server\100\Tools\Binn\VSShell\Common7\IDE\
;C:\Program Files\Microsoft Visual Studio 9.0\Common7\IDE\PrivateAssemblies\;C:\
WINDOWS\system32\WindowsPowerShell\v1.0;C:\Program Files\Java\jdk1.6.0_16\bin;C:
\Program Files\IronPython 2.6
PATHEXT=.COM;.EXE;.BAT;.CMD;.VBS;.VBE;.JS;.JSE;.WSF;.WSH;.PSC1
PROCESSOR_ARCHITECTURE=x86
PROCESSOR_IDENTIFIER=x86 Family 15 Model 47 Stepping 0, AuthenticAMD
PROCESSOR_LEVEL=15
PROCESSOR_REVISION=2f00
ProgramFiles=C:\Program Files
PROMPT=$P$G
SESSIONNAME=Console
SystemDrive=C:
SystemRoot=C:\WINDOWS
TEMP=C:\DOCUME~1\John\LOCALS~1\Temp
TMP=C:\DOCUME~1\John\LOCALS~1\Temp
USERDOMAIN=MAIN
USERNAME=John
USERPROFILE=C:\Documents and Settings\John
VS100COMNTOOLS=C:\Program Files\Microsoft Visual Studio 10.0\Common7\Tools\
VS90COMNTOOLS=C:\Program Files\Microsoft Visual Studio 9.0\Common7\Tools\
windir=C:\WINDOWS

C:\0255 - Source Code\Chapter10>
```

FIGURE 10-6: Most computers have a wealth of environment variables.

As you can see from Figure 10-6, environment variables appear as a name/value pair. An environment variable with a specific name has a certain value. Some environment variables in this list are common to all Windows machines. For example, the system wouldn't be able to find applications without the Path environment variable. Environment variables such as COMPUTERNAME and USERNAME can prove helpful for your applications. You can also discover facts such as the processor type and system drive using environment variables.

It's possible to create environment variables using a number of techniques. However, the method used to create the environment variable determines its scope (personal or global), visibility (command prompt only or command prompt and Windows application), and longevity (session or permanent). For example, if you type Set MyVar=Hello (notice that there are no quotes for the value) and press Enter, you create a personal environment variable that lasts for the current session and is visible only in the command prompt window. You can see any environment variable by typing Echo %VarName% and pressing Enter. Try it out with MyVar. Type Echo %MyVar% and press Enter to see the output shown in Figure 10-7.

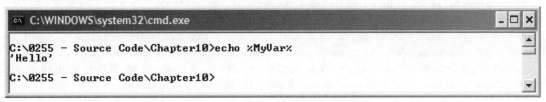

FIGURE 10-7: Use the Echo command to see environment variable content.

The most common way to set a permanent environment variable is to click Environment Variables on the Advanced tab of the System Properties dialog box. You see the Environment Variables dialog box shown in Figure 10-8. This dialog box has two environment variable settings areas. The upper area manages personal settings that affect just one person — the current user. The lower area manages environment variables that affect everyone who uses the system.

To create a new environment variable, simply click New. You see the New User Variable (shown in Figure 10-9) or the New System Variable dialog box. In both cases, you type an environment variable name in the Variable Name field and an environment variable value in the Variable Value field. Click OK and you see the environment variable added to the appropriate list. Editing an environment variable is just as easy. Simply highlight the environment variable you want to change in the list and click Edit. You'll see a dialog box similar to the one shown in Figure 10-9 where you can change the environment variable value. To remove an environment variable, simply highlight its entry in the list and click Delete.

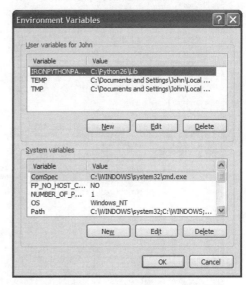

FIGURE 10-8: Personal environment variables affect just one person; system environment variables affect everyone.

Any changes you make to environment variables won't show up until you close and reopen any command prompt windows. Windows provides the current set of environment variables to every command prompt window when it opens the window, but it doesn't perform updates.

The interesting thing about environment variables you set using the Environment Variables dialog box is that they are also available to Windows applications. You can read these environment variables just as easily in a graphical application as you can in a character mode application (as described in the "Using the .NET Method" section of the chapter).

FIGURE 10-9: Create an environment variable by supplying a name/value pair.

You may find that you want to create environment variables for just the command prompt. Of course, you can always use the Set command approach described earlier in this section. However, most developers will want something a little more automated. If you need to set command line–only environment variables for the entire machine, then you need to modify the AutoExec.NT file found in the \WINDOWS\system32 folder of your system. Figure 10-10 shows a typical view of this file.

```
@echo off

REM AUTOEXEC.BAT is not used to initialize the MS-DOS environment.
REM AUTOEXEC.NT is used to initialize the MS-DOS environment unless a
REM different startup file is specified in an application's PIF.

REM Install CD ROM extensions
lh %SystemRoot%\system32\mscdexnt.exe

REM Install network redirector (load before dosx.exe)
lh %SystemRoot%\system32\redir

REM Install DPMI support
lh %SystemRoot%\system32\dosx

REM The following line enables Sound Blaster 2.0 support on NTVDM.
REM The command for setting the BLASTER environment is as follows:
REM     SET BLASTER=A220 I5 D1 P330
REM     where:
REM         A       specifies the sound blaster's base I/O port
REM         I       specifies the interrupt request line
REM         D       specifies the 8-bit DMA channel
REM         P       specifies the MPU-401 base I/O port
REM         T       specifies the type of sound blaster card
REM                 1 - Sound Blaster 1.5
REM                 2 - Sound Blaster Pro I
REM                 3 - Sound Blaster 2.0
REM                 4 - Sound Blaster Pro II
REM                 6 - Sound Blaster 16/AWE 32/32/64
REM
REM     The default value is A220 I5 D1 T3 and P330.  If any of the switches is
REM     left unspecified, the default value will be used. (NOTE, since all the
REM     ports are virtualized, the information provided here does not have to
REM     match the real hardware setting.)  NTVDM supports Sound Blaster 2.0 only.
REM     The T switch must be set to 3, if specified.
SET BLASTER=A220 I5 D1 P330 T3

REM To disable the sound blaster 2.0 support on NTVDM, specify an invalid
REM SB base I/O port address.  For example:
REM     SET BLASTER=A0
```

FIGURE 10-10: Some people forget that AutoExec.NT contains environment variables.

Simply open the file using a text editor, such as Notepad (don't use WordPad), and add a `Set` command to it. Every time someone opens a command prompt, Windows reads this file and uses the settings in it to configure the command prompt window. Many people forget that the `AutoExec.NT` file even exists, but it's a valuable way to add `Set` commands in certain cases.

It's also possible to set individualized command prompt environment variables for a specific application. In this case, create a batch (`.BAT`) file using a text editor. Add `Set` commands to it for the application, and then add a line to start the application, such as `IPY MyApp.py`. In short, you can make environment variables appear whenever and wherever you want by simply using the correct method to create them.

Using the Python Method

Python provides operating system–generic methods of reading and writing variables. As with many things in IronPython, the Python techniques work great across platforms, but probably won't provide the greatest flexibility. The following sections describe the techniques you use to read and set environment variables using the Python method.

Reading the Environment Variables Using Python

This example looks at a new Python module, `os`, which contains a number of interesting classes. In this case, you use the `environ` class, which provides access to the environment variables and lets you manipulate them in various ways, as shown in Listing 10-6.

LISTING 10-6: Displaying the environment variables using the Python method

```python
# Import the required Python modules.
import os

# Obtain the environment variable keys.
Variables = os.environ.keys()

# Sort the keys in alphabetic order.
Variables.sort()

# Display the keys and their associated values.
for Var in Variables:
    print '%30s %s' % (Var,os.environ[Var])

# Pause after the debug session.
raw_input('\nPress any key to continue...')
```

The code begins by importing the required modules, as normal. It then places the list of environment variable keys, the names, in `Variables` using `os.environ.keys()`. In most cases, you want to view the environment variables in sorted order because there are too many of them to simply peruse a list, so the code sorts the list using `Variables.sort()`.

At this point, the code is ready to display the list. It uses a simple `for` loop to perform the task. Notice the use of formatting to make the output more readable. Remember that the values don't appear in the Variables list, so you must obtain them using os.environ[Var]. Figure 10-11 shows typical output from this example.

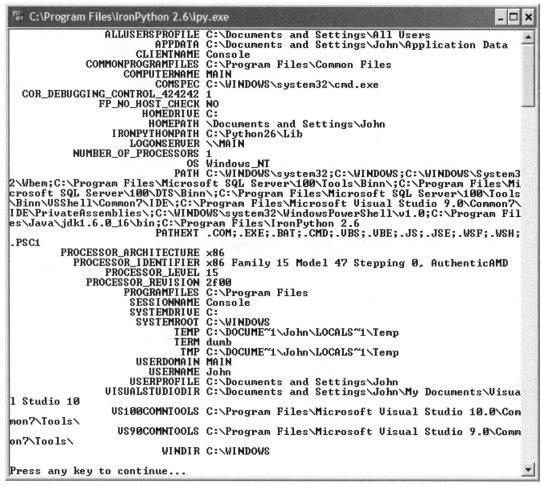

FIGURE 10-11: The environment variables are displayed in alphabetical order.

Setting the Environment Variables Using Python

Python makes it relatively easy to set environment variables. However, the environment variables you create using IronPython affect only the current command prompt session and the current user. Consequently, if you start another application in the current session (see the section "Starting Other Command Line Applications" later in the chapter for details), it can see the environment variable, but if you start an application in a different session or start a graphical application, the environment variable isn't defined. In addition, changes you make to existing environment variables affect only the current session. Nothing is permanent. Listing 10-7 shows how to modify environment variables using the Python method.

LISTING 10-7: Setting an environment variable using the Python method

```
# Import the required Python modules.
import os

# Create a new environment variable.
os.environ.__setitem__('MyVar', 'Hello')

# Display its value on screen.
print 'MyVar =', os.environ['MyVar']

# Change the environment variable and show the results.
os.environ.__setitem__('MyVar', 'Goodbye')
print 'MyVar =', os.environ['MyVar']

# Delete the variable, and then try to show it.
try:
    os.environ.__delitem__('MyVar')
    print 'MyVar =', os.environ['MyVar']
except KeyError as (KeyName):
    print 'Can\'t display', KeyName

# Pause after the debug session.
raw_input('\nPress any key to continue...')
```

Setting and changing an environment variable use the same method, `os.environ.__setitem__()`. In both cases, you supply a name/value pair (`MyVar`/`Hello`). When you want to see the value of the environment variable, you request the value by supplying the name, such as `os.environ['MyVar']` for this example.

Deleting an environment variable requires use of `os.environ.__delitem__()`. In this case, you supply only the name of the environment variable you want to remove.

If you try to display an environment variable that doesn't exist, the interpreter raises a `KeyError` exception. The example shows the result of trying to print `MyVar` after you remove it using `os.environ.__delitem__()`. Figure 10-12 shows the output from this example.

FIGURE 10-12: IronPython makes it easy to set, modify, and delete environment variables for the current session.

Using the .NET Method

Working with environment variables using the .NET method isn't nearly as easy as working with them using the Python method. Then again, you can make permanent environment variable changes using .NET. In fact, .NET provides support for three levels of environment variables.

➤ **Process:** Affects only the current process and any processes that the current process starts

➤ **User:** Affects only the current user

➤ **Machine:** Affects all users of the host system

An important difference between the Python and .NET methods is that any change you make using the .NET method affects both command line and graphical applications. You have significant control over precisely how and where an environment variable change appears because you specify precisely what level the environment variable should affect. The following sections provide more information on reading and setting environment variables using the .NET method.

Reading the Environment Variables Using .NET

As previously mentioned, the .NET method is more flexible than the Python method, but also requires a little extra work on your part. Some of the extra work comes in the form of flexibility. The .NET method provides several ways to obtain environment variable data.

➤ Use one of the `Environment` class properties to obtain a standard environment variable value. You can find a list of these properties at `http://msdn.microsoft.com/library/system.environment_properties.aspx`.

➤ Check a specific environment variable using `GetEnvironmentVariable()`.

➤ Obtain all the environment variables for a particular level using `GetEnvironmentVariables()` with an `EnvironmentVariableTarget` enumeration value.

➤ Obtain all the environment variables regardless of level using `GetEnvironmentVariables()`.

It's important to note that these techniques let you answer questions such as whether a particular environment variable is a standard or custom setting. You can also determine whether the environment variable affects the process, user, or machine as a whole. In short, you obtain more information using the .NET method, but at the cost of additional complexity. Listing 10-8 shows how to read environment variables using each of the .NET methods.

LISTING 10-8: Displaying the environment variables using the .NET method

```
# Obtain access to Environment class properties.
from System import Environment

# Obtain all of the Environment class methods.
from System.Environment import *
```

```
# Import the EnvironmentVariableTarget enumeration.
from System import EnvironmentVariableTarget

# Display specific, standard environment variables.
print 'Standard Environment Variables:'
print '\tCurrent Directory:', Environment.CurrentDirectory
print '\tOS Version:', Environment.OSVersion
print '\tUser Name:', Environment.UserName

# Display any single environment variable.
print '\nSpecific Environment Variables:'
print '\tIronPython Path:', GetEnvironmentVariable('IronPythonPath')
print '\tSession Name:', GetEnvironmentVariable('SessionName')

# Display a particular kind of environment variable.
print '\nUser Level Environment Variables:'
for Var in GetEnvironmentVariables(EnvironmentVariableTarget.User):
    print '\t%s: %s' % (Var.Key, Var.Value)

# Display all of the environment variables in alphabetical order.
print '\nAll of the environment variables.'

# Create a list to hold the variable names.
Keys = GetEnvironmentVariables().Keys
Variables = []
for Item in Keys:
    Variables.Add(Item)

# Sort the resulting list.
Variables.sort()

# Display the result.
for Var in Variables:
    print '\t%s: %s' % (Var, GetEnvironmentVariable(Var))

# Pause after the debug session.
raw_input('\nPress any key to continue...')
```

The code begins by importing some .NET assemblies. Notice that the example reduces clutter by importing only what the code actually needs.

As mentioned earlier, you can obtain standard environment variable values by using the correct property value from the System.Environment class. In this case, the code retrieves the current directory, operating system version, and the user name, as shown in Figure 10-13.

The next code segment in Listing 10-8 shows how to obtain a single environment variable. All you need is the GetEnvironmentVariable() with a variable name, such as, IronPythonPath.

If you want to work with the environment variables found at a particular level, you use GetEnvironmentVariables() with an EnvironmentVariableTarget enumeration value, as shown in the next code segment in Listing 10-8. Unless you create a custom environment variable, you won't see any output at the EnvironmentVariableTarget.Process level.

You might remember from Listing 10-6 the ease of sorting the environment variables when using the Python method. Sorting the environment variables when using the .NET method isn't nearly as easy because the .NET method relies on a `System.Collections.Hashtable` object for the output of the `GetEnvironmentVariables()` method call. The easiest method to sort the environment variables is to obtain a list of the keys using `GetEnvironmentVariables()`.`Keys`, the `Keys` object; place them in a list object, `Variables`; and then sort as normal using `Variables.sort()`.

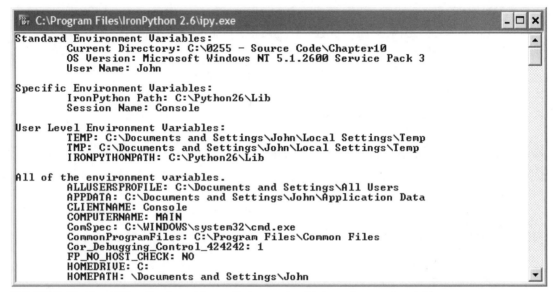

FIGURE 10-13: The .NET method provides multiple ways to obtain environment variables.

Now that the code has a sorted list, it uses a `for` loop to enumerate each environment variable using `GetEnvironmentVariable()`. Figure 10-13 does show the entire list, but when you try the example, you'll see that the list is indeed sorted. There are definitely times where .NET objects will cause problems for your IronPython application and this is one of them.

Setting the Environment Variables Using .NET

The .NET method provides some additional setting capabilities when compared to the Python method. For one thing, you can make the environment variable settings permanent. The reason for this difference is that the .NET method lets you write the settings directly to the registry. You won't manipulate the registry directly, but the writing does take place in the background, just as it would if you used the Environment Variables dialog box.

You do have some limitations. For example, you can't change an Environment class property value. This restriction makes sense because you don't want to change an environment variable that a number of applications might need. Listing 10-9 shows how to set environment variables as needed.

LISTING 10-9: Setting an environment variable using the .NET method

```
# Obtain access to Environment class properties.
from System import Environment

# Obtain all of the Environment class methods.
from System.Environment import *

# Import the EnvironmentVariableTarget enumeration.
from System import EnvironmentVariableTarget

# Create a temporary process environment variable.
SetEnvironmentVariable('MyVar', 'Hello')
print 'MyVar =', GetEnvironmentVariable('MyVar')

# Create a permanent user environment variable.
SetEnvironmentVariable('Var2', 'Goodbye', EnvironmentVariableTarget.User)
print 'Var2 =', GetEnvironmentVariable('Var2')
print 'Var2 =', GetEnvironmentVariable('Var2', EnvironmentVariableTarget.User)
raw_input('\nOpen the Environment Variables dialog box...')

# Delete the temporary and permanent variables.
print '\nDeleting the variables...'
SetEnvironmentVariable('MyVar', None)
SetEnvironmentVariable('Var2', None, EnvironmentVariableTarget.User)
print 'MyVar =', GetEnvironmentVariable('MyVar')
print 'Var2 =', GetEnvironmentVariable('Var2', EnvironmentVariableTarget.User)

# Pause after the debug session.
raw_input('\nPress any key to continue...')
```

The example begins with the usual assembly imports. It then creates a new environment variable using the `SetEnvironmentVariable()` method. If you call `SetEnvironmentVariable()` without specifying a particular level, then the .NET Framework creates a temporary process environment variable that only lasts for the current session.

The next step creates a permanent user environment variable. In this case, you must supply an `EnvironmentVariableTarget` enumeration value as the third argument. This portion of the example also demonstrates something interesting. If you create a new permanent environment variable in a process, the .NET Framework won't update that process (or any other process for that matter). Consequently, the first call to `GetEnvironmentVariable()` fails, as shown in Figure 10-14.

To see the environment variable, you must either restart the process or you must call `GetEnvironmentVariable()` with an `EnvironmentVariableTarget` enumeration value. As a result, the second call succeeds. At this point, the example pauses so you can open the Environment Variables dialog box and see for yourself that the environment variable actually does exist as a permanent value.

Deleting an environment variable is as simple as setting it to `None` using the `SetEnvironmentVariable()` method. However, you need to delete permanent environment variables by including the `EnvironmentVariableTarget` enumeration value, or the .NET Framework won't delete it. Unlike the Python method, you won't get an error when checking for environment variables that don't exist using the .NET method. Instead, you'll get a value of `None`, as shown in Figure 10-14.

```
C:\Program Files\IronPython 2.6\ipy.exe                          _ □ ×
MyVar = Hello
Var2 = None
Var2 = Goodbye

Open the Environment Variables dialog box...

Deleting the variables...
MyVar = None
Var2 = None

Press any key to continue...
```

FIGURE 10-14: You can create permanent environment variables using the .NET method.

Environment Variable Considerations

Some developers don't think too hard about how the changes they make to the environment will affect other applications. One application, which will remain nameless, actually changed the path environment variable and caused other applications to stop working. Users won't tolerate such behavior because it impedes their ability to perform useful work. In addition, companies lose a lot of money when administrators have to devote time to fixing such problems.

The standard rules for using environment variables is that you should only read environment variables created by others. You may find a situation where you need to change a non-standard environment variable, but proceed with extreme caution. It's never allowed to change a standard environment variable, such as USERNAME, created by the operating system because doing so can cause a host of problems.

If you want to have an environment variable you can change, create a custom environment variable specifically for your application. Even if you have to copy the value of another environment variable into this custom environment variable, you can be sure you won't cause problems for other applications if you always use custom environment variables for your application.

STARTING OTHER COMMAND LINE APPLICATIONS

You can start other applications using IronPython. In fact, Python provides a number of techniques for performing this task. If you've worked with a .NET language for a while, you know that the .NET Framework also provides several methods of starting applications. However, most developers want to do something simple with the applications they start as subprocesses. For example, you might want to get the operating system to perform a task that IronPython won't perform for you directly.

IronPython sports a plethora of methods to execute external applications. However, the simplest of these methods is os.popen(). Using this method, you can quickly open an external application, obtain any output it provides, and work with that output in your application. These three steps are all that many developers need. Listing 10-10 shows how to use os.popen() to execute an external application.

LISTING 10-10: Starting applications directly in IronPython

```
# Import the required module.
import os

# Open a copy of Notepad.
os.popen('Notepad C:/Test.TXT')

# Use the Dir command to get a directory listing and display it.
Listing = os.popen('Dir C:\\ /OG /ON')
for File in Listing.readlines():
    print File,

# Pause after the debug session.
raw_input('\nPress any key to continue...')
```

This example begins by opening a copy of Notepad with C:/Test.TXT. Notice that the command uses a slash, not a backslash. In many cases, you can use a standard slash to avoid having to use a double backslash (\\) in your command. When this command executes, you see a copy of Notepad open with the file loaded. Of course, you need to create C:/Test.TXT before you execute the example to actually see the file loaded into Notepad.

In some cases, you need to read the output from a command after it executes. For example, you might want to obtain a directory listing using particular command line switches. The second part of the example shows how to perform this task. When the Dir command returns, Listing 10-10 has a directory listing in it similar to the one shown in Figure 10-15. In this case, you must provide the double backslash because, for some reason, Dir won't work with the / when called from IronPython.

```
C:\Program Files\IronPython 2.6\ipy.exe                              _ □ ×
 Volume in drive C is Windows XP
 Volume Serial Number is 40B3-46F6

 Directory of C:\

01/21/2009  09:52 AM    <DIR>          0153 - Source Code
01/21/2009  09:52 AM    <DIR>          0174 - Source Code
06/26/2009  12:42 PM    <DIR>          0184 - Source Code
05/23/2009  03:00 PM    <DIR>          0188 - Source Code
01/22/2009  07:01 PM    <DIR>          0195 - Source Code
01/21/2009  09:53 AM    <DIR>          0217 - Source Code
01/21/2009  09:53 AM    <DIR>          0247 - Source Code
11/17/2009  06:05 PM    <DIR>          0248 - Source Code
07/15/2009  10:50 AM    <DIR>          0249 - Source Code
03/03/2009  04:20 PM    <DIR>          0252 - Source Code
11/04/2009  05:34 PM    <DIR>          0253 - Source Code
11/16/2009  07:14 PM    <DIR>          0255 - Source Code
08/12/2009  06:49 AM    <DIR>          0256 - Source Code
07/26/2006  08:38 AM    <DIR>          BIBLEU
01/21/2009  09:53 AM    <DIR>          Countdown
01/20/2009  05:05 PM    <DIR>          Documents and Settings
01/23/2009  06:10 PM    <DIR>          Email
01/21/2009  09:55 AM    <DIR>          Excel Data
01/24/2009  03:41 PM    <DIR>          Games
01/21/2009  09:56 AM    <DIR>          GrabAPicture
```

FIGURE 10-15: Use the results of executing a command to display results in IronPython.

If you really need high-powered application management when working with IronPython, then you want to use the subprocess *module, which contains a single method,* Popen(). *This approach is for those few who really need extreme control over the applications they execute. You can read about this module at* http://docs.python.org/library/subprocess.html. *The* os *module also has a number of* popen() *versions, ranging from* popen() *to* popen4(). *Generally, if* popen() *won't meet your needs, it's probably a good idea to use the* subprocess .Popen() *method because it provides better support for advanced functionality.*

PROVIDING STATUS INFORMATION

Your administrative application often performs tasks without much user interaction, which means that the user might not even be aware of errors that occur. Consequently, you need to provide some means of reporting status information. The following sections provide a quick overview of some techniques you can use to report status information to the user.

Reporting Directly to the User

The time honored method of reporting status information to the user is to display it directly onscreen. In fact, most of the applications in this book use this approach. If you know that the user will be watching the display or at least checking it from time-to-time, it's probably a good idea to provide direct information. Make sure you provide all the details, including error numbers and strings as appropriate. Depending on the skill of the user, you'll want to provide messages that are both friendly and easy to understand. Otherwise, less-skilled users are apt to do something rash because they don't understand what the message is telling them.

If you know that less skilled users will rely on your application, you should provide a secondary method of reporting status information such as an event log. Log files are also helpful, but can prove troublesome for the administrator to access from a remote location. The Microsoft Management Console (MMC) provides easy methods for administrators to gain access to remote event logs as necessary.

You can probably provide a remote paging system or similar contact techniques for the administrator as well. However, such methods are somewhat complex and not directly supported by IronPython through the Python libraries. The implementation of these techniques is outside the scope of this book. However, you'll probably want to use a .NET Framework methodology, such as the one described at http://code.msdn.microsoft.com/sendemail, to perform this task.

Creating Log Files

At one time, administrators relied on text log files to store information from applications. However, most applications today output complex information that's hard to read within a text file. If you plan to create log files for your application, you probably want to store them in XML format to make them easy to ready and easy to import into a database. Chapter 13 describes how to work with XML files.

Using the Event Log

Many applications rely on the event log as a means to output data to the administrator. Of all of the methods that Microsoft has created for outputting error and status information, the event log has been around the longest and is the most successful. Fortunately, for the IronPython developer, using the event log is extremely easy and it's the method that you should use most often. Listing 10-11 shows just how easy it is to write an event log entry.

LISTING 10-11: Writing an event log entry

```
# Import the required assemblies.
from System.Diagnostics import EventLog, EventLogEntryType

# Create the event log entry.
ThisEntry = EventLog('Application', 'Main', 'SampleApp')

# Write data to the entry.
ThisEntry.WriteEntry('This is a test!', EventLogEntryType.Information)

# Pause after the debug session.
raw_input('Event log entry written...')
```

The `EventLog()` constructor accepts a number of different inputs. The form shown in the example defines the log name, machine name, and the application name. In most cases, this is all the information you need to start writing event log entries.

After you create `ThisEntry`, you can use it to begin writing event log entries as needed using the `WriteEntry()` method. The `WriteEntry()` is overloaded to accept a number of information formats — the example shows what you'll commonly use for simple entries. You can see other forms of the `WriteEntry()` method at `http://msdn.microsoft.com/library/system.diagnostics .eventlog.writeentry.aspx`.

In this case, the `WriteEntry()` provides a message and defines the kind of event log entry to create. You can also create warning, error, success audit, and failure audit messages. Figure 10-16 shows the results of running this example.

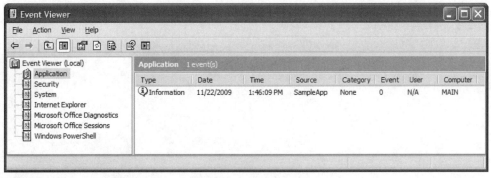

FIGURE 10-16: The example outputs data to the event log.

USING IRONPYTHON CONSTRUCTIVELY

This chapter has provided you with the basic information required to write a good command line application that an administrator (or anyone else for that matter) can use to work at the command line. The basic idea you should take away from this chapter is that while command line applications are normally more difficult to work with, they're also much more flexible, faster, and more adaptable to automation than graphical applications are. In short, you won't write command line applications for the novice user — you write them for an experienced user who is normally a developer, administrator, or someone else who needs to perform low-level tasks.

It's amazing to think that some developers don't even have a strong grasp of the command line any longer. If you haven't done so already, take some time to discover the command line. Work with some applications that look interesting. You can find a basic reference of command line utilities at `http://www.microsoft.com/resources/documentation/windows/xp/all/proddocs/en-us/ntcmds.mspx`, but Microsoft and other vendors provide a wealth of other utilities for you to use. My book, *Administering Windows Server 2008 Server Core* (Sybex, 2008), provides a complete command line reference and documents a few of those undocumented utilities as well. Check out the help for each of the utilities (normally you use the `/?` command line switch) to discover differences in command line utility design that you can use when creating your own applications.

If you're really interested in the command line, consider getting a book on command utilities. The help provided with command line applications, especially utilities and commands, is notoriously poor. Besides discovering an entirely different side of Windows, these utilities help you discover what works, and what doesn't, when creating utilities of your own. Book authors often make you aware of utility and command problems that you want to fix in your own applications.

Chapter 11 helps you discover the ASP.NET application in IronPython. You might be amazed at how simple ASP.NET application development can be in IronPython. In fact, you'll learn that IronPython has certain advantages when compared to other languages.

11

Developing ASP.NET Applications

WHAT'S IN THIS CHAPTER?

➤ Discovering and overcoming Web Application compatibility issues

➤ Downloading and installing ASP.NET dynamic language support

➤ Developing a simple Web site

➤ Using IronPython to add content to a basic Web site

Chapter 8 introduces the idea of building Windows Forms applications using IronPython. In that chapter, you discovered you can create a Windows Forms application of any complexity using IronPython as long as you understand what the Visual Studio IDE is doing in the background for you. It shouldn't be too surprising, then, that you can also build Webforms applications using ASP.NET. Again, you need to consider what is happening in the background when you create a Webform using another language such as C# or Visual Basic.NET.

Unlike Windows Forms applications, a Webforms application relies on a server such as Internet Information Server (IIS) to execute. Using IIS adds another layer of complexity to the application development process. Unfortunately, Microsoft didn't have IronPython in mind when it built IIS, so there are some compatibility issues to consider when using IronPython to build Web applications. Some of these problems you can overcome by installing dynamic language support (the process is discussed later in this chapter), but other issues will remain a problem and you need to know how to overcome them.

One of the best kept secrets of the .NET Framework is that it provides a miniature Web server you can use for testing purposes. In fact, Visual Studio calls on this Web server every time you test your Webforms applications. Fortunately, you can access this Web server from the command line and use it to work with your IronPython Web applications as well. This chapter demonstrates how to use the WebDev.WebServer utility to test your application quickly, even if you don't have IIS installed on your machine. Using WebDev.WebServer isn't only a real time saver, but it makes your system considerably more secure as well, so it's a good idea to work with this utility whenever you can.

CONSIDERING IRONPYTHON WEB APPLICATION COMPATIBILITY

IronPython (and Python for that matter) have huge potential for making Web sites significantly easier to build and manage. In fact, there are a lot of options for using Python (and IronPython) to perform Web development tasks that you can see at `http://wiki.python.org/moin/WebProgramming` and `http://www.fredshack.com/docs/pythonweb.html`. The problem with IronPython is that it can't use the C/C++ libraries used by Python, which means that some of these solutions won't work. For example, it's unlikely that you could use IronPython in a Common Gateway Interface (CGI) application because CGI relies on modules written in C/C++. Consequently, the first rule for Web development with IronPython is to make sure that IronPython can actually interact with the desired modules.

Unfortunately, IronPython isn't integrated into Visual Studio. Because Visual Studio relies on some level of integration to provide full Web development support, you'll almost certainly find that some projects are out of reach. It's not that you can't create them using IronPython; it's that the process would be so horribly time consuming and error prone that using another language would be a better idea. You do have full .NET capability when working with IronPython, as demonstrated by the example in this chapter. All you really need is to add Dynamic Language Runtime (DLR) support to the picture and things will work out just fine.

The picture isn't all gloom. IronPython actually proves to be a good development language for some tasks. As you progress through this chapter, you'll find that IronPython actually makes code behind tasks exceptionally easy. It's conceivable that you can build and test simple Web projects using IronPython considerably faster than using another language such as C# or Visual Basic.NET.

It's important to remember that you don't have to work with IronPython alone. Your Web application can include other technologies, such as Silverlight. You can also rely on other languages, such as C# or Visual Basic.NET, to fill in the gaps in IronPython coverage. Having another language at your disposal is all about flexibility, and IronPython is a great add-on language for any Web application project.

OBTAINING ASP.NET DYNAMIC LANGUAGE SUPPORT

Microsoft built ASP.NET with extensibility in mind, but the native support tends to focus more on static languages such as Visual Basic.NET and C#, rather than dynamic languages such as IronPython. The Dynamic Language Runtime (DLR) is an add-on for ASP.NET that makes it possible to use languages, such as IronPython, that make typing decisions at run time, rather than compile time. You must download and install this support before you can use IronPython to create a Web application. The following sections describe DLR in more detail.

DLR Limitations

The DLR is currently a work in progress. The overall feel is of an alpha product that shows promise, but still has more than a few warts. In addition, the product currently lacks these features (in order of their importance to you as a developer):

➤ **IntelliSense:** Most developers depend on IntelliSense to provide clues as to what works and what doesn't — in essence, what to write next. Without IntelliSense support, most developers find themselves peaking at the documentation and spending hours being frustrated with the development environment. Because a default relies so heavily on IntelliSense during the entire development process, its lack is keenly felt. Let's hope that Microsoft will choose to add this feature sooner rather than later.

➤ **Limited designer support:** If you worked through the examples in Chapter 8, you probably have a good idea of why designer support is so important. Sure, you can create a perfectly usable interface without a designer, but doing so becomes time consuming and many developers give up before they get their user interface completely right. The better the designer support, the faster you can work.

➤ **Project templates:** The lack of templates isn't anything new. You've created examples throughout this book without them, so not having them now isn't that big a deal. However, it will be nice to have the convenience of project templates when Microsoft creates them.

➤ **ASP.NET Model-View-Controller (MVC) pattern:** MVC is a development pattern that Microsoft is pushing very hard because it provides better control over the development process. You can learn more about ASP.NET MVC at `http://www.asp.net/mvc/`. Microsoft eventually plans to add MVC to DLR by extending MVC for IronRuby (see `http://github.com/jschementi/ironrubymvc` for additional details).

➤ **Language Services Support:** A new language feature that Microsoft plans to provide sometime in the future. Details about this feature are unavailable as of this writing, but it's likely that Language Services Support will somehow make DLR more flexible and able to support a myriad of languages.

If you read the information at `http://www.asp.net/DynamicLanguages/` *carefully, you notice that it contains a wealth of caveats. The DLR is essentially an alpha version of a product that may not even appear as part of ASP .NET. Consequently, you need to use DLR to see what's possible, rather than as a production tool for needs you have today. Anything you create using DLR today is likely to require updates and changes tomorrow (assuming you can use DLR at all). The lack of solid DLR commitment by Microsoft is one reason this chapter provides an overview of ASP.NET application development, rather than in-depth information.*

Getting DLR

Before you can use DLR, you must download and install it. The files you need for the installation appear at `http://aspnet.codeplex.com/Release/ProjectReleases.aspx?ReleaseId=17613`. Download both the documentation and binaries files so that you have a complete setup. The documentation file is very small, so you might not think you even received the download at first.

The files are simple ZIP files, so you can extract them to your root directory. The examples in this chapter use a source folder of `C:\ironpython-2.6-beta1-aspnet-200905` for the DLR-specific examples. You need to change the path in the examples to match the location you used to extract the files on your machine.

The `ironpython-2.6-beta1-aspnet-200905.ZIP` file contains two folders: `bin` and `examples`. The `bin` folder contains a complete set of IronPython files, including the files required to make an IronPython script work as an ASP.NET application (you can read more about these files in the section "Creating a Web Site" later in this chapter). The `examples` folder contains two examples that you work with in the next section, "Using the Sample Applications."

Using the Sample Applications

The `\ironpython-2.6-beta1-aspnet-200905\examples\` folder contains two example applications. You should run at least one of these examples to ensure you have a good installation (simple as it is, sometimes there's a configuration on your machine that prevents the examples from working as intended). To start as simply as possible, use the following steps to run the basic Hello Web forms example:

1. Open a command prompt. It doesn't have to be a VS2010 command prompt — any command prompt will do. If you're using Vista or above, make sure you open the command prompt with administrator rights by right-clicking the Command Prompt icon in the Start menu and choosing Run As Administrator from the context menu.

2. Type `CD \WINDOWS\Microsoft.NET\Framework\v2.0.50727` and press Enter to change directories to the .NET Framework 2.0 folder on your system. If you don't have the .NET Framework 2.0 installed on your system, then type `CD \Program Files\Common Files\ Microsoft Shared\DevServer\10.0\` and press Enter to gain access to the ASP.NET Development Server folder on your system.

3. Type `WebDev.WebServer /port:85 /path:C:\ironpython-2.6-beta1-aspnet-200905\ examples\hello-webforms` and press Enter (change your path information if you need to do so). You may need to type `WebDev.WebServer20` if you're using an alternate folder location. This action will start the ASP.NET Development Server on port 85. You'll see an ASP.NET Development Server icon appear in the Notification Area. (Don't worry about the details of the ASP.NET Development Server for now — they appear in the section "Starting the Visual Studio Built-In Web Server" later in this chapter.)

4. Right-click the ASP.NET Development Server icon and choose Open in Web Browser from the context menu. Your Web browser should open up and you should see a simple Web page like the one shown in Figure 11-1.

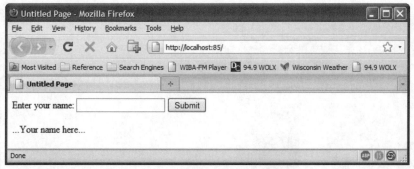

FIGURE 11-1: This simple Web page relies on IronPython for support.

5. Test the Web page to see if it works. Type your name in the Enter Your Name field and click Submit. You should see your name appear in place of the Your Name Here label shown in Figure 11-1. It's a really simple example, but it will tell you whether you're getting the right results.

6. Right-click the ASP.NET Development Server icon and choose Stop from the context menu. The server is no longer available.

The DLR package includes a second example. To use it, simply type `WebDev.WebServer /port:85 / path:C:\ironpython-2.6-beta1-aspnet-200905\examples\album-handler` and press Enter at the command prompt (again, make sure you use a path that matches your machine setup). This example is a little more complicated. When you initially display the browser, you see a list of filenames, which isn't particularly helpful. Click the `album-ipy.aspx` entry and wait a few seconds. Eventually, you'll see the Test icon shown in Figure 11-2.

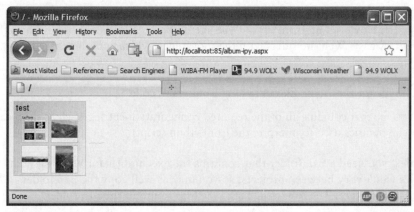

FIGURE 11-2: The second example is a little more interesting — at least it has graphics.

Click the Test icon and you'll see more graphics. You can click the La Flore icon to see some flowers, or click one of the scenic images, as shown in Figure 11-3. Spend a bit of time with this application and you'll find that it really is pretty interesting. Now, consider that this application is written in IronPython. Even though DLR isn't a fully supported technology yet, it does have some amazing capabilities.

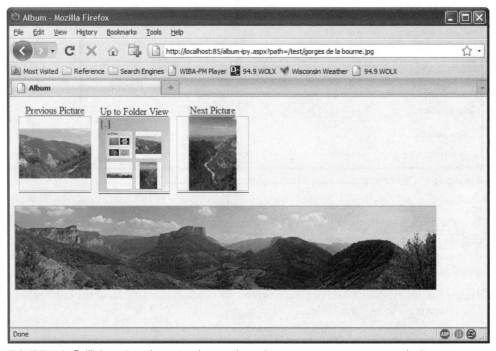

FIGURE 11-3: Drill down into the second example and you start to see some complexity.

CREATING A WEB SITE

You might think that creating an IronPython Web site is going to be complex at first — especially with a lack of IDE support. However, an IronPython Web site doesn't really contain many parts that you have to worry about. A basic Web site starts with the root folder, which contains three items:

➤ An Active Server Page Framework (.ASPX) file containing the user interface

➤ The code behind file for the .ASPX file containing IronPython code

➤ The Web.CONFIG file that contains all of the required configuration entries (such as the location of the special binaries used to interpret the IronPython script)

In addition to these files, you need a bin folder that contains the executables for working with IronPython. These files won't vary between projects, so you may as well copy the bin folder whenever you create a new project. The following list is the files found in the bin folder.

➤ IronPython.DLL

➤ IronPython.Modules.DLL

➤ Microsoft.Dynamic.DLL

➤ Microsoft.Scripting.Core.DLL

- ➤ `Microsoft.Scripting.DLL`

- ➤ `Microsoft.Scripting.ExtensionAttribute.DLL`

- ➤ `Microsoft.Web.Scripting.DLL`

It's important to remember that IronPython is scripted. As a consequence, much of the compiled language baggage that you might have had to consider in the past isn't an issue when working with IronPython. Don't let the seeming simplicity of the Web site fool you, however; IronPython is just as capable as any other language.

BUILDING A BASIC ASP.NET SITE USING IRONPYTHON

You've seen someone else's examples for working with IronPython on a Web site. Now it's time to create an IronPython Web site of your own. The example in this section isn't meant to do anything too impressive. This section focuses on a process you can use to build ASP.NET applications of your own instead. The following sections describe every step you need to take to create any ASP.NET application using IronPython.

Creating the Project

Neither Visual Studio nor DLR provides a project template for you to use. In addition, you have more work to do when creating an ASP.NET application, so creating a project isn't quite as easy as it should be. The DLR instructions suggest copying the `hello-webforms` folder to another location and using it as a starting point, which will work but will prove cumbersome. The following steps create a different kind of setup, one that will prove better in the long run, but require more work on your part now.

1. Create a folder for your application. The example uses `Calculator`, but you can use any name you want.

2. Copy the `hello-webforms\bin` folder to your project folder.

3. Create a `.BAT` file (the example uses `Start.BAT`) with the following content:

```
@Echo Off

REM Change this directory to the location of WebDev.Webserver
CD \WINDOWS\Microsoft.NET\Framework\v2.0.50727

REM Start the Web server.
Start /B WebDev.WebServer /port:%1 /path:%2

REM Open the Web browser to the right Web site.
Start "C:\Program Files\Mozilla Firefox\Firefox" http://localhost:%1/

@Echo On
```

This batch file changes directories to the correct location for the WebDev.Webserver utility. It then starts the WebDev.Webserver utility with the port and path information you provide as part of the project arguments. Finally, it starts your browser so you can see the results.

4. Start Visual Studio and choose File ⇨ Open ⇨ Project/Solution. Locate CMD.EXE found in the \Windows\System32 folder and click Open. This step creates a project based on the command processor.

5. Right-click cmd in Solution Explorer and choose Properties from the context menu. You see the General tab of the cmd Properties window, as shown in Figure 11-4.

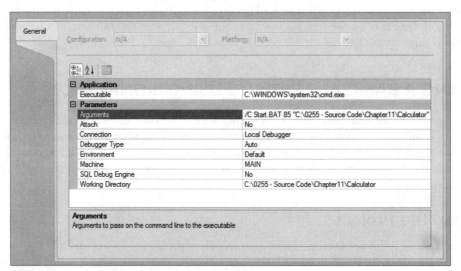

FIGURE 11-4: Set the properties for your project.

6. Type /C Start.BAT 85 "C:\0255 - Source Code\Chapter11\Calculator" in the Arguments field. The arguments start with the /C command line switch, which tells the command processor to process all of the commands you've requested, and then terminate itself. The Start.BAT argument is the file you created in Step 3. This batch file requires two input arguments, the port number you want to use and the location of the example application.

7. Type the location of your project, such as C:\0255 - Source Code\Chapter11\ Calculator, in the Working Directory folder.

8. Right-click the Solution entry in Solution Explorer and choose Add ⇨ New Item from the context menu. You'll see the Add New Item dialog box shown in Figure 11-5.

9. Highlight the HTML Page template and type Default.ASPX in the Name field. Click Add. Visual Studio adds a new ASPX file to your project.

10. Right-click the Solution entry in Solution Explorer and choose Add ⇨ New Item from the context menu to display the Add New Item dialog box again.

11. Highlight the Text File template and type Default.ASPX.py in the Name field. Click Add. Visual Studio adds the code behind file for the Default.ASPX page.

12. Copy the Web.CONFIG file from the hello-webforms folder to your project folder.

13. Right-click the Solution entry in Solution Explorer and choose Add ⇨ Existing Item from the context menu to display the Add Existing Item dialog box shown in Figure 11-6.

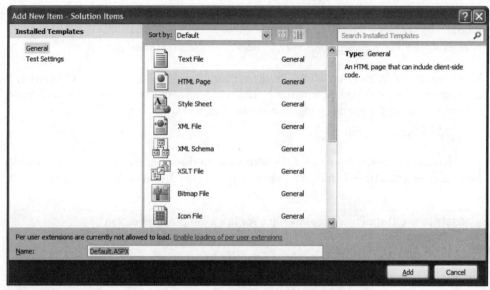

FIGURE 11-5: Select items to add from the Add New Item dialog box.

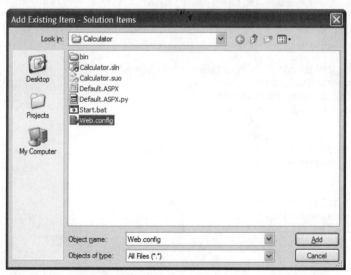

FIGURE 11-6: Copy the Web.CONFIG file from an existing project.

14. Locate and highlight the Web.CONFIG file as shown in Figure 11-6. Click Add. Your project is now ready to go.

Defining the User Interface

The template used for this example is actually an .HTM file so it doesn't contain a few essential entries; you need to use it as an .ASPX file. First, you must tell the Web service which language to use and where to find the code behind file. Add the following code as the first line in the .ASPX file.

```
<%@ Page Language="IronPython" CodeFile="Default.aspx.py" %>
```

When you complete this step, close and then reopen the Default.ASPX file. Otherwise, the IDE is going to spend a lot of time complaining. The next step is to change where the code runs. You want it to run at the server so you change the <head> tag, as shown in the following code:

```
<head runat="server">
```

Now you need to create content for the Web page. In this case, the user interface provides a simple four-function calculator. Listing 11-1 shows the code needed to perform this task.

LISTING 11-1: Defining a user interface for the example application

```
<form ID="form1" runat="server">
    <div>
        <asp:Label ID="lblInput" runat="server"
            text="Type an input value:"/>
        <asp:TextBox ID="txtInput" runat="server" />
        <asp:Label ID="lblError" runat="server"
            text="Type a number in the input field!"
            style="color:red"
            visible="false" />
    </div>
    <div>
        <asp:Button ID="btnAdd" runat="server" text="+"
            OnClick="btnAdd_Click" />
        <asp:Button ID="btnSub" runat="server" text="-"
            OnClick="btnSub_Click" />
        <asp:Button ID="btnMul" runat="server" text="*"
            OnClick="btnMul_Click" />
        <asp:Button ID="btnDiv" runat="server" text="/"
            OnClick="btnDiv_Click" />
    </div>
    <div>
        <asp:Label ID="lblResult" runat="server"
            text="Current Value:" />
        <asp:TextBox ID="txtResult" runat="server" text="0"
            readonly="true" />
    </div>
    <div>
        <asp:Button ID="btnClear" runat="server" text="Clear"
            OnClick="btnClear_Click" />
    </div>
</form>
```

As the listing shows, you work with IronPython code in the same way that you work with any .ASPX file. Unfortunately, the designer has not a clue as to what to do with your code, so you have to write it all by hand. Theoretically, you could start a Web project and then simply move the .ASPX file from that project to your IronPython project, but that seems like a lot of work unless your interface is relatively complex. If you find that you can't quite remember all the ASP.NET controls at your disposal, you can find a complete list at `http://www.w3schools.com/ASPNET/aspnet_refwebcontrols.asp` in an easily accessible form.

In this case, the controls appear in four separate groups: input, control, result, and clearing. Figure 11-7 shows a typical view of the example form. Some common errors that developers make are not including the `runat="server"` attribute and not providing the proper connectivity to events in the code behind, such as `OnClick="btnClear_Click"`. Notice that you can use styles, just as you normally do, with the `style` attribute. One of the attributes that developers can forget about is `visible="false"`, which makes the control invisible.

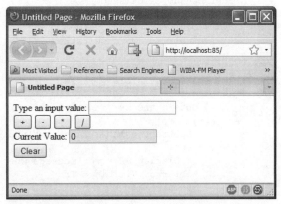

FIGURE 11-7: The example form is a simple four-function calculator.

Creating the Code Behind

The code behind for this example is in pure IronPython. So, while you won't see much difference in `Default.ASPX`, you'll find that `Default.ASPX.py` looks completely different from any Web project you've worked with in the past. Listing 11-2 shows the code for this example.

LISTING 11-2: Creating the code behind for the example

```python
# Import the required assemblies.
from System import *

# Respond to an Add button click.
def btnAdd_Click(sender, e):

    # Get the current value.
    Value = Int32.Parse(txtResult.Text)

    # Reset the error message label.
    lblError.Visible = False

    # Obtain the new input value.
    try:
        Addition = Int32.Parse(txtInput.Text)
    except:
        # Display an error message when necessary.
        lblError.Visible = True
        return
```

continues

LISTING 11-2 *(continued)*

```
    # Perform the task and return the result.
    Value = Value + Addition
    txtResult.Text = str(Value)

# Respond to a Subtraction button click.
def btnSub_Click(sender, e):

    # Get the current value.
    Value = Int32.Parse(txtResult.Text)

    # Reset the error message label.
    lblError.Visible = False

    # Obtain the new input value.
    try:
        Subtract = Int32.Parse(txtInput.Text)
    except:
        # Display an error message when necessary.
        lblError.Visible = True
        return

    # Perform the task and return the result.
    Value = Value - Subtract
    txtResult.Text = str(Value)

# Respond to a Multiplication button click.
def btnMul_Click(sender, e):

    # Get the current value.
    Value = Int32.Parse(txtResult.Text)

    # Reset the error message label.
    lblError.Visible = False

    # Obtain the new input value.
    try:
        Multiply = Int32.Parse(txtInput.Text)
    except:
        # Display an error message when necessary.
        lblError.Visible = True
        return

    # Perform the task and return the result.
    Value = Value * Multiply
    txtResult.Text = str(Value)

# Respond to a Division button click.
def btnDiv_Click(sender, e):

    # Get the current value.
```

```
        Value = Int32.Parse(txtResult.Text)

        # Reset the error message label.
        lblError.Visible = False

        # Obtain the new input value.
        try:
            Divide = Int32.Parse(txtInput.Text)
        except:
            # Display an error message when necessary.
            lblError.Visible = True
            return

        # Perform the task and return the result.
        Value = Value / Divide
        txtResult.Text = str(Value)

    # Respond to a Clear button click.
    def btnClear_Click(sender, e):
        txtResult.Text = '0'
```

The code begins by importing the required assemblies. As with any IronPython application, you can use a combination of Python modules and .NET assemblies to create your application. You also have full access to both Python and .NET functionality in your application, so the considerable flexibility that IronPython provides is still available in this environment.

Each of the event handlers must provide both the sender and e arguments as shown. You don't include a self argument in this case, as you would with other IronPython code. As you might expect, the sender argument contains a reference to the control that called the event handler, while e contains a list of event arguments (normally set to None).

The four math buttons begin by obtaining the current value of txtResult (the output TextBox) as an Int32 value. Because txtResult is read-only, you don't need to worry about someone putting an incorrect value into it. Consequently, this task doesn't provide any error trapping code.

The next step is to obtain the new value for the math operation from txtInput. In this case, you're relying on the user to provide the correct input value, which means that the application code could receive anything. Someone might even try to enter a script in order to fool your application into doing something improper. Using the Int32.Parse() method means that any input other than a number triggers an exception, which your code can handle by simply not processing the input. The try...except structure does just that. If the user inputs an incorrect value, the Web page displays an error message, rather than doing anything with the input.

Now that the code has two inputs to process, it performs the required math operation. After the math operation is complete, the code outputs the result to txtResult.Text.

The btnClear_Click() event handler is relatively simple. All it does is place a 0 in txtResult .Text. The next math operation starts with a zero value, which means that txtResult is cleared.

Starting the Visual Studio Built-In Web Server

It's time to begin testing your application. Many developers don't realize it, but the .NET Framework includes a special utility that makes it possible to host Web sites without having a full-fledged Web server. The WebDev.WebServer utility originally appeared as part of the .NET Framework 2.0. When you build an application for testing purposes with Visual Studio, you're using this built-in Web server to execute the code.

You find the `WebDev.WebServer.EXE` file in the `\WINDOWS\Microsoft.NET\Framework\v2.0.50727` folder on your system. Alternatively, you can also find versions of this utility in the `\Program Files\ Common Files\Microsoft Shared\DevServer\10.0\` folder as `WebDev.WebServer20.EXE` or `WebDev.WebServer40.EXE`.

The amazing part of the built-in Web server is that it works fine for any Web site using any kind of code. If you want to test your standard HTML pages, that's fine — just point the built-in Web server to the correct directory on your hard drive. Of course, you can't run some types of applications because the built-in Web server isn't designed to handle them. For example, you can't execute your PHP code. This little deficiency doesn't matter for your IronPython application, however, because the built-in Web server will see it as a standard ASP.NET application.

Unlike your full-fledged Web server, the built-in Web server doesn't provide outside access, which is the reason you want to use it to test your unsecured, experimental IronPython Webforms application. You don't have to worry about prying eyes seeing your tests and possibly using them as a means to gain entrance to your machine. More important, because this server is virtual, it's less likely that a failed experiment will cause your system to crash. The following sections describe the WebDev.WebServer utility in more detail.

Understanding the WebDev.WebServer Command Line Syntax

The WebDev.WebServer utility provides only a few command line switches because you perform most configuration tasks using a special Notification Area icon. Here's the command line syntax for this utility.

```
WebDev.WebServer /port:<PortNumber> /path:<PhysicalPath> [/vpath:<VirtualPath>]
WebDev.WebServer20 /port:<PortNumber> /path:<PhysicalPath>
    [/vpath:<VirtualPath>]
WebDev.WebServer40 /port:<PortNumber> /path:<PhysicalPath>
    [/vpath:<VirtualPath>]
```

The following list provides an explanation of each of the command line switches.

➤ **/port:*PortNumber*:** Defines the port number used to host the application. Because your application isn't accessible to the outside world and you use a local browser to access the Web server, the port you use isn't as important as it usually is. You can't select port 80 if you also have IIS installed on the system. Any port number between 1 and 65,535 will work as long as the port you select isn't in use.

➤ **/path:*PhysicalPath*:** Specifies the physical location of the application you want to host in the browser. You must provide the full path, but you don't include a filename.

➤ **/vpath:***VirtualPath***:** Provides a virtual path for the application where *VirtualPath* is normally the application name, such as /MyApp. The default setting provides a virtual path of /.

➤ **?:** Displays the help information for the WebDev.WebServer utility.

Using the Built-In Web Server with a Batch File

When you use a batch (.BAT) file to start the application, use the Start utility to execute WebDev .WebServer. Otherwise, the Web server won't start properly. In addition, you should include the Start utility's /B command line switch (it isn't mandatory). The /B command line switch tells Windows not to open a new window to start the application. If Windows opens a new window, the Web server will start, but it may not display the Web page. Here's a modified command line for batch files.

```
Start /B WebDev.WebServer /port:7171 /path:"F:\My Web Site"
```

Interacting with the Built-In Web Server

The WebDev.WebServer utility creates an icon in the Notification Area ( ) when you start it. In fact, a popup message alerts you to the presence of this icon. Right-click this icon and you see three options:

➤ **Open in Web Browser:** Tells the utility to start the default Web browser and navigate to the Web page hosted by the Web server. In most cases, WebDev.WebServer uses the same defaults as any full Web server you have set up on your machine. Otherwise, you can count on these defaults working:

    ➤ Default.HTM

    ➤ Default.ASP

    ➤ Default.ASPX

    ➤ Index.HTM

➤ **Stop:** Stops the server and makes any Web pages inaccessible.

➤ **Show Details:** Displays the ASP.NET Development Server dialog box shown in Figure 11-8 where you can see details about the Web server. In addition, this dialog box provides a link to access the default Web page.

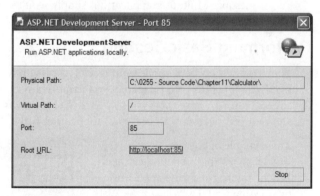

FIGURE 11-8: The ASP.NET Development Server dialog box provides details about the Web server.

Considering the Built-In Web Server Limitations

It's important to realize that we're not using the WebDev.WebServer utility for production purposes. The following list helps you better understand why you can't use this utility for every purpose.

➤ **Functionality:** The WebDev.WebServer utility doesn't create a full-fledged Web server. Some of the functionality you rely on, such as the ability to add users or work with virtual directories, simply isn't available.

➤ **Security:** Any security that you want to set up has to appear as part of your application in a Web.CONFIG file. The WebDev.WebServer utility does tend to follow whatever rules you set for Internet Information Server (IIS) if you have it installed. However, you can't count on this behavior when working on your own and you certainly can't count on it when you send the application to other machines.

➤ **Administrative tools support:** Anything you normally configure through the Internet Information Services console located in the Administrative Tools folder of the Control Panel is unavailable when working with the WebDev.WebServer utility. Consequently, if your application relies on a special ISAPI Filter, you won't be able to execute it using the WebDev.WebServer utility. The same holds true for anything else that you normally have to add using the Internet Information Services console.

 Savvy developers can get around some of the WebDev.WebServer configuration limitations through judicious use of the Web.CONFIG file and by creating resources locally. Make sure you don't assume that an application won't work simply because you have to configure it in a new way.

➤ **Single user Web server:** It's important to remember that this is a single-user Web server. No one outside the local machine can access the Web server because theoretically, it doesn't exist — it's virtual. This means that you can't perform some types of testing using the built-in Web server. The feature that makes it so secure also prevents you from performing some kinds of real-world testing. Multi-user applications simply won't work with the built-in Web server.

Performing Basic Testing

Your IronPython Web application works just like any other Web application you create. Because IronPython is fully .NET capable, you can use any control set you want within the application. Of course, you also have access to standard Web controls. All of this flexibility increases complexity and makes it necessary to test your application fully.

The example application is relatively simple, so testing isn't cumbersome. When you first start the application by pressing Ctrl+F5, you see the Web page shown in Figure 11-7. When you type a value into the Type an Input Value field and click one of the math buttons (+, -, *, or /), the application performs the desired task. Trying to input an invalid value triggers an error message like the one shown in Figure 11-9.

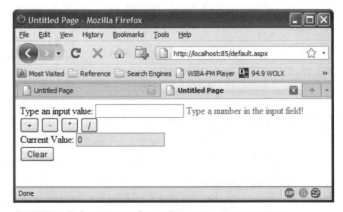

FIGURE 11-9: Incorrect values trigger an error message.

Interestingly enough, the scripting nature of IronPython makes it possible to use IronPython to test your Web application. This gives you an advantage over compiled languages such as C# and Visual Basic.NET. Chapter 18 tells you more about using IronPython for application testing.

Considering Debugging

You may be wondering whether this project can provide any debugging. The fact is that you don't get direct debugging when working with DLR, even if you use a full Web server. However, there are four ways in which you can debug your application.

➤   Use print statements and other old standbys to determine what your application is doing.

➤   Attach the debugger to the running process after the fact by choosing Debug ➪ Attach to Process within Visual Studio.

➤   Import the `Microsoft.Scripting.Debugging.DLL` found in the `\Program Files\ IronPython 2.6` folder and add debugging information manually.

➤   Rely on the output error message from the Web server, such as the one shown in Figure 11-10.

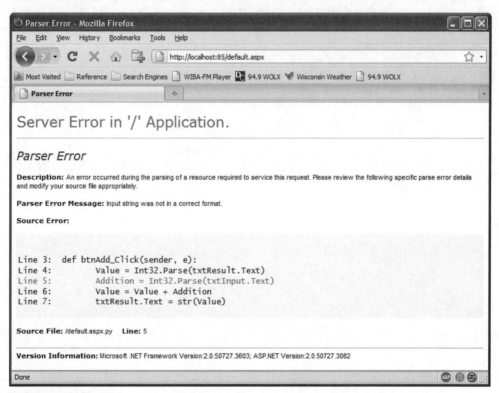

FIGURE 11-10: The Web server provides you with error messages as needed.

USING IRONPYTHON CONSTRUCTIVELY

This chapter demonstrates that it's possible to use IronPython to create a Webforms application. In fact, given enough time, you can create a Webforms application of any complexity. However, it's the time factor that's a problem right now. Without proper support for project templates and IntelliSense, you'll spend a lot of time using IronPython to create a production Webforms application. In addition, unlike a Windows Forms application, you have to use DLR to make Webforms applications work and DLR isn't in released form yet. Experimentation is the name of the game for now. Even so, as you've seen, IronPython can be a lot of fun to use for Webforms development.

Even though Webforms use isn't quite ready for prime time, you should still take time to experiment. At the very least, try the example programs that come with DLR to see that IronPython is a viable Web development language. Use the example application in this chapter as a starting point for your own experimentation. In short, have a bit of fun using IronPython to create Web pages. Consider how the dynamic nature of IronPython could help you in future Web application development, because DLR won't remain in alpha status forever.

Chapter 12 considers an extremely important need for any developer — application debugging. Unlike debugging a C# or Visual Basic.NET application, IronPython holds a few surprises — mainly because this language isn't built into the Visual Studio IDE. Even so, you can use the Visual Studio IDE to debug an IronPython application and many developers do just that. Chapter 12 helps you understand the ins and outs of this process.

12

Debugging IronPython Applications

WHAT'S IN THIS CHAPTER?

➤ Diagnosing and understanding IronPython warnings

➤ Getting error information using sys

➤ Using the Python debugger to debug an application

➤ Using the CLR debugger to debug an application

➤ Using Visual Studio to debug an application

➤ Adding exceptions to your application

Most applications have a bug or two in them at some point. In fact, unless your application is mind-numbingly simple (making it of dubious value), you can probably count on seeing at least a few bugs. When working with a language such as C#, the debugging process can be difficult, but at least you know directly where to start for debugging. You simply use the debugger built into Visual Studio. Unfortunately, IronPython isn't built into Visual Studio and lacks a dedicated Integrated Development Environment (IDE) of its own. As a result, debugging is more difficult for IronPython developers because you don't have a ready-made debugging solution.

IronPython developers aren't without resources. Debugging requires a different approach in IronPython, but in many respects you can use the same techniques you normally do to work through the debugging process. For example, most developers don't go directly to the debugger — they begin with warnings and error messages. Fortunately, IronPython has a robust set of both warning and error-handling features, which makes your job easier.

You can also use any of a number of debuggers with IronPython — these debuggers simply won't have the built-in feel that you might expect from other languages. This chapter discusses two debuggers: the Common Language Runtime (CLR) debugger and the Visual Studio debugger. Neither of these solutions is perfect and you might have to combine them to locate the precise source of the bug in your application.

Easy debugging actually begins with good exception handling. When you understand the potential sources of bugs in your application, you can add exceptions and exception handlers to alert you to these conditions. A sudden rise in exceptions can signal a change in environment, new threats to your application, or modifications in user patterns. IronPython tends to force you to create robust error-handling routines, which really isn't a bad feature to add to an application.

UNDERSTANDING IRONPYTHON WARNINGS

Warnings are simply indicators that something could be wrong with your application or might not work under all conditions. For example, if you use a deprecated (outdated) function, you might later find that the application refuses to work on all machines. You can use warnings for all kinds of purposes, including providing debugging messages for your application.

The main difference between a warning and an exception is that a warning won't stop the application. When the interpreter encounters a warning, it outputs the warning information to the standard error device unless the interpreter is ignoring the warning. In some cases, you need to tell the interpreter to ignore a warning because the warning is due to a bug in someone else's code, a known issue that you can't fix, or simply something that is obscuring other potential errors in your code. A standard warning looks like this:

```
__main__:1: UserWarning: deprecated
```

The elements are separated by colons (:) and each warning message contains the following elements (unless you change the message formatting to meet a specific need).

➤ Function name (such as __main__)

➤ Line number where the warning appears

➤ Warning category

➤ Message

You'll discover more about these elements as the chapter progresses. In the meantime, it's also important to know that you can issue warnings, filter them, change the message formatting, and perform other tasks using the warning-related functions shown in Table 12-1. You see these functions in action in the sections that follow.

TABLE 12-1: Warning-Related Functions and Their Purpose

FUNCTION	PURPOSE
filterwarnings()	Adds rules to a warning that affects when it triggers and how the interpreter reacts to the warning.
formatwarning()	Displays a warning in the standard way.

FUNCTION	PURPOSE
resetwarnings()	Resets the warning state to its default settings.
showwarning()	Displays the specified warning. You can use this function to write the warning to a file. The function defaults to writing the warning to the `sys.stderr` device.
simplefilter()	Provides a simplified version of the `filterwarnings()` function that doesn't require the use of Regular Expressions.
warn()	Used to issue a warning of a particular category.
warn_explicit()	Provides low-level access to the `warn()` function so that you can output extended warning information.
warnpy3k()	Issues warnings for Python 3.x–related deprecations. This function doesn't do anything unless you start IronPython using the `-3` command line switch.

This chapter doesn't describe every argument you can use with every function; it concentrates on actual usage instead. The site at `http://docs.python.org/library/warnings.html` *provides information about all of the arguments you can use with each of these functions.*

Working with Actions

Before you do too much with warnings, it's important to know that warnings have an action associated with them. For example, you can choose to turn a particular warning into an exception or to ignore it completely. You can apply actions to warnings in a number of ways using either the `filterwarnings()` or `simplefilter()` function. Table 12-2 shows the list of standard warning actions.

TABLE 12-2: Standard Warning Actions

ACTION TYPE	DESCRIPTION
error	Turns all matching warnings into exceptions, which means the application will terminate when it encounters the warning unless you provide the required exception handling.
ignore	Disregards the matching warnings so that the interpreter doesn't print them and they don't affect application execution. Using this action can hide potentially useful warnings from view and make debugging significantly harder.

continues

TABLE 12-2 *(continued)*

ACTION TYPE	DESCRIPTION
always	Prints the matching warnings, even if the interpreter would normally ignore it. Using this action displays more information, which could make debugging easier, but also means that the screen will become clogged with unnecessary warnings at times.
default	Performs the default warning action of printing the first occurrence of matching warnings for each location where the interpreter issues the warning. A warning could appear more than once for each module. For example, it can appear once in each class within the module.
module	Prints the first occurrence of matching warnings just one time for each module, even if the interpreter would print the warning more often. Using this action displays less information than the default action, which means that the console screen will remain clearer. However, you could miss essential warnings you need to debug your application.
once	Prints only the first occurrence of matching warnings no matter where the warning appears. This action is useful when you want to fix each warning immediately. However, it'll definitely hide useful debugging information if you plan to run your application for an extended interval.

It's important to work with a few warnings to see how filtering works because filters are exceptionally important. In order to use warnings, you import the warnings module. Figure 12-1 shows a typical instance of the default action. Notice that the first time the code issues the `warnings.warn("deprecated", DeprecationWarning)` warning, the interpreter displays a message. (Don't worry too much about the specific arguments for the `warnings.warn()` function for right now; you see them explained in the "Working with Messages" and "Working with Categories" sections of the chapter.) However, the interpreter ignores the same warning the second time. If you change the message, however, the interpreter displays another message.

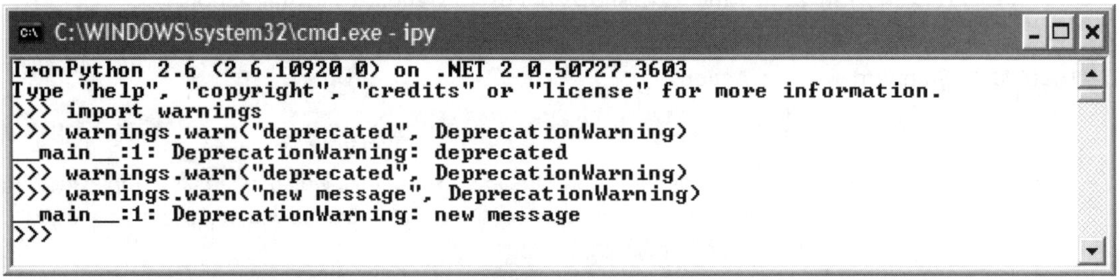

```
C:\WINDOWS\system32\cmd.exe - ipy

IronPython 2.6 (2.6.10920.0) on .NET 2.0.50727.3603
Type "help", "copyright", "credits" or "license" for more information.
>>> import warnings
>>> warnings.warn("deprecated", DeprecationWarning)
__main__:1: DeprecationWarning: deprecated
>>> warnings.warn("deprecated", DeprecationWarning)
>>> warnings.warn("new message", DeprecationWarning)
__main__:1: DeprecationWarning: new message
>>>
```

FIGURE 12-1: The default action displays each message just one time.

Of course, you could always associate a different action with the `warnings.warn("deprecated", DeprecationWarning)` warning. To make this change, you can use the `simplefilter()` function as shown in Figure 12-2. Now when you issue the warning, it appears every time.

```
C:\WINDOWS\system32\cmd.exe - ipy
>>> warnings.simplefilter('always', category=DeprecationWarning)
>>> warnings.warn("deprecated", DeprecationWarning)
__main__:1: DeprecationWarning: deprecated
>>> warnings.warn("deprecated", DeprecationWarning)
__main__:1: DeprecationWarning: deprecated
>>> warnings.warn("deprecated", DeprecationWarning)
__main__:1: DeprecationWarning: deprecated
>>> warnings.warn("newmessage", DeprecationWarning)
__main__:1: DeprecationWarning: newmessage
>>> warnings.warn("newmessage", DeprecationWarning)
__main__:1: DeprecationWarning: newmessage
>>>
```

FIGURE 12-2: You can set the warning to appear every time.

Unfortunately, as shown in the figure, the change affects every message. Using the `simplefilter()` function affects every message in every module for a particular message category. Both the `newmessage` and `deprecated` messages always appear. Let's say you want to make just the deprecated message always appear. To perform this task, you use the `filterwarnings()` function as shown in Figure 12-3 (after first resetting the category using the `resetwarnings()` function).

```
C:\WINDOWS\system32\cmd.exe - ipy
>>> warnings.resetwarnings()
>>> warnings.filterwarnings('always', message='deprecated', category=Deprecation
Warning)
>>>
>>> warnings.warn("deprecated", DeprecationWarning)
__main__:1: DeprecationWarning: deprecated
>>> warnings.warn("deprecated", DeprecationWarning)
__main__:1: DeprecationWarning: deprecated
>>>
>>> warnings.warn("newmessage", DeprecationWarning)
__main__:1: DeprecationWarning: newmessage
>>> warnings.warn("newmessage", DeprecationWarning)
>>>
```

FIGURE 12-3: Use the filterwarnings() function when you need better control over filtering.

In this case, the `warnings.warn("deprecated", DeprecationWarning)` warning appears every time because its action is set to `always`. However, the `warnings.warn("newmessage", DeprecationWarning)` warning appears only once because it uses the default action.

 You can also set an action at the command line using the –W command line switch. For example, to set the interpreter to always display warning messages, you'd use the –W always command line switch. The –W command line switch accepts an action, message, category, module, or line number (lineno) as input. You can include as many –W command line switches as needed on the command line to filter the warning messages.

The `resetwarnings()` function affects every warning category and every message in every module. You might not want to reset an entire filtering configuration by using the `resetwarnings()` function. In this case, simply use the `filterwarnings()` or `simplefilter()` function to set the warning back to the default action.

At this point, you might wonder how to obtain a list of the filters you've defined. For that matter, you don't even know if there are default filters that the interpreter defines for you. Fortunately, the `warnings` class provides two attributes, `default_action` and `filters`, which provide this information to you. Listing 12-1 shows how to use these two attributes.

LISTING 12-1: Discovering the default action and installed filters

```
# Import the required modules.
import warnings

# Display the default action.
print 'Default action:', warnings.default_action

# Display the default filters.
print '\nDefault Filters:'
for filter in warnings.filters:
    print 'Action:', filter[0],
    print 'Msg:', filter[1],
    print 'Cat:', str(filter[2]).split("'")[1].split('.')[1],
    print 'Module:', filter[3],
    print 'Line:', filter[4]

# Add new filters.
warnings.filterwarnings('always', message='Test', category=UserWarning)
warnings.filterwarnings('always', message='Test2', category=UserWarning,
    module='Test')
warnings.filterwarnings('always', message='Test3', category=UserWarning,
    module='Test', append=True)

# Display the updated filters.
print '\nUpdated Filters:'
for filter in warnings.filters:
    print 'Action:', filter[0],

    try:
        print 'Msg:', filter[1].pattern,
    except AttributeError:
        print 'None',

    print 'Cat:', str(filter[2]).split("'")[1].split('.')[1],

    try:
        if len(filter[3].pattern) == 0:
            print 'Module: Undefined',
        else:
            print 'Module:', filter[3].pattern,
    except AttributeError:
```

```
        print 'Module: None',

    print 'Line:', filter[4]

# Pause after the debug session.
raw_input('\nPress any key to continue...')
```

The code begins by importing the `warnings` module. It then displays (using `warnings.default_action`) the default action that the interpreter will take when it encounters a warning. As shown in Figure 12-4 and described in Table 12-2, the default action is `'default'`.

```
C:\Program Files\IronPython 2.6\ipy.exe                                    _ □ ×
Default action: default

Default Filters:
Action: ignore Msg: None Cat: PendingDeprecationWarning Module: None Line: 0
Action: ignore Msg: None Cat: ImportWarning Module: None Line: 0
Action: ignore Msg: None Cat: BytesWarning Module: None Line: 0

Updated Filters:
Action: always Msg: Test2 Cat: UserWarning Module: Test Line: 0
Action: always Msg: Test Cat: UserWarning Module: Undefined Line: 0
Action: ignore Msg: None Cat: PendingDeprecationWarning Module: None Line: 0
Action: ignore Msg: None Cat: ImportWarning Module: None Line: 0
Action: ignore Msg: None Cat: BytesWarning Module: None Line: 0
Action: always Msg: Test3 Cat: UserWarning Module: Test Line: 0

Press any key to continue..._
```

FIGURE 12-4: The example shows the default actions and filters, along with the output of filter changes.

Because of space limitations in this book, the text of Listing 12-1 shows two lines of code as being split, when they should appear on a single line. You would type the `warnings.filterwarnings('always', message='Test2', category=UserWarning, module='Test')` *and* `warnings.filterwarnings('always', message='Test3', category=UserWarning, module='Test', append=True)` *lines of code on a single line. The example won't work if you type the code on multiple lines as shown.*

The next step is to show the default filters that the interpreter provides for you. It may surprise you to know that the interpreter does include some default filters for the `PendingDeprecationWarning`, `ImportWarning`, and `BytesWarning`, as shown in Figure 12-4. These default filters make the interpreter easier and more enjoyable to use, but could also hide important bugs, so you need to be aware of them.

In order to show how actions and filters work, the example adds three filters using the `warnings.filterwarnings()` function. The first filter simply tells the interpreter to always display warnings about the `Test` message provided in the `UserWarning` category. The second filter specifies that the `Test2` warning will appear in the `Test` module. The third filter specifies that the interpreter should append the warning filter to the end of the filter list, rather than add it to the front of the list as is traditional. You can see the result of all three filter additions in Figure 12-4.

The code used to display the filter information is different in this case because the simple display method used earlier won't work. What you'll see as output for the message and module information is something like

```
<RE_Pattern object at 0x000000000000002C>
```

which isn't particularly useful. In order to get information from the message and module elements, you must access the `pattern` attribute. Unfortunately, this attribute isn't available with the default filters, so the solution is to create a `try...except AttributeError` structure, as shown in the code. When the code encounters a default filter entry, it simply prints `None` as it would have done in the past.

Working with modules presents a special problem. If you look at the first filter declaration, it doesn't include the `Module` attribute. Unfortunately, the interpreter takes this omission to mean that you want to create a blank entry, not a null entry. Consequently, the module code also handles the empty entry scenario by saying the module is undefined. If you want to create a null module entry, you must use `Module=None` as part of your filter declaration.

Notice in Figure 12-4 that the first two filters appear at the front of the list and in reverse order. That's because the interpreter always adds new filters to the beginning of the list unless you include the `append=True` attribute. Because the third filter includes this attribute, it appears at the end of the list.

UNDERSTANDING THE WARNING TYPE EXTRACTION CODE

You've probably noticed that the code for extracting the type string from `filter[2]` is somewhat complex. Some extraction sequences can become this way in IronPython. Let's start simply. When you `print filter[2]` directly you get

```
<type 'exceptions.PendingDeprecationWarning'>
```

While this output is descriptive, it doesn't really make type apparent in a friendly way. Consequently, you can `print str(filter[2]).split("'")` to obtain the following array with three elements

```
['<type ', 'exceptions.PendingDeprecationWarning', '>']
```

The next step is to extract the second array element and split the remaining text in two. You use `print str(filter[2]).split("'")[1].split('.')` to perform this task and the output looks like this:

```
['exceptions', 'PendingDeprecationWarning']
```

The final step is to extract the second array element again and print it to screen. So the final statement is `print str(filter[2]).split("'")[1].split('.')[1]`. Even though this code looks complex, it really isn't once you take it apart.

Working with Messages

A *message* is simply the text that you want to appear as part of the warning. The message is specific information about the warning so that someone viewing the warning will know precisely why the warning is issued. For example, if you issue a `DeprecationWarning` category warning, the output will automatically tell the viewer that something is deprecated. As a result, your message doesn't have to tell the viewer that something is deprecated, but it does have to tell the viewer what is deprecated. In many cases, this means supplying the name of the feature such as a method name, attribute, function, or even a class.

Simply telling someone that a feature is deprecated usually isn't enough information. At a minimum, you must include information about an alternative. For example, you might want to suggest another class or a different function. Even if there is no alternative, you should at least tell the viewer that there isn't an alternative. Otherwise, the viewer is going to spend hours looking for something that doesn't exist.

You can't always tell someone why something is deprecated, but you should when you can. For example, it would be helpful to know that an old function is unstable and that the new function fixes this problem. It's a good idea to extend this information by saying that the old function is supplied for backward compatibility (assuming that this really is the case).

In some cases, you also need to provide some idea of when a feature is deprecated, especially if the action occurs in the future. Perhaps your organization knows that a function is unstable but hasn't come up with a fix yet. The fix will appear in the next version of a module as a new function. Having this information will help organizations that rely on your module to plan ahead for required updates.

The point of messages is that they should provide robust information — everything that someone needs to make good decisions. Of course, you don't want to provide too much information either (anything over three well-written sentences is too much). If you feel the viewer needs additional information, you can always provide it as part of the feature's help. That way, people who are curious can always find more information. Make sure you note the availability of additional information as part of your message.

Message consistency is another consideration. Remember that filters work with messages as well as categories and other warning elements. If two modules require the same message, make sure you use the same message to ensure filtering works as anticipated. In fact, copying and pasting the message is encouraged to reduce the risk of typographical errors.

If you ever want to see how your message will appear to others, you can use the `formatwarning()` function to perform the task. Try it out now. Open a copy of the IronPython console and try the following code.

```
import warnings
warnings.formatwarning('Bad Input', UserWarning, 'My.py', 5, 'import warnings')
```

You'll see results similar to those shown in Figure 12-5. Notice that the output contains linefeeds like this: `'My.py:5: UserWarning: Bad Input\n  import warnings\n'`. When you work with the printed version, the warning appears on multiple lines, as shown near the bottom of Figure 12-5.

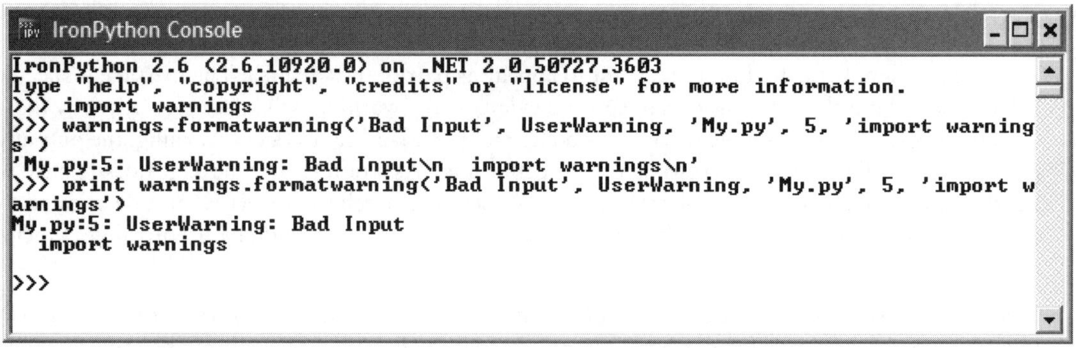

FIGURE 12-5: Use formatwarning() to see how your warning will appear.

Of course, it's handy to know the arguments for the `formatwarning()` function. The following list provides a brief description of each argument.

➤ **Message:** The message you want to display to the user.

➤ **Category:** The warning category you want to use.

➤ **Filename:** The name of the file where the warning occurred (not necessarily the current file).

➤ **Line number:** In most cases, this value contains the line at which the warning is detected, which isn't always the line at which the warning occurs. For example, it's possible for a warning to appear at the end of a structure, rather than at the appropriate line within the structure.

➤ **Line of code:** An optional entry that shows the line of code at which the warning occurs. If you don't supply this argument, the `formatwarnings()` function defaults to a value of `None`. The IronPython implementation differs from the standard in this regard. According to the standard, the interpreter is supposed to read the file, obtain the correct line of code, and display the specified line when you don't provide the appropriate text.

Working with Categories

A warning *category* is a means of identifying a particular kind of warning. The category makes it possible to group like warnings together and reduces the risk that someone will misinterpret the meaning of a message. In short, a category is a way to pigeonhole a particular message so that others know what you intend. Of course, filtering considers the warning category, so you also need to use the correct category to ensure filtering works as expected. Table 12-3 contains a list of the warning message categories, including a general `Warning` class that you shouldn't ever use because it's too general.

TABLE 12-3: Warning Message Categories

CLASS	DESCRIPTION
DeprecationWarning	Used to display warnings about applications that use deprecated (outdated) features. Normally, these warnings provide an alternative feature you should use in place of the deprecated feature.

CLASS	DESCRIPTION
FutureWarning	Used to display warnings about applications that use features that will change sometime in the future. For example, the class, method, attribute, or function might change in an update of the Python specification. In most cases, you should keep the future update in mind, but not change your application today unless the new feature is available and debugged.
ImportWarning	Triggered when an application imports a module. The module is still usable and likely doesn't contain any problems (unless you see other warnings). The interpreter generally ignores these warnings.
PendingDeprecationWarning	Used to display warnings about applications that use features that will be deprecated sometime in the future (as opposed to the change indicated by the FutureWarning category). In most cases, you won't need to change your application immediately, but you should change it to use an updated feature soon.
RuntimeWarning	Specifies that one or more features are based on suspect runtime functionality (such as modules that aren't fully tested). In most cases, this warning indicates that your application is likely to fail more often or suffer other reliability issues.
SyntaxWarning	Indicates that the application will run, but that it contains some suspect syntax. Perhaps the syntax isn't approved or is simply non-standard. Finding standardized methods for creating the application syntax is a good way to avoid this warning.
UnicodeWarning	Triggered whenever an application experiences some problem with Unicode implementation. Although this warning may not affect some languages, it could affect languages that rely on an extended character set.
UserWarning	Provides the default category for the `warn()` function. This warning level is for issues related to user code. For example, input from a user code function is supposed to provide the location of a logging file on disk, but your module can't find the logging file. Your code won't fail without the information, but it can't create the logging information either.
Warning	Provides the implementation of all warning subclasses. It's a subclass of the `Exception` class. This is a warning category that you use to create new warning categories. There is never a good reason to use this category to generate warning messages.

The warning categories are used with almost every `warnings` module function. For example, you supply a category when setting a filter or creating a new message. There is always an exception. The `resetwarnings()` function doesn't require any input, not even a warning category, because it resets the entire warning environment to a default state.

OBTAINING ERROR INFORMATION

Errors will happen in your application, even if you use good exception handling. The handlers you create only react to the errors you know about. Applications also encounter unknown errors. In this case, your application has to have a way to obtain error information and display it to the user (or at least record it in a log file).

It's important to remember that you normally obtain error information in an application using the exception process described in the "Defining and Using Exceptions" section of this chapter. This section of the chapter is more designed for those situations where you need to work with a generic exception or obtain more detailed information than the specific exceptions provide.

As with many things, IronPython provides a number of methods for obtaining error information. In fact, you might be surprised at how many ways you can retrieve information once you really start looking. The following sections discuss the most common methods for obtaining error information.

Using the sys Module

The `sys` module contains a wealth of useful functions and attributes you use to obtain, track, and manage error information. One of the first things you should know about the `sys` module is that it contains the `sys.stderr` attribute, which defines where the interpreter sends error output. Normally, the output goes to the console window, but you can redirect the error output to any object that has a `write()` method associated with it, such as a file. If you want to later reset the `sys.stderr` attribute to the console, the `sys.__stderr__` attribute always contains the original output location, so using `sys.stderr = sys.__stderr__` performs a reset.

Obtaining error information seems like it should be straightforward, but it's harder than most developers initially think because obtaining error information often affects application execution in unforeseen ways. In addition, ensuring that the caller receives the right information in a multithreaded application is difficult. The caller could also make unfortunate changes to error information objects, such as the `traceback` object, creating problems with circular references that the garbage collector is unable to handle. Consequently, you find a lot of functions in `sys` that look like they should do something useful (and this section covers them), but the two functions you need to keep in mind when working with IronPython are.

➤ **sys.exc_info():** Returns a `tuple` containing three items:

➤ **type:** The type of the error, such as `ZeroDivisionError`. You can find a list of all standard exception types in the `exceptions` module.

➤ **value:** The human readable string that defines the error. For example, a `ZeroDivisionError` might provide `ZeroDivisionError('Attempted to divide by zero.',)` as a value.

➤ **traceback:** An object that describes the stack trace for an exception. Normally, you won't use this information directly unless you truly need to obtain the stack trace information, which can prove difficult. If you need stack trace information, consider using the `traceback` module features instead (see the "Using the traceback Module" section of this chapter for details).

➤ `sys.exc_clear()`: Clears the existing exceptions from the current thread. After you call this function, `sys.exc_info()` returns `None` for all three elements in the `tuple`.

The `sys.exc_info()` function isn't very hard to use, but you can't really try it out by executing it directly in the IronPython console. You need to place it within a `try...except` structure instead. The following code shows a quick demonstration you can type directly into the console window.

```
try:
    5/0
except:
    type, value = sys.exc_info()[:2]
    print type
    print value
```

The example uses a simple division by zero to create an exception. As previously noted, you normally need just the first two elements of the `tuple`, which you can obtain using `sys.exc_info()[:2]`. When you execute this code, you see the following output.

```
<type 'exceptions.ZeroDivisionError'>
Attempted to divide by zero.
```

Some IronPython `sys` module functions affect only the interactive thread (which means they're safe to use in multithreaded applications because there is only one interactive thread in any given session). You could use these functions to determine the current type, value, and `traceback` for an exception, but only for the interactive session, which means these functions are completely useless for your application. In most cases, you avoid using these three functions.

➤ `sys.last_traceback()`

➤ `sys.last_type()`

➤ `sys.last_value()`

You could run into problems when working with some functions in the `sys` module. For example, these three functions are global, which means they aren't specific to the current thread and are therefore, unsafe to use in a multithreaded application.

➤ `sys.exc_type()`

➤ `sys.exc_value()`

➤ `sys.exc_traceback()`

Interestingly enough, these three functions are also listed as deprecated (outdated) in most Python implementations (including IronPython). As with all IronPython modules, you also have access to low-level functions in the `sys` module. The following list is low-level modules you can use for special needs, but won't normally use in your application.

➤ **sys.excepthook(*type, value, traceback*):** The system calls this low-level function each time it generates an exception. To use this function, you supply the same tuple of values as you receive when you call `sys.exc_info()`.

➤ **sys._getframe([*depth*]):** The system calls this low-level function to display a frame object from the call stack. If the caller supplies a *depth* value, the frame object is at that call stack depth. The default *depth* value setting is 0. IronPython doesn't appear to implement this function, but you may encounter it in other versions of Python, so it pays to know about this function.

If you want to control how much information the interpreter provides when you request a `traceback`, you can always set the `sys.tracebacklimit` attribute. The `sys.tracebacklimit` attribute defaults to 1,000. It doesn't actually appear when you perform a `dir()` command. In fact, until you set it, printing the `sys.tracebacklimit` attribute returns an `AttributeError`. Use code like this

```
sys.tracebacklimit = 3
```

to modify the `traceback` level. Now when you try to print the `sys.tracebacklimit` attribute, you get back the value you supplied.

Using the traceback Module

The `traceback` module adds to the capabilities of the `sys` module described in the "Using the sys Module" section of the chapter. In addition, it adds to the standard exception handling capabilities of IronPython by making it easier to obtain complex information about exceptions in general. The `traceback` module does focus on `tracebacks`, which are the IronPython equivalent of a call stack.

The most common call is `traceback.print_exc()`. Essentially, this call prints out the current exception information. You can use it in a `try...except` structure, much as you'd use the `sys.exc_info()` function, but with fewer limitations. Figure 12-6 shows a typical view of the `traceback.print_exc()` function in action.

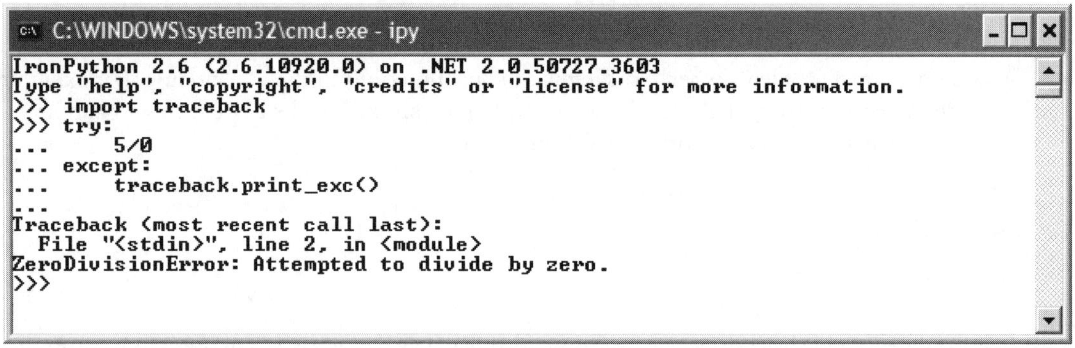

FIGURE 12-6: Obtain traceback information with ease using the traceback.print_exc() function.

You may find that you want a string that you can manipulate, rather than direct output. In this case, you use the `traceback.format_exc()` function and place its output in a variable. The information is the same as shown in Figure 12-6, but you have the full capability of string manipulation functions to output the information in any form desired.

All of the `traceback` output functions include a *level* argument that defines how many levels of trace information you want. The default setting provides 1,000 levels, which may be a little more information than you want. Many of the `traceback` output functions also include a *file* argument that accepts the name of a file you can use for output (such as application logging). If you don't provide the *file* argument, it defaults to using the `sys.stderr` device (normally the console).

Some of the `traceback` functions are macros for longer function combinations. For example, when you type `traceback.print_last()`, what you're really doing is executing `print_exception(sys.last_type, sys.last_value, sys.last_traceback, limit, file)`. Obviously, typing `traceback.print_last()` is a lot less work!

IronPython is missing some extremely important functionality when it comes to the `traceback` module. You can't use `traceback.print_stack()`, `traceback.extract_stack()`, or `traceback.format_stack()` to obtain current stack information. The code shown in Figure 12-7 is standard output when working with Python. Figure 12-8 shows what happens when you execute this code in IronPython. Instead of getting a nice stack trace you can use for debugging (see Figure 12-7), you get nothing at all (see Figure 12-8). This is a known issue (see the issue information at `http://ironpython.codeplex.com/WorkItem/View.aspx?WorkItemId=25543`).

```
Python (command line)                                                    _ □ ✕
Python 2.6.4 (r264:75708, Oct 26 2009, 08:23:19) [MSC v.1500 32 bit (Intel)] on
win32
Type "help", "copyright", "credits" or "license" for more information.
>>> import traceback
>>> def function1():
...     function2()
...
>>> def function2():
...     function3()
...
>>> def function3():
...     print 'Printing Stack'
...     traceback.print_stack()
...     print '\nExtracting Stack'
...     print repr(traceback.extract_stack())
...     print '\nFormatting Stack'
...     print repr(traceback.format_stack())
...
>>> function1()
Printing Stack
  File "<stdin>", line 1, in <module>
  File "<stdin>", line 2, in function1
  File "<stdin>", line 2, in function2
  File "<stdin>", line 3, in function3

Extracting Stack
[('<stdin>', 1, '<module>', None), ('<stdin>', 2, 'function1', None), ('<stdin>'
, 2, 'function2', None), ('<stdin>', 5, 'function3', None)]

Formatting Stack
['  File "<stdin>", line 1, in <module>\n', '  File "<stdin>", line 2, in functi
on1\n', '  File "<stdin>", line 2, in function2\n', '  File "<stdin>", line 7, i
n function3\n']
>>>
```

FIGURE 12-7: Python provides full stack information you can use for debugging.

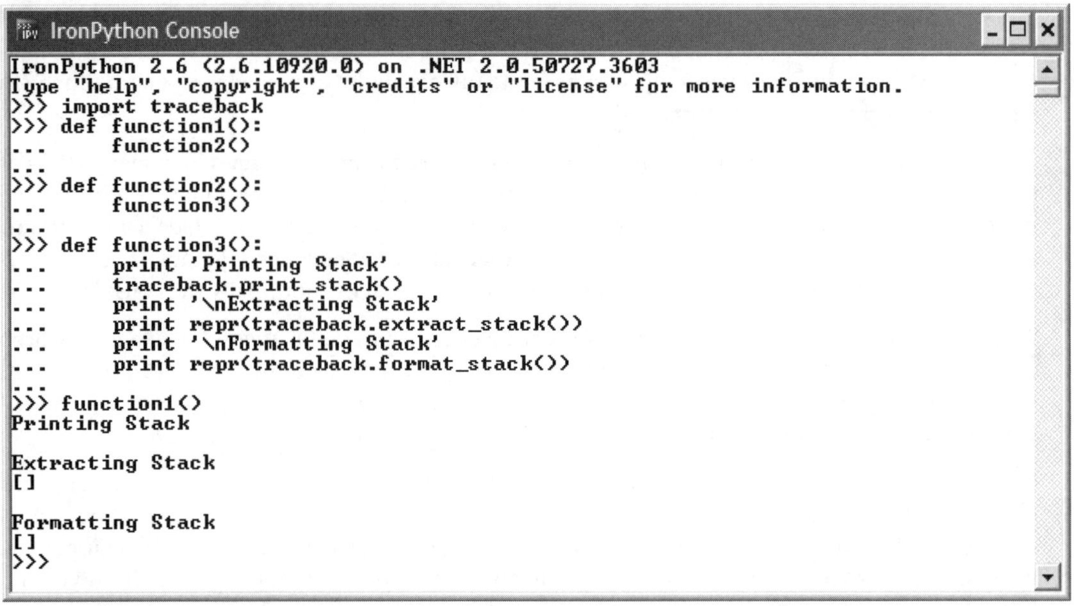

```
IronPython Console                                              _ □ ×
IronPython 2.6 (2.6.10920.0) on .NET 2.0.50727.3603
Type "help", "copyright", "credits" or "license" for more information.
>>> import traceback
>>> def function1():
...     function2()
...
>>> def function2():
...     function3()
...
>>> def function3():
...     print 'Printing Stack'
...     traceback.print_stack()
...     print '\nExtracting Stack'
...     print repr(traceback.extract_stack())
...     print '\nFormatting Stack'
...     print repr(traceback.format_stack())
...
>>> function1()
Printing Stack

Extracting Stack
[]

Formatting Stack
[]
>>>
```

FIGURE 12-8: IronPython lacks support for stack traces, making debugging significantly more difficult.

The traceback module contains a number of interesting functions that you can use to debug your application. You can see these functions described at http://docs.python.org/library/traceback .html. Don't assume that all of these functions work as they do in Python. There are currently a number of outstanding traceback module issues for IronPython.

DEBUGGING WITH THE PYTHON DEBUGGER

You might not know it, but Python and IronPython come with a debugger module, pdb (for Python debugger). Like any module, you have full access to the debugger source code and can modify it as needed. This section describes the default debugger performance.

It's possible to use pdb with any Python file by invoking the debugger at the command line using the –m command line switch. Here's how you'd invoke it for the example shown in Listing 12-1.

```
IPY -m pdb ShowFilters.py
```

Unfortunately, using this command line format limits what you can do with the debugger. Although you can single step through code, you can't work with variables easily and some other debugger commands may not work as anticipated.

The debugger works better if you configure your application to use a main() module. Most of the examples in this book don't use a main() function for the sake of simplicity, but you should use one for any production code you create. The ShowFilters2.py file contains the modifications to provide a `main()` function. Essentially, you encase the code in Listing 12-1 in the `main()` function and then call it using the following code:

```
# Create an entry point for debugging.
if __name__ == "__main__":
    main()
```

Using the debugger is very much like old-style DOS debuggers such as the Debug utility. You issue commands and the debugger responds without output based on the application environment and variable content. The lack of a visual display may prove troublesome to developers who have never used a character-mode debugger, but `pdb` is actually more effective than any of the graphical alternatives in helping you locate problems with your application — at least, in the Python code. Use these steps to start the `pdb`:

1. Start the IronPython console by selecting it from the Start menu or typing IPY at the command line.

2. Type `import pdb` and press Enter to import the Python debugger.

3. Type `import ApplicationName` where `ApplicationName` is the name of the file that contains your application and press Enter. For example, if your application appears in `ShowFilters2.py`, then you'd type `import ShowFilters2` (without the file extension) and press Enter.

4. Type `pdb.run('ApplicationName.FunctionName()')` where `ApplicationName` is the name of the application and `FunctionName` is the name of the function you want to test, and press Enter. For example, if your application is named `ShowFilters2` and the function you want to test is `main()`, you'd type `pdb.run('ShowFilters2.main()')` and press Enter. The standard console prompt changes to a `pdb` prompt, as shown in Figure 12-9.

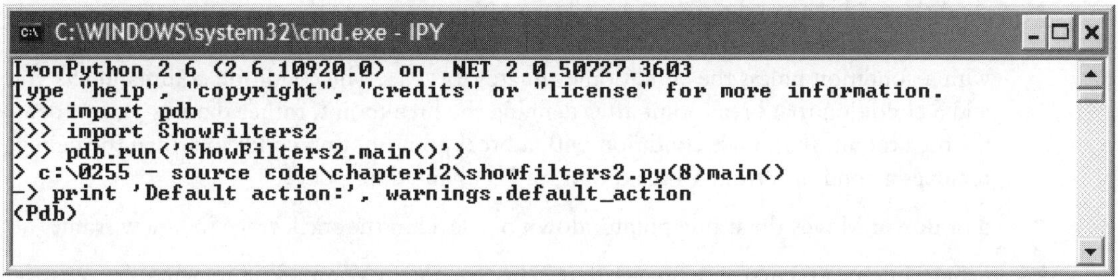

FIGURE 12-9: The Python debugger uses a special pdb prompt where you can enter debugging commands.

Now that you have a debugger prompt, you can begin debugging your application. Here is a list of standard debugger commands you can issue:

➤ **a or args:** Displays the list of arguments supplied to the current function. If there aren't any arguments, the call simply returns without displaying anything.

➤ **alias:** Creates an alias for a complex command. For example, you might need to use a `for` loop to drill down into a `list` to see its contents. You could use an alias to create a command to perform that task without having to write the complete code every time. An alias can include replaceable variables, just as you would use for a batch file.

➤ **b or break:** Defines a breakpoint when you supply a line number or a function name. When you provide a function name, the breakpoint appears at the first executable line within the function. If an application spans multiple files, you can specify a filename, followed by a colon, followed by a line number (no function name allowed), such as `ShowFilters2:1`. A breakpoint can also include a condition. To add the condition, follow the breakpoint specification with a comma and the condition you want to use, such as `ShowFilters2:2, Filter == None`. If you type just b or break, the debugger shows the current breakpoints. Use the `cl` or `clear` command to clear breakpoints you create.

➤ **bt, w, or where:** Prints a stack trace with the most current frame at the bottom of the list. You can use this feature to see how the application arrived at the current point of execution.

➤ **c, cont, or continue:** Continues application execution until the application ends or the debugger encounters a breakpoint.

➤ **cl or clear:** Clears one or more breakpoints. You can specify the breakpoint to clear by providing one or more breakpoint numbers separated by spaces. As an alternative, you can supply a line number or a filename and line number combination (where the filename and line number are separated by a colon).

➤ **commands:** Defines one or more commands that execute when the debugger arrives at a line of code specified by a breakpoint. You include the optional breakpoint as part of the commands command. If you don't supply a breakpoint, then the commands command refers to the last breakpoint you set. To stop adding commands to a breakpoint, simply type **end**. If you want to remove the commands for a breakpoint, type **commands**, press Enter, type **end**, and press Enter again. A command can consist of any interactive Python or debugger command. For example, if you want to automatically move to the next line of code, you'd simply add step as one of the commands.

➤ **condition:** Adds a condition to a breakpoint. You must supply a breakpoint number and a Boolean statement (in string format) as arguments. The debugger doesn't honor a breakpoint with a condition unless the condition evaluates to `True`. The condition command lets you add a condition to a breakpoint after defining the breakpoint, rather than as part of defining the breakpoint. If you use condition with a breakpoint, but no condition, then the debugger removes a condition from a breakpoint, rather than adding one.

➤ **d or down:** Moves the frame pointer down one level in the stack trace to a new frame.

➤ **debug:** Enters a recursive debugger that helps you debug complex statements.

➤ **disable:** Disables one or more breakpoints so that they still exist, but the debugger ignores them. You can separate multiple breakpoint numbers with spaces to disable a group of breakpoints at once.

➤ **enable:** Enables one or more breakpoints so that the debugger responds to them. You can separate multiple breakpoint numbers with spaces to enable a group of breakpoints at once. Enabling a breakpoint doesn't override any conditions that are set on the breakpoint. The condition must still evaluate to `True` before the debugger reacts to the breakpoint.

➤ **EOF:** Tells the debugger to handle the End of File (EOF) as a command. Normally, this means ending the debugger session once the debugger reaches EOF.

➤ **exit or q or quit:** Ends the debugging session. Make sure you type `exit`, and not `exit()`, which still ends the IronPython console session.

➤ **h or help:** Displays information about the debugger. If you don't provide an argument, help displays a list of available debugging commands. Adding an argument shows information about the specific debugging command.

➤ **ignore:** Creates a condition where the debugger ignores a breakpoint a specific number of times. For example, you might want to debug a loop with a breakpoint set at a specific line of code within the breakpoint. You could use the ignore command to ignore the first five times through the loop and stop at the sixth. You must supply a breakpoint number and a count to use this command. The debugger automatically ignores the breakpoint until the count is 0.

➤ **j or jump:** Forces the debugger to jump to the line of code specified as an argument.

➤ **l or list:** Displays the specified lines of code. If you don't supply any arguments with the command, the debugger displays 11 lines of code starting with the current line. When you supply just a starting point (a code line number), the debugger displays 11 lines of code starting with the starting point you specify. To control the listing completely, supply both a starting and ending point.

➤ **n or next:** Continues execution to the next line of code. If the current line of code is a function, the debugger executes all of the code within the function and stops at the next line of code in the current function. In sum, this command works much like a step over command in most other debuggers. (See return, step, and until for other stepping commands.)

➤ **p:** Prints the value of an expression as the debugger sees it. Don't confuse this command with the IronPython `print()` function, which prints an expression based on how IronPython sees it.

➤ **pp:** Performs a pretty print. Essentially, this command is the same as the p command, except that the debugger interprets any control characters within the output so that the output appears with line feeds, carriage returns, tabs, and other formatting in place.

➤ **r or return:** Continues execution until the current function returns. This command works much like a step out command in most other debuggers (see next, step, and until for other stepping commands).

➤ **restart:** Restarts the current application at the beginning so that you can retest it. The command lets you supply optional arguments that appear as part of the `sys.argv` attribute. This command preserves debugger history, breakpoints, actions, and options.

➤ **run:** Starts the application when used within Python as demonstrated earlier in this section. However, this command is simply an alias for restart when used within the debugger environment.

➤ **s or step:** Executes the current line of code and then moves to the next line of code, even if that line of code appears within another function. This command works much like a step into command in most other debuggers (see next, return, and until for other stepping commands).

➤ **tbreak:** Performs precisely like a break command, except that the debugger removes the breakpoint when the debugger stops at it the first time. This is a useful command when you want to execute a breakpoint just one time.

➤ **u or up:** Moves the frame pointer up one level in the stack trace to an old frame.

➤ **unalias:** Removes the specified alias (see the alias command for additional details).

➤ **unt or until:** Continues execution until such time as the line number is greater than the current line number or the current frame returns. This command works much like a combination of the step over and step out commands in most other debuggers (see next, return, and step for other stepping commands).

➤ **whatis:** Displays the type of the argument that you supply.

DEBUGGING WITH THE CLR DEBUGGER

The CLR debugger, `CLRDbg.EXE`, is part of the .NET Framework SDK. You find it in the `GuiDebug` folder of your .NET Framework installation or in the `\Program Files\Microsoft.NET\SDK\v2.0\GuiDebug\` folder. However, if you installed Visual Studio without installing the SDK, you might not see a `GuiDebug` folder. In this case, you can download and install the .NET Framework SDK separately. You can obtain the .NET Framework SDK for various platforms at these locations.

➤ **.NET Framework 2.0:** `http://msdn.microsoft.com/en-us/netframework/aa731542.aspx`

➤ **.NET Framework 3.0:** `http://msdn.microsoft.com/en-us/netframework/bb264589.aspx`

➤ **.NET Framework 3.5:** `http://msdn.microsoft.com/en-us/netframework/cc378097.aspx`

➤ **.NET Framework 3.5 SP1:** `http://msdn.microsoft.com/en-us/netframework/aa569263.aspx`

This section relies on the `CLRDbg.EXE` version found in the .NET Framework 2.0 SDK. However, the instructions work fine for every other version of the CLR debugger as well. The newer versions of the debugger may include a few additional features that you won't likely use or need when working with IronPython. The following steps describe how to start the debugger.

1. Start the CLR debugger. If you installed the .NET Framework SDK separately, choose Start ➪ Programs ➪ Microsoft .NET Framework SDK v2.0 ➪ Tools ➪ Microsoft CLR Debugger. It's also possible to start the CLR debugger from the command line by typing **CLRDbg** and pressing Enter as long as the debugger's location appears in the path. You see the Microsoft CLR Debugger window.

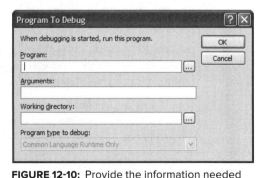

FIGURE 12-10: Provide the information needed to debug your application.

2. Choose Debug ➪ Program to Debug. You see the Program to Debug dialog box shown in Figure 12-10. This dialog box is where you enter the IronPython executable and script information, along with any command line switches you want to use.

3. Click the ellipsis (…) in the Program field and use the Find Program to Debug dialog box to locate the IPY.EXE file. Click Open to add the IPY.EXE information to the dialog box.

4. Type –D *NameOfScript*.py in the Arguments field (the example uses -D ShowFilters2 .py). Type any additional command line arguments you want to use while working with the application.

5. Click the ellipses in the Working Directory field and use the Browse for Working Directory dialog box to locate the script directory (not the IPY.EXE directory). Click Open to select the working directory.

6. Click OK. The CLR debugger prepares the debugging environment. However, you don't see any files opened. You must open any files you wish to interact with as a separate step.

7. Choose File ⇨ Open ⇨ File. Locate the source files you want to debug (ShowFilters2.py for the example). Click Open. You see the source file opened in the Microsoft CLR Debugger window. Figure 12-11 shows an example of how your display should look when working with the example. (The figure shows the debugger in debugging mode.)

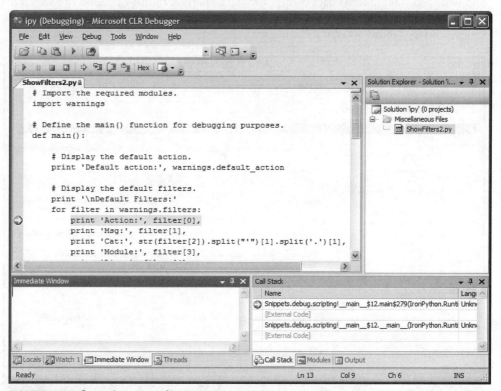

FIGURE 12-11: Open the source files you want to debug.

At this point, you can begin working with the script just as you would with the Visual Studio debugger. The next section, "Using Visual Studio for IronPython Debugging," discusses this debugger in more detail. Make sure you review the debugger basics described in the "Debugging the Project" section of Chapter 2 as well.

USING VISUAL STUDIO FOR IRONPYTHON DEBUGGING

When you create a project for your IronPython application using the techniques described in the "Using Visual Studio to Create IronPython Applications" section of Chapter 2, you also have access to the Visual Studio debugger. The "Debugging the Project" section of Chapter 2 provides a good overview of the functionality you have available to you. However, working with the ShowFilters2 example can provide a few additional insights not found in Chapter 2.

As mentioned in Chapter 2, you can set breakpoints, use the History window, and set watches for your application. It's the watches that really shine when working with complex objects. For example, set a breakpoint at this line of code.

```
print 'Action:', filter[0]
```

When you click Start Debugging, the debugger stops at the line of code as you might expect. Now, create a watch for both `filter` and `filters`. As shown in Figure 12-12, you can drill down into a complex object and examine it. In many cases, you must look through the Non-Public Members to find what you want, but the data is there for you to peruse. In this case, you can see all five elements in `filters` and even see the `pattern` data. Notice that the Type column is truly helpful in showing you which types to use when interacting with the data.

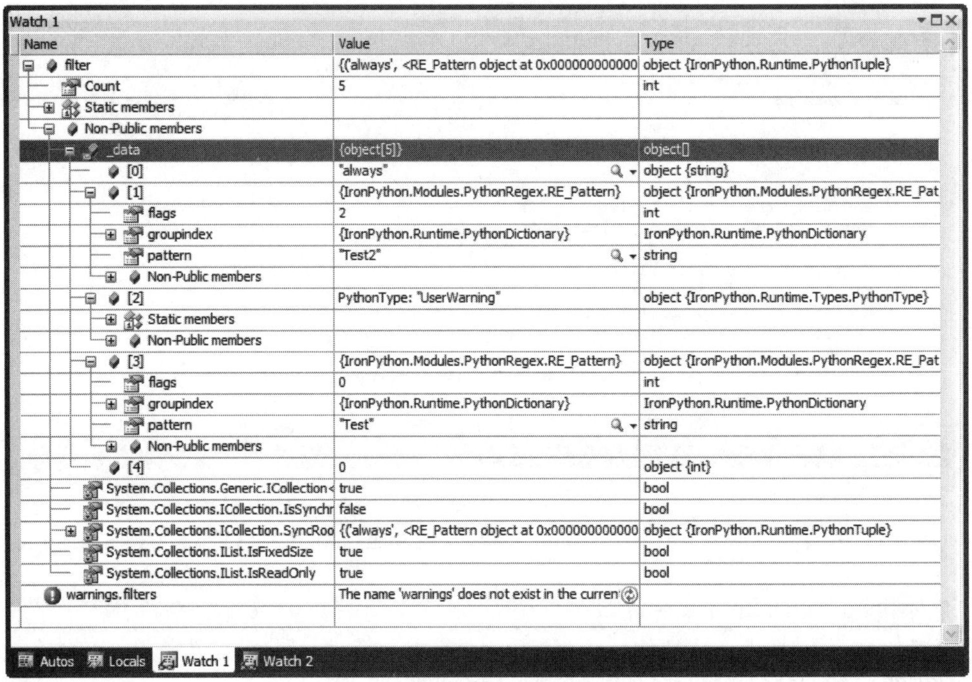

FIGURE 12-12: Watches let you drill down into both Python and .NET data.

Unfortunately, Figure 12-12 also shows the other side of the coin. You can't access `warnings`
`.filters` even though it should be available. The Visual Studio debugger often produces poor

results when working with Python-specific objects. If you have a need for working with these objects, the Python debugger described in the "Debugging with the Python Debugger" section of this chapter is a better choice.

If you're used to working with the Immediate window while debugging, it does have some use when working with IronPython. As shown in Figure 12-13, you can use the Immediate window to query objects directly. However, you can't drill down into an object as you might have in the past. Consequently, entering **? filter** works just fine, but entering **? filter[0]** doesn't.

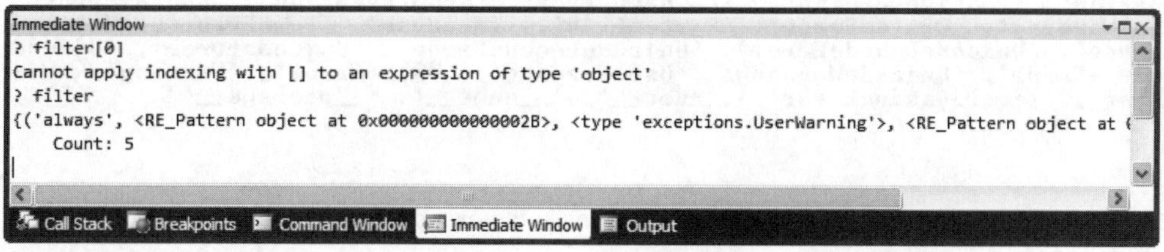

```
Immediate Window                                                              ▾ □ ×
? filter[0]
Cannot apply indexing with [] to an expression of type 'object'
? filter
{('always', <RE_Pattern object at 0x000000000000002B>, <type 'exceptions.UserWarning'>, <RE_Pattern object at (
    Count: 5
```

🔁 Call Stack 🔲 Breakpoints 🔲 Command Window 🔲 Immediate Window 🔲 Output

FIGURE 12-13: The Immediate window is only partially useful when working with IronPython.

In general, you'll find that using the Python debugger works better for some Python-specific applications. Even though the Visual Studio debugger does provide a nice visual display, the quality of information isn't quite as good. Of course, the picture changes when your application mixes Python and .NET code. In this case, the Visual Studio debugger can be your best friend because it knows how to work with the .NET objects.

DEFINING AND USING EXCEPTIONS

Exceptions are an essential part of any application. In fact, most developers have no problem using them at all. Unfortunately, many developers also misuse exceptions. Instead of providing robust code that handles common problems, the developer simply raises an exception and hopes someone else does something about the issue. Exceptions are generally used to address conditions that you couldn't anticipate.

IronPython provides access to both Python exception and .NET exceptions, so the developer actually has twice as many opportunities to catch errors before they become a problem. It's important to use the correct kind of exception handling. If you're working with .NET code, you'll normally use a .NET exception. Python exceptions address anything that isn't .NET-specific. The following sections provide additional information about exceptions.

Implementing Python Exceptions

Python provides a number of standard exceptions, just as the .NET Framework does. You find these exceptions in the `exceptions` module. To see the list of standard exceptions, import the `exceptions` module and perform a `dir()` command on it, as shown in Figure 12-14.

```
IronPython Console                                              _ □ ×
IronPython 2.6 (2.6.10920.0) on .NET 2.0.50727.3603
Type "help", "copyright", "credits" or "license" for more information.
>>> import exceptions
>>> dir(exceptions)
['ArithmeticError', 'AssertionError', 'AttributeError', 'BaseException', 'Buffer
Error', 'BytesWarning', 'DeprecationWarning', 'EOFError', 'EnvironmentError', 'E
xception', 'FloatingPointError', 'FutureWarning', 'GeneratorExit', 'IOError', 'I
mportError', 'ImportWarning', 'IndentationError', 'IndexError', 'KeyError', 'Key
boardInterrupt', 'LookupError', 'MemoryError', 'NameError', 'NotImplementedError
', 'OSError', 'OverflowError', 'PendingDeprecationWarning', 'ReferenceError', 'R
untimeError', 'RuntimeWarning', 'StandardError', 'StopIteration', 'SyntaxError',
 'SyntaxWarning', 'SystemError', 'SystemExit', 'TabError', 'TypeError', 'Unbound
LocalError', 'UnicodeDecodeError', 'UnicodeEncodeError', 'UnicodeError', 'Unicod
eTranslateError', 'UnicodeWarning', 'UserWarning', 'ValueError', 'Warning', 'Win
dowsError', 'ZeroDivisionError', '__doc__', '__name__', '__package__']
>>>
```

FIGURE 12-14: Python stores its list of standard exceptions in the exceptions module.

The various exceptions provide different amounts of information. For example, when working with
an IOError, you can access the errno, filename, message, and strerror attributes. On the other
hand, a ZeroDivisionError provides only the message attribute. You can use the dir(exceptions
.ExceptionName) command to obtain information about each of the exception attributes.

As with .NET, you can create custom exceptions using Python. The documentation for creating
a custom exception is a bit sketchy, but you can create a custom exception (usually with the word
Error in the name by convention) for every need. Listing 12-2 shows all of the Python exception
basics, including creating a relatively flexible custom exception.

LISTING 12-2: Discovering the default action and installed filters

```
# Import the required modules.
import exceptions

# Define a custom exception.
class MyError(exceptions.Exception):
    errno = 0
    message = 'Nothing'
    def __init__(self, errno=0, message='Nothing'):
        self.errno = errno
        self.message = message
    def __str__(self):
        return repr(self.message)

# Display the Error exception list.
for Error in dir(exceptions):
    if 'Error' in Error:
        print Error

# Create a standard exception.
try:
    5/0
```

```
    except ZeroDivisionError as (errinfo):
        print "\nDivide by Zero error: {0}".format(errinfo)

    # Create a custom exception.
    try:
        raise MyError(5, 'Hello from MyError')
    except MyError, Info:
        print "Custom Error({0}): {1}".format(Info.errno, Info.message)

    # Pause after the debug session.
    raw_input('\nPress any key to continue...')
```

The code begins by importing exceptions. The for loop lists all of the exceptions
(the names of the types) found in exceptions, as shown in Figure 12-15. Notice how the code uses
if 'Error' in Error to locate just the exceptions in the module. This technique is useful for a lot
of tasks in IronPython where you need to filter the output in some way.

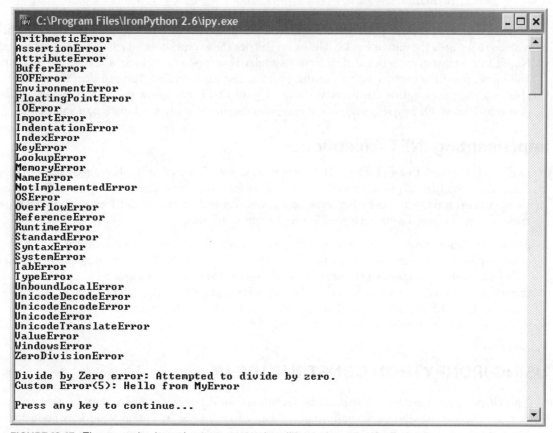

FIGURE 12-15: The example shows basic exception handling and creation for Python.

The next bit of code raises a standard exception and then handles it. The output shows just a message.
Notice that this exception relies on the as clause to access the error information.

It's time to look at a custom exception, which begins with the `MyError` class definition. At a minimum, you should define both __init__() and __str__() or the exception won't work as intended. Notice how __init__() assigns default values to both `errno` and `message`. You can't depend on the caller to provide this information, so including default values is the best way to approach the problem. You can always assign other values later in the code based on the actual errors.

Make sure you create attributes for any amplifying information you want the caller to have. In this case, the example defines two attributes `errno` and `message`.

The __str__() method should return a human-readable message. You can return just the text portion of the exception or return some combination of exception attributes. The important thing is to return something that the developer will find useful should the exception occur. You can test this behavior out with the example by typing `raise MyError`. Here's the output you'll see.

```
Traceback (most recent call last):
  File "<stdin>", line 1, in <module>
__main__.MyError: 'Nothing'
```

Because you didn't provide any arguments, the output shows the default values. Try various combinations to see how the output works. The example tries the exception in a `try...except` statement. Notice that a custom exception differs from a standard exception in that you don't use the `as` clause and simply provide a comma with a variable (`Info` in this case) instead. You can then use the variable to access the exception attributes as shown. Figure 12-15 shows how the custom exception outputs information. Of course, your custom exception can provide any combination of values.

Implementing .NET Exceptions

In general, you want to avoid using .NET exceptions in your IronPython applications, except in those cases where you need to provide specific functionality for .NET code. The problem is that IronPython views such exceptions from a Python perspective. Consequently, trapping .NET exceptions can prove tricky unless you spend some time working with them in advance.

Many .NET exceptions are available in the `System` assembly so you need to import it before you can perform any serious work. After that, you can `raise` a .NET exception much as you do a Python exception. Handling the exception follows the same route as using a `try...except` statement. However, the problem is that the exception you get isn't the exception you raised. Look at Figure 12-16 and you see that the `ArgumentException` becomes a `ValueError` and the `ArithmeticException` becomes an `ArithmeticError`.

USING IRONPYTHON CONSTRUCTIVELY

This chapter has shown you some practical techniques for debugging your IronPython application. In some respects, IronPython actually makes things easier for you by forcing you to use good coding practice to write your applications. Sloppy programming will cost you so much time as to make the programming experience a nightmare. Using a combination of warnings, error trapping, and exceptions will make your code significantly easier to debug. Of course, choosing the right debugging tool is also a requirement if you want to go home this weekend, rather than spending it in your office debugging your latest application.

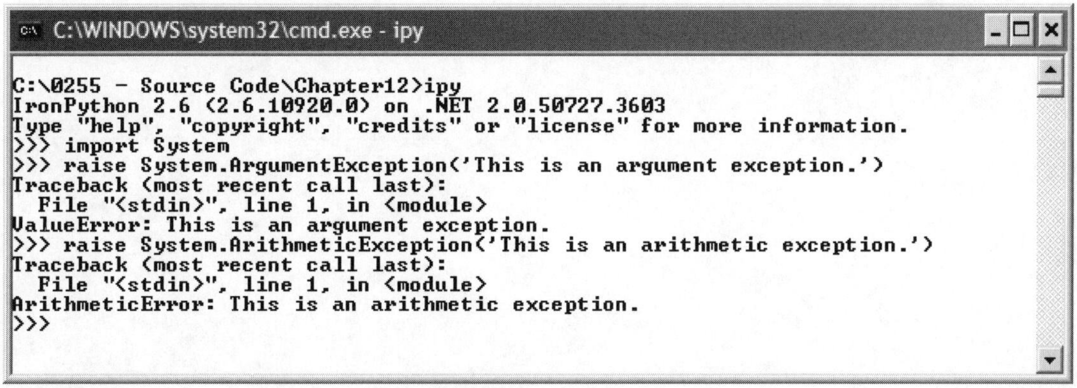

FIGURE 12-16: IronPython tends to change the name of .NET exceptions.

You'll get plenty of practice debugging applications. Even experts create applications that don't behave as expected. However, sometimes it's educational to create an application that you use to experiment. Write the application, make sure it doesn't actually contain any bugs, and then introduce bugs to see how various tools work in finding them. Working with known bugs can help you discover what unknown bugs look like based on their pattern. Fixing known bugs also helps you discover new techniques for handling bugs so that you can locate and repair bugs in production applications faster.

Chapter 13 begins a new part of the book. In this part, you begin working through some advanced IronPython capabilities — some of which you can also perform in Python (such as reading and writing XML), and some that might prove difficult when working with Python (such as interacting with another .NET language). Chapter 13 begins simply by working through the intricacies of XML development. You'll find that IronPython provides many methods of working with XML. Of course, you might find uses for the debugging techniques covered in this chapter as you work through these advanced IronPython topics.

PART IV
Advanced IronPython Topics

13

Working with XML Data

WHAT'S IN THIS CHAPTER?

➤ Interacting with XML using the .NET XML classes

➤ Interacting with XML using the XMLUtil module

➤ Interacting with XML using the Python modules

The eXtensible Markup Language (XML) is one of the easiest ways to move data between systems without losing the data context. (Although every system on the planet accepts text data, you can't incorporate context with text data.) In addition, Web services and many applications use XML as an essential data storage strategy. In short, anyone writing an application today is bound to run into some form of XML. Fortunately, IronPython provides robust XML handling capabilities that don't require you to jump through too many hoops (unlike some languages that make it nearly impossible to perform some XML tasks).

When working with IronPython, you have three choices for working with XML: the .NET Framework, XMLUtil, and Python modules. This chapter provides an overview of all three techniques. When you finish this chapter, you should have a good idea of what each technique can do for you and understand the basics of using each technique.

XML comes in a number of forms. In fact, XML comes in so many forms that it would be quite easy to write an entire book on just one of the techniques described in this chapter, much less all three. Consequently, you shouldn't consider this chapter the end of the IronPython XML experience. Rather, you should consider it a good start that you can use to find additional information that meets your specific programming needs. The chapter does provide online references as needed to help you obtain more information about IronPython's support for XML.

USING THE .NET XML FUNCTIONALITY

If you know how to work with XML in .NET languages such as C#, then you already know how to perform the same tasks in IronPython because you can import the System.Xml assembly to gain full access to this functionality. Because the XML capabilities of the .NET Framework are so well defined, using the System.Xml assembly may be all you need to perform tasks within your application. The main issue to consider is how you plan to use your application later. For example, if you plan to move your application to another platform, then using the .NET Framework solution won't work. In addition, you need to consider data type translation in IronPython. The .NET data types that you use normally are translated into their IronPython counterparts, which could prove confusing for some developers. With these factors in mind, the following sections provide an overview of XML support in the .NET Framework from the IronPython perspective.

Considering the System.Xml Namespace

The System.Xml namespace provides access to the various classes used to interact with XML data. You use these classes to read, write, interpret, edit, build, and otherwise manage XML data. For example, you might use the XmlDeclaration class to begin building an XML data file from scratch when needed. All of these classes depend heavily on standards to ensure the file you create using IronPython is readable by other languages and applications. In fact, the System.Xml namespace supports these standards and specifications.

➤ **XML 1.0 (including Document Type Definition, DTD, support):** http://www.w3.org/TR/1998/REC-xml-19980210

➤ **XML Namespaces (both stream level and Document Object Model, DOM):** http://www.w3.org/TR/REC-xml-names/

➤ **XSD Schemas:** http://www.w3.org/2001/XMLSchema

➤ **XPath expressions:** http://www.w3.org/TR/xpath

➤ **XSLT transformations:** http://www.w3.org/TR/xslt

➤ **DOM Level 1 Core:** http://www.w3.org/TR/REC-DOM-Level-1/

➤ **DOM Level 2 Core:** http://www.w3.org/TR/DOM-Level-2/

Developing a Basic .NET XML Application

A .NET XML application will follow most of the same principles you use when working with a static language such as C# or Visual Basic.NET. In fact, you might not notice much difference at all except for the obvious structural requirements of a Python application. Consequently, you should find it easy to move your XML code over to IronPython because you really don't have anything new to worry about. Listing 13-1 shows a simple XML application that creates an XML document, saves it to disk, reads it from disk, and then displays the content onscreen.

DOM-ONLY SUPPORT IN THE .NET FRAMEWORK

It's important to note that the .NET Framework supports DOM and not Simple API for XML (SAX). However, if you want SAX support, you can use the Python modules instead (see the "Working with xml.sax" section of this chapter). XML files include both data and context. In order to reconstruct the original dataset described by an XML file, you need a parser to read the text and then convert it to a usable object. DOM and SAX represent two different methods for interacting with XML documents without forcing the developer to create a parser. If you want more information about the DOM versus SAX approach to parsing XML parsers, check out the information at `http://developerlife.com/tutorials/?p=28` and `http://www.jamesh.id.au/articles/libxml-sax/libxml-sax.html`. Here's a summary of the DOM features.

➤ Object-based.

➤ Object module is created automatically.

➤ Element sequencing is preserved.

➤ High memory usage.

➤ Slow initial data retrieval.

➤ Best for complex data structures.

➤ In-memory document updates are supported.

SAX takes a completely different approach than DOM. Here's a summary of the SAX features.

➤ Event-based.

➤ Object module is created by the application.

➤ Element sequencing is ignored in favor of single events.

➤ Low memory usage.

➤ Fast initial data retrieval.

➤ Best for simple data structures.

➤ No document updates.

LISTING 13-1: Reading and writing an XML document

```
# Import clr to add references.
import clr

# Add the required reference.
clr.AddReference('System.Xml')
```

continues

LISTING 13-1 *(continued)*

```
# Import the System.Xml classes.
from System.Xml import *

# This function creates the document and writes it to disk.
def CreateDocument():

    # Create a document.
    Doc = XmlDocument()

    # Add the XML Declaration.
    Declaration = Doc.CreateXmlDeclaration('1.0', 'utf-8', 'yes')
    Doc.AppendChild(Declaration)

    # Create the root node.
    Root = Doc.CreateNode(XmlNodeType.Element, 'root', None)

    # Add child elements to the root.
    MsgNode = Doc.CreateNode(XmlNodeType.Element, 'Message', None)
    MsgNode.InnerXml = 'Hello'
    Root.AppendChild(MsgNode)

    MsgNode = Doc.CreateNode(XmlNodeType.Element, 'Message', None)
    MsgNode.InnerXml = 'Goodbye'
    Root.AppendChild(MsgNode)

    # Add the root node to the document.
    Doc.AppendChild(Root)

    # Save the document to disk.
    Doc.Save('Test.XML')

def DisplayDocument():

    # Create a document.
    XMLDoc = XmlDocument()

    # Load the XML data.
    XMLDoc.Load('Test.XML')

    # Process the document.
    for Nodes in XMLDoc:
        if type(Nodes) == XmlElement:
            for MsgNodes in Nodes:
                print 'Message:', MsgNodes.InnerXml

# Interact with an XML document.
CreateDocument()
DisplayDocument()

# Pause after the debug session.
raw_input('\nPress any key to continue...')
```

The code begins by importing `clr`, which the application uses to add the required reference to `System.Xml` using the `clr.AddReference()` method. The code then imports the `System.Xml` classes.

The example relies on two functions to keep the code simple: `CreateDocument()`, which creates and saves the document to disk, and `DisplayDocument()`, which reads the document from disk and displays the content on screen. The example calls each of these functions in turn.

The `CreateDocument()` function begins by creating an `XmlDocument` object, `Doc`. As with any .NET application, `Doc` doesn't contain anything when you create it. The first task is to add the XML declarations so that the result is a well-formed XML document using `Doc.CreateXmlDeclaration()`. Calling `Doc.AppendChild()` adds the declaration to the document.

Now it's time to create some content. All XML documents have a root node, which is `Root` for this example. The code creates `Root` using `Doc.CreateNode()` with an `XmlNodeType.Element` type and `'root'` for a name. The example doesn't work with XML namespaces, so the third argument is set to `None`.

The most efficient way to create an XML document from scratch is to add all the child nodes to `Root` before you add `Root` to the document. The code creates `MsgNode` using the same technique as for `Root`. It adds content to `MsgNode` using the `MsgNode.InnerXml` property and then adds the node to `Root` using `Root.AppendChild()`. The example provides two `'Message'` nodes.

At this point, the code adds `Root` to the document using `Doc.AppendChild()`. It then saves the document to disk using `Doc.Save()`. Figure 13-1 shows the typical output from this example when viewed in Notepad (you can use any text editor to view the output because the `Doc.Save()` method includes spaces and line feeds).

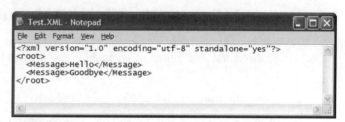

FIGURE 13-1: The XML document output looks much as you might expect.

The `DisplayDocument()` function begins by creating a document, `XMLDoc`, using the `XmlDocument` class constructor. It then loads the previously created XML document using `XMLDoc.Load()`. At this point, `XMLDoc` contains everything the code created earlier and you can easily explore it using the IronPython console.

If you've worked with XML documents using C# or Visual Basic.NET, you know that these languages sometimes make it hard to get to the data you really want. IronPython makes things very easy. All you need is a `for` loop, as shown in the code. Simple `if` statements make it easy to locate nodes of a particular type, `XmlElement` in this case.

By the time the code reaches the second `for` loop, it's working with the `'Message'` elements. The code simply prints the `MsgNodes.InnerXml` property value to the screen, as shown in Figure 13-2. By now you can see that IronPython makes it incredibly simple to work with XML documents using the .NET Framework approach.

FIGURE 13-2: The example outputs the message content in the XML document.

USING XMLUTIL

The IronPython `Tutorial` directory contains an interesting module, `XMLUtil.py`. Normally, a tutorial module wouldn't require much discussion in a book because the tutorial modules normally address the special need of teaching someone how to use IronPython. This module is a little different, however, because you could possibly use it in an application to reduce the work you must perform. It's important to remember that `XMLUtil.py` is a tutorial script, so you should make a copy of it and modify it as needed to meet specific needs in your application. The following sections describe `XMLUtil.py` in more detail.

Loading and Viewing the XMLUtil Module

The example in this section assumes that you've loaded the `XMLUtil` module from the IronPython `Tutorial` directory. The following steps show you how to load this module manually so you can see the content.

1. Open the IronPython console.

2. Type `import sys` and press Enter. This command imports the `sys` module so that you can add the required directory to it.

3. Type `sys.path.append('C:/Program Files/IronPython 2.6/Tutorial')` and press Enter (make sure you change the path information to match the location of your IronPython installation). The `XMLUtil.py` module exists in the `Tutorial` directory. Using this module is fine for experimentation, but be sure you copy the `XMLUtil.py` module to another location for other uses.

 Remember that you can use forward slashes (/) for a path to avoid using double backslashes (\\). Either form works fine with IronPython, but the forward slashes tend to be easier to read.

4. Type `print sys.path` and press Enter. You should see the new path added to the list.

5. Type `import XMLUtil` and press Enter. This step makes the `XMLUtil.py` module available for use.

6. Type `dir(XMLUtil)` and press Enter. You see the list of methods available in `XMLUtil` (as shown in Figure 13-3), which includes the `Walk()` method used in the example.

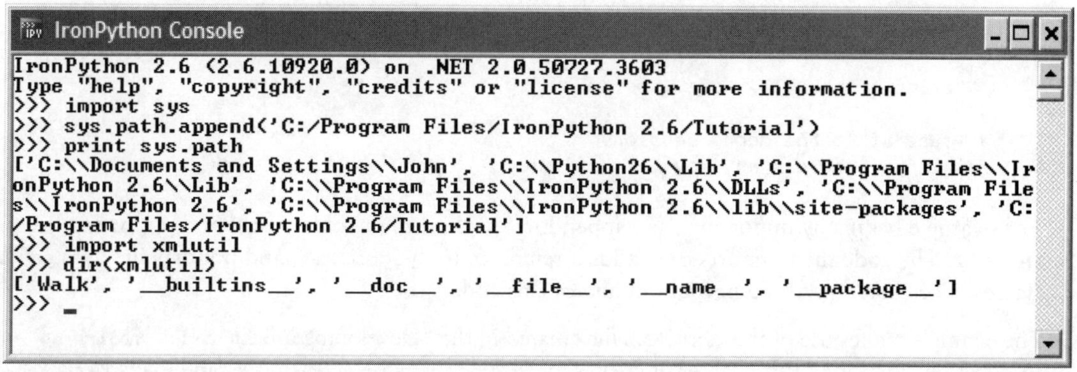

IronPython Console

```
IronPython 2.6 (2.6.10920.0) on .NET 2.0.50727.3603
Type "help", "copyright", "credits" or "license" for more information.
>>> import sys
>>> sys.path.append('C:/Program Files/IronPython 2.6/Tutorial')
>>> print sys.path
['C:\\Documents and Settings\\John', 'C:\\Python26\\Lib', 'C:\\Program Files\\Ir
onPython 2.6\\Lib', 'C:\\Program Files\\IronPython 2.6\\DLLs', 'C:\\Program File
s\\IronPython 2.6', 'C:\\Program Files\\IronPython 2.6\\lib\\site-packages', 'C:
/Program Files/IronPython 2.6/Tutorial']
>>> import xmlutil
>>> dir(xmlutil)
['Walk', '__builtins__', '__doc__', '__file__', '__name__', '__package__']
>>> _
```

FIGURE 13-3: The Walk() method makes viewing XML data easier.

Using the XMLUtil Module to View XML Data

As previously mentioned, the XMLUtil.py file isn't anything so advanced that you couldn't put it together yourself, but it's an interesting module to work with and use. Listing 13-2 shows a short example of how you could use this module in an application.

Available for download on Wrox.com

LISTING 13-2: Walking an XML document using XMLUtil

```python
# Add the path required to import xmlutil.
import sys
sys.path.append('C:/Program Files/IronPython 2.6/Tutorial')

# Import xmlutil to access the Walk() function.
import xmlutil

# Import clr to add references.
import clr

# Add the required reference.
clr.AddReference('System.Xml')

# Import the System.Xml classes.
from System.Xml import *

# Create a document.
XMLDoc = XmlDocument()

# Load the XML data.
XMLDoc.Load('Test.XML')

# Walk the file contents.
print 'Contents of Test.XML'
for Node in xmlutil.Walk(XMLDoc):
    print '\nName:', Node.Name
    print 'Value:', Node.Value
```

continues

LISTING 13-2 *(continued)*

```
    print 'InnerXml', Node.InnerXml

# Pause after the debug session.
raw_input('\nPress any key to continue...')
```

The example begins by importing `sys`, appending the `Tutorial` folder path, and importing `XMLUtil`. The code then imports `clr`, adds a reference to `System.Xml`, and imports the `System.Xml` classes. There isn't anything new about any of this code.

The example makes use of the `Text.XML` file created in the "Developing a Basic .NET XML Application" section of this chapter. It creates an `XmlDocument` object, `XMLDoc`, and loads `Text.XML` into it using the `XMLDoc.Load()` method. At this point, you have an XML document that you can walk (go from node-to-node and examine). The `XMLUtil.Walk()` method can walk any sort of XML document, so you should try it out with other files after you've worked with the example for a while.

The next step is to call on `XMLUtil.Walk()` to walk the XML document for you. The example shows output from the `Name`, `Value`, and `InnerXml` properties. However, you have access to all the properties provided for the various XML data types that the .NET Framework provides. Consequently, you can use `XMLUtil.Walk()` to display any information needed, or to manage that information. Just because the example displays properties doesn't mean you have any limitation on how you interact with the output of `XMLUtil.Walk()`. Figure 13-4 shows the output of this example.

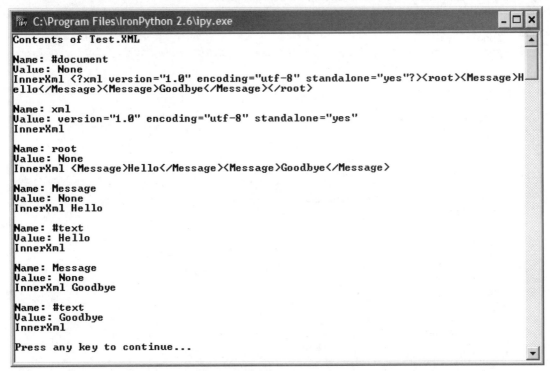

FIGURE 13-4: Screen shows the output of the Walk() method for Test.XML.

The `XMLUtil.Walk()` function is so important because it demonstrates a Python generator (described later in the section when you have the required background). Most languages don't provide support for generators, so they require a little explanation. The issue at the center of this whole discussion is the variant list. You know that an application will need to process some number of items during run time, but you have no idea of how long this list is or whether the list will exist at all. A *producer* function is one that outputs values one at a time in response to a request. The producer keeps processing items until it runs out, so the length of the list is no longer a concern (even if the list contains no items at all). Most languages rely on a *callback*, an address to the requestor, to provide a place to send the producer output. The problem with using a callback is that the code must provide some means of retaining state information to remember previous values. In some cases, using callbacks leads to unnatural, convoluted coding techniques that are hard to write, harder to understand, and nearly impossible to update later.

Developers have a number of alternatives they can use. For example, the developer could simply use a very large `list`. However, `list`s require that the developer know what values should appear in the `list` during design time, and lists can consume large quantities of memory, making them a less than helpful solution in many cases. Another solution is to use an `iterator` to perform the task. Using an `iterator` makes it easier to get out of a loop when the processing is finished and eliminates the memory requirements. However, using an `iterator` shifts the burden of maintaining state information to the producer, complicating an already difficult programming task because the producer may not know anything about the caller. There are other solutions, as well, such as running the requestor and producer on separate threads so that each object can maintain state information without worrying about the potential corruption that occurs when running the code on a single thread. Unfortunately, multithreaded applications can run slowly and require a platform that fully supports multithreading, making your application less portable. In short, most languages don't provide a good solution to the problem of working with data of variant length.

A *generator* creates a situation where the producer continuously outputs individual results as in a loop, maintaining its state locally. The requestor actually views the function as a type of `iterator`, even though the producer isn't coded to provide an `iterator`. To accomplish this task, Python provides the `yield` statement shown in Figure 13-5. The `yield` statement returns an intermediate result from the producer to the requestor, while the producer continues to process a list of items.

The code in Figure 13-5 begins with the definition of a function named `Walk()`. This function accepts some kind of XML as input. The first `yield` statement sends the entire `xml` input back to the requestor (the example application shown in Listing 13-2). Consequently, you see `#document` as the `Name` and the entire XML document as the `InnerXml`.

The second call to `Walk()` moves past the first `yield` statement. Because the second item doesn't meet the `hasattr(xml, "Attributes")` requirement, the code moves onto the loop statement at the bottom of the code listing shown in Figure 13-5. The effect of this loop is to obtain the child elements of the entire document. So the second call to `Walk()` ends with `yield c`, which returns the XML declaration element. As a result, you see `xml` for the `Name`, `version="1.0" encoding="utf-8" standalone="yes"` for the `Value`, and nothing for the `InnerXml`. This second call ends processing of the XML declaration.

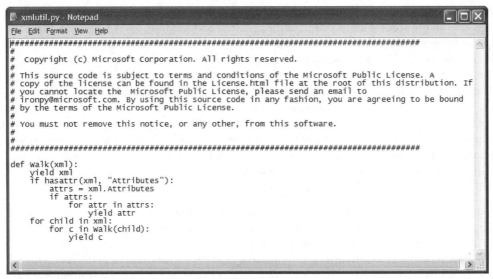

FIGURE 13-5: The XMLUtil.Walk() function is interesting because it provides a generator.

The third call to Walk() begins processing of the root node. It's interesting to trace through the code in the debugger because you see the for loops in XMLUtil.Walk() used to trace through each element of the input xml as if it were using recursion or perhaps some type of iteration, but the fact is that the code merely combines the for loop with a yield statement to feed each partial result back to the requestor. Using the Python debugger is actually a bit more helpful in this case than using the Visual Studio debugger because the Visual Studio debugger won't show you the value of xml, child, or c so that you can see the changing values. The example code for this book includes XMLUtilDemo2.py for the purpose of using the Python debugger. Follow these steps to load the debugger so you can trace through the example yourself.

1. Open the IronPython console.

2. Type import sys and press Enter. This command imports the sys module so that you can add the required directory to it.

3. Type sys.path.append('C:/Program Files/IronPython 2.6/Tutorial') and press Enter (make sure you change the path information to match the location of your IronPython installation).

4. Type import XMLUtil and press Enter to import the support file (important if you want to see how the generator works).

5. Type import XMLUtilDemo2 and press Enter to import the source code file.

6. Type import pdb and press Enter to import the debugger.

7. Type pdb.run('XMLUtilDemo2.main()') to start the debugger. At this point, you can single step through the code to see how everything works. The "Debugging with the Python Debugger" section of Chapter 12 provides additional details.

USING THE PYTHON MODULES

At one point, the Python modules were stable and straightforward to use, but later versions are less stable and, when it comes to IronPython, may be missing required elements completely. Consequently, you might see tutorials such as the one at `http://www.boddie.org.uk/python/XML_intro.html` and wonder why they don't work. These tutorials are based on earlier versions of Python and don't account for the missing CPython elements in IronPython. The following sections describe how to overcome these problems in your application when you use the Python approach to XML file management in IronPython.

Working with xml.dom.minidom

The `xml.dom.minidom` module is designed to help you work with XML using the DOM approach. However, this module is far from complete in IronPython, partly due to the CPython support required in standard Python. The actual document support is complete, so you won't have a problem building, editing, and managing XML documents. It's the write and read support that are lacking.

Fortunately, you can overcome write issues by using a different approach to outputting the document to disk (or other media). Standard Python development practice is to use the `xml.dom.ext.PrettyPrint()` method, which simply doesn't exist in IronPython. You get around the problem by performing the task in two steps, rather than one, as shown in Listing 13-3.

The reading problem isn't as easy to solve. Standard Python development practice is to use the `xml.dom.minidom.parse()` method. This method does exist in IronPython, but it outputs an error stating

```
ImportError: No module named pyexpat
```

This module actually is missing. In order to fix this problem, you must download the `pyexpat.py` file from `https://fepy.svn.sourceforge.net/svnroot/fepy/trunk/lib/`. Place this file in your `\Program Files\IronPython 2.6\Lib`, not the `\Program Files\IronPython 2.6\Lib\xml\dom` folder as you might think. As shown in Listing 13-3, the standard Python techniques work just fine now.

Available for download on Wrox.com

LISTING 13-3: Managing XML documents using the Python approach

```python
# Import the required XML support.
import xml.dom.minidom

def CreateDocument():
    # Create an XML document.
    Doc = xml.dom.minidom.Document()

    # Create the root node.
    Root = Doc.createElement('root')

    # Add the message nodes.
    MsgNode = Doc.createElement('Message')
    Message = Doc.createTextNode('Hello')
    MsgNode.appendChild(Message)
```

continues

LISTING 13-3 *(continued)*

```
        Root.appendChild(MsgNode)

        MsgNode = Doc.createElement('Message')
        Message = Doc.createTextNode('Goodbye')
        MsgNode.appendChild(Message)
        Root.appendChild(MsgNode)

        # Append the root node to the document.
        Doc.appendChild(Root)

        # Create the output document.
        MyFile = open('Test2.XML', 'w')

        # Write the output.
        MyFile.write(Doc.toprettyxml(encoding='utf-8'))

        # Close the document.
        MyFile.close()

def DisplayDocument():
    # Read the existing XML document.
    XMLDoc = xml.dom.minidom.parse('Test2.XML')

    # Print the message node content.
    for ThisChild in XMLDoc.getElementsByTagName('Message'):
        print 'Message:', ThisChild.firstChild.toxml().strip('\n\t')

CreateDocument()
DisplayDocument()

# Pause after the debug session.
raw_input('\nPress any key to continue...')
```

The first thing you should notice is that the code for this example is much shorter than its .NET counterpart, even though the result is essentially the same. Despite the problems with the Python libraries, you can write concise code for manipulating XML using Python.

The code begins by importing the only module it needs, xml.dom.minidom. It then calls CreateDocument() and DisplayDocument() in turn, just as the .NET example does. In fact, the output from this example is precisely the same. You see the same output shown in Figure 13-2 when you run this example.

The CreateDocument() function begins by creating an XML document, Doc, using xml.dom .minidom.Document(). The XML document automatically contains the XML declaration, so unlike the .NET version of the code, you don't need to add it manually. So the first processing task is to create the root node using Doc.createElement('root').

As with the .NET example, this example creates two MsgNode elements that contain different messages. The technique used is different from the .NET example. Instead of setting an InnerXml property, the code creates an actual text node using Doc.createTextNode(). However, the result is the same, as shown in Figure 13-6. The last step is to add Root to Doc using Doc.appendChild().

A big difference between IronPython and Python is how you write the XML to a file. As previously mentioned, you can't use the `xml.dom.ext.PrettyPrint()` method. In this case, the code creates a file, `MyFile`, using `open()`. The arguments define the filename and the mode, where `'w'` signifies write. In order to write the text to a file, you use a two-step process. First, the code creates formatting XML by calling `Doc.toprettyxml()`. The function accepts

FIGURE 13-6: The Python output is similar, but not precisely the same as the .NET output.

an optional encoding argument, but there isn't any way to define the resulting XML document as stand-alone using the `standalone="yes"` attribute (see Figure 13-1). Second, the code writes the data to the file buffer using `MyFile.write()`.

 Calling `MyFile.write()` *doesn't write the data to disk. In order to clear the file buffer, you must call* `MyFile.close()`. *Theoretically, IronPython will call* `MyFile.close()` *when the application ends, but there isn't any guarantee of this behavior, so you must specifically call* `MyFile.close()` *to ensure there isn't any data loss.*

The `DisplayDocument()` function comes next. Reading an XML document from disk and placing it in a variable is almost too easy when using IronPython. All you need to do is make a single call to `xml.dom.minidom.parse()`. That's it! The document is immediately ready for use.

The second step is to display the same output shown in Figure 13-2. Again, all you need in IronPython is a simple `for` loop, rather than the somewhat lengthy .NET code. In this case, you ask IronPython to retrieve the nodes you want using `XMLDoc.getElementsByTagName()`. The output is a list that you can process one element at a time. The `print` statement calls on a complex-looking call sequence.

```
ThisChild.firstChild.toxml().strip('\n\t')
```

However, if you take this call sequence apart, it really isn't all that hard to understand. Every iteration of the loop places one of the `MsgNode` elements in `ThisChild`. The first (and only) child of `MsgNode` is the `Message` text node, so you can retrieve it using the `firstChild` property. The `firstChild` property contains a DOM `Text` node object, so you convert it to XML using the `toxml()` method. Unfortunately, the resulting string contains control characters, so you remove them using the `strip('\n\t')` method. The result is a simple value output.

Working with xml.sax

It's important to remember that SAX is an event-driven method of working with XML. An application looks at a small number of bits out of an entire document. Consequently, SAX can be a good method for processing larger documents that you can't read into memory at one time. A SAX application normally relies on three constructs:

➤ One or more sources as input

➤ A parser (normally, only one is used)

➤ One or more handlers to respond to input events

There are many different Python SAX modules. Each of these modules provides different implementations of the three constructions. The default SAX implementation provides just four handlers. These handlers are implemented as classes that you use to interact with the events generated by the input file.

➤ **ContentHandler:** Provides the main SAX interface for handling document events. Most applications use this interface as a minimum because it provides the basic support required for any document. The example shows how to use this handler, which is provided as part of the xml.sax module.

➤ **DTDHandler:** Manages all of the Document Type Definition (DTD) events.

➤ **EntityResolver:** Resolves external entities such as files referenced by processing instructions.

➤ **ErrorHandler:** Reports any errors or warnings that the parser encounters when it processes the XML. Provided as part of the xml.sax module.

Now that you have a little better idea of what to expect, it's time to look at an actual example. Listing 13-4 shows a simple SAX implementation that includes all of the constructs you normally need. Of course, you can easily add to this example to make it do considerably more than it does now.

LISTING 13-4: Parsing an XML document using SAX

```python
# Import the required module.
import xml.sax

# Create a handler based on the default ContentHandler class.
class MessageHandler(xml.sax.ContentHandler):

    # Contains the message text.
    Message = ''

    # Determines when the content is a message.
    IsMessage = False

    # Check for the kind of element before processing it.
    def startElement(self, name, attrs):
        if name == 'Message':
            self.IsMessage = True
            self.Message = ''
        else:
```

```
            self.IsMessage = False

        # If this is the right kind of element, display the message for it.
        def endElement(self, name):
            if name == 'Message':
                print 'Message:', self.Message.strip('\n\t')

        # Add each of the characters of the message to the Message variable.
        def characters(self, ch):
            if self.IsMessage:
                self.Message += ch

# Create a parser.
Parser = xml.sax.make_parser()

# Create a handler for the parser and tell the parser to use it.
Handler = MessageHandler()
Parser.setContentHandler(Handler)

# Open a source and parse it using the parser with the custom handler.
Parser.parse(open('Test2.XML'))

# Pause after the debug session.
raw_input('\nPress any key to continue...')
```

The code begins by importing the required xml.sax module. You don't need anything fancy to create a basic SAX handler. Remember that SAX processes the file one character at a time and generates events based on the characters that the parser sees. Consequently, the code may seem a little odd for someone who is used to working with complete elements, but SAX gives you fine control over the processing cycle, including locating errors within the file.

The centerpiece of this example is the MessageHandler class. This class includes a variable to hold the message (Message), an indicator of whether an element is a message (IsMessage), and the three methods described in the following list.

➤   **startElement():** The parser calls this method at the beginning of an element.

➤   **endElement():** The parser calls this method at the end of an element.

➤   **characters():** Every character read from the source generates a call to characters().

For this example, the startElement() method checks the element name. If the element is a 'Message' element, then the code sets IsMessage to True and clears Message of any existing content. This is a preparatory step.

When the characters() method sees that IsMessage is True, it appends every character it receives to Message. Remember that these are individual characters, so you can't assume much about the content except that the flow is from the beginning of the file to the end of it. In other words, you won't receive characters out of order.

The endElement() checks the element name again. When the element name is 'Message', the code prints the content of Message. Because Message contains all of the characters from the source, you must use `strip('\n\t')` to remove any control characters. The output from this example is the same as shown in Figure 13-2.

Now that you understand the handler, it's time to see how you put it to work. The main part of the code begins by creating a parser, `Parser`, using `xml.sax.make_parser()`. Remember that the parser simply generates events based on the input characters it sees. The handler performs the actual interpretation of those characters.

The next step is to create an instance of `MessageHandler` named `Handler`. The code uses `Parser.setContentHandler()` to assign the handler to `Parser`. Otherwise, `Parser` won't know which handler to use to process the XML characters.

In order to process the XML file, the code still requires a source — the third construct. The `open('Test2.XML')` call opens `Test2.XML` as a source and passes this source to `Parser` through the `Parser.parse()` method. It's the call to the `Parser.parse()` method that actually begins the process of generating events.

USING IRONPYTHON CONSTRUCTIVELY

This chapter has demonstrated basic XML usage in IronPython using three basic techniques. It's important to remember that this chapter presents an overview of XML usage with IronPython and that it isn't intended to tell the whole story of XML usage for your specific application. What you should take away from this chapter is a basic understanding of which techniques work best for a particular need. In addition, because IronPython does offer so many choices, you should consider just how to use it to access the XML you need from any location. When working with IronPython, you don't have to follow someone else's rules — you make your own.

A major issue that most companies face when working with XML is that the developers don't truly understand the format of the XML data with which they want to work. The flexibility that IronPython offers is a double-edged sword. If you don't truly understand the data you want to manipulate, the flexibility that IronPython offers can become more of a hindrance than a help. Take time now to work through the XML data formats that your application uses and create a plan for managing them using IronPython. After you take this step, consider which IronPython technique will work best for your application and then spend more time researching that technique before you begin building your application.

Chapter 11 introduced the Dynamic Language Runtime (DLR) as it applies to ASP.NET application development. However, the information in Chapter 11 was just an appetizer. Now that you've had time to work through more of the capabilities that IronPython has to offer, it's time for the main course. Chapter 14 helps you understand the capabilities that DLR provides in more detail. You'll be amazed at what DLR can do for your application and how it can make your development efforts both simpler and less error-prone. Of course, you'll find a few usage caveats in Chapter 14 as well.

14

Interacting with the DLR

WHAT'S IN THIS CHAPTER?

➤ Getting your copy of the DLR

➤ Considering hosting APIs

➤ Employing extensions to the LINQ ExpressionTree

➤ Working with DynamicSite

➤ Understanding IDynamicObject

➤ Using the ActionBinder

➤ Considering the other DLR Features

The Dynamic Language Runtime (DLR) is a new feature of the .NET platform. Its intended purpose is to support dynamic languages, such as Python (through IronPython) and Ruby (through IronRuby). Without DLR, the .NET Framework can't really run dynamic languages. In addition, DLR provides interoperability between dynamic languages, the .NET Framework, and static languages such as C# and Visual Basic.NET. Without DLR, dynamic and static languages can't communicate (see the section "Understanding the Relationship between Dynamic and Static Languages" in Chapter 15 for additional details). In order to meet these goals, DLR must provide basic functionality that marshals data and code calls between the dynamic and static environments. This functionality comes in a number of forms that are discussed in this chapter. You might be surprised to find that you've already used many of these features throughout the book. Here's the list of features that DLR supports in order to accomplish its goals.

➤ **Hosting Application Programming Interfaces (APIs):** In order to run dynamic language scripts, the host language must have access to the scripting engine. The Hosting APIs provide the support needed to host the dynamic language within the host environment through the scripting engine. This marshaling of code and data makes it possible to seamlessly integrate static and dynamic languages.

➤ **Extensions to Language Integrated Query (LINQ) ExpressionTree:** Normally, a language would need to convert data, objects, and code into Microsoft Intermediate Language (MSIL) before it could translate anything into another language. Because all .NET languages eventually end up as MSIL, MSIL is the common language for all higher-level .NET languages. These extensions make it possible for language compilers to create higher-level constructs for communication purposes, rather than always relying on MSIL. The result is that the marshaling process takes less time and the application runs faster.

➤ **DynamicSite:** This feature provides a call-site cache that dynamic languages use in place of making constant calls to other .NET languages. Because the call-site cache is already in a form that the dynamic language can use, the overall speed of the dynamic language application improves.

➤ **IDynamicObject:** An interface used to interact with dynamic objects directly. If you create a class that implements IDynamicObject, DLR lets the class perform the required conversions, rather than rely on the built-in functionality. Essentially, you create an object that can have methods, properties, and events added dynamically during run time. You use IDynamicObject when you want to implement custom behaviors in your class.

➤ **ActionBinder:** The ActionBinder is a utility that helps support .NET interoperability. The ActionBinder is language specific. It ensures that conversions of variable data, return values, and arguments all follow language-specific behaviors so that the host language sees the data in a form it understands.

These are the main tasks that DLR performs. Of course, it also provides other compiler utilities that you need to know about. The final section in this chapter provides an overview of these other features.

 DLR is a constantly changing technology today, so you'll want to keep up with the additions and changes to DLR. One of the better places to find general DLR resources online is at http://blogs.msdn.com/ironpython/archive/2008/03/16/dlr-resources.aspx. *This chapter also provides a number of specific resources you can use to discover more about DLR. The point is to keep track of what's going on with this exciting technology and review your code as things change.*

OBTAINING DLR

It's important to remember that IronPython relies on DLR to perform just about every task that IronPython executes. Therefore, you already have access to a certain level of DLR, even if you don't install anything or do anything special. In fact, you're using DLR in the background every time you use IronPython. However, you're using DLR without really knowing it exists and without understanding what DLR itself can do for your application. So while you can use the direct approach to DLR, it can prove frustrating and less than friendly.

In order to truly understand DLR, you at least need documentation. Better yet, you can download the entire DLR package and begin to understand the true impact of this product. If nothing else, spend some time viewing the available components at `http://www.codeplex.com/dlr`. The following sections describe various methods of gaining access to DLR so you can use it to perform some custom tasks.

> *This chapter relies on DLR version 0.92, which is a pre-release version of the product. It's never a good idea to use pre-release software in a production environment unless you're willing to live with the potential issues that pre-release software brings, such as reliability, speed, and security problems. This chapter is better viewed as food for thought for future production projects and as a means of experimenting with new technology.*

Using the Direct Method

The direct method is the easiest way to obtain the benefits of DLR, but it's also the most limited. You simply add a reference to the `IronPython.DLL` file located in the `\Program Files\IronPython 2.6` folder of your hard drive. This technique works fine for embedding IronPython scripts in your C# or Visual Basic.NET application. In fact, you gain access to the following classes:

- ➤ `IronPython`
- ➤ `IronPython.Compiler`
- ➤ `IronPython.Compiler.Ast`
- ➤ `IronPython.Hosting`
- ➤ `IronPython.Modules`
- ➤ `IronPython.Runtime`
- ➤ `IronPython.Runtime.Binding`
- ➤ `IronPython.Runtime.Exceptions`
- ➤ `IronPython.Runtime.Operations`
- ➤ `IronPython.Runtime.Types`

For many developers, this is all the DLR support you need, especially if your application only requires cross-language support through the Hosting APIs. (You'll still want to download the documentation that's available on the main DLR Web site — the section "Downloading the Documentation" later in this chapter explains how to perform this task.) The following steps describe how to add the required reference to gain access to these classes.

1. Create the .NET project.

2. Right-click References in Solution Explorer and choose Add Reference from the context menu. You see the Add Reference dialog box.

3. Select the Browse tab and locate the IronPython.DLL file, as shown in Figure 14-1.

4. Click OK. Visual Studio adds the required reference to your project.

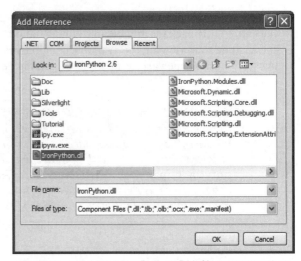

You make use of `IronPython.DLL` as you would any other .NET assembly. Simply add the required `use` or `Imports` statement to your code. The examples throughout the book tell you about these requirements for the individual example.

Downloading the Full DLR

If you really want to experience DLR, you need the complete package. The full DLR

FIGURE 14-1: Add the IronPython.DLL file to your project.

consists of a number of components and even the source code weighs in at a hefty 10.5 MB. You must build the full DLR from the source code as described in the section "Building the Full DLR" later in this chapter.

Before you begin the download, check out the release notes at `http://dlr.codeplex.com/ wikipage?title=0.92_release_notes` for additional information about DLR. For example, you might decide to get an IronPython- or IronRuby-specific download. The full release includes both language products (which can be helpful, even if you use only one of them).

You obtain the full DLR from `http://dlr.codeplex.com/Release/ProjectReleases .aspx?ReleaseId=34834`. When you click the DLR-0.92-Src.zip link, you see a licensing dialog box. Click I Agree to begin the download process.

After the download completes, extract the resulting `DLR-0.92-Src.ZIP` file into its own folder. The resulting `\Codeplex-DLR-0.92` folder contains the following items.

➤ **License.HTML and License.RTF:** You can read the same licensing information in two different formats. Use whichever form works best for you.

➤ **\Docs:** A folder containing the complete documentation for DLR. The best place to begin is the `DLR-Overview.DOC` file.

➤ **\Samples:** A folder containing a number of sample applications that demonstrate DLR features. There's only one IronPython sample in the whole batch — you'll find it in the `\Codeplex-DLR-0.92\Samples\Silverlight\App\Python\python` folder.

➤ **\Source:** A folder that contains the complete DLR source code that you need to compile in order to use DLR to create applications. This folder should be your first stop after you read the `DLR-Overview.DOC` file.

At this point, you can proceed with the instructions in the next section, "Building the Full DLR."

Building the Full DLR

Before you can use DLR, you must build it. The previous section explains how to download a copy of the DLR source. The following sections describe three methods you can use to build DLR. For most developers, the easiest and fastest method is the command line build. However, if you want to review the code before you use it, you might want to load the solution in Visual Studio and take a peek.

Performing a Command Line Build

The command line build option requires that you use the Visual Studio command line, not a standard command line (which doesn't contain a path to the utilities you need). The following steps describe how to perform the command line build:

1. Choose Start ➪ Programs ➪ Microsoft Visual Studio 2008 ➪ Visual Studio Tools ➪ Visual Studio 2008 Command Prompt or Start ➪ Programs ➪ Microsoft Visual Studio 2010 ➪ Visual Studio Tools ➪ Visual Studio Command Prompt (2010). You'll see a command prompt.

2. Type `CD \Codeplex-DLR-0.92\Src` and press Enter. This command places you in the DLR source code directory.

3. Type `MSBuild Codeplex-DLR.SLN` (when using Visual Studio 2008) or `MSBuild Codeplex-DLR-Dev10.SLN` (when using Visual Studio 2010) and press Enter. By default, you get a debug build. Use the `/p:Configuration=Release` command line switch (as in `MSBuild Codeplex-DLR.SLN /p:Configuration=Release` or `MSBuild Codeplex-DLR-Dev10.SLN /p:Configuration=Release`) to obtain a release build. You see a lot of text appear onscreen as MSBuild creates the DLR DLLs for you. Some of the text will appear unreadable (Microsoft uses some odd color combinations). When the build process is complete, you should see `0 Error(s)` as the output, along with a build time, as shown in Figure 14-2. (If you don't see a 0 error output, you should probably download the files again because there is probably an error in the files you downloaded.)

FIGURE 14-2: The build process should show 0 Error(s) as the output message.

 Don't look for the output in the source code folders. The output from the build process appears in the `\Codeplex-DLR-0.92\Bin\40` *folder when working with Visual Studio 2010, no matter which technique you use to build DLR. Visual Studio 2008 developers will find their output in the* `\Codeplex-DLR-0.92\Bin\Debug` *or* `\Codeplex-DLR-0.92\Bin\Release` *folders, depending on the kind of build created. Visual Studio 2008 developers will also find a separate* `\Codeplex-DLR-0.92\Bin\Silverlight Debug` *or* `\Codeplex-DLR-0.92\Bin\Silverlight Release` *folder for Silverlight use.*

Performing a Visual Studio 2008 Build

Some developers will want to perform a build from within Visual Studio 2008. To perform this task, simply double-click the Codeplex-DLR.SLN icon in the `\Codeplex-DLR-0.92\Src` folder. Choose Build ➪ Build Solution or press Ctrl+Shift+B. You'll see a series of messages in the Output window. When the process is complete, you should see, "Build: 23 succeeded or up-to-date, 0 failed, 1 skipped" as the output.

 You must select each of the options in the Solution Configurations combo box in turn and perform a build to create a complete setup. Otherwise, you'll end up with just the Release build or just the Debug build. If you need Silverlight or FxCop support, you must also create these builds individually.

Don't worry if you see a number of messages stating

```
Project file contains ToolsVersion="4.0", which is not supported by this
version of MSBuild. Treating the project as if it had ToolsVersion="3.5".
```

because this is normal when using Visual Studio 2008. You'll also see a number of warning messages (a total of 59 for the current DLR build) in the Errors window, which you can ignore when using the current release.

Performing a Visual Studio 2010 Build

A release version of DLR will build better if you have a copy of Visual Studio 2010 on your system. To perform this task, simply double-click the Codeplex-DLR-Dev10.SLN icon in the `\Codeplex-DLR-0.92\Src` folder. Set the Solution Configurations option to Release or Debug as needed (there aren't any options to build Silverlight or FxCop output). Choose Build ➪ Build Solution or press Ctrl+Shift+B. You'll see a series of messages in the Output window. When the process is complete, you should see, "Build: 15 succeeded or up-to-date, 0 failed, 2 skipped" as the output. The Warnings tab of the Error List window should show 24 warnings.

Downloading the Documentation

The download you performed earlier provides code and documentation, but you might find that the documentation is outdated. As with everything else about DLR, the documentation is in a constant state of flux. If you want to use DLR directly, then you need the documentation found at `http://dlr.codeplex.com/wikipage?title=Docs and specs&referringTitle=Home`. Unfortunately, you have to download each document separately.

Reporting Bugs and Other Issues

At some point, you'll run into something that doesn't work as expected. Of course, this problem even occurs with production code, but you'll definitely run into problems when using the current release of DLR. In this case, check out the listing of issues at `http://www.codeplex.com/dlr/`

`WorkItem/List.aspx`. If you don't find an issue entry that matches the problem you're experiencing, make sure you report the bug online so it gets fixed. Of course, reporting applies equally to code and documentation. Documentation errors are often harder to find and fix than coding errors — at least where developers are concerned — because it's easier to see the coding error in many cases.

WORKING WITH HOSTING APIS

As you've progressed through the book, you probably found that IronPython is a reasonably easy language to learn, yet it provides considerable flexibility and functionality. In fact, you may have even wondered whether it's possible to use IronPython as a scripting language for your next application. Fortunately, you can use IronPython as the scripting language for your next application by relying on the Hosting APIs. It turns out that a lot of people have considered IronPython an optimal language for the task. The following sections consider a number of Hosting API questions, such as how you can use it in an actual application, what the host application needs in order to use the Hosting APIs, and what you'd need to do to embed IronPython as a scripting language in an application.

 A single section of a book can't provide everything needed to use the Hosting APIs. In fact, the authors of the Hosting APIs specification required 87 pages just to document the specification. You can find the specification in the `DLR-Spec-Hosting.DOC` *file found in the* `\Codeplex-DLR-0.92\Docs` *folder of your DLR installation. Of course, you may find that some of the information in this file is outdated, so be sure to check on* `http://www.iunknown.com/2008/01/latest-dlr-host.html` *for additional information or download the updated specification from* `http://www.iunknown.com/files/dlr-spec-hosting.pdf`*.*

Using the Hosting APIs

The DLR specification lists a number of hosting scenarios, such as operating on dynamic objects you create within C# or Visual Basic.NET applications. (See the section "Working with IDynamicObject" later in this chapter for details on dynamic objects in C# and Visual Basic.NET.) It's also possible to use the Hosting APIs to create a scripting environment within Silverlight or other types of Web applications.

Whatever sort of host environment you create, you can use it to execute code snippets or entire applications found in files. The script run time can appear locally or within a remote application so you can use this functionality to create agent applications or scripting that relies on server support. The Hosting APIs make it possible to choose a specific scripting engine to execute the code or to let DLR choose the most appropriate scripting engine for the task. This second option might seem foolhardy, but it can actually let your code use the most recent scripting engine, even if that engine wasn't available at the time you wrote the host environment code.

Chaos could result if you couldn't control the extent (range) of the script execution in some way. For example, two developers could create variables with the same name in different areas of the application. The Hosting APIs make it possible to add scope to script execution. The scope acts much like a namespace does when writing code. Just as a namespace eliminates naming conflicts in assemblies, scoping eliminates them in the scripting environment. Executing the code within a scope also provides it with an execution context (controlled using a `ScriptScope`). Scopes are either public or private, with private scopes providing a measure of protection for the scripting environment. A script can also import scopes for use within the environment or require the host to support a certain scope to execute the script.

The Hosting APIs also provide support for other functionality. For example, you can employ reflection to obtain information about object members, obtain parameter information, and view documentation. You can also control how the scripting engine resolves file content when dynamic languages import code files.

Understanding the Hosting APIs Usage Levels

The DLR documentation specifies that most developers will use the Hosting APIs at one of three levels that are dictated by application requirements. Here are the three basic levels.

- ➤ **Basic code:** The basic code level (Level 1 in the documentation) relies on a few basic types to execute code within scopes. The code can interact with variable bindings within those scopes.

- ➤ **Advanced code execution:** The next level (Level 2 in the documentation) adds intermediate types that provide additional control over how code executes. In addition, this level supports using compiled code in various scopes and permits use of various code sources.

- ➤ **Support overrides:** The final level (Level 3 in the documentation) provides methods to override how DLR resolves filenames. The application can also use custom source content readers, reflect over objects for design-time tool support, provide late bound variable values from the host, and use remote `ScriptRuntime` objects.

The concept of a `ScriptRuntime` object is central to working with the Hosting APIs. A host always begins a session by creating the `ScriptRuntime` object and then using that object to perform tasks. You can create a `ScriptRuntime` object using several methods. Of course, the easiest method is to use the standard constructor, which requires a `ScriptRuntimeSetup` object as input. It's also possible to create a `ScriptRuntime` object using these methods

- ➤ `ScriptRuntime.CreateFromConfiguration():` A factory method that lets you use a pre-configured scope to create the `ScriptRuntime` object. In fact, this factor method is just short for `new ScriptRuntime(ScriptRuntimeSetup.ReadConfiguration())`.

- ➤ `ScriptRuntime.CreateRemote():` A factory method that helps you to create a `ScriptRuntime` object in another domain. The code must meet strict requirements to perform remote execution. See Section 4.1.3, "Create* Methods," in the Hosting APIs specification for details.

At its name implies, a `ScriptRuntimeSetup` object gives a host full control over the `ScriptRuntime` object configuration. The `ScriptRuntimeSetup` object contains settings for debug mode, private execution, the host type, host arguments, and other setup features. Simply creating a `ScriptRuntimeSetup` object sets the defaults for executing a script. Once you use a `ScriptRuntimeSetup` object to create a `ScriptRuntime` object, you can't change the settings — doing so will raise an exception.

The Hosting APIs actually support a number of objects that you use to create a scripting environment, load the code you want to execute, and control the execution process. The figure at `http://www.flickr.com/photos/john_lam/2220796647/` provides an overview of these objects and how you normally use them within the hosting session.

It's important to isolate code during execution. The Hosting APIs provide three levels of isolation.

➤ **AppDomain:** The highest isolation level, which affects the entire application. The `AppDomain` lets you execute code at different trust levels, and load and unload code as needed.

➤ **ScriptRuntime:** Every `AppDomain` can have multiple `ScriptRuntimes` within it. Each `ScriptRuntime` object can have different name bindings, use different .NET assemblies, have different settings (one can be in debug mode, while another might not), and provide other settings and options support.

➤ **ScriptScope:** Every `ScriptRuntime` can contain multiple `ScriptScopes`. A `ScriptScope` can provide variable binding isolation. In addition, you can use a `ScriptScope` to give executable code specific permissions.

Now that you have a better idea of how the pieces fit together, it's important to consider which pieces you use to embed scripting support within an application. Generally, if you want basic code (Level 1) support, all you need are the objects shown in green at `http://www.flickr.com/photos/john_lam/2220796647/`. In fact, if you want to use the default `ScriptScope` settings, all you really need to do is create the `ScriptRuntime` and then use the default `ScriptScope`.

Considering the Host Application

A host has to meet specific requirements before it can run IronPython as a scripting language. Chapter 15 discusses more of the details for C# and Visual Basic.NET developers. You'll find that C# and Visual Basic.NET provide everything you need. However, it's interesting to see just what the requirements are, especially if you're using an older version of these languages. Section 3 of the `DLR-Spec-Hosting.DOC` file found in the `\Codeplex-DLR-0.92\Docs` folder contains complete information about the hosting requirements. Section 3.3 (and associated subsections) are especially important for most developers to read if they plan to use the Hosting APIs for anything special.

Embedding IronPython as a Scripting Language

Imagine that you've created a custom editor in your application where users can write IronPython scripts. They then save the script to disk (or you could read it from memory), and then they assign the script to a button or menu in your application. When the user selects the button or menu, your application executes the script. Creating this scenario isn't as hard as you might imagine. DLR comes with most of the functionality you need built in.

Of course, you need a test script to start. Listing 14-1 shows the test script for this example. The example is purposely simple so that the example doesn't become more focused on the IronPython code than the code that executes it. However, you could easily use any script you want as long as it's a legitimate IronPython script.

LISTING 14-1: A simple IronPython script to execute

```
# A simple function call.
def mult(a, b):
    return a * b

# Create a variable to hold the output.
Output = mult(5,10)

# Display the output.
print('5 * 10 ='),
print(Output)

# Pause after the debug session.
raw_input('\nPress any key to continue...')
```

In this case, the example has a simple function, `mult()`, that multiplies two numbers together. The `__main__()` part of the script multiplies two numbers and displays the result using the `print()` function. In short, the script isn't very complicated.

Now that you have a script, you need to create an application to execute it. The example is a simple console application. In order to create the IronPython `ScriptRuntime` object, you need access to some of the IronPython assemblies. Right-click References in Solution Explorer and choose Add Reference from the context menu. You see the Add Reference dialog box shown in Figure 14-3. Ctrl+click each of the entries shown in Figure 14-3, then click OK to add them to your project.

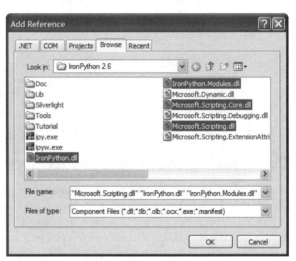

FIGURE 14-3: Add the required references from your IronPython setup.

The example also requires that you add `using` statements for a number of the assemblies. Here are the `using` statements that you must add for this example.

```
using System;
using IronPython.Hosting;
using IronPython.Runtime;
using Microsoft.Scripting.Hosting;
```

Now that the console project is set up, you can begin coding it. This example is very simple, but it actually works. You can execute an IronPython script using this technique. Of course, you can't interact with it much. Chapter 15 provides more detailed examples, but this example is a good starting place. Listing 14-2 shows the minimum code you need to execute an IronPython script and display the result of executing it onscreen.

You may wonder why Figure 14-3 shows so many assemblies selected when the example code only uses one of them directly. The other assemblies are dependencies that the assemblies you use directly require to execute. The code will compile just fine without these other assemblies, but the application will raise an exception when you try to execute it. If you run into a situation where you think that the application should execute, but it keeps raising an exception, read the exception information carefully to determine whether a missing assembly is the problem.

LISTING 14-2: Executing the IronPython script

```
static void Main(string[] args)
{
    // Create an IronPython ScriptRuntime.
    ScriptRuntime Runtime = IronPython.Hosting.Python.CreateRuntime();

    // Execute the script file and return scope information about
    // the task.
    ScriptScope Scope = Runtime.ExecuteFile("Test.py");

    // Display the name of the file executed.
    Console.WriteLine("\r\nExecuted {0}",
        Scope.GetVariable<string>("__name__"));

    // Keep the output visible.
    Console.WriteLine("\r\nPress any key...");
    Console.ReadLine();
}
```

The code begins by creating the `ScriptRuntime` object, `Runtime`. Notice that you create this object by directly accessing the IronPython assemblies, rather than the DLR assemblies. There are many ways to accomplish this task, but using the technique shown is the simplest. The `Runtime` object contains default settings for everything. For example, this `ScriptRuntime` doesn't provide debugging capability. Consequently, this technique is only useful when you have a debugged script to work with and may not do everything needed in a production environment where you let users execute their own scripts as part of an application.

The `Runtime.ExecuteFile()` method is just one of several ways to execute a script. You use it when a script appears in a file on disk, as is the case for this example. When you call the `Runtime` `.ExecuteFile()` method, your application actually calls on the IronPython interpreter to execute the code. The output from the script appears in Figure 14-4. As you can see, the code executes as you expect without any interference from the host. In fact, you can't even tell that the application has a host.

```
file:///C:/0255 - Source Code/Chapter14/UsingHostAPIs/UsingHostAPIs/bin/Debug/UsingHos...   _ □ ×
5 * 10 = 50

Press any key to continue..._
```

FIGURE 14-4: The script output appears as you might expect.

When the `Runtime.ExecuteFile()` method call returns, the C# application that executed the script receives a `ScriptScope` object that it can use to interact with the application in various ways. This `ScriptScope` object, like the `ScriptRuntime` object, contains all the usual defaults. It's a good idea to examine both `Runtime` and `Scope` in the debugger to see what these objects contain because you'll find useful information in both.

The script is running in a host application. In fact, they share the same console window. To show how this works, the example writes output to the console window. It retrieves the __name__ property from `Scope` and displays it onscreen with the message, as shown in Figure 14-5. The point of this example is that the IronPython script truly is hosted and not running on its own. The technique shown here lets you perform simple interactions between C# or Visual Basic.NET and IronPython.

```
file:///C:/0255 - Source Code/Chapter14/UsingHostAPIs/UsingHostAPIs/bin/Debug/UsingHos...

5 * 10 = 50

Press any key to continue...

Executed Test

Press any key...
```

FIGURE 14-5: The output shows that the host and the IronPython environment share the same console.

You may have heard that hosting DLR requires that you create entries in the App.CONFIG *file. While it's true that you gain additional flexibility using the* App.CONFIG *file approach, it's not true that you must use this approach to execute scripts. Many developers will find that their scripts execute just fine using the technique shown in this section and with far less code than using the* App.CONFIG *file approach. However, Chapter 15 does demonstrate this technique so that you can see the best of both worlds when it comes to working with scripts.*

UNDERSTANDING THE EXTENSIONS TO LINQ EXPRESSION TREE

Part of the premise behind DLR is that every .NET language eventually ends up in Microsoft Intermediate Language (MSIL) form. Whether you use C# or Visual Basic.NET, or even managed C++, the output from the compiler is MSIL. That's how the various languages can get along. They rely on MSIL as an intermediary so that managed languages can work together.

Earlier versions of IronPython let you compile your application code using the -X:SaveAssemblies *command line switch. For example, you could type* IPY -X:SaveAssemblies Test.py *and press Enter to create an executable file (it still requires that you supply IronPython.DLL). The latest version of IronPython doesn't supply this feature, so you can't actually see IronPython turned into MSIL.*

The problem with compiling everything to MSIL is that MSIL doesn't necessarily perform tasks quickly or easily when working with dynamic languages such as IronPython. It would be far easier if there were a mechanism for translating the code directly into something that C# or Visual Basic .NET could use. That's where the LINQ Expression Tree (ET) comes into play. A LINQ ET can represent IronPython or other code (such as JavaScript) in a tree form that DLR can then translate into something that C# or Visual Basic.NET can understand. The result is a DLR tree that presents the code in an easily analyzable and mutable form. The example at `http://blogs.msdn.com/hugunin/archive/2007/05/15/dlr-trees-part-1.aspx` explains how DRL trees work graphically. In this case, the author explains how a DLR tree can represent a JavaScript application — the same technique also applies to IronPython.

The LINQ ET originally appeared in the .NET Framework 3.5. In its original form, Microsoft used the LINQ ET to model LINQ expressions written in C# and Visual Basic.NET. In the .NET Framework 4.0, Microsoft added extensions for a number of reasons. For the purposes of this book, the most important reason to extend LINQ ETs is to accommodate the DLR semantics used to translate IronPython code into something that C# and Visual Basic.NET can understand.

A single section of a book can't provide everything needed to use the DLR Trees. In fact, the authors of the Expression Trees specification required 173 pages just to document the specification. You can find the specification in the `Expr-Tree-Spec.DOC` *file found in the* `\Codeplex-DLR-0.92\Docs` *folder of your DLR installation. Of course, you may find that some of the information in this file is outdated, so be sure to check on* `http://dlr.codeplex.com/wikipage?title=Docs%20and%20specs` *for the latest documentation.*

DLR trees work in the background. It's helpful to know they exist, but you generally won't worry about them when working with IronPython so this section is short. However, let's say you want to create a scripting language for your application that isn't as complex as IronPython. Perhaps you want to implement an editor and everything that goes with it in your application. In this case, you may very well want to work with DLR trees. The examples found at `http://weblogs.asp.net/podwysocki/archive/2008/02/08/adventures-in-compilers-building-on-the-dlr.aspx` show what you need to do to create your own language compiler. Once you have a compiler like this built, you could execute the code using a technique similar to the one shown in Listing 14-2.

It's important to consider one word of warning, however, when working with the current version of DLR trees. As you scan through the specification, you'll find that the authors have left behind copious notes about issues that aren't resolved now or features that were left out of the current implementation due to a lack of time. The result is conversations such as the one at `http://stackoverflow.com/questions/250377/are-linq-expression-trees-turing-complete`. If you look at section 2.4.1 of the specification, you find that a higher-level looping mechanism was indeed cut, but Microsoft is aware of the problem and plans to implement the feature in the future. In short, DLR trees have limits that you need to consider before implementing them in your application.

CONSIDERING DYNAMICSITE

When working with a static language such as C# or Visual Basic.NET, the compiler knows what to emit in the form of MSIL based on the code the developer provides. However, dynamic code isn't static — it can change based on any of a number of factors. One problem with dynamic languages is that DLR doesn't always know what to emit during compile time because the real time event hasn't occurred yet. Of course, the static language still needs some code in place because static languages need to know what to do at compile time. This seeming conundrum is handled by invoking a `DynamicSite` object. Using a `DynamicSite` object means that the static language knows what to call at compile time and DLR can fill the `DynamicSite` object with executable code during run time.

As with many parts of DLR, the action takes place behind the scenes — you don't even know it occurs. However, it's useful to know what happens so you at least know what to suspect when an error occurs. The act of invoking the `DynamicSite` method creates an operation to perform and a delegate. The delegate contains caching logic that is updated every time the arguments change. In short, as the dynamic language changes, DLR generates events that change the content of the cache as well.

At the center of working with `DynamicSite` is the `UpdateBindingAndInvoke()` method. The first time that application code calls the `DynamicSite` object, the `UpdateBindingAndInvoke()` method queries the arguments for the specified code. For example, the code might be something simple such as x + y, so the query would request the types of x and y. At this point, `UpdateBindingAndInvoke()` generates a delegate that contains the implementation of the code.

The next time the application invokes the `DynamicSite` object, the delegate checks the arguments in the call against those in the cache. If the argument types match, then the delegate simply uses the current implementation of the code. However, if the arguments are different, then the delegate calls `UpdateBindingAndInvoke()`, which creates a new delegate that contains a definition of the new code with the updated arguments. The new delegate contains checks for both sets of argument types and calls the appropriate implementation based on the arguments it receives. Of course, if none of the argument sets match the call, then the process starts over again with a call to `UpdateBindingAndInvoke()`.

WORKING WITH IDYNAMICOBJECT

This section discusses the `IDynamicObject` interface provided as part of DLR, which doesn't affect IronPython directly, but could affect how you use other languages to interact with IronPython. You can easily skip this section and leave it for later reading if you plan to work exclusively with IronPython for the time being. This is a very short discussion of the topic that is meant to fill in the information you have about DLR and its use with IronPython.

As mentioned throughout the book, C# and Visual Basic.NET are both static languages. Microsoft doesn't appear to have any desire to change this situation in upcoming versions of either language. Consequently, you can't create dynamic types using C# or Visual Basic. There isn't any technique for defining missing methods or dynamic classes using either language. However, you can consume dynamic types defined using a new interface, `IDynamicObject`.

The `IDynamicObject` interface tells DLR that the class knows how to dispatch operations on itself. In some respects, `IDynamicInterface` is a kind of managed form of the `IQueryable` interface that C++ developers use when creating COM objects. The concept isn't new, but the implementation of it in the .NET environment is new.

There are many levels of complexity that you can build into your dynamic implementation. The example in this section is a very simple shell that you can build on when creating a full-fledged application. It's designed to show a common implementation that you might use in an application. You can see another simple example at `http://blogs.msdn.com/csharpfaq/archive/2009/10/19/dynamic-in-c-4-0-creating-wrappers-with-dynamicobject.aspx`.

The starting point for this example is a class that implements `DynamicObject`. In order to create such a class, you need to include the following `using` statements:

```
using System;
using System.Dynamic;
```

The class is called `ADynamicObject` and appears in Listing 14-3.

LISTING 14-3: Creating a class to handle dynamic objects

```csharp
// Any dynamic object you create must implement IDynamicObject.
public class ADynamicObject : DynamicObject
{

    // Calls a method provided with the dynamic object.
    public override bool TryInvokeMember(InvokeMemberBinder binder,
        object[] args, out object result)
    {
        Console.WriteLine("InvokeMember of method {0}.", binder.Name);
        if (args.Length > 0)
        {
            Console.WriteLine("\tMethod call has {0} arguments.", args.Length);
            for (int i = 0; i < args.Length; i++)
                Console.WriteLine("\t\tArgument {0} is {1}.", i, args[i]);
        }
        result = binder.Name;
        return true;
    }

    // Gets the property value.
    public override bool TryGetMember(GetMemberBinder binder,
        out object result)
    {
        Console.WriteLine("GetMember of property {0}.", binder.Name);
        result = binder.Name;
        return true;
    }

    // Sets the property value.
    public override bool TrySetMember(SetMemberBinder binder, object value)
    {
```

continues

LISTING 14-3 *(continued)*

```
        Console.WriteLine("SetMember of property {0} to {1}.",
                           binder.Name, value);
        return true;
    }
}
```

In this case, the code provides the ability to call methods, get property values, and set property values. Amazingly, DLR automatically calls the correct method without any hints from you.

Notice that each of the methods uses a different binder class: `InvokeMemberBinder`, `GetMemberBinder`, or `SetMemberBinder` as needed. The binder provides you with information about the member of interest. In most cases, you use the member name to locate the member within the dynamic object. In this case, the code simply displays the member name onscreen so you can see that the code called the correct member.

Two of these methods, `TryInvokeMember()` and `TryGetMember()`, return something to the caller. It's important to remember that the data is marshaled, so you must use the `out` keyword for the argument that returns a value or the application will complain later (the compiler may very well accept the error without comment). In both cases, the code simply returns the `binder.Name` value. If you were building this dynamic object class for an application, you'd use the `binder.Name` value to access the actual property or method.

When invoking a method, the `TryInvokeMember()` method receives an array of arguments to use with the method call. The code shows how you detect the presence of arguments and then displays them onscreen for this example. In an actual application, you'd need to compare the arguments provided by the caller against those required by the method to ensure the caller has supplied enough arguments of the right type.

All three methods return `true`. If the code were to return `false` instead, you'd see a `RuntimeBinderException` in the caller code. This exception tells the caller that the requested method or property doesn't exist.

When a C# application desires to create a dynamic object, it simply creates an instance of the dynamic class. The instance can create properties, methods, or other constructs as needed. Listing 14-4 shows an example of how a test application might appear.

LISTING 14-4: Using the ADynamicObject class

```
class Test
{
    static void Main()
    {
        // Create a new dynamic object.
        dynamic DynObject = new ADynamicObject();

        // Set a property to a specific value.
        Console.WriteLine("Setting a Property to a Value");
        DynObject.AProp = 5;
```

```
                // Use one property to set another property.
                // You would see a property get, followed by a property set.
                Console.WriteLine("\r\nSetting a Property to another Property");
                DynObject.Prop1 = DynObject.AProp;

                // Call a method and set its output to a property.
                // You would see a method call, followed by a property set.
                Console.WriteLine("\r\nSetting a Property to a Method Output");
                DynObject.Prop2 = DynObject.AMethod();

                // Call a method with a property argument and set a new property.
                // You would see a property get, a method call, and finally a
                // property set.
                Console.WriteLine("\r\nSetting a Property to Method Output with Args");
                DynObject.Prop3 = DynObject.AMethod(DynObject.AProp);

                // Wait to see the results.
                Console.WriteLine("\r\nPress any key when ready...");
                Console.ReadLine();
            }
        }
```

Notice that the code begins by creating a new dynamic object using the `dynamic` keyword. At this point, you can begin adding properties and methods to the resulting `DynObject`. Properties can receive values directly, from other properties, or from methods. Methods can use arguments to change their output. Figure 14-6 shows the output from this example. The path that the code takes through the various objects helps you understand how dynamic objects work.

The `DynamicObject` class actually provides support for a number of members. You can use these members to provide a complete dynamic implementation for your application. Here's a list of the `DynamicObject` members you can override.

- ➤ `GetDynamicMemberNames()`
- ➤ `GetMetaObject()`
- ➤ `TryBinaryOperation()`
- ➤ `TryConvert()`
- ➤ `TryDeleteIndex()`
- ➤ `TryDeleteMember()`
- ➤ `TryGetIndex()`
- ➤ `TryGetMember()`
- ➤ `TryInvoke()`
- ➤ `TryInvokeMember()`
- ➤ `TrySetIndex()`
- ➤ `TrySetMember()`
- ➤ `TryUnaryOperation()`

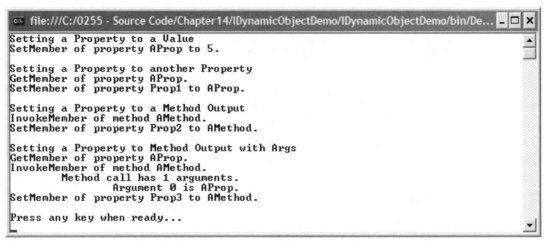

FIGURE 14-6: The output shows the process used to work with dynamic objects.

The point of all this is that you can implement a kind of dynamic object strategy for static languages, but it's cumbersome compared to IronPython. You might use this approach when you need to provide a dynamic strategy for something small within C# or Visual Basic. This technique is also useful for understanding how IronPython works, at a very basic level. IronPython is far more robust than the code shown in this example, but the theory is the same.

UNDERSTANDING THE ACTIONBINDER

In the section "Considering DynamicSite" earlier in this chapter, you discovered how DLR makes it possible to invoke dynamic code from within a static environment using a `DynamicSite` object. The actual process for creating the method invocation call is to create an Abstract Syntax Tree (AST). The AST has functions assigned to it using an `Assign()` method. When DLR wants to assign a new function to AST, it supplies a function name and provides a calling syntax using the `Call()` method. The `Call()` method accepts four arguments.

➤ An object used to hold the function. Normally, the code calls the `Create()` method of the host class using `GetMethod("Create")`.

➤ A constant containing the name of the function as it appears within the host object.

➤ The array of arguments supplied to the function.

➤ A delegate instance used to invoke the code later. It's this argument that you consider when working with an `ActionBinder`.

At this point, you have an object that holds the parameters of the function call, as well as a delegate used to execute the function. The problem now is one of determining how to call the function. After all, the rest of your code knows nothing about the delegate if you create it during run time, as is the case when working with dynamic languages. If none of the code knows about the delegate, there must be some way to call it other than directly.

The most common way to call a delegate of this sort is to create a rule that DLR can use to call it. Of course, you still have to know what to call. DLR supports a number of methods to perform this task, but the method that works with an `ActionBinder` is to create an object that implements `IDynamicObject` as described in the section "Working with IDynamicObject" earlier in this chapter.

To make rules work, your code has to include a `GetRule()` method that returns a `StandardRule` object. Inside `GetRule()` is a switch that selects an action based on the kind of action that DLR requests, such as a call (`DynamicActionKind.Call`). When DLR makes this request, the code creates a `StandardRule` object that contains an `ActionBinder`. The `ActionBinder` determines what kind of action the call performs. For example, you might decide that the `ActionBinder` should be `LanguageContext.Binder`, which defines a language context for the function. The *language context* is a definition of the language's properties, such as its name, identifier, version, and specialized features. (You can learn more about how a language context works at `http://www.dotnetguru` `.org/us/dlrus/DLR2.htm`.) The code then calls `SetCallRule()` with the `StandardRule` object, the `ActionBinder`, and a list of arguments for the function.

Now, here's the important consideration for this section. The `ActionBinder` is actually part of the language design. If you wanted to create a new language, then part of the design process is to design an `ActionBinder` for it. The `ActionBinder` performs an immense amount of work. For example, a call to `ActionBinder.ConvertExpression()` provides conversion information about the data types that the language supports. Of course, IronPython already performs this task for you, but it's important to know how things work under the hood in case you encounter problems.

UNDERSTANDING THE OTHER DLR FEATURES

DLR is a moving target at the time of this writing. The latest release, 0.92, isn't even considered production code as of yet. Consequently, you might find that the version of DLR that you use has features not described in this chapter because they weren't available at the time of this writing.

This chapter doesn't discuss some of the DLR features because you see them in use in other chapters or they're of a type that you normally won't implement directly. For example, to go along with the `DynamicObject` class (and associated `IDynamicObject` interface), you can create an `ExpandoObject` object.

An `ExpandoObject` is a dynamic property bag. Essentially, you fill it with data you want to move from one language to another. It works just like any other property bag you've used in the past. Because the `ExpandoObject` class implements `IDynamicMetaObjectProvider`, you can use it with dynamic languages such as IronPython. You use this object when moving data from C# or Visual Basic.NET to IronPython.

USING IRONPYTHON CONSTRUCTIVELY

This chapter has provided a comprehensive overview of DLR. You probably noticed that you've already used some of these features in the book without really viewing them as DLR. Of course, later chapters, especially Chapter 15, will demonstrate how to use more DLR functionality. The point is that you now know what DLR has to offer you as a developer. It's important to realize that

DLR is there as the base of IronPython, even though you don't see it, and you don't have to see DLR to use it effectively. What this chapter tells you is that there's more functionality available should you want to use it.

Many of you probably won't want to use the full functionality of DLR until you become proficient using IronPython. However, you should at least consider working with the Hosting APIs because they provide powerful ways for developers to interact with IronPython. Make sure you read and understand at least that part of the chapter before you move on to Chapter 15. In addition, make sure you understand the section "Using the Direct Method" earlier in this chapter or you'll quickly become lost as the book progresses. The more adventurous will want to try all the techniques explored in this chapter and use them to build a few new applications.

Chapter 15 is possibly one of the most exciting chapters in the book because you close a loop. You already know how to access the .NET Framework from IronPython — previous chapters provide plenty of examples of using this technique. However, Chapter 15 shows how to go in the other direction — accessing IronPython from .NET languages such as C# and Visual Basic.NET. The reason this chapter is so exciting is that you can finally create applications that exchange data and objects in two directions, enabling you to make full use of all of the IronPython capabilities to create your next application.

15

Using IronPython from Other .NET Languages

WHAT'S IN THIS CHAPTER?

➤ Considering the dynamic and static language relationship

➤ Developing an externally accessible IronPython module

➤ Using the external module from C#

➤ Using the external module from Visual Basic.NET

➤ Testing the external module

➤ Finding bugs in external modules

One of the essential features of IronPython is that it relies on the .NET Framework as a basis for its functionality and is designed to interact with the .NET Framework. You've seen examples of using the .NET Framework in a number of previous chapters. For example, Chapter 13 demonstrates how to tap the .NET Framework for the functionality needed to manage XML data. This chapter considers the other side of the coin — accessing IronPython from a .NET language such as C# or Visual Basic.NET.

You may have noticed that IronPython is great when it comes to processing lists of information and it excels at working with various sorts of data, including ragged datasets. However, Chapters 8 and 11 demonstrated that IronPython isn't always the easiest language to use for user interface needs. The language currently lacks designer and other visual tool support, which means you have to write all of the interface code by hand. Of course, writing the code by hand isn't a very big deal for an application with just a few dialog boxes, but imagine the complexity of developing an application with 40 or 50 different windows, dialog boxes, and other visual elements. In this case, combining C# or Visual Basic.NET with IronPython makes sense because you can leverage the forte of each language to develop applications faster and with fewer errors.

Before you can use IronPython in another language, you need to create a module that works with that other language. This chapter demonstrates a relatively simple IronPython module that offers enough functionality to do something useful. Of course, a major part of this task is discovering how to use the script engine to access IronPython functionality. The IronPython module you create will work fine with either C# or Visual Basic.NET.

The next task is to create an application that can consume the IronPython module. Using IronPython from C# or Visual Basic.NET isn't nearly as easy as using .NET from IronPython — the dynamic nature of IronPython makes consuming it in the static languages much harder. The examples in this chapter show all the steps you need to take to use the sample IronPython module.

Once you get the IronPython module working from within C# or Visual Basic.NET, you need to test it. The testing process will likely reveal bugs in both the IronPython and the C# or Visual Basic.NET code, so you also need to perform debugging. This chapter considers both issues and offers insights on how to make the task easier.

UNDERSTANDING THE RELATIONSHIP BETWEEN DYNAMIC AND STATIC LANGUAGES

Something that most developers fail to consider is that, at some point, all languages generate the same thing — machine code. Without machine code, the software doesn't execute. Your computer cares nothing at all about the idiosyncrasies of human language and it doesn't care about communicating with you at all. Computers are quite selfish when you think about it. The circuitry that makes up your computer relies on software to change the position of switches — trillions of them in some cases. So computers use machine code and only machine code; languages are for humans.

When it comes to dynamic and static languages, it's the way that humans view the languages that make them useful. A dynamic language offers the developer freedom of choice, call it the creative solution. A static language offers a reliable and stable paradigm — call it the comfort solution, the one that everyone's used. How you feel about the languages partly affects your use of them. In the end, both dynamic and static language output ends up as machine code. Dynamic and static languages end up being tools that help you create applications faster and with fewer errors. If you really wanted to do so, you could write any application today using assembler (a low-level language just above machine code, see `http://www.bing.com/reference/semhtml/Assembly_language` for more information), but assembler is hardly the correct tool any longer — humans need a better tool to put applications together. The point is that you should use the tool that works best for a particular development process and not think that the tool is doing anything for your computer.

Anytime you use multiple languages, you must consider issues that have nothing to do with the dynamic or static nature of that language. For example, you must consider the data types that the languages support and provide a method for marshaling data from one language to the other. In fact, marshaling data is an important element in many areas of coding. If you want to communicate with the Win32 API from a .NET-managed language such as C# or Visual Basic.NET, you must marshal the data between the two environments. It's important not to confuse communication and infrastructure requirements with differences between dynamic and static languages. Many resources you find do confuse these issues, which makes it hard for anyone to truly understand how dynamic and static languages differ.

Before you can use IronPython from other languages, it's important to consider the way in which IronPython performs tasks. When an IronPython session starts, nothing exists — the environment begins with an empty slate. You've discovered throughout this book that IronPython calls upon certain script files as it starts to configure the environment automatically. These configuration tasks aren't part of the startup; they are part of the configuration — something that occurs after the startup. The dynamic nature of IronPython means that all activity begins and ends with adding, changing, and removing environment features. There aren't any compiled bits that you can examine statically. Everything in IronPython is dynamic.

When a static language such as C# or Visual Basic.NET attempts to access IronPython, it must accommodate the constant change. If you got nothing else out of Chapter 14 but this one fact, then the chapter was worth reading. In order to do this, C# and Visual Basic.NET rely upon events because they can't actually accommodate change as part of the language. An event signals a change — an IronPython application has modified a class to contain a new method or property. It isn't just the idea that the output or value has changed, but the method or property itself is new. In some cases, C# or Visual Basic.NET will also need to deal with the situation where a method or property simply goes away as well. The underlying mechanism of events, delegates, and caches is inspired and all but invisible, but to be successful at using the languages together, you must know they're present.

The differences between dynamic and static languages go further than simply not knowing what code will execute next in a dynamic language. There's also the matter of data typing. A static language assigns a type to the data it manages, which means that the compiler can make assumptions about the data and optimize access to it. A dynamic language also assigns types to the data it manages, but only does so at run time and even then the data type can change. Now, consider how this changeability complicates the matter of marshaling data from one language to the other. Because the data no longer has a stable type, the marshaling code can't assume anything about it and must constantly check type to ensure the data it marshals appears in the right form in the target language.

The difference between dynamic and static languages, at least from a programming perspective, comes down to flexible coding and data typing. Everything else you may have heard either relates to differences between any two languages (such as the need to marshal data) or the political drama of which tool works best. This book won't endeavor to tell you what tool to use. Certainly, I don't tell anyone that a hammer works best for driving screws or that screwdrivers make wonderful ice picks (not that I believe either of these statements myself). The tool you use for a particular task is the one you can use best or the one called for by a particular job requirement. The point of this chapter and the rest of the book is to demonstrate that dynamic and static languages can work together successfully and in more than one way. The tool you use is up to you.

CREATING AN EXTERNALLY ACCESSIBLE IRONPYTHON MODULE

The first requirement for building an application that allows external access is to create the IronPython script you want to use. Ideally, this script will contain code that is fully debugged. You also want to test the code before you try to use it within C# or Visual Basic.NET. The following sections provide you with the techniques you use to create an IronPython script that you access from C# or Visual Basic .NET. Later sections of this chapter will show the actual access techniques.

CONSIDERING AN ALTERNATIVE EDITOR

Visual Studio 2010 doesn't have IronPython built into it, so you may find that it doesn't always provide the best functionality for working with your IronPython applications. Yes, it provides a means for starting and stopping your application from within the IDE. It's even possible to perform some basic application debugging. Yet, everything about using Visual Studio seems like an afterthought — you're adding IronPython into an environment in which it doesn't actually belong.

In the "Working with IDLE" section of Chapter 6, you discovered one alternative editor, the Integrated DeveLopment Environment. The only problem with IDLE is that it doesn't help much with .NET Framework specific features, such as DLR. Fortunately, you have another alternative to consider, IronEditor (`http://ironeditor.codeplex.com/`). IronEditor is specifically designed to work with DLR languages such as IronPython and IronRuby.

One of the more interesting features of IronEditor is that it actually works with both the .NET Framework and with Mono (see Chapter 19), so you can use it on both the Linux and Mac OS X platforms. IronEditor provides some nice features, such as keyword highlighting. You don't get anything like IntelliSense with this application. It also doesn't include a debugger at present. However, IronEditor is a nice editor that works well with IronPython and supports multiple platforms should you require such support.

Considering Requirements for Externally Accessible Modules

It's easy to access a .NET assembly from within IronPython. For example, in Chapter 9, you accessed the managed code assembly to work with the Windows Media Player, among other things. You could just as easily build a DLL using C# of Visual Basic.NET and use the techniques shown in Chapter 9 to access the DLL. The DLL can contain anything, including Windows forms or other resources you need.

Unfortunately, accessing IronPython from C# or Visual Basic.NET is more difficult. The section "Embedding IronPython as a Scripting Language" in Chapter 14 shows a bare minimum example of accessing an IronPython script from C#, but this example is hardly functional. In order to use IronPython fully, you need more.

The mistake that many developers will make is to think they must do something special in IronPython to make the code accessible. What you really need to do is create an IronPython script using the same techniques as always, and then test it directly. After you test the script using IronPython code, work with the target static language to gain the required access. This pretesting process is important to ensure that you aren't fighting with a bad script in addition to potential problems marshaling data or interacting with methods that change.

Creating the IronPython Script

The IronPython script used for this example is quite simple in approach. All that the example call really does is add two numbers together. You could perform the task with far less code, but the point of this class is to demonstrate access techniques, so it's purposely simple. Listing 15-1 shows the external module code and the code used to test it. As previously mentioned, testing your IronPython script is essential if you want the application to work properly.

LISTING 15-1: A test IronPython class for use in the examples

```python
# The class you want to access externally.
class DoCalculations():

    # A method within the class that adds two numbers.
    def DoAdd(self, First, Second):

        # Provide a result.
        return First + Second

# A test suite in IronPython.
def __test__():

    # Create the object.
    MyCalc = DoCalculations()

    # Perform the test.
    print MyCalc.DoAdd(5, 10)

    # Pause after the test session.
    raw_input('\nPress any key to continue...')

# Execute the test.
# Comment this call out when you finish testing the code.
__test__()
```

The class used for this example is `DoCalculations()`. It contains a single method, `DoAdd()`, that returns the sum of two numbers, `First` and `Second`. Overall, the class is simple.

The `TestClass.py` file also contains a `__test__()` function. This function creates an instance of `DoCalculations()`, `MyCalc`. It then prints the result of calling the `DoAdd()` method with values of `5` and `10`. The example waits until you press Enter to exit.

In `__main__()`, you see a call to `__test__()`. You can execute the example at the command line, as shown in Figure 15-1. Make sure you use the `-D` command line switch to place the interpreter in debug mode. You could also open `IPY.EXE` interactively, load the file, and execute it inside the interpreter. When you know that the code works properly, be sure to comment out the call to `__test__()` in `__main__()`.

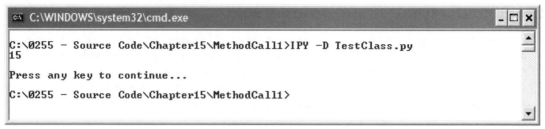

FIGURE 15-1: Test the external module before you use it with your application.

 Make absolutely certain that you comment out the call to __test__() after you finish testing the code. Otherwise, the IronPython module will be in test mode when you use it in your application.

ACCESSING THE MODULE FROM C#

Now that you have an external module to use, you'll probably want to access from an application. This section considers the requirements for accessing IronPython from C#. Don't worry; the section "Accessing the Module from Visual Basic.NET" later in this chapter discusses access from Visual Basic. NET as well. The sections that follow provide everything you need to access the external module created in the section "Creating an Externally Accessible IronPython Module" earlier in this chapter. If you follow these steps, you'll find that access is relatively straightforward, even if it does get a bit convoluted at times. Microsoft promises the future versions of C# will make dynamic language access even easier.

Adding the Required C# References

Any application you create requires access to the dynamic language assemblies. The IronPython assemblies appear in the `\Program Files\IronPython 2.6` folder on your machine. Right-click References and choose Add Reference from the content menu to display the Add Reference dialog box. Select the Browse tab. In most cases, you only need the three DLLs shown in Figure 15-2 to access any IronPython script. (You may also need to add the `IronPython .Modules.DLL` file to the list in some cases.)

Select the assemblies you require by Ctrl-clicking them in the Add Reference dialog box. Click OK when you're finished. You'll see the assemblies added to the References folder in Solution Explorer.

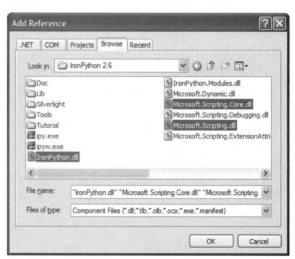

FIGURE 15-2: Add the required references from your IronPython setup.

Adding the Required References to the Host Language

You can perform a multitude of tasks with IronPython. In fact, later chapters in the book show how to perform tasks such as testing your static application code. IronPython really is quite flexible. However, most people will start by executing external scripts and only need a few of the namespaces in the IronPython assemblies to do it. The following `using` statements provide everything needed to execute and manage most IronPython scripts.

```
using System;
using IronPython.Hosting;
using IronPython.Runtime;
using Microsoft.Scripting.Hosting;
```

Understanding the Use of ScriptEngine

You have many options for working with IronPython scripts. This first example takes an approach that works fine for Visual Studio 2008 developers, as well as those using Visual Studio 2010. It doesn't require anything fancy and it works reliably for most scripts. Ease and flexibility concerns aside, this isn't the shortest technique for working with IronPython scripts. This is the Method1 approach to working with IronPython scripts — the technique that nearly everyone can use and it appears in Listing 15-2.

LISTING 15-2: Using the script engine to access the script

```
static void Main(string[] args)
{
    // Create an engine to access IronPython.
    ScriptEngine Eng = Python.CreateEngine();

    // Describe where to load the script.
    ScriptSource Source = Eng.CreateScriptSourceFromFile("TestClass.py");

    // Obtain the default scope for executing the script.
    ScriptScope Scope = Eng.CreateScope();

    // Create an object for performing tasks with the script.
    ObjectOperations Ops = Eng.CreateOperations();

    // Create the class object.
    Source.Execute(Scope);

    // Obtain the class object.
    Object CalcClass = Scope.GetVariable("DoCalculations");

    // Create an instance of the class.
    Object CalcObj = Ops.Invoke(CalcClass);

    // Get the method you want to use from the class instance.
    Object AddMe = Ops.GetMember(CalcObj, "DoAdd");

    // Perform the add.
    Int32 Result = (Int32)Ops.Invoke(AddMe, 5, 10);
```

continues

LISTING 15-2 *(continued)*

```
        // Display the result.
        Console.WriteLine("5 + 10 = {0}", Result);

        // Pause after running the test.
        Console.WriteLine("\r\nPress any key when ready...");
        Console.ReadKey();
    }
```

This example builds on the example you saw in Chapter 14. In this case, the code begins by creating a script engine. Think of this engine as a means to access IPY.EXE without actually loading IPY.EXE. If you don't really understand the ScriptEngine object, Eng, make sure you read through the theory section in Chapter 14. What this code is showing you is the practical application of that theory.

Now that you have access to Eng, you can use it to perform various tasks. For example, you must tell Eng what scope to use when executing code, so the example creates a ScriptScope object, Scope. In order to perform tasks, you must also have an ObjectOperations object, Ops. The example uses the defaults provided for each of these objects. However, in a production application, you might decide to change some properties to make the application execute faster or with better security.

At this point, you can execute the script. The act of executing the script using Source.Execute() loads the script into memory and compiles it in a form that the static application can use. The Source.Execute() method associates Scope with the execution environment. At this point, the parameters for executing the script are set in stone — you can't change them.

The script is in memory, but you can't access any of its features just yet. The script contains a DoCalculations class that you access by calling Scope.GetVariable() to create CalcObj. The code gains access to the class by creating an instance of it, CalcObj, using Ops.Invoke(). At this point, CalcObj contains an instance of DoCalculations() in the IronPython module, but you can't use it directly. Remember that you must marshal data between C# and IronPython. In addition, C# has to have a way to deal with the potential changes in the IronPython script.

In order to use the DoAdd() method in DoCalculations(), the static application must create an object to hold a call-site cache, as explained in Chapter 14. To do this, the code calls Ops.GetMember() with the instance of DoCalculations(), CalcObj, and the name of the method it wants to access, DoAdd(). The result is the AddMe object.

This seems like a lot of work just to gain access to DoAdd, but you can finally use AddMe to perform the addition. A call to Ops.Invoke() with AddMe and the arguments you want to use performs all of the required marshaling for you. You must coerce the output to an Int32 (something that C# understands). Finally, the application outputs the result, as shown in Figure 15-3.

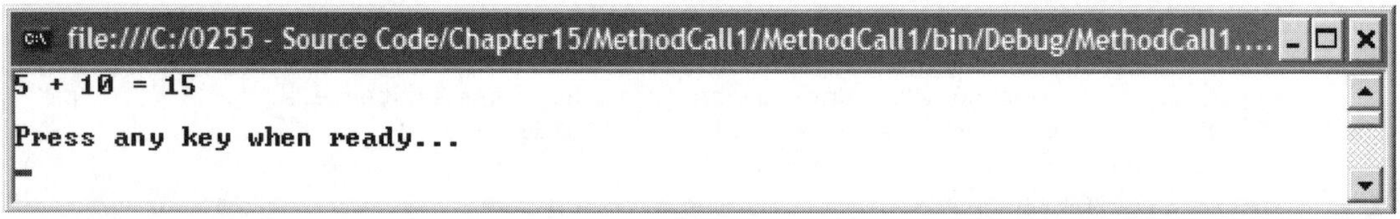

FIGURE 15-3: The example application calls the DoAdd() method and displays the result onscreen.

Using the dynamic Keyword

One of the new ways in which you can access IronPython in C# 4.0 is to use the `dynamic` keyword. This keyword makes it possible for you to cut out a lot of the code shown in Listing 15-2 to perform tasks with IronPython. It's still not perfect, but you'll do a lot less work. Listing 15-3 shows a short example that accesses the `__test__()` function found in Listing 15-1.

LISTING 15-3: Accessing IronPython using the dynamic keyword

```
static void Main(string[] args)
{
    // Obtain the runtime.
    var IPY = Python.CreateRuntime();

    // Create a dynamic object containing the script.
    dynamic TestPy = IPY.UseFile("TestClass.py");

    // Execute the __test__() method.
    TestPy.__test__();
}
```

This example has a few differences from previous examples. The first is the use of `var` as the type for `IPY`. Calling `Python.CreateRuntime()` creates a `ScriptRuntime` object, much like the example in Chapter 14. In this case, the code works with `IPY` in a different manner by relying on the `dynamic` type.

The next step is to load the script. The dynamic type, `TestPy`, contains all the features of the `TestClass.py` script after you load it using `IPY.UseFile()`. Figure 15-4 shows how `TestPy` appears after the script loads. Notice that the Locals window correctly identifies all the IronPython types in the file. This approach gives you far better access with a lot less code than other techniques in this chapter, but it only works with C# 4.0 (Visual Basic.NET developers will have to wait for an update).

In this case, the example calls the `__test__()` function. This function outputs the same information shown in Figure 15-1.

Locals		
Name	Value	Type
⚲ args	{string[0]}	string[]
⊞ ⚲ IPY	{Microsoft.Scripting.Hosting.ScriptRuntime}	Microsoft.Scripting.Hosting.ScriptRuntime
⊟ ⚲ TestPy	{Microsoft.Scripting.Hosting.ScriptScope}	dynamic {Microsoft.Scripting.Hosting.ScriptScope}
⊞ 🔧 Language	"IronPython 2.6"	Microsoft.Scripting.Hosting.ScriptEngine
⊟ 🔧 Variables	Count = 6	System.Collections.Hashtable
⊞ ⚲ ["DoCalculations"]	{<module>.DoCalculations}	
⊞ ⚲ ["__builtins__"]	{IronPython.Runtime.PythonDictionary}	
⊞ ⚲ ["__name__"]	"<module>"	
⊞ ⚲ ["__doc__"]	null	
⊞ ⚲ ["__file__"]	".\\TestClass.py"	
⊞ ⚲ ["__test__"]	{IronPython.Runtime.PythonFunction}	
⊞ ⚲ Raw View		
⊞ ⚲ Raw View		
🖳 Autos 🖳 Locals 🖳 Watch 1 🖳 Watch 2		

FIGURE 15-4: Loading the script provides access to all of the features it contains.

CONSIDERING THE DYNAMIC TYPE IN C# 4.0

Visual Basic.NET has always had a kind of dynamic lookup in the form of late binding. However, C# has always used early binding. That has changed with C# 4.0 with the new dynamic lookup functionality found in the DLR. Dynamic lookup provides you with these additional capabilities when working with C#:

➤ A shared infrastructure for runtime name resolution across all .NET languages.

➤ Enhanced support for the Office Primary Interoperability Assemblies (PIA) and Component Object Model (COM) interoperability that negates the need to use bulky type libraries and optional arguments in function calls.

➤ The ability to consume dynamic languages by making it possible to interact with dynamic language types.

➤ Improved reflection support, which makes it possible to easily instantiate classes and call arbitrary methods that are not known at compile time.

The `dynamic` type has considerably more to offer than a sidebar can hold. For more information check out the article at `http://msdn.microsoft.com/library/dd264736(VS.100).aspx`. This article provides a good example of how the `dynamic` keyword comes into play.

Working with the App.CONFIG File

In some cases, you might want to configure your application using an `App.CONFIG` file. Using the `App.CONFIG` file tends to ensure that your application works better between development machines. In addition, using the `App.CONFIG` file can make it easier to work with DLR using older versions of Visual Studio. Most important of all, using the `App.CONFIG` file ensures that anyone working with the application uses the correct version of the DLLs so that any DLL differences aren't a problem.

Your project won't contain an `App.CONFIG` file at the outset. To add this file, right-click the project entry in Solution Explorer and choose Add ➪ New Item from the context menu. You see the Add New Item dialog box shown in Figure 15-5. Highlight the Application Configuration File entry as shown and click Add. Visual Studio automatically opens the file for you.

The `App.CONFIG` file contains entries that describe the Microsoft scripting configuration. In most cases, you begin by defining a `<section>` element, which describes a `<microsoft.scripting>` element. The `<microsoft.scripting>` element contains a list of languages you want to use in a `<languages>` element, as shown in Listing 15-4.

Available for
download on
Wrox.com

LISTING 15-4: Defining the App.CONFIG file content

```
<?xml version="1.0" encoding="utf-8" ?>
<configuration>
  <configSections>
    <section name="microsoft.scripting"
```

```
            type="Microsoft.Scripting.Hosting.Configuration.Section,
                Microsoft.Scripting, Version=1.0.0.0, Culture=neutral,
                PublicKeyToken=31bf3856ad364e35"
            requirePermission="false" />
    </configSections>
    <microsoft.scripting>
        <languages>
            <language names="IronPython,Python,py"
                    extensions=".py"
                    displayName="IronPython 2.0 Beta"
                    type="IronPython.Runtime.PythonContext,IronPython,
                        Version=2.6.10920.0, Culture=neutral,
                        PublicKeyToken=31bf3856ad364e35" />
        </languages>
    </microsoft.scripting>
</configuration>
```

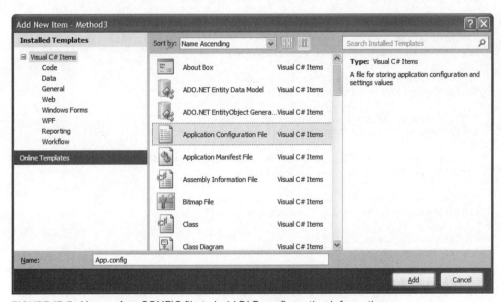

FIGURE 15-5: Use an App.CONFIG file to hold DLR configuration information.

The `<section>` element includes attributes for `name`, `type`, and `requirePermission`. The `type` attribute should appear on one line, even though it appears on multiple lines in the book. This attribute describes the `Microsoft.Scripting.DLL` attributes. Especially important is the `Version` and `PublicKeyToken` entries.

The `<microsoft.scripting>` element contains a `<languages>` element at a minimum. Within the `<languages>` element you find individual `<language>` elements that are descriptions of the languages you want to use in your application.

For this example, you create a `<language>` element for IronPython that starts with a `names` attribute. It's important to define all the names you plan to use to access the language — the example defines three of them. The `extensions` attribute describes the file extensions associated with the language, which is .py in this case. The displayName attribute simply tells how to display the language. Finally, the type attribute contains a description of the IronPython.DLL file. As with the type element for Microsoft.Scripting.DLL, this element should appear on a single line, even though it appears on multiple lines in the book. Again, you need to exercise special care with the Version and PublicKeyToken entries.

Now that you have the App.CONFIG file created, it's time to look at the application code. Listing 15-5 contains the source for this example.

LISTING 15-5: Using the App.CONFIG file in an application

```
static void Main(string[] args)
{
    // Read the configuration information from App.CONFIG.
    ScriptRuntimeSetup srs = ScriptRuntimeSetup.ReadConfiguration();

    // Create a ScriptRuntime object from the configuration
    // information.
    ScriptRuntime runtime = new ScriptRuntime(srs);

    // Create an engine to access IronPython.
    ScriptEngine Eng = runtime.GetEngine("Python");

    // Describe where to load the script.
    ScriptSource Source = Eng.CreateScriptSourceFromFile("TestClass.py");

    // Obtain the default scope for executing the script.
    ScriptScope Scope = Eng.CreateScope();

    // Create an object for performing tasks with the script.
    ObjectOperations Ops = Eng.CreateOperations();

    // Create the class object.
    Source.Execute(Scope);

    // Obtain the class object.
    Object CalcClass = Scope.GetVariable("DoCalculations");

    // Create an instance of the class.
    Object CalcObj = Ops.Invoke(CalcClass);

    // Get the method you want to use from the class instance.
    Object AddMe = Ops.GetMember(CalcObj, "DoAdd");

    // Perform the add.
    Int32 Result = (Int32)Ops.Invoke(AddMe, 5, 10);

    // Display the result.
    Console.WriteLine("5 + 10 = {0}", Result);

    // Pause after running the test.
    Console.WriteLine("\r\nPress any key when ready...");
    Console.ReadKey();
}
```

The biggest difference between this example and the one shown in Listing 15-2 is that you don't create the script engine immediately. Rather, the code begins by reading the configuration from the `App.CONFIG` file using `ScriptRuntimeSetup.ReadConfiguration()`. This information appears in `srs` and is used to create a `ScriptRuntime` object, `runtime`.

At this point, the code finally creates the `ScriptEngine`, `Eng`, as in the previous example. However, instead of using `Python.CreateEngine()`, this example relies on the `runtime.GetEngine()` method. For this example, the result is the same, except that you've had better control over how the `ScriptEngine` is created, which is the entire point of the example — exercising control over the IronPython environment. The rest of the example works the same as the example shown in Listing 15-2. The output is the same, as shown in Figure 15-3.

ACCESSING THE MODULE FROM VISUAL BASIC.NET

You might get the idea from the lack of Visual Basic.NET examples online that Microsoft has somehow forgotten Visual Basic.NET when it comes to DLR. Surprise! Just because the examples are nowhere to be seen (send me an e-mail at JMueller@mwt.net if you find a stash of Visual Basic.NET examples somewhere) doesn't mean that you can't work with IronPython from Visual Basic. In fact, the requirements for working with Visual Basic.NET are much the same as those for working with C#, as shown in the following sections.

One limitation of Visual Basic.NET is that it doesn't appear to support an equivalent of the `dynamic` keyword. Consequently, you might find that some techniques which work fine for C# won't work at all for Visual Basic.NET. Let's hope Microsoft will remedy this situation sometime in the future. In the meantime, a little extra thought and creativity should give you complete access to every IronPython script you might want to access from Visual Basic.NET.

Adding the Required Visual Basic.NET References

Visual Basic requires the same DLL references as C# does to work with IronPython. Figure 15-2 shows the assemblies you should add to your application to make it work properly. In this case, you right-click the project entry and choose Add Reference from the context menu to display an Add Reference dialog box similar to the one shown in Figure 15-2. Select the Browse tab and add the IronPython assemblies shown in Figure 15-2 by Ctrl-clicking on each of the assembly entries. Click OK. Visual Basic will add the references, but you won't see them in Solution Explorer unless you click Show All Files at the top of the Solution Explorer window.

As with C#, you need to add some Imports statements to your code to access the various IronPython assemblies with ease. Most applications will require the following Imports statements at a minimum.

```
Imports System
Imports IronPython.Hosting
Imports IronPython.Runtime
Imports Microsoft.Scripting.Hosting
```

Creating the Visual Basic.NET Code

This example uses the same `TestClass.py` file as every other example in this chapter. As with all the other examples, you shouldn't let the IronPython example dictate what you do in your own applications. You can obtain full access to any IronPython script from Visual Basic.NET and fully use every feature it provides.

Accessing IronPython scripts from Visual Basic.NET is much the same as accessing them from C# using the `ScriptEngine` object. Listing 15-6 shows the code you need to access the IronPython script used for all the examples in this chapter.

LISTING 15-6: Accessing IronPython from Visual Basic.NET

```vb
Sub Main()
    ' Create an engine to access IronPython.
    Dim Eng As ScriptEngine = Python.CreateEngine()

    ' Describe where to load the script.
    Dim Source As ScriptSource = Eng.CreateScriptSourceFromFile("TestClass.py")

    ' Obtain the default scope for executing the script.
    Dim Scope As ScriptScope = Eng.CreateScope()

    ' Create an object for performing tasks with the script.
    Dim Ops As ObjectOperations = Eng.CreateOperations()

    ' Create the class object.
    Source.Execute(Scope)

    ' Obtain the class object.
    Dim CalcClass As Object = Scope.GetVariable("DoCalculations")

    ' Create an instance of the class.
    Dim CalcObj As Object = Ops.Invoke(CalcClass)

    ' Get the method you want to use from the class instance.
    Dim AddMe As Object = Ops.GetMember(CalcObj, "DoAdd")

    ' Perform the add.
    Dim Result As Int32 = Ops.Invoke(AddMe, 5, 10)

    ' Display the result.
    Console.WriteLine("5 + 10 = {0}", Result)

    ' Pause after running the test.
    Console.WriteLine(vbCrLf + "Press any key when ready...")
    Console.ReadKey()
End Sub
```

As you can see from the listing, Visual Basic.NET code uses precisely the same process as C# does to access IronPython scripts. In fact, you should compare this listing to the content of Listing 15-2. The two examples are similar so that you can compare them. The output is also precisely the same. You'll see the output shown in Figure 15-3 when you execute this example.

DEVELOPING TEST PROCEDURES FOR EXTERNAL MODULES

Many developers are beginning to realize the benefits of extensive application testing. There are entire product categories devoted to the testing process now because testing is so important. Most, if not all, developer tools now include some idea of application testing with them. In short, you should have all the testing tools you need to test the static portion of your IronPython application.

Unfortunately, the testing tools might not work particularly well with the dynamic portion of the application. Creating a test that goes from the static portion of the application to the dynamic portion of the application is hard. (Chapter 18 shows that the opposite isn't true — IronPython makes an excellent tool for testing your static application.) Consequently, you need to include a test harness with your dynamic code and perform thorough testing of the dynamic code before you use it with the static application. (When you think about a test harness, think about a horse, your application that has a harness added externally for testing purposes. You add the harness for testing and remove it for production work without modifying the application.) Listing 15-1 shows an example of how you might perform this task.

The test harness you create has to test everything, which is a daunting task to say the least. In addition, you need to expend extra effort to make the test harness error free — nothing would be worse than to chase an error through your code, only to find out that the error is in the test harness. At a minimum, your test harness should perform the following checks on your dynamic code:

➤   Outputs with good inputs

➤   Outputs with erroneous inputs

➤   Exception handling within methods

➤   Property value handling

➤   Exceptions that occur on public members that would normally be private

Of course, you want to check every method and property of every class within the dynamic code. To ensure you actually test everything, make sure you create a checklist to use to verify your test harness. Because IronPython isn't compiled, you'll find that you must manually perform some checks to ensure the code works precisely as planned, but use as much automation as possible.

DEBUGGING THE EXTERNAL MODULE

Debugging isn't hard, but it also isn't as straightforward as you might think when working with IronPython. The debugger won't take you directly to an error. You can't test variables using the debugger from within the static language. In short, you have to poke and prod the external script to discover what ails it. Fortunately, you do have three tools at your disposal for discovering errors.

➤   Exceptions

➤   `print` Statements

➤   An `ErrorListener` object

Let's begin with the easiest of the three tools. The static language application won't ignore outright errors in the script code. For example, you might have the following error in the script:

```
# Introduce an error.
print 1/0
```

If your code has this error (and it really shouldn't), you'll see an exception dialog box like the one shown in Figure 15-6. Unfortunately, when you click View Detail, the content of the View Detail dialog box is nearly useless. The exception information won't tell you where to find the error in your script. In fact, it may very well lead you on a wild goose chase that ends in frustration.

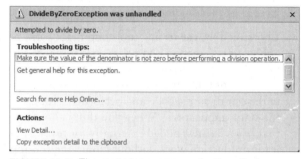

FIGURE 15-6: The static language application displays exceptions for your script.

The name of the exception will provide clues as to where the error might exist, but you can't confirm your suspicions without help. The only tool, besides vigorous script testing, is to include `print` statements such as these in your code.

```
# Display the values of First and Second.
print 'Values in IronPython Script'
print 'First = ', First
print 'Second = ', Second
```

When you run the script, you see the output shown in Figure 15-7. Most developers view `print` statements as a bit old school, but they do work if you use them correctly. Make sure you provide enough information to know where the script is failing to perform as expected. Even so, using `print` statements may feel a bit like wandering around in the dark, so you should place an emphasis on testing the script before you use it and after each change you make.

```
file:///C:/0255 - Source Code/Chapter15/Debugging/Debugging/bin/Debug/Debugging.EXE
Values in IronPython Script
First =  5
Second =  10

5 + 10 = 15

Press any key when ready...
```

FIGURE 15-7: Using print statements may seem old school, but they work.

In some cases, you might make a small change to a script and it stops running completely — you might not see a script exception, just an indicator that something's wrong because the application raises an unrelated exception. Syntax errors and other problems where the interpreter simply fails can cause the developer a lot of woe. For example, your application might have the following syntax error:

```
# Create a syntax error.
while True print 'This is an error!'
```

This code obviously won't run. Because of the nature of the error, you might even pass it by while looking through your code. The answer to this problem is to create an ErrorListener class like the one shown in Listing 15-7.

LISTING 15-7: Create an ErrorListener to hear script semantic errors

```
class MyListener : ErrorListener
{

    public override void ErrorReported(ScriptSource source,
                                       string message,
                                       SourceSpan span,
                                       int errorCode,
                                       Severity severity)
    {
        Console.WriteLine("Script Error {0}: {1}", errorCode, message);
        Console.WriteLine("Source: {0}", source.GetCodeLine(span.Start.Line));
        Console.WriteLine("Severity: {0}", severity.ToString());
    }

}
```

The ErrorListener contains just one method, ErrorReported(). This method can contain anything you need to diagnose errors. The example provides an adequate amount of information for most needs. However, you might decide to provide additional information based on the kind of script you're using.

In order to use this approach, you must compile the script before you execute it. The compilation process must include the ErrorListener, as shown here.

```
// Compile the script.
Source.Compile(new MyListener());
```

When you run the application now, you get some useful information about the syntax error, as shown in Figure 15-8.

```
file:///C:/0255 - Source Code/Chapter15/Debugging/Debugging/bin/Debug/Debugging.EXE
Script Error 16: unexpected token 'print'
Source:                 while True print 'This is an error!'
Severity: FatalError
```

FIGURE 15-8: The ErrorListener provides useful output on syntax errors.

USING IRONPYTHON CONSTRUCTIVELY

This chapter has demonstrated how to access an IronPython module from C# or Visual Basic.NET. All this work may seem counterproductive, but you really can gain a lot from using this approach. Not only can you create extremely fast and flexible IronPython modules to perform tasks such as list processing, but you gain the user interface development flexibility offered by both C# and Visual Basic.NET. The one essential concept you should take from this chapter is that using multiple languages in an application to gain access to the best features of each language nets considerable flexibility and development speed once you overcome the initial development hurdles.

There isn't any way that a single chapter of a book can address every possible need for every possible reader. However, before this technology becomes real to you, you have to see it do something that you couldn't ordinarily do with ease in your development environment. Before you move on to the next chapter, consider creating a list of applications that could benefit from a combined IronPython and C# or Visual Basic.NET approach. Try creating examples that exemplify key features of these applications. As you gain experience using IronPython with the .NET languages you use now, you'll begin to understand why using multiple language tools is so beneficial. The important thing is to try more than just the one example in this chapter.

So far you've used .NET from IronPython and IronPython from a .NET static language. There's a third relationship that you need to try before you can consider your essential IronPython experience complete — extending IronPython using another language. Chapters 16 and 17 show how to create extensions for IronPython so that you can begin building special libraries that enhance basic IronPython functionality. For example, you might create a basic library of dialog boxes to use with IronPython and overcome that user interface problem (at least partially). Chapter 16 discusses C# extensions, while Chapter 17 discusses Visual Basic.NET extensions. Interestingly enough, the two languages require a slightly different approach when extending IronPython; it pays to read both chapters so you can see the full range of extension requirements.

16

Extending IronPython Using C#

WHAT'S IN THIS CHAPTER?

➤ Defining the requirements for an extension

➤ Understanding how static language differences affect extensions

➤ Developing a simple C# extension

➤ Providing user interface support through a C# extension

➤ Providing Win32 API support through a C# extension

Many developers view C# as the new C. It's true that C# does provide many of the low-level characteristics of C, but it's not really a replacement. Even so, C# is a good language choice for many tasks, especially when it comes to working through difficulties with Win32 API (the programming interface that native code executables use). Because IronPython lacks support for certain low-level operations, you'll find many ways to use C# to extend IronPython to perform amazing new tasks.

Of course, it's important to know precisely what an extension is, so this chapter spends some time exploring the issue. As with many software constructs, extensions aren't a complete fix for every problem — they have both advantages and disadvantages that you need to consider during the design process. Extensions are an important tool in your IronPython toolkit and act as a replacement for the lack of CPython support in many cases.

This chapter provides a simple extension. You can use this simple example as a starting point for other extensions you might want to create. Of course, even a simple example can take you a long way in understanding extension techniques.

After you complete the simple extension, you see two other examples. The first example shows how to build a library of Windows forms. You see how to work with both message boxes and Windows Forms classes using an extension. Even though you could perform this task using IronPython, many developers will find it significantly easier to use a C# extension to perform the task. With careful planning, you could create an entire library containing all the forms required to address every need in an IronPython application. The second example is a Win32 API extension that helps you better understand how extensions can provide access to low-level calls that you might not ordinarily be able to make — at least, not with ease. Even though the Python language is supposed to shield you from the vagaries of platform-specific coding, sometimes you really do need to know something more about the platform on which you're working.

UNDERSTANDING THE REQUIREMENTS FOR AN EXTENSION

It's important to understand that an extension, any extension, probably ties your code to Windows. Whenever you use an extension with IronPython, you rely on something other than the Python libraries to perform a task, which means you lose the platform independence for which Python is so famous. In short, extensions provide considerable flexibility and help you provide additional capabilities for IronPython, but this flexibility isn't without cost. Every time you make a design decision of this sort, you must pay a price in the following:

➤ **Reduced reliability:** Due to increased failure points.

➤ **Weakened security:** More languages mean more places where someone could leave a security hole.

➤ **Impaired speed:** Marshaling data between language barriers takes time.

➤ **Fewer platforms:** In order to use an extension, you must find a platform that supports both IronPython and the extension language.

Writing an extension isn't always straightforward. It isn't as simple as writing some class library code and putting it in a DLL. In fact, you must spend considerable effort thinking about how an extension should be designed to make it useable. The following list considers just a few of the most important factors for your extension.

➤ **Python language requirements:** IronPython may not support every feature that the static language supports. For example, you may find that IronPython doesn't support a particular static language operator, such as the ++ operator.

➤ **IronPython developer mentality:** An extension that performs tasks in a way that runs completely counter to the way that an IronPython developer normally does them isn't very useful, because the IronPython developer will have to think too hard about using the extension. The best kind of extension is one that feels natural to the IronPython developer.

➤ **Flexibility:** An extension should provide some significant advantage in flexibility. When you write an extension, write it with the benefit to the IronPython developer in mind, not simply because the functionality the extension provides is interesting.

The one factor that you don't need to consider is whether something is doable. Normally, if you can perform a task with the static language you want to use to build the extension, then you can do it with IronPython as well. Sometimes, you have to massage the data or present the technique in a way that doesn't match your normal methodology, but you can normally perform the task with a bit of effort.

CONSIDERING IRONPYTHON AND STATIC LANGUAGE DIFFERENCES

IronPython is a dynamic language (a language that does things like decide variable type at run time, which is contrasted with a static language that decides everything during compile time). As such, it has some significant advantages for the human developer that a static language can't provide. It's true that the concept of language is foreign to the computer, but the human developer relies on certain characteristics of language to accomplish tasks quickly and with few errors. Consequently, as part of defining the reason to use an extension, you must consider the differences between IronPython and the static language of your choice.

Defining Why You Use a Static Language with IronPython

Typically, you use a static language with IronPython to gain a specific advantage. For example, IronPython doesn't create graphical user interfaces very well, so using a static language to perform this task could provide a significant advantage in development time. In addition, you could probably reuse code that you already have on hand, which may reduce debugging time as well. Look for the advantages that you can gain when using a static language with IronPython. If you have problems describing the material benefit of an extension, then perhaps you really should look at another solution.

Make sure you consider the strengths of the static language when making your selections. For example, C# is often the best choice for Win32 API interaction because it supports unsafe pointers — a requirement for certain specialized Win32 API tasks. Of course, you should make sure that the use of the Win32 API is actually required. Perhaps a third-party library already has the solution you require and with a lot less work. Visual Basic.NET is often the best choice for database work because it takes care of so many tasks in the background for the developer. You don't have to worry so much about coercing data types because Visual Basic addresses the need for you in the background.

Sometimes the use of a static language is practical. For example, you might have an overwhelming number of developers on your team who know C# or Visual Basic.NET, but know nothing about IronPython. In general, this is one of the poorest reasons to use a static language with IronPython, but the reality of development today is that you often use the tools you have on hand to accomplish the task. No one can afford to have developers sitting on their hands simply because the dynamic language is the best choice for a particular job.

Understanding Line Noise

There are good reasons to avoid using a static language with IronPython. You can write most code in IronPython using far fewer lines than a static language requires. Fewer lines of code translate into higher developer productivity and sometimes into fewer coding errors as well.

The additional code that a static code developer must write is often referred to as line noise. The code doesn't substantially translate into useful output, but the static language requires it. For example, IronPython doesn't require that you declare the type of a variable — you simply leave this task to IronPython.

While the extra code in a static language does tend to reduce the potential for unintended output, it can also make the code harder to read. With every benefit, there's a corresponding negative. When you decide to use an extension with IronPython, you need to consider when it's appropriate to work through the extra code and cumbersome features of static languages and when IronPython is truly the better choice.

Let's look at a quick example. Say you want to create an array of names in a function and pass them back to a caller. Here's the C# code to perform the task.

```
public String[] GetNames()
{
    String[] Result = new String[4];
    Result[0] = "John";
    Result[1] = "Amy";
    Result[2] = "Jose";
    Result[3] = "Carla";
    return Result;
}

public void ShowNames()
{
    String[] TheNames = GetNames();

    foreach (String Name in TheNames)
    {
        Console.WriteLine(Name);
    }
}
```

The code in `GetNames()` creates an array of `String`, fills it with names, and returns those names to the caller, `ShowNames()`. At this point, `ShowNames()` uses a `foreach` loop to display each name individually. Now take a look at the same functionality written in IronPython.

```
def GetNames():
    return "John", "Amy", "Jose", "Carla"

def ShowNames():
    for Name in GetNames():
        print Name
```

The code performs the same task in both cases, but as you can see, the IronPython code is significantly shorter. In addition, the IronPython code is actually easier to read.

Considering Scoping Issues

One of the most important differences between IronPython and static languages such as C# is that IronPython doesn't have the concept of scope within classes. Everything in an IronPython class is public, so you always have access to every element. Of course, this presents a dilemma for languages that do support scope. When creating an IronPython extension, your static language scope declarations will change as follows:

➤ `Public` members remain public.

➤ `Protected` members become public.

➤ `Protected Internal` members become public.

➤ `Private` members remain private and don't appear at all to IronPython.

➤ `Internal` members become private and don't appear at all to IronPython.

CREATING THE SIMPLE C# EXTENSION

The example in the following sections provides a simple set of calculations. Think of it as the basic four-function calculator with a bit extra added. The example doesn't do anything fancy, but it does demonstrate techniques you need to build any C# extension for IronPython. The rest of the examples in this chapter build on this example, so you should at least scan the techniques presented in the sections that follow.

Creating the Project

A C# extension project in Visual Studio is nothing more than the typical class library. The following steps help you create the project for this example. You can use the same steps when working with the other examples — all you need to do is change the project name.

1. Choose File ➪ New ➪ Project. You see the New Project dialog box shown in Figure 16-1.

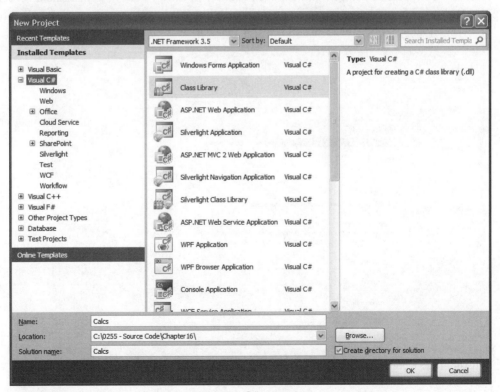

FIGURE 16-1: Create a new project to hold your C# extension.

2. Choose the Visual C# folder in the Installed Templates list.

3. Select .NET Framework 3.5 or an earlier version of the .NET Framework. Don't select the .NET Framework 4.0 entry. The list of templates changes when you change the .NET Framework version.

4. Select the Class Library template.

5. Type **Calcs** in the Name field and click OK. Visual Studio creates a class library project for you.

6. Right-click `Class1.cs` in Solution Explorer and choose Rename from the context menu. Visual Studio makes the filename editable.

7. Type `Calcs.CS` for the new filename and press Enter. Visual Studio displays a dialog box that asks whether you'd like to rename all of the `Class1.cs` references to match the new filename.

8. Click Yes. The project is ready for use.

At the time of this writing, IronPython doesn't support extensions written using the .NET Framework 4.0. You must create your extensions using the .NET Framework 3.5 or earlier. Otherwise, the extension will simply fail to load and IronPython won't provide anything in the way of an explanation (at least, nothing useable). If you suspect that you've targeted the wrong .NET Framework version, choose Project ➪ *ProjectName* Properties. Select the Application tab of the Properties window and change the entry in the Target Framework field to .NET Framework 3.5, as shown in Figure 16-2. The IDE may ask permission to modify features in your setup and require that you restart your project to see the effects of the change.

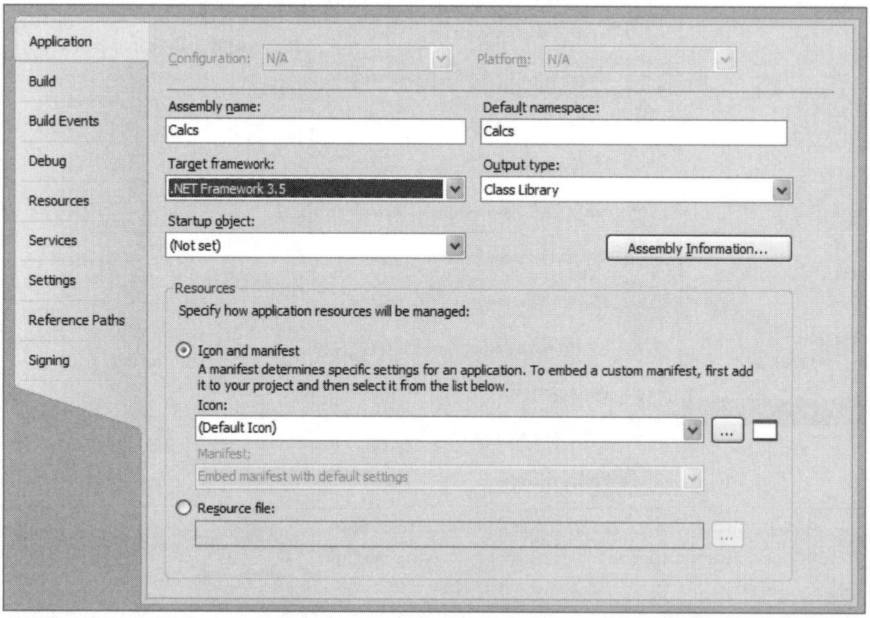

FIGURE 16-2: Modify the Target Framework field to a version of the .NET Framework that works with IronPython.

Developing the C# Extension

The C# extension does have a few tricks to it, but generally speaking, if you know how to create a class library, you already know how to create the code for a C# extension. Listing 16-1 shows the code for the example extension.

LISTING 16-1: A simple calculations extension

```csharp
public class Calcs
{
    private Int32 Data;

    public Calcs(Int32 Value)
    {
        this.Data = Value;
    }

    public override string ToString()
    {
        return Data.ToString();
    }

    public static Calcs operator +(Calcs Value1, Calcs Value2)
    {
        return new Calcs(Value1.Data + Value2.Data);
    }

    public static Calcs operator -(Calcs Value1, Calcs Value2)
    {
        return new Calcs(Value1.Data - Value2.Data);
    }

    public static Calcs operator *(Calcs Value1, Calcs Value2)
    {
        return new Calcs(Value1.Data * Value2.Data);
    }

    public static Calcs operator /(Calcs Value1, Calcs Value2)
    {
        return new Calcs(Value1.Data / Value2.Data);
    }

    public Calcs Inc()
    {
        return new Calcs(this.Data + 1);
    }

    public Calcs Dec()
    {
        return new Calcs(this.Data - 1);
    }
}
```

In most cases, you want to create a constructor that accepts the kind of data you want to manipulate with the extension. In this case, the constructor accepts an Int32 value. Interestingly enough, the constructor is the only place where you normally reference the data type of the data directly. In all other cases, you work with the data type indirectly by using the extension class.

Another issue is displaying the data in IronPython. The default implementation of the ToString() method displays the class name, which isn't helpful. Consequently, you must override the default implementation of ToString() and provide your own output. In this case, the method simply returns the current value of the private variable Data as a string.

This example deals with operators. Of course, there are two kinds of operators, unary and binary. The method you implement for each kind of operator is different.

To create a binary operator, you must consider that the operator will work with two instances of the Calcs class. In short, the operator works with the base class and you must declare it as static. In this example, the + operator is binary, so the code declares it as static. The method also accepts the two instances of the Calcs class as input. In order to return output, the method must create a new instance of the Calcs class with the sum of the two input values. Notice that the method never defines what kind of data it works on, simply that the data is contained in an instance of the Calcs class.

Creating a unary operator is different because you're working with a single instance of the Calcs class in this instance. To create a unary operator, you simply declare the method as a non-static member of the class, as shown for the Inc() and Dec() methods. In this case, because you're working with a single value, the code uses this.Data (the internal representation of the data value of the single value) to perform the math. You may wonder why the code simply doesn't create a ++ operator method. A ++ operator method would look like this and wouldn't work in a unary manner within IronPython.

```
public static Calcs operator ++(Calcs Value1)
{
    return new Calcs(Value1.Data + 1);
}
```

If you compiled the class now, you could view it in the IronPython console. The following code provides the steps for loading the extension into memory.

```
import clr
clr.AddReferenceToFile('Calcs.DLL')
import Calcs
dir(Calcs.Calcs)
```

Figure 16-3 shows the output of the dir(Calcs.Calcs) call. Notice that Inc() and Dec() appear as you expect. However, there aren't any entries for +, -, *, and / methods. These operators still work as you expect, but IronPython shows a Python equivalent for the operators in the form of the __add__(), __radd__(), __sub__(), __rsub__(), __mul__(), __rmul__(), __div__(), and __rdiv__(). These methods don't appear unless you define the operators in your class.

If you're looking at the class in the IronPython console, you might want to give it a quick try before you close up the console and move on to the next part of the example. Try this code and you'll see an output of 15 from the __add__() method.

```
Value1 = Calcs.Calcs(10)
Value2 = Calcs.Calcs(5)
print Value1.__add__(Value2)
```

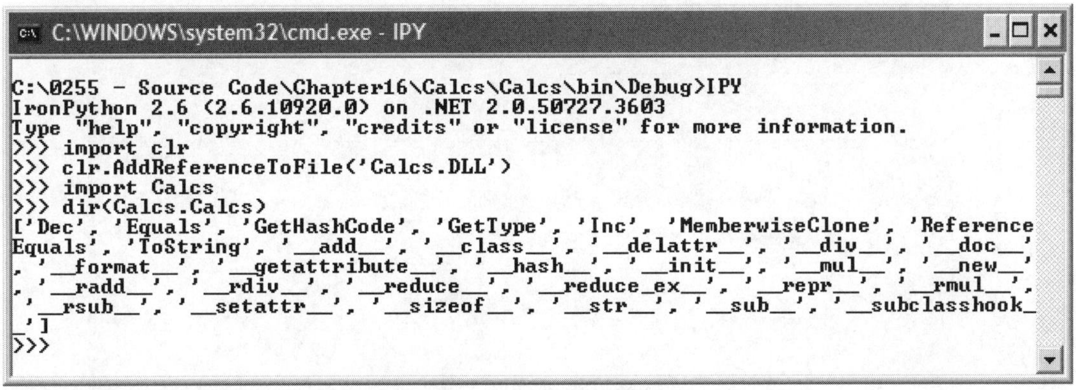

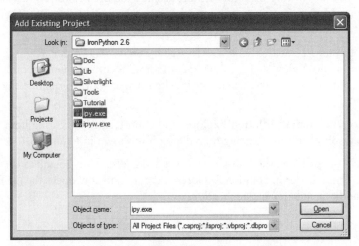

FIGURE 16-3: The dir() function shows the content of the Calcs class.

Adding the IronPython Project

At this point, you have a C# extension (or module) to use with IronPython. Of course, you'll want to test it. The easiest way to do this is to add the IronPython project directly to the current solution. The following steps describe how to perform this task.

1. Right-click the solution entry in Solution Explorer and choose Add ⇨ Existing Project from the context menu. You see the Add Existing Project dialog box shown in Figure 16-4.

FIGURE 16-4: Locate IPY.EXE and add it to your solution.

2. Locate IPY.EXE on your hard drive and highlight it. Click Open. You see a new project entry added to the solution.

3. Right-click the ipy entry in Solution Explorer and choose Set as Startup Project from the context menu. This step ensures that choosing one of the startup options from the Debug menu starts the IronPython application.

4. Right-click the ipy entry in Solution Explorer and choose Properties from the context menu. You'll see the General tab of the ipy Properties window shown in Figure 16-5.

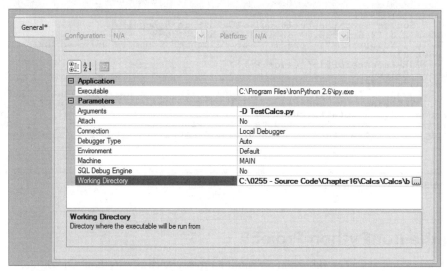

FIGURE 16-5: Configure the IronPython application to work with Calcs.DLL.

5. Type **-D TestCalcs.py** in the Arguments field.

6. Click the ellipses in the Working Directory field to display the Browse for Folder dialog box. Locate the output folder of the Calcs.DLL (or other extension) file. Click OK. The IDE adds the correct directory information to the Working Directory field.

7. Open Windows Explorer. Locate the \Calcs\Calcs\bin\Debug folder. Right-click in the right pane and choose New ⇨ Text Document from the context menu. Name the file TestCalcs.py and press Enter. Click Yes if asked if you want to rename the file extension.

8. Right-click the solution item in Solution Explorer and choose Add ⇨ Existing Item from the context menu to display the Add Existing Item dialog box shown in Figure 16-6.

9. Locate the TestCalcs.py file in the solution and click Add. Visual Studio adds TestCalcs.py to the Solution Items folder in Solution Explorer and automatically opens the file for you. You're ready to add test code for the application.

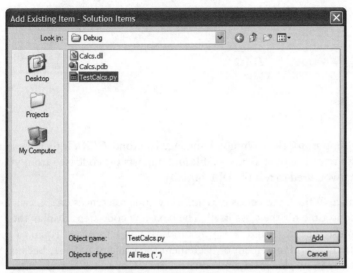

FIGURE 16-6: Add the TestCalcs.py file to the solution.

Creating the IronPython Application

Now that you have a file to use for the IronPython application, it's time to add some code to it. The example code fully exercises everything you can do with the C# extension. Listing 16-2 shows the code you add to the `TestCalcs.py` file.

LISTING 16-2: Testing the extension using IronPython

```python
# Add a reference to the CLR
import clr

# Obtain access to the extension.
clr.AddReferenceToFile('Calcs.DLL')
import Calcs

# Create an instance of the class and fill it with data.
Value1 = Calcs.Calcs(10)

# Print the original value, then decrement and increment it.
print 'Original Value1 Content: ', Value1
print 'Value1 + 1: ', Value1.Inc()
print 'Value1 - 1: ', Value1.Dec()

# Create a second value and display it.
Value2 = Calcs.Calcs(5)
print '\nOriginal Value2 Content: ', Value2

# Use the two values together in different ways.
print '\nValue1 + Value2 = ', Value1 + Value2
```

continues

LISTING 16-2 *(continued)*

```
print 'Value1 - Value2 = ', Value1 - Value2
print 'Value1 * Value2 = ', Value1 * Value2
print 'Value1 / Value2 = ', Value1 / Value2

# Pause after the debug session.
raw_input('\nPress any key to continue...')
```

The example begins by importing support for the Common Language Runtime (CLR). It then uses the
`AddReferenceToFile()` method to reference the `Calcs.DLL` file and imports the code into IronPython.
These steps are similar to those that you used to test the DLL initially.

The next step is to create an instance of the `Calcs` class, `Value1`. The code references `Calcs` twice —
once for the namespace and a second time for the class itself. The next few code steps display the
value of `Value1` and show how to use the `Inc()` and `Dec()` methods. If you set `Value1` equal to
the output of `Inc()` or `Dec()`, it truly would increment or decrement the value of `Value1`. Because
IronPython doesn't support the ++ operator, however, you can't use the ++ operator in your extension. On the other hand, you could implement the += and -= operators.

You can't really test binary operators without a second variable, so the code creates a second
instance of `Calcs`, `Value2`. The example then shows how the +, -, *, and / operators work.
Figure 16-7 shows the output from this example.

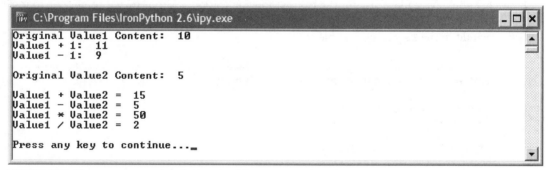

FIGURE 16-7: Here are the results of using the C# extension within IronPython.

USING C# FOR USER INTERFACE SUPPORT

Chapter 8 demonstrates that you can create Windows Forms applications using IronPython. It's a
painful process because you don't have access to any designers, but the process is definitely doable.
You may very well decide to use IronPython directly for all your graphics needs, simply to avoid
using another language. However, C# or Visual Basic.NET make better choices for creating a user
interface because you do get access to the designer support that these languages provide. With this
in mind, the following sections describe how you can add graphic support to IronPython using a C#
extension. (Chapter 17 shows how to perform essentially the same task using Visual Basic.NET.)

Defining a Library of Dialog Boxes

If you're using IronPython as your main application language and relying on a static language for ancillary support, such as the user interface requirements, it makes sense to create all the dialog boxes you require and place them in a library. Of course, if the application is relatively complex, you might use several physical DLLs to perform the task or rely on a single DLL, but rely on multiple projects to accommodate a team of developers The point is that you need to plan how to store the dialog boxes in a manner that makes it efficient to work on the project.

There's a tendency by some developers to create generic dialog boxes and then manipulate them in code. This technique does work well when you use the dialog boxes in the static language. However, the approach can become counterproductive when using the dialog boxes in IronPython. The IronPython code can become so complicated that it becomes unreliable and hard to maintain. In general, use specific dialog boxes whenever possible, which won't require many (or any) changes.

IronPython doesn't have a representation of every C# or Visual Basic.NET feature. For example, in the section "Developing the C# Extension" section earlier in this chapter, you'll discover that IronPython doesn't support the C# ++ operator, but it does support the += operator. It's best to perform data manipulation in the static language environment when possible or pass the raw data to IronPython in a form it can readily use. For example, you might pass a list of field values to IronPython as a dictionary.

Marshaling data between languages can reduce application performance. You may find situations where you need to process data in a thread to maintain acceptable performance for the user. However, before you take time to create a complex threading solution, ask users to try the application in a test environment to determine whether the performance is acceptable.

Creating the Dialog Box Library in C#

Your dialog box library can support dialog boxes at two levels. It's possible to meet some IronPython needs using a simple message box or prompt box. Because these solutions are already programmed for you, supporting them through the static language, where the features are easily accessed, is a good way to save on development and debugging time. You can customize the implementation of these standardized features to make them easy to use within IronPython — reducing the need to import a lot of managed assemblies into IronPython.

Of course, many user-interface needs require something more advanced than a simple message box. The following sections describe how to create simple message boxes and complex Windows Forms in C# that you can use in your IronPython application. The goal is to use the right kind of interface element for a given task and to make the interface element easy to access and process from within IronPython. The section "Creating the Simple C# Extension" earlier in this chapter describes how to set up the solution used for this example.

Defining Simple Message Boxes

This example is interesting because it shows how you can create overrides of your methods. The `MessageBox.Show()` method has 21 overrides in C#. Of course, you might not need all those overrides and the example shows only five of them. Before you can work with message boxes in a

C# class, you need to add a reference to the System.Windows.Forms.DLL and add the following using statement.

```
using System.Windows.Forms;
```

Now that you have the prerequisites in place, it's time to look at some code. Listing 16-3 shows the code used to create this example.

LISTING 16-3: Creating a simple message box class

```csharp
public class Dialogs
{
    public Dialogs()
    {
    }

    public String ShowMessage(String Msg)
    {
        return MessageBox.Show(Msg).ToString();
    }

    public String ShowMessage(String Msg, String Title)
    {
        return MessageBox.Show(Msg, Title).ToString();
    }

    public String ShowMessage(String Msg, String Title, Int16 Buttons)
    {
        return MessageBox.Show(Msg, Title,
            (MessageBoxButtons)Buttons).ToString();
    }

    public String ShowMessage(String Msg, String Title, Int16 Buttons,
        Int16 Icon)
    {
        return MessageBox.Show(Msg, Title,
            (MessageBoxButtons)Buttons, (MessageBoxIcon)Icon).ToString();
    }

    public String ShowMessage(String Msg, String Title, Int16 Buttons,
        Int16 Icon, Int16 DefaultButton)
    {
        return MessageBox.Show(Msg, Title,
            (MessageBoxButtons)Buttons, (MessageBoxIcon)Icon,
            (MessageBoxDefaultButton)DefaultButton).ToString();
    }
}
```

The code begins with the usual constructor. The constructor doesn't really need to do anything in this case. Of course, you could set up the constructor to accept some of the required inputs, such as the message and message box title, but sending the information with the ShowMessage() method works just fine, too. The constructor could also set up default settings, if desired, that the developer could override with specific versions of ShowMessage().

The `ShowMessage()` method declarations come next. The methods are relatively simple. Each one calls a different override of the `MessageBox.Show()` method. Notice that you must coerce the `MessageBoxButtons`, `MessageBoxIcon`, `MessageBoxDefaultButton` values from the inputs. You could ask the caller to provide the actual enumerated values, but that approach would reduce the benefit of using this approach for working with message boxes, because the developer would need to load the required .NET assemblies anyway.

Even when working with simple message boxes, you can encounter a few problems. For example, the enumerations provided in the static environment make it simple to select a particular button combination or icon. IntelliSense displays the list of values from which you can choose. However, IronPython doesn't provide IntelliSense, so there isn't any simple method of selecting a button combination or icon from a list. The example uses numbers, which works fine for the button combinations because they're numbered 0 through 5. However, the icons have values of 0, 16, 32, 48, and 64, which are hardly easy to remember. The default button values are equally odd at 0, 256, and 512. Tables 16-1 through 16-3 show the values for the message box enumerations. In a production environment, you'd probably create text equivalents for the developer, which you could translate in the extension, or provide some type of enumeration for the developer.

TABLE 16-1: Message Box Button Combinations

ENUMERATED VALUE	INT16 VALUE
MessageBoxButtons.AbortRetryIgnore	2
MessageBoxButtons.OK	0
MessageBoxButtons.OKCancel	1
MessageBoxButtons.RetryCancel	5
MessageBoxButtons.YesNo	4
MessageBoxButtons.YesNoCancel	3

TABLE 16-2: Message Box Icon Combinations

ENUMERATED VALUE	INT16 VALUE
MessageBoxIcon.Asterisk	64
MessageBoxIcon.Error	16
MessageBoxIcon.Exclamation	48
MessageBoxIcon.Hand	16
MessageBoxIcon.Information	64
MessageBoxIcon.None	0

continues

TABLE 16-2 *(continued)*

ENUMERATED VALUE	INT16 VALUE
MessageBoxIcon.Question	32
MessageBoxIcon.Stop	16
MessageBoxIcon.Warning	48

TABLE 16-3: Message Box Default Button Options

ENUMERATED VALUE	INT16 VALUE
MessageBoxDefaultButton.Button1	0
MessageBoxDefaultButton.Button2	256
MessageBoxDefaultButton.Button3	512

Using Enumerations with IronPython

There's a way around the issue of enumerated values in .NET calls. You can simply choose to create your own enumeration. For example, let's say you want to overcome the problem of working with the `MessageBoxButtons` enumeration. In this case, you create an enumeration and a new override of the `ShowMessage()` method as shown here.

```
public enum ButtonTypes
{
    OK,
    OKCancel,
    AbortRetryIgnore,
    YesNoCancel,
    YesNo,
    RetryCancel
}

public String ShowMessage(String Msg, String Title, ButtonTypes Buttons)
{
    return MessageBox.Show(Msg, Title,
        (MessageBoxButtons)Buttons).ToString();
}
```

Notice that you must still use coercion to make the `MessageBox.Show()` call. However, the IronPython developer now has an enumeration to use when making the call. Here's a typical call from within IronPython.

```
MyDialog.ShowMessage('Hello', 'Title', MyDialog.ButtonTypes.OKCancel)
```

The resulting message box would contain `'Hello'` as the message, `'Title'` as the message box title, and two buttons, OK and Cancel.

Considering Developer Help

As your extensions gain in complexity, you need to start providing some help to the IronPython developer. Most IronPython developers will spend part of their time in the interpreter trying things out. The developer will look to your documentation for help in using the extension you create. There are two forms of help, as shown here.

```
help(MyDialog.ShowMessage)
MyDialog.ShowMessage.__doc__()
```

It turns out that IronPython automatically provides a form of the `help()` function help for you as shown in Figure 16-8. In this case, you see all of the method calls that the `Dialogs` class provides, along with the enumeration described in the section "Using Enumerations with IronPython" earlier in this chapter.

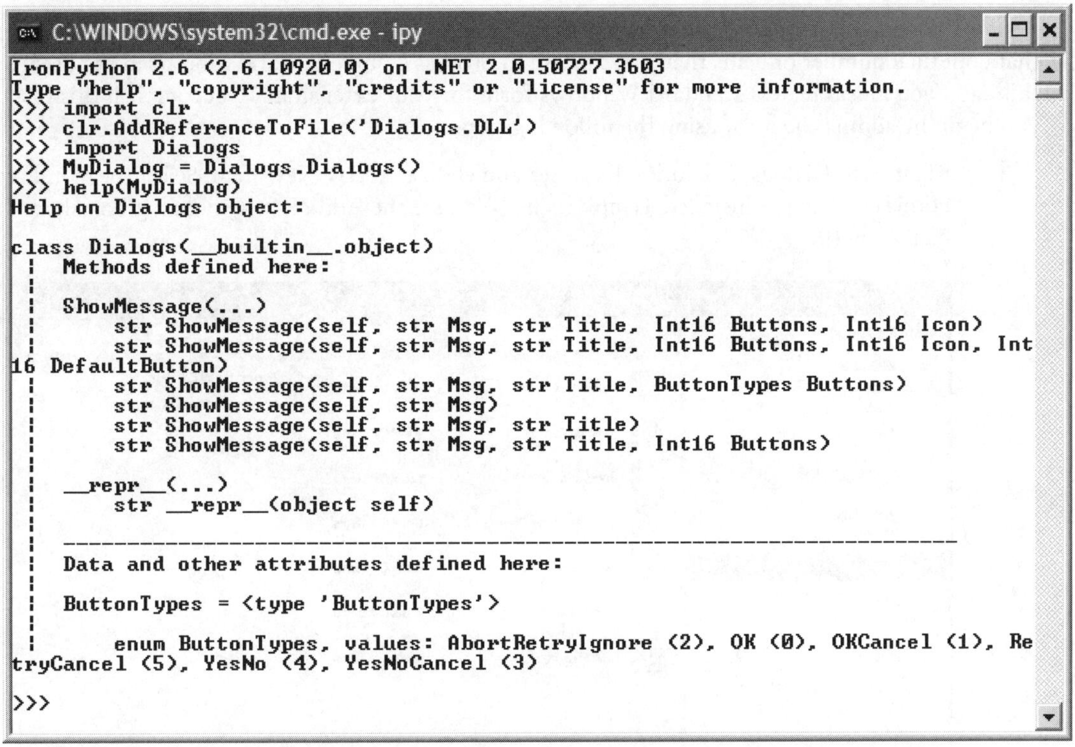

FIGURE 16-8: IronPython provides a kind of help for you automatically.

Unfortunately, IronPython doesn't provide the `__doc__()` method by default. You must define it for yourself as part of the class you create. Here's a simple `__doc__()` method you can use with the example. Of course, a production version would contain far more information.

```
public String __doc__()
{
    return "This is a help string";
}
```

When you try this method out at the Python prompt, you see the outline shown in Figure 16-9. You can use all of the normal formatting characters to make the help provided by the __doc__() method look nice. For that matter, you could store the information externally and simply read it in as needed.

```
C:\WINDOWS\system32\cmd.exe - ipy
>>> MyDialog.__doc__()
'This is a help string'
>>>
```

FIGURE 16-9: You must define your own version of the __doc__() method.

Defining Complex Forms

At some point, simple message boxes simply won't do the job for you. After all, you'll want forms that contain a number of fields that you can use to process complex information from the user. In this case, you must create a standard Windows form for your extension. To accomplish this task, you begin by adding the form using the following steps.

1. Right-click Dialogs in Solution Explorer and choose Add ➪ New Item. Select the Windows Forms entry in the Installed Templates list. You see the Add New Item dialog box shown in Figure 16-10.

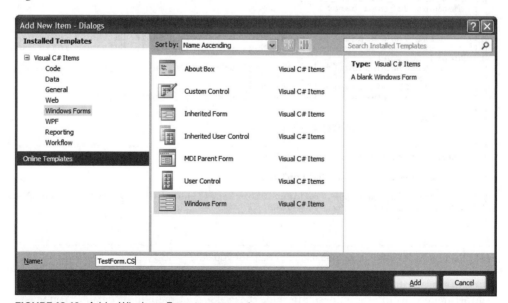

FIGURE 16-10: Add a Windows Form to your project.

2. Highlight the Windows Form entry. Type **TestForm.CS** in the Name field and click Add. Visual Studio adds the new form to your project and automatically opens it for editing.

At this point, you can create the form just as you normally would for any static application. Figure 16-11 shows the form used for this example. It's simple, but it contains multiple data-entry fields and multiple exit options.

Before you assume anything about this form, note that it does differ in a few ways from the forms you've created for your static applications. The first difference is that the buttons that close the form, rather than do something within the form, must have the DialogResult property set to a unique value or you won't be able to tell which button the user clicked. For this example, the DialogResult for btnOK is OK, while the DialogResult for btnCancel is Cancel.

FIGURE 16-11: The Windows Form can contain any level of complexity you desire.

The second difference involves a problem with getting information from the form you create to the IronPython application. You could contrive all sorts of odd methods for accomplishing the task, but the simplest method is to set the Modifiers property for the individual controls (txtName and txtColor) to Public. In this case, using Public doesn't create a problem because IronPython sets everything to public. In all other respects, there's no difference between this form and any other form you've created in the past.

To make things simple, this example doesn't use any code-behind for the form itself. Any code-behind works as you'd expect. There isn't any difference between calling the form from IronPython than calling it from within your C# application.

Accessing the Dialog Box Library from IronPython

At this point, you have a nice collection of dialog box and form classes to use in an IronPython application. Of course, a production application would probably have quite a few more forms in it, but you have enough for testing and experimentation purposes. The following sections describe how to use these classes.

An Alternative Method for Adding the IronPython Project

There are a number of ways to configure a test setup for your extensions. The section "Adding the IronPython Project" earlier in this chapter shows one technique. The technique works well when you want to maintain separate builds of your extension. However, you might want to maintain just one build — the build you're currently using for debugging, testing, or experimentation. Use the following steps to create a centralized test configuration.

1. Right-click Dialogs in Solution Explorer and choose Properties from the context menu. Select the Build tab. You see the Properties window shown in Figure 16-12.

2. Click Browse next to the Output Path field to display the Select Output Path dialog box shown in Figure 16-13. Because you'll add the IronPython test file at the solution level, you need to send the output to the solution level as well.

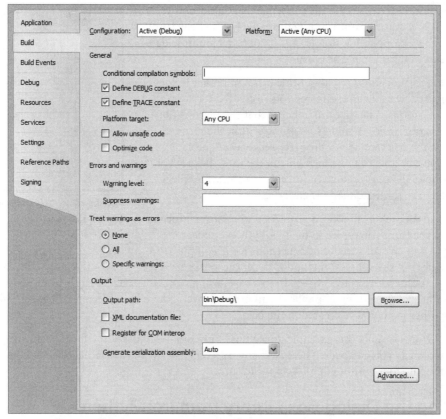

FIGURE 16-12: Configure the build to use a central output location.

3. Select the first Dialogs entry in the list and click OK. Visual Studio adds an absolute path to the Output Path field that you must change for every machine that uses the application. As an alternative, you could type ..\(two periods and a backslash) in the field to place the output in the solution folder.

4. Select the next configuration in the Configuration field.

5. Perform Steps 2 through 4 for each configuration. Make sure each configuration uses the same output directory. Normally, your project will only contain Debug and Release configurations.

6. Right-click the solution entry in Solution Explorer and choose Add ➪ Existing Project from the context menu. You see the Add Existing Project dialog box shown in Figure 16-4.

FIGURE 16-13: Modify the output path as required for your application.

7. Locate IPY.EXE on your hard drive and highlight it. Click Open. You'll see a new project entry added to the solution.

8. Right-click the ipy entry in Solution Explorer and choose Set as Startup Project from the context menu.

9. Right-click the ipy entry in Solution Explorer and choose Properties from the context menu. You see the General tab of the ipy Properties window shown in Figure 16-5.

10. Type **-D DialogTest.py** in the Arguments field.

11. Click the ellipses in the Working Directory field to display the Browse for Folder dialog box. Locate the solution folder for the project (the first Dialogs folder). Click OK. The IDE adds the correct directory information to the Working Directory field.

12. Right-click the solution entry in Solution Explorer and choose Add ➪ New Item from the context menu. You see the Add New Item dialog box shown in Figure 16-14.

FIGURE 16-14: Add the IronPython test file to your project.

13. Type **DialogTest.py** in the Name field and click Add. Visual Studio adds the new file to the Solution Items folder in Solution Explorer and opens the file automatically for editing.

Performing the Message Box and Form Tests

It's finally time to test the message boxes and forms you've created. The code in this section performs a few simple tests and demonstrates how to obtain output from the message boxes and forms you've created. You can use this code as a starting point for more complex processing in your own application. Listing 16-4 shows the test code for this application.

LISTING 16-4: Testing the extension using IronPython

```python
# Define the message box tests.
def TestMessages():

    # Create a message box object.
    MyDialog = Dialogs.Dialogs()

    # Test a simple message box.
    print 'Testing a simple message box.'
    print 'Simple message box output: ',
    print MyDialog.ShowMessage('Hello')

    # Perform a more complex test.
    print '\nA more complex message box.'
    print 'Complex message box output: ',
    print MyDialog.ShowMessage('Hello Again', 'Title 2', 3, 64, 256)

# Define the form test.
def TestForm():

    # Create the form instance.
    MyForm = Dialogs.TestForm()

    # Display the form and test the dialog result.
    print '\nThe form example.'
    if MyForm.ShowDialog().ToString() == 'OK':

        # Display the results.
        print 'The user clicked OK.'
        print 'User Name: ', MyForm.txtName.Text
        print 'Favorite Color: ', MyForm.txtColor.Text

    # Display an alternate result.
    else:
        print 'The user clicked cancel.'

# Import the Common Language Runtime.
import clr

# Access the extension.
clr.AddReferenceToFile('Dialogs.DLL')
import Dialogs

# Test the message box code.
TestMessages()

# Test the form code.
TestForm()

# Pause after the debug session.
raw_input('\nPress any key to continue...')
```

The test code begins by importing CLR and gaining access to the `Dialogs` namespace. This example demonstrates one of the benefits of using a namespace, easy access to multiple classes. It's a good way to organize a library of forms to make them easy to access and to avoid naming conflicts.

The `TestMessages()` function contains the code to test the `Dialogs.Dialogs` class. This code begins by creating a `Dialogs.Dialogs` instance, `MyDialog`. In this case, the application begins by creating a simple message box and displaying it onscreen. This message box lacks a title and contains only an OK button. When the user clicks OK, the program prints the dialog result to screen.

The second test is a little more complex. This time the code relies on the most complex form of the `ShowMessage()` method to display a dialog box that contains a message, title, icon, and multiple buttons as shown in Figure 16-15. Notice that the figure shows that the message box also has the middle button selected by default. Pressing Enter will automatically select this default option. Normally, message boxes select the first button as the default. Depending on which button the user clicks, the application will display a message with the appropriate dialog result. You could also use this dialog result as part of an `if...else` statement to choose an appropriate course of action.

FIGURE 16-15: A more complex message box includes multiple buttons, a title, and an icon.

The `TestForm()` method begins by creating an instance of `Dialogs.TestForm`, `MyForm`. The `dir()` function will show you that `MyForm` now has access to all of the functionality normally associated with a Windows Forms class, but without importing any of the bulk associated with the `System.Windows.Forms` assembly. As with any Windows Form, you call `ShowDialog()` to display the form. However, the result of displaying the form is going to be something that IronPython can't use directly. The way to overcome this problem is to call `ShowDialog().ToString()`. In this case, the output is a string that describes which button the user has clicked.

This portion of the example shows how to process the form data locally. When the user clicks OK, the dialog result is `'OK'` and the `if` statement succeeds. The code accesses the `MyForm.txtName.Text` and `MyForm.txtColor.Text` properties to determine what the user has typed. When the `if` statement fails, the code displays a message telling you that the user clicked Cancel. Figure 16-16 shows typical output from this example.

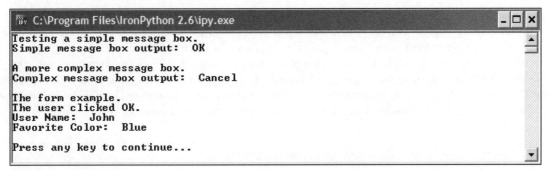

FIGURE 16-16: Here are the results of using the C# extension within IronPython.

USING C# FOR WIN32 SUPPORT

The Python language doesn't really support much in the way of platform-specific functionality and that's by design. One of the tenets of cross-platform compatibility is not to make an issue out of the platform on which the code runs. However, in some cases, you really do need to access the platform and discover things about it. For example, you might want to know more about the environment in which your application is executing, such as the size of the console window. You might even want to clear the console window (a feature that is missing from the IronPython console, without which your sessions can appear messy). An application may need to know something about the security in place for the current session. In short, you might have many reasons for wanting to know something more, but Python (and by extension, IronPython) largely lacks the functionality to provide this information.

The example in the following sections plays to a strength of C#, which is to interact with the Windows platform through a feature called Platform Invoke (P/Invoke). This example goes outside the managed .NET environment and relies on the Win32 API to access Windows functionality that you can't access through .NET.

Creating the P/Invoke Code

Before you can write any P/Invoke code, you need to add the following `using` statement.

```
using System.Runtime.InteropServices;
```

This statement provides access to the various special programming features that C# provides for accessing the Win32 API.

 You may find that you have little interest in precisely how P/Invoke works. It's possible to skip the details found in this section, proceed to the sections that follow, and still understand how the whole application works. However, working through the P/Invoke code will give you a better understanding of the power that C# provides in accessing features you might not have used in the past (and potentially a few that you might not even know exist now).

If you haven't worked with the Win32 API in the past, you might find the use of structures, enumerations, and pointers confusing. In reality, all these events take place somewhere in the background when you execute any application. At some point, your managed code ends up interacting with the Win32 API to perform tasks because the basic Windows DLLs still rely on the Win32 API. Normally, CLR hides all these details from view so you don't need to worry about them. Listing 16-5 shows the Win32 API access code — the lower-level code that does all the hard work for this example.

LISTING 16-5: Win32 API access code and structures

```
// This special class contains an enumeration of
// standard handles.
class StdHandleEnum
```

```
{
    public const int STD_INPUT_HANDLE   = -10;
    public const int STD_OUTPUT_HANDLE  = -11;
    public const int STD_ERROR_HANDLE   = -12;
};

// The GetStdHandle() function returns a handle to any
// standard input or output.
[DllImport("kernel32.dll", SetLastError=true)]
public static extern IntPtr GetStdHandle(int nStdHandle);

// This sructure contains a screen coordinate.
[StructLayout(LayoutKind.Sequential, Pack=1)]
public struct COORD
{
    public short X;
    public short Y;
}

// Obtains the current display mode--fullscreen or fullscreen hardware.
[DllImport("Kernel32.DLL")]
public static extern bool GetConsoleDisplayMode(ref UInt32 lpModeFlags);

// An enumeration used to determine the current display mode.
public enum ConsoleDispMode
{
    CONSOLE_WINDOWED            = 0, // Only implied by function.
    CONSOLE_FULLSCREEN          = 1, // The console is fullscreen.
    CONSOLE_FULLSCREEN_HARDWARE = 2  // The console owns the hardware.
}

// Obtains the size of the largest console window possible.
[DllImport("Kernel32.DLL")]
public static extern COORD
    GetLargestConsoleWindowSize(IntPtr hConsoleOutput);

// Returns the console mode information.
[DllImport("Kernel32.DLL")]
public static extern bool GetConsoleMode(
    IntPtr hConsoleHandle,
    ref UInt32 lpMode);

public enum ModeFlags
{
    // Input mode flags
    ENABLE_PROCESSED_INPUT     = 0x0001,
    ENABLE_LINE_INPUT          = 0x0002,
    ENABLE_ECHO_INPUT          = 0x0004,
    ENABLE_WINDOW_INPUT        = 0x0008,
    ENABLE_MOUSE_INPUT         = 0x0010,

    // Output mode flags
    ENABLE_PROCESSED_OUTPUT    = 0x0001,
    ENABLE_WRAP_AT_EOL_OUTPUT  = 0x0002
}
```

Many of the Win32 API functions require you to know specific integer or hexadecimal values. Even C++ developers can't remember these numbers. Normally, a C++ developer relies on `define` statements that put the numbers into human-readable form. The P/Invoke code used in this chapter does the same thing, but sometimes it places the numbers in an enumeration to make them even easier to use. The `StdHandleEnum` class provides a list of standard handles (pointers) for Windows devices: input, output, and error. However, these aren't the actual handles.

In order to get the standard Windows handle, an application must call the `GetStdHandle()` function. This function is in `kernel32.dll`. The `[DllImport()]` attribute tells the compiler where to look for an external Win32 API function that you want to use in your code. In this case, the attribute also tells the compiler that you want any error information that the Win32 API can provide. The use of `extern` before the function name tells the compiler that the requested DLL contains a function of the name that follows. You can now call this function directly and CLR will automatically perform any required marshaling for you.

Many of the Win32 API calls provide coordinates — x and y locations that tell where something is or how large it is. The `COORD` structure provides a means of transferring this kind of information between the .NET environment and the Win32 API environment. Windows uses a very basic view of structures. Unfortunately, .NET often causes problems by trying to optimize the data structures and causes P/Invoke calls to fail even though they should succeed. The `[StructLayout()]` attribute tells the compiler how to create a data structure in memory, which overrides the normal optimization process.

You may create applications that need to run in full-screen mode, if for no other reason than that they require the additional screen real estate to present information to the user. The `GetConsoleDisplayMode()` function tells you what mode the console is currently in. If the console is in the wrong mode, you can ask the user to change the mode or simply stop the application before the screen mode causes any problems. This function returns flags, not an enumerated value. At least one of the flags is always set, but the return value can have multiple flags set. The `ConsoleDispMode` enumeration makes it easier to work through the flag settings and provide usable output. The section "Defining the GetCurrentDisplayMode() Method" later in this chapter provides more information about this function.

In some cases, you need to know the largest size console window that the system will support. The `GetLargestConsoleWindowSize()` function provides this information. You can use other Win32 API functions to adjust the size of the window to meet application requirements (which is a topic for another book). The section "Defining the GetConsoleWindowSize() Method" provides more information about this function.

It's also handy to know what kinds of operations the console window will support. For example, it's good to know whether the console window will respond to the mouse. The `GetConsoleMode()` function provides this kind of information. The output is in the form of flags that you must interpret in your code. The `GetConsoleMode()` function is special in that the output you receive depends on the kind of device handle you provide. The output differs when you provide an input handle, versus an output handle. The section "Defining the GetConsoleInfo() Method" provides additional information about how this technique works.

Developing the IronPython Callable Methods

The P/Invoke code shown in Listing 16-5 does expose the Win32 API calls needed to perform certain tasks with IronPython. Theoretically, you could rely on just the code in Listing 16-5 to gain the access you require in IronPython. However, the task would be difficult because you'd need to work through the required bit manipulations. It's better to place the code you need to access the Win32 API in easily called methods, which is the purpose of the code in the following sections.

Defining Common Variables and the Constructor

Win32 API calls often reuse information. It's not uncommon for functions to ask for the same information over and over. For example, any function that works with a window will probably need the handle for that window. With this requirement in mind, Listing 16-6 shows the common variables and the constructor used for this example.

LISTING 16-6: Common variables and constructor

```
UInt32 DisplayMode = 0;      // The current display mode.
IntPtr hOut;                 // Handle to the output device.
IntPtr hIn;                  // Handle to the input device.
UInt32 ConsoleMode = 0;      // The console mode information.

public ConMode()
{
    // Obtain a handle to the console screen and console input.
    hIn = GetStdHandle(StdHandleEnum.STD_INPUT_HANDLE);
    hOut = GetStdHandle(StdHandleEnum.STD_OUTPUT_HANDLE);
}
```

The common variables include the current display mode (such as windowed), the console mode information (such as whether it accepts mouse input), and the handles for the input and output devices. These variables represent common pieces of information that the developer requires for multiple calls.

The constructor initializes the input and output handles using the GetStdHandle() function. The input argument simply tells Windows which handle you want. The output is an IntPtr, a special kind of variable that points to something. An IntPtr is a safe pointer, meaning you can use it without problems in a managed language. C# also supports unsafe pointers that you should use only as a last resort.

An IntPtr provides an integer value that represents a pointer. The size of the integer is platform-specific and you should never view a standard Int16 or Int32 type as an acceptable substitute. Always use an IntPtr when you need to access a pointer or handle supplied by a Win32 API call.

Defining the GetCurrentDisplayMode() Method

Sometimes you need to know whether the console is presented in a windowed or full-screen mode. A windowed console can get covered up and needs to share resources with other windows. In addition, the text in a windowed console can be small and hard to read. On a positive note, using a windowed console makes it easier to share data between applications. In most cases, the user will prefer that you use a windowed console to make it easier to multitask between applications. Listing 16-7 shows how to detect the current console display mode.

LISTING 16-7: Obtaining the current display mode

```
public OutputMode GetCurrentDisplayMode()
{

    // Get the current display mode.
    if (GetConsoleDisplayMode(ref DisplayMode))

        // Determine if the console is in windowed mode.
        if (DisplayMode == (UInt32)ConsoleDispMode.CONSOLE_WINDOWED)
            return OutputMode.Windowed;
        else
        {

            // If the console is fullscreen mode, determine which
            // of the potential conditions are true.
            switch (DisplayMode)
            {
                case (UInt32)ConsoleDispMode.CONSOLE_FULLSCREEN:
                    return OutputMode.Fullscreen;
                case (UInt32)ConsoleDispMode.CONSOLE_FULLSCREEN_HARDWARE:
                    return OutputMode.HadwareAccess;
                case (UInt32)ConsoleDispMode.CONSOLE_FULLSCREEN +
                     (UInt32)ConsoleDispMode.CONSOLE_FULLSCREEN_HARDWARE:
                    return OutputMode.FullscreenHardwareAccess;
            }
        }

    // Return a default value.
    return OutputMode.Unknown;
}
```

The code begins by calling `GetConsoleDisplayMode()` to obtain the display mode as a numeric value. The information is returned in `DisplayMode`, not as a return value from the function call. The function itself returns a success value that indicates the call was successful. The first `if` statement says that if the call is successful, then `DisplayMode` will contain the console display mode, and that the application should proceed to process it. Because `DisplayMode` provides a return value, you must include the `ref` keyword when passing it to the Win32 API.

Now that the code has a display mode value, it needs to process it. If a console is in windowed mode, all the code has to do is return a value that says it's windowed. However, full-screen mode requires some additional processing. When a console is in full-screen mode, it can also have access to the hardware. This is virtual hardware access, but it still feels to the application as if the access is direct. Consequently, the code must now determine whether the console is simply in full-screen mode or it's in full-screen mode with hardware access.

The call could fail, but it's unlikely to. Even so, the `GetCurrentDisplayMode()` handles the potential problem by providing the `OutputMode.Unknown` return value. This value simply says that the method couldn't determine the current console display mode.

Defining the GetConsoleWindowSize() Method

Sometimes an application needs to know the maximum windowed console that a machine can accommodate. You might need additional room to display complex textual information. The Win32 API returns this information in a `COORD` structure that simply states the number of rows and columns of text that a console can support at maximum size. The following code shows the `GetConsoleWindowSize()` method used to obtain this information.

```
public COORD GetConsoleWindowSize()
{
    // Determine the largest screen size possible.
    return GetLargestConsoleWindowSize(hOut);
}
```

This method is easy. All it does is call the `GetLargestConsoleWindowSize()` function with the output handle. Make sure you provide the output handle, and not the input handle, when making this call. The X and Y members of `COORD` contain the maximum screen size on return from the call.

 If you compare how the `GetConsoleDisplayMode()` *function works with the* `GetLargestConsoleWindowSize()` *function, you'll see that they're inconsistent. The inconsistency of the Win32 API calls is one of the reasons that developers don't like to work with them and why using the .NET Framework is better. When working with the Win32 API, make sure you know precisely how a function works before you use it. Calling some functions using the wrong technique can have terrifying results (such as rebooting your system or damaging data).*

Defining the GetConsoleInfo() Method

Consoles can support a number of input and output methods. For example, a console can support the mouse, which may make it easier for the user to interact with your character-mode application. If a console provides support for echo, it re-displays commands sent to it from batch files and other forms of automation. Consequently, you might find it useful to know just what the console will do for you. Listing 16-8 shows how to determine the input and output handling that a console provides.

LISTING 16-8: Obtaining the console characteristics

```csharp
public struct ConsoleData
{
    public Boolean Echo;
    public Boolean LineInput;
    public Boolean MouseInput;
    public Boolean ProcessedInput;
    public Boolean WindowInput;
    public Boolean ProcessedOutput;
    public Boolean LineWrap;
}

public ConsoleData GetConsoleInfo()
{
    // Create the required structure.
    ConsoleData Output = new ConsoleData();

    // Retrieve the input information.
    if (GetConsoleMode(hIn, ref ConsoleMode))
    {
        if ((ConsoleMode & (UInt32)ModeFlags.ENABLE_ECHO_INPUT) ==
        (UInt32)ModeFlags.ENABLE_ECHO_INPUT)
            Output.Echo = true;
        else
            Output.Echo = false;

        if ((ConsoleMode & (UInt32)ModeFlags.ENABLE_LINE_INPUT) ==
        (UInt32)ModeFlags.ENABLE_LINE_INPUT)
            Output.LineInput = true;
        else
            Output.LineInput = false;

        if ((ConsoleMode & (UInt32)ModeFlags.ENABLE_MOUSE_INPUT) ==
        (UInt32)ModeFlags.ENABLE_MOUSE_INPUT)
            Output.MouseInput = true;
        else
            Output.MouseInput = false;

        if ((ConsoleMode & (UInt32)ModeFlags.ENABLE_PROCESSED_INPUT) ==
        (UInt32)ModeFlags.ENABLE_PROCESSED_INPUT)
            Output.ProcessedInput = true;
        else
            Output.ProcessedInput = false;

        if ((ConsoleMode & (UInt32)ModeFlags.ENABLE_WINDOW_INPUT) ==
        (UInt32)ModeFlags.ENABLE_WINDOW_INPUT)
            Output.WindowInput = true;
        else
            Output.WindowInput = false;
    }

    // Retrieve the output information.
    if (GetConsoleMode(hOut, ref ConsoleMode))
```

```
    {
        if ((ConsoleMode & (UInt32)ModeFlags.ENABLE_PROCESSED_OUTPUT) ==
        (UInt32)ModeFlags.ENABLE_PROCESSED_OUTPUT)
            Output.ProcessedOutput = true;
        else
            Output.ProcessedOutput = false;

        if ((ConsoleMode & (UInt32)ModeFlags.ENABLE_WRAP_AT_EOL_OUTPUT)
        == (UInt32)ModeFlags.ENABLE_WRAP_AT_EOL_OUTPUT)
            Output.LineWrap = true;
        else
            Output.LineWrap = false;
    }

    // Return the results.
    return Output;
}
```

This is one of the few situations in the chapter where you need to send a number of pieces of information back to IronPython. The `ConsoleData` structure contains an entry of each piece of information that the `GetConsoleInfo()` provides. An IronPython application can set the output of the call to a variable and then use the variable content to determine precisely how the console is configured.

The `GetConsoleInfo()` method is a little more complicated than the other calls in the extension. This method relies on the `GetConsoleMode()` function to obtain console information. However, notice that the method calls the `GetConsoleMode()` function twice, once with the input handle and again with the output handle. This method demonstrates how the use of the wrong handle could cause problems because the output from the `GetConsoleMode()` function differs with the handle you provide as input.

The return value from the `GetConsoleMode()` function is a series of flags. Notice how the code uses `if` statements to determine whether each flag is set. When a flag is set, the feature is enabled and the code sets that value in the `ConsoleData` data structure, `Output`, to `true`. The method ends by returning the fully completed `ConsoleData` data structure to the caller.

Writing an IronPython Application to Use P/Invoke

If you've been following along with the example, you know it's finally time to use the `ConMode` class with IronPython. It's now possible to determine the display mode, the size of the console window, and the capabilities it provides. Listing 16-9 shows the code used for testing this extension.

LISTING 16-9: Testing the Win32 API extension

```
# Import the Common Language Runtime.
import clr

# Access the extension.
clr.AddReferenceToFile('Win32API.DLL')
import Win32API

# Create an instance of the class.
```

continues

LISTING 16-9 *(continued)*

```
TestWin32 = Win32API.ConMode()

# Check the display mode.
print 'The display mode is: ',
print TestWin32.GetCurrentDisplayMode()

# Obtain the largest possible window size.
print '\nThe largest possible window size is: '
Size = TestWin32.GetConsoleWindowSize()
print '\tColumns: ', Size.X
print '\tRows: ', Size.Y

# Display the console characteristics.
print '\nThe console has these characteristics:'
Chars = TestWin32.GetConsoleInfo()
print '\tEcho Enabled: ', Chars.Echo
print '\tLine Input Enabled: ', Chars.LineInput
print '\tMouse Input Enabled: ', Chars.MouseInput
print '\tProcessed Input Enabled: ', Chars.ProcessedInput
print '\tWindow Input Enabled: ', Chars.WindowInput
print '\tConsole Can Produce Processed Output:', Chars.ProcessedOutput
print '\tConsole Uses Line Wrap: ', Chars.LineWrap

# Pause after the debug session.
raw_input('\nPress any key to continue...')
```

The code begins by importing CLR support. It then creates a reference to Win32API.DLL and imports the Win32API namespace into the IronPython environment. The next step is to create an instance of the Win32API.ConMode class, TestWin32.

At this point, the code begins checking each console feature in turn, beginning with the console display mode, which doesn't require any additional processing. The GetConsoleWindowSize() method call requires that the code display the Size.X (columns) and Size.Y (rows) values separately.

The GetConsoleInfo() method call comes next. This particular call requires a little more processing because it returns more information. The output of the call appears in Chars as a ConsoleData data structure. As you can see, the code simply displays the true or false value of each of the data structure members. Figure 16-17 shows the output from this example.

One of the most important issues when making Win32 API calls from IronPython is to ensure that the C# extension processes the data in an easy-to-use manner. In addition, you should provide a consistent method for returning the data from the C# extension to IronPython, such as using data structures (as shown in the example).

USING IRONPYTHON CONSTRUCTIVELY

When you complete this chapter, you should have gained a number of new skills related to extensions. Remember to use the simple extension example as the starting point for extensions that you create. The more complex examples provide techniques you can use, but not necessarily implement directly in your own extensions. Of course, the starting point for this chapter describes how to work with extensions in general and helps you consider issues related to extension design. This information applies equally well to Visual Basic.NET extensions.

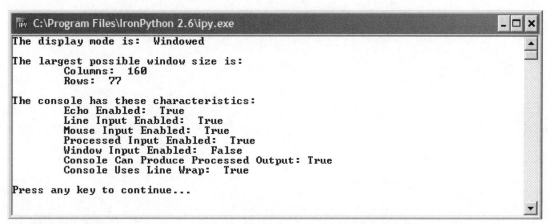

FIGURE 16-17: The P/Invoke code tells you about the console window characteristics.

Before you move on to the next chapter, try all the examples in this chapter and discover how they work. It's important to choose the right extension language. Even though there's overlap between the tasks you can perform with C# and Visual Basic.NET, each language also has features that make it the right choice for a particular task. In this chapter, you discover that C# works great for low-level tasks that you might not be able to perform otherwise, such as directly accessing the Windows security features. After you work through the examples in this chapter, make a list of tasks that you might want to perform for your organization that involve C# extensions and IronPython. Weigh the value of the C# and IronPython combination against other language choices. As you gain experience in more languages, choosing the right language becomes harder because each language has so much to offer.

Now that you've discovered the C# extension, it's time to see the Visual Basic.NET extension in action. Chapter 17 shows how to create extensions using Visual Basic.NET. Just like this chapter, Chapter 17 provides you with a basic example you can use to build your own extensions with ease. However, Chapter 17 also compares and contrasts the kinds of extensions you build using C# with those that you typically build using Visual Basic.NET. For example, Visual Basic.NET excels at database management tasks. You may actually want to come back to this chapter after you read through and try out the examples in Chapter 17 so that you get the full amount of information available from both chapters.

17

Extending IronPython Using Visual Basic.NET

WHAT'S IN THIS CHAPTER?

➤ Understanding the differences between C# and Visual Basic.NET extensions

➤ Developing a simple Visual Basic.NET extension

➤ Providing user interface support through a Visual Basic.NET extension

➤ Providing database support through a Visual Basic.NET extension

Visual Basic is a great language for many tasks, especially when it comes to database management. Sure, you can write great database management code using C#, but many developers feel that Visual Basic does a better job in this area. In addition, many developers find that Visual Basic is easier to work with for user interface tasks. Whether you agree with this assessment or not, Visual Basic should be another tool in your IronPython extension toolkit.

 This chapter assumes that you already know the requirements for building an extension. If you haven't already read the section "Understanding the Requirements for an Extension" in Chapter 16, you should do so before you start this chapter. The first section of this chapter describes the few differences between C# and Visual Basic.NET extensions.

This chapter begins with a simple Visual Basic.NET extension. You can use this example as the basis for your own extensions. Simply remove the example code and use the project itself

to start your own extensions. Of course, this simple example is also useful for demonstrating how to create extensions. This chapter provides the complete Visual Basic.NET view of working with extensions, so you only need to view a few common items in Chapter 16 (and may not need to view them at all). The example in this chapter is complete and you should follow it when working with Visual Basic.NET code.

The chapter includes two additional examples that demonstrate some of the better ways to use Visual Basic.NET to create extensions for IronPython. The first example provides you with a library of dialog boxes that you can use within IronPython. In many cases, your existing Visual Basic.NET dialog boxes are your best resource when working with IronPython — there isn't a good reason to recreate them in IronPython. The second example is a little more complex. It demonstrates how to work with databases in Visual Basic.NET and then extend that code to IronPython.

CONSIDERING C# AND VISUAL BASIC.NET EXTENSION SIMILARITIES

Most of the techniques you use to create an extension in C# also work with Visual Basic.NET. You configure your projects essentially the same way and the layout of the code itself is the same. Both C# and Visual Basic.NET extensions require the same forms of type conversion and marshaling to work with IronPython. Consequently, most of the materials contained in the sections "Understanding the Requirements for an Extension" and "Considering IronPython and Static Language Differences" in Chapter 16 also apply to Visual Basic.NET extensions. Make sure you read these sections before you proceed further in this chapter.

Visual Basic.NET does have some distinct advantages over C# when building an extension. The most important of these distinctions is that Visual Basic.NET does more for you in the background. For example, Visual Basic.NET automatically creates a namespace for you — it isn't something you have to think about. Visual Basic.NET also performs some type conversions automatically, so you don't have to think about type conversions as much either. When you do need to perform a type conversion, you use the `CType()` function, which makes the kind of conversion a little more apparent.

You can easily use either C# or Visual Basic.NET to perform simple tasks. For example, either language works fine for creating a math library or for working with files. It's also possible to use either language to create a library of dialog boxes. The language you choose comes down to a matter of personal preference. As presented in Chapter 16, C# probably has an advantage in working with low-level extensions, especially those that interact with the Win32 API. On the other hand, the tendency of Visual Basic.NET to hide some of the gory details of programming works to your advantage when working with higher-level programming requirements, such as database access. Consequently, this chapter describes the requirements for creating a database extension.

CREATING THE SIMPLE VISUAL BASIC.NET EXTENSION

The best place to begin learning how to create extensions is to create a very simple one. The sections that follow explore a simple Visual Basic.NET extension. This project creates a simple math library. In the process, it demonstrates some unique principles of creating extensions using Visual Basic.NET.

Creating the Project

A Visual Basic.NET extension project is nothing more than the typical class library. The following steps help you create the project for this example. You can use the same steps when working with the other examples — simply change the project name.

1. Choose File ➪ New ➪ Project. You'll see the New Project dialog box shown in Figure 17-1.

FIGURE 17-1: Create a new project to hold your Visual Basic.NET extension.

2. Choose the Visual Basic folder in the Installed Templates list.

3. Select .NET Framework 3.5 or an earlier version of the .NET Framework if you're using Visual Studio 2010. Don't select the .NET Framework 4.0 entry because IronPython won't load extensions based on the .NET Framework 4.0. The list of templates changes when you change the .NET Framework version.

4. Select the Class Library template.

5. Check Create Directory for Solution if it isn't already checked. When working with extensions, creating a solution directory provides a place for putting solution-level objects.

6. Type **Calcs** in the Name field and click OK. Visual Studio creates a class library project for you.

7. Right-click Class1.vb in Solution Explorer and choose Rename from the context menu. Visual Studio makes the filename editable.

8. Type **Calcs.VB** for the new filename and press Enter. Visual Studio displays a dialog box that asks whether you'd like to rename all of the Class1.vb references to match the new filename.

9. Click Yes. The project is ready for use.

Renaming the class file also renames any hidden elements. For example, the namespace for this project is hidden, but it's renamed to Calcs. *It's important to keep the renaming of hidden elements in mind as you work with the IronPython code.*

Developing the Visual Basic.NET Extension

The Visual Basic.NET extension code for this example is relatively simple. Listing 17-1 shows the constructor, operator overrides, and methods used for this example.

LISTING 17-1: A simple calculations extension

```vbnet
Public Class Calcs

    Private Data As Int32

    Public Sub New(ByVal Value As Int32)
        Me.Data = Value
    End Sub

    Public Overrides Function ToString() As String
        Return Data.ToString()
    End Function

    Public Shared Operator +(ByVal Value1 As Calcs, _
                             ByVal Value2 As Calcs) As Calcs
        Return New Calcs(Value1.Data + Value2.Data)
    End Operator

    Public Shared Operator -(ByVal Value1 As Calcs, _
                             ByVal Value2 As Calcs) As Calcs
        Return New Calcs(Value1.Data - Value2.Data)
    End Operator

    Public Shared Operator *(ByVal Value1 As Calcs, _
                             ByVal Value2 As Calcs) As Calcs
        Return New Calcs(Value1.Data * Value2.Data)
    End Operator

    Public Shared Operator /(ByVal Value1 As Calcs, _
                             ByVal Value2 As Calcs) As Calcs
        Return New Calcs(Value1.Data / Value2.Data)
    End Operator

    Public Function Inc() As Calcs
        Return New Calcs(Me.Data + 1)
    End Function
```

```
Public Function Dec() As Calcs
    Return New Calcs(Me.Data - 1)
End Function

End Class
```

The code begins with a constructor that accepts an `Int32` value as input. The example doesn't include a default constructor because IronPython needs to assign a value to the object during the instantiation process. A default constructor would still need to assign a value to the private `Data` member, so it's just better to assign a valid value to `Data` at the outset.

The `ToString()` override comes next. The default behavior for `ToString()` is to display the name of the class. You must override this behavior to display the value of `Data`. Notice that you must access `Data` as `Me.Data` — the copy of `Data` associated with this particular instance of the `Calcs` class.

The four `Operator` methods are defined as `Shared`, rather than `Overrides`. The `Operator` methods act as static class members so that you can use them naturally in IronPython. The input arguments for each method are the objects you create within IronPython. Consequently, there isn't any concept of numeric type for `Value1` or `Value2` (you could theoretically use the same methods for any numeric value). The actual math operation occurs on the `Data` member of each object.

IronPython doesn't support the ++ or -- operators that are supported by Visual Basic for increment and decrement. Consequently, the class provides an `Inc()` and `Dec()` method. Notice that these methods aren't defined as `Shared` because they work with a single object. You need to consider the differences between binary (those that work with two objects) and unary (those that work with a single object) operators when creating your extension. Binary operators are always declared as `Shared`, while unary operators appear as a standard method.

At this point, you can compile the class if desired. Start a copy of the IronPython console and type the following commands to load the extension.

```
import clr
clr.AddReferenceToFile('Calcs.DLL')
import Calcs
dir(Calcs.Calcs)
```

The `dir()` function shows the content of the `Calcs` extension as shown in Figure 17-2. Notice that `Inc()` and `Dec()` appear as you expect. However, there aren't any entries for +, -, *, and / methods. These operators still work as you expect, but IronPython shows a Python equivalent for the operators in the form of `__add__()`, `__radd__()`, `__sub__()`, `__rsub__()`, `__mul__()`, `__rmul__()`, `__div__()`, and `__rdiv__()`. These methods don't appear unless you define the operators in your class.

If you're looking at the class in the IronPython console, you might want to give it a quick try before you close up the console and move on to the next part of the example. Try this code and you'll see an output of 15 from the `__add__()` method. Figure 17-2 shows the results of the calculation.

```
Value1 = Calcs.Calcs(10)
Value2 = Calcs.Calcs(5)
print Value1.__add__(Value2)
```

```
C:\WINDOWS\system32\cmd.exe - ipy

IronPython 2.6 (2.6.10920.0) on .NET 2.0.50727.3603
Type "help", "copyright", "credits" or "license" for more information.
>>> import clr
>>> clr.AddReferenceToFile('Calcs.DLL')
>>> import Calcs
>>> dir(Calcs.Calcs)
['Dec', 'Equals', 'GetHashCode', 'GetType', 'Inc', 'MemberwiseClone', 'Reference
Equals', 'ToString', '__add__', '__class__', '__delattr__', '__div__', '__doc__'
, '__format__', '__getattribute__', '__hash__', '__init__', '__mul__', '__new__'
, '__radd__', '__rdiv__', '__reduce__', '__reduce_ex__', '__repr__', '__rmul__',
'__rsub__', '__setattr__', '__sizeof__', '__str__', '__sub__', '__subclasshook_
_']
>>> Value1 = Calcs.Calcs(10)
>>> Value2 = Calcs.Calcs(5)
>>> print Value1.__add__(Value2)
15
>>>
```

FIGURE 17-2: The dir() function shows the content of the Calcs class.

Adding the IronPython Project

At this point, you have a Visual Basic.NET extension (or module) to use with IronPython. Of course, you'll want to test it. The easiest way to do this is to add the IronPython project directly to the current solution. The following steps describe how to perform this task.

1. Right-click the solution entry in Solution Explorer and choose Add ⇨ Existing Project from the context menu. You'll see the Add Existing Project dialog box shown in Figure 17-3.

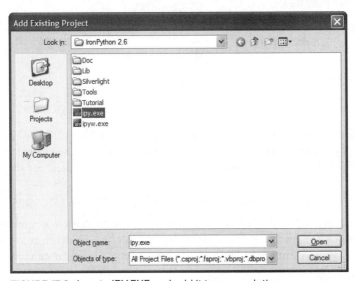

FIGURE 17-3: Locate IPY.EXE and add it to your solution.

2. Locate `IPY.EXE` on your hard drive and highlight it. Click Open. You'll see a new project entry added to the solution.

3. Right-click the ipy entry in Solution Explorer and choose Set as Startup Project from the context menu. This step ensures that choosing one of the startup options from the Debug menu starts the IronPython application.

4. Right-click the ipy entry in Solution Explorer and choose Properties from the context menu. You'll see the General tab of the ipy Properties window shown in Figure 17-4.

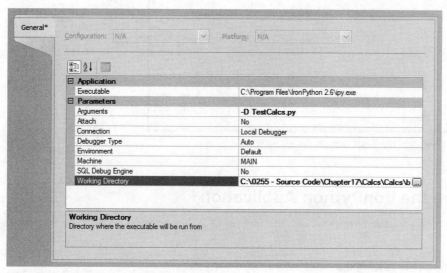

FIGURE 17-4: Configure the IronPython application to work with Calcs.DLL.

5. Type **-D TestCalcs.py** in the Arguments field.

6. Click the ellipses in the Working Directory field to display the Browse for Folder dialog box. Locate the output folder of the `Calcs.DLL` (or other extension) file. Click OK. The IDE adds the correct directory information to the Working Directory field.

7. Open Windows Explorer. Locate the `\Calcs\Calcs\bin\Debug` folder. Right-click in the right pane and choose New ⇨ Text Document from the context menu. Name the file `TestCalcs.py` and press Enter. Click Yes if asked if you want to rename the file extension.

8. Right-click the solution item in Solution Explorer and choose Add ⇨ Existing Item from the context menu to display the Add Existing Item dialog box shown in Figure 17-5.

9. Locate the `TestCalcs.py` file in the solution and click Add. Visual Studio adds `TestCalcs.py` to the `Solution Items` folder in Solution Explorer and automatically opens the file for you. You're ready to add test code for the application.

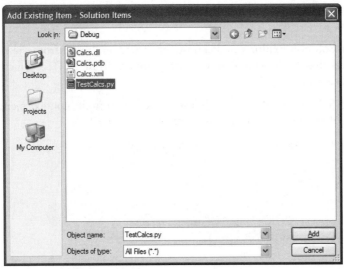

FIGURE 17-5: Add the TestCalcs.py file to the solution.

Creating the IronPython Application

It's time to write code to test Calcs.DLL. Listing 17-2 shows the code you'll use for testing purposes.

LISTING 17-2: Testing the extension using IronPython

```
# Add a reference to the CLR
import clr

# Obtain access to the extension.
clr.AddReferenceToFile('Calcs.DLL')
import Calcs

# Create an instance of the class and fill it with data.
Value1 = Calcs.Calcs(10)

# Print the original value, then decrement and increment it.
print 'Original Value1 Content: ', Value1
print 'Value1 + 1: ', Value1.Inc()
print 'Value1 - 1: ', Value1.Dec()

# Create a second value and display it.
Value2 = Calcs.Calcs(5)
print '\nOriginal Value2 Content: ', Value2

# Use the two values together in different ways.
print '\nValue1 + Value2 = ', Value1 + Value2
print 'Value1 - Value2 = ', Value1 - Value2
print 'Value1 * Value2 = ', Value1 * Value2
```

```
print 'Value1 / Value2 = ', Value1 / Value2

# Pause after the debug session.
raw_input('\nPress any key to continue...')
```

The code begins by importing the Common Language Runtime (CLR). It then uses the `AddReferenceToFile()` method to create a reference to `Calcs.DLL`. The final step is to import the `Calcs` code.

 Visual Basic automatically creates a hidden namespace for you. Even though the namespace is hidden in the Visual Basic editor, you must still use it when accessing the class in IronPython. Consequently, you see the `Calcs` accessed as `Calcs.Calcs`, where the first reference is the namespace and the second is the class.

Before the code can use the `Calcs` code, it must create an instance of it, `Value1`. Notice that the code calls the `Calcs.Calcs()` constructor with an initial value. Any time you want to assign a value to `Value1`, you must use the `Calcs.Calcs()` constructor. If you were to assign a value using `Value1 = 15`, it would change the type of `Value1`. A consequent addition, such as `Value1 + Value2`, would produce the following error:

```
Traceback (most recent call last):
  File "<stdin>", line 1, in <module>
TypeError: unsupported operand type(s) for +: 'int' and 'Calcs'
```

One way to overcome this problem would be to override the = operator.

After the code creates `Value1`, it demonstrates the use of the `Inc()` and `Dec()` methods. These two methods simply add or remove 1 from the value of `Value1`. If you want to change the actual value of `Value1`, you need to make `Value1` equal to the output of the method like this:

```
Value1 = Value1.Inc()
```

The next step is to create `Value2`, a second `Calcs` object you can use for binary operations. The code outputs the initial value of `Value2`. The remainder of the example demonstrates the use of the various operators. As you can see, they work precisely as you would expect. You could even use them to create a third value like this:

```
Value3 = Value1 + Value2
```

Figure 17-6 shows the output from this example. Except for the absence of the ++ and -- operators, everything works much as you would expect.

USING VISUAL BASIC.NET FOR USER INTERFACE SUPPORT

It's certainly possible to create message boxes and even Windows Forms applications using IronPython. Chapter 8 shows how to perform this task and most people will consider the process quite painful by the time they're finished. The biggest issue is that IronPython lacks support for the designers that make the task of writing Windows Forms code so easy. You have to be able to picture the form you want in your mind and then use trial and error to get it to appear in the application. Consequently, most developers will probably want to use a language such as Visual Basic.NET to create their Windows Forms applications and then make those forms accessible from IronPython as part of an extension.

FIGURE 17-6: Here are the results of using the Visual Basic.NET extension within IronPython.

The examples in the sections that follow aren't all that complicated, but they do demonstrate the principles required to build your own library of message boxes and Windows Forms classes. By the time you finish these examples, you'll have everything needed to create your own user interface library for use in IronPython.

Creating the User Interface Library Module

From an IronPython perspective, user interface elements come in two forms: messages boxes and Windows Forms. Obviously, Visual Basic.NET can create a host of user interface presentations, but if you start at this basic level, you'll find the task of creating a user interface library module easier. The following sections describe how to create both a message box class and a Windows Forms class that you place in a single DLL for use with your IronPython application. Of course, a production DLL could have hundreds of different forms, depending on the user interface requirements for the application.

Defining Simple Message Boxes

Message boxes (created using the `MessageBox` class) are extremely useful for displaying short messages and getting canned responses. Depending on the buttons you provide, a user could tell you that the application should retry an operation or answer yes to simple questions. If you need a little more input, you can always rely on an input box (created with the `InputBox()` method of the `Interaction` class). Of course, an input box is still limited to a single field, but even so, it does extend the kinds of input you can receive from the user.

Listing 17-3 demonstrates both the `MessageBox.Show()` and `InputBox()` methods. In addition, you'll see how to implement the `__doc__()` method that most IronPython developers rely upon to obtain information about your extension. The section "Considering Developer Help" in Chapter 16 provides additional information about developer help needs.

> *The content of the* `Interaction` *class is something that some Visual Basic.NET developers tend to forget. These methods, such as* `Beep()`, *are useful in IronPython. Visual Basic.NET developers get these features automatically as part of the* `Microsoft.VisualBasic` *namespace. Other language developers, such as C#, can use these features, too, but will need to add a reference to* `Microsoft.VisualBasic.DLL` *and provide the proper* `using` *statements.*

LISTING 17-3: Working with simple message boxes

```vbnet
Imports System.Windows.Forms

Public Class Dialogs

    Public Function ShowMessage(ByVal Msg As String) As String
        Return MessageBox.Show(Msg).ToString()
    End Function

    Public Function ShowMessage(ByVal Msg As String, _
                                ByVal Title As String) As String
        Return MessageBox.Show(Msg, Title).ToString()
    End Function


    Public Function ShowMessage(ByVal Msg As String, ByVal Title As String, _
                                ByVal Buttons As Int16) As String
        Return MessageBox.Show(Msg, Title, CType(Buttons, MessageBoxButtons) _
                            ).ToString()
    End Function

    Public Function ShowMessage(ByVal Msg As String, ByVal Title As String, _
                                ByVal Buttons As Int16, ByVal Icon As Int16 _
                                ) As String
        Return MessageBox.Show(Msg, Title, CType(Buttons, MessageBoxButtons), _
                            CType(Icon, MessageBoxIcon)).ToString()
    End Function

    Public Function ShowMessage(ByVal Msg As String, ByVal Title As String, _
                                ByVal Buttons As Int16, ByVal Icon As Int16, _
                                ByVal DefaultButton As Int16) As String
        Return MessageBox.Show(Msg, Title, CType(Buttons, MessageBoxButtons), _
                            CType(Icon, MessageBoxIcon), _
                            CType(DefaultButton, MessageBoxDefaultButton) _
                            ).ToString()
    End Function

    Public Function GetInput(ByVal Msg As String, ByVal Title As String)
        Return InputBox(Msg, Title, "Type a value")
```

continues

LISTING 17-3 *(continued)*

```
    End Function

    Public Function __doc__() As String
        Return "This is a help string"
    End Function
End Class
```

Before you can compile this code, you need to add a reference to `System.Windows.Forms.DLL`. Right-click Dialogs in Solution Explorer and choose Add Reference from the context menu. You'll see the Add Reference dialog box shown in Figure 17-7. Highlight the `System.Windows.Forms` entry and click OK. At this point, you also need to add an `Imports System.Windows.Forms` entry to your project and you're ready to work with message boxes.

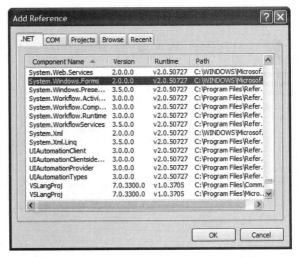

FIGURE 17-7: Add the System.Windows.Forms.DLL entry to your project.

The code begins by creating a series of `ShowMessage()` methods. The first is relatively simple and the complexity increases with each `ShowMessage()` method entry. Notice that the `ShowMessage()` method uses `Int16` input values to select the buttons, icon, and default button. You could also use enumerations to provide input values. The one thing you don't want to do is ask the IronPython developer to provide a `MessageBoxButtons`, `MessageBoxIcon`, or `MessageBoxDefaultButton` value, because then the IronPython developer would need to import all the required .NET Framework functionality, reducing the usefulness of your extension. The `CType()` function helps you convert the `Int16` values into the appropriate enumeration value. Interestingly enough, there are 21 forms of the `MessageBox.Show()` method, even though the example shows only five of them.

> *The enumeration values used to access message box features aren't consistent. For example, the `MessageBoxIcon` enumeration has values of 0, 16, 32, 48, and 64, which are hardly easy to remember. The `MessageBoxDefaultButton` enumeration values are equally odd at 0, 256, and 512. Fortunately, the `MessageBoxButtons` enumeration is a straightforward list of 0 through 5. In Chapter 16, Tables 16-1 through 16-3 show the values for the message box enumerations.*

The `GetInput()` method shows just one of several `InputBox()` method variations you can use. In this case, the IronPython developer supplies the prompt (or message) and title to display onscreen. The `GetInput()` method supplies a default `InputBox()` value. Normally, you want to supply a value so that the user knows to type something and what you want the user to type. Even if the required input seems obvious to you, many users won't know what to provide.

The `__doc__()` provides a help string for the IronPython developer. The example shows something quick, but in reality, you'd provide complete documentation for your class. The output string can use all the standard formatting characters. You could even read the content in from an external source, such as a file, to make it easy to provide updates without having to recompile the extension. Using an external file would also allow the IronPython developer to personalize the content.

Defining Complex Forms

A Windows Forms class can contain anything you want. It can even call other forms as needed. In fact, anything you can do with a Visual Basic.NET Windows Forms application is doable with IronPython. Of course, you do need to maintain interaction with the IronPython application. The following steps describe how to create a simple Windows Forms class for your extension.

1. Right-click Dialogs in Solution Explorer and choose Add ⇨ New Item. Select the Windows Forms entry in the Installed Templates list. You see the Add New Item dialog box shown in Figure 17-8.

FIGURE 17-8: Add a Windows Form to your project.

One of the advantages of using Visual Basic.NET rather than C# to create Windows Forms classes is that Visual Basic.NET includes several additional predefined templates. In fact, Visual Basic.NET provides 11 templates rather than the seven templates provided in C#. The additional Visual Basic.NET templates include Dialog, Explorer Form, Login Form, and Splash Screen, all of which are usable in IronPython.

2. Highlight the Windows Form entry. Type **TestForm.VB** in the Name field and click Add. Visual Studio adds the new form to your project and automatically opens it for editing.

3. Create the form just as you normally would for any static application. Figure 17-9 shows the form used for this example. It's simple, but it contains multiple data entry fields and multiple exit options.

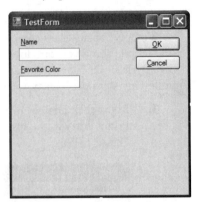

The form shown in Figure 17-9 is a little deceptive. Before you assume anything about this form, it does have a few differences from the forms you've created for your static applications.

➤ Buttons that close the form, rather than do something within the form, must have the `DialogResult` property set to a unique value or you won't be able to tell which button the user clicked. For this example, the `DialogResult` for `btnOK` is `OK`, while the `DialogResult` for `btnCancel` is `Cancel`.

FIGURE 17-9: The Windows Form can contain any level of complexity you desire.

➤ Getting information from the form you create to the IronPython application can prove problematic. You could contrive all sorts of odd methods for accomplishing the task, but the simplest method is to set the `Modifiers` property for the individual controls (`txtName` and `txtColor`) to `Public`. In this case, using `Public` doesn't create a problem because IronPython sets everything to public. In all other respects, there's no difference between this form and any other form you've created in the past.

To make things simple, this example doesn't use any code-behind for the form itself. Any code-behind works as you'd expect. There isn't any difference between calling the form from IronPython than calling it from within your Visual Basic.NET application.

Accessing the User Interface Library Module from IronPython

It's time to use the extension you've created with an IronPython application. The following sections describe an alternative way to set up your project so that you don't have to create the IronPython file using Windows Explorer and show how to use the extension.

An Alternative Method for Adding the IronPython Project

There are a number of ways to configure a test setup for your extensions. The "Adding the IronPython Project" section shows one technique. The technique shown in that section works well when you want to maintain separate builds of your extension. For example, you might want to maintain separate debug and release builds.

Unfortunately, that earlier method is a bit clumsy — you have to create the IronPython file using Windows Explorer. The technique in this section avoids that problem. In addition, this technique shows how to maintain just one build — the build you're currently using for debugging, testing, or experimentation. Use the following steps to create a centralized test configuration:

1. Right-click Dialogs in Solution Explorer and choose Properties from the context menu. Select the Compile tab. You'll see the Properties window shown in Figure 17-10.

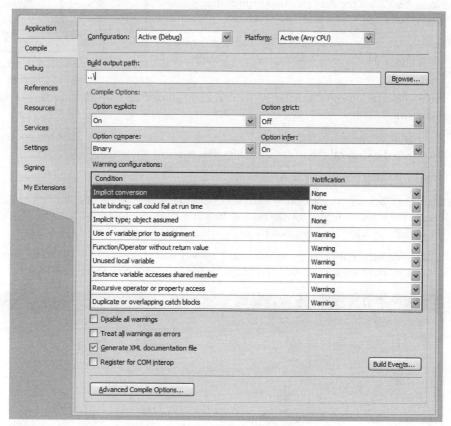

FIGURE 17-10: Configure the build to use a central output location.

2. Click Browse next to the Build Output Path field to display the Select Output Path dialog box shown in Figure 17-11. Because you'll add the IronPython test file at the solution level, you need to send the output to the solution level as well.

3. Select the first Dialogs entry in the list and click OK. Visual Studio adds an absolute path to the Output Path field that you must change for every machine that uses the application. As an alternative, you could type ..\ (two periods and a backslash) in the field to place the output in the solution folder.

4. Select the next configuration in the Configuration field.

5. Perform Steps 2 through 4 for each configuration. Make sure each configuration uses the same output directory. Normally, your project will contain only Debug and Release configurations.

6. Right-click the solution entry in Solution Explorer and choose Add ⇨ Existing Project from the context menu. You'll see the Add Existing Project dialog box shown in Figure 17-3.

7. Locate IPY.EXE on your hard drive and highlight it. Click Open. You'll see a new project entry added to the solution.

FIGURE 17-11: Modify the output path as required for your application.

8. Right-click the ipy entry in Solution Explorer and choose Set as Startup Project from the context menu.

9. Right-click the ipy entry in Solution Explorer and choose Properties from the context menu. You'll see the General tab of the ipy Properties window shown in Figure 17-4.

10. Type -D DialogTest.py in the Arguments field.

11. Click the ellipses in the Working Directory field to display the Browse for Folder dialog box. Locate the solution folder for the project (the first Dialogs folder). Click OK. The IDE adds the correct directory information to the Working Directory field.

12. Right-click the solution entry in Solution Explorer and choose Add ⇨ New Item from the context menu. You see the Add New Item dialog box shown in Figure 17-12.

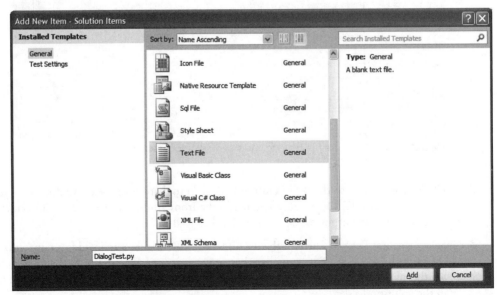

FIGURE 17-12: Add the IronPython test file to your project.

13. Type `DialogTest.py` in the Name field and click Add. Visual Studio adds the new file to the Solution Items folder in Solution Explorer and opens the file automatically for editing.

Performing the Message Box and Form Tests

The example is ready except for the test code. Listing 17-4 shows the IronPython code you need for this example.

LISTING 17-4: Testing the message boxes and forms

```python
# Define the message box tests.
def TestMessages():

    # Create a message box object.
    MyDialog = Dialogs.Dialogs()

    # Show the help information.
    print 'Dialogs Class Help Information.'
    print MyDialog.__doc__()

    # Test a simple message box.
    print '\nTesting a simple message box.'
    print 'Simple message box output: ',
    print MyDialog.ShowMessage('Hello')

    # Perform a more complex test.
    print '\nA more complex message box.'
    print 'Complex message box output: ',
    print MyDialog.ShowMessage('Hello Again', 'Title 2', 3, 64, 256)

    # Get some user input.
    print '\nUsing an InputBox.'
    print 'InputBox Output: ',
    print MyDialog.GetInput('Type Your Name:', 'User Name Entry')

# Define the form test.
def TestForm():

    # Create the form instance.
    MyForm = Dialogs.TestForm()

    # Display the form and test the dialog result.
    print '\nThe form example.'
    if MyForm.ShowDialog().ToString() == 'OK':

        # Display the results.
        print 'The user clicked OK.'
        print 'User Name: ', MyForm.txtName.Text
        print 'Favorite Color: ', MyForm.txtColor.Text

    # Display an alternate result.
    else:
```

continues

LISTING 17-4 *(continued)*

```
        print 'The user clicked cancel.'

# Import the Common Language Runtime.
import clr

# Access the extension.
clr.AddReferenceToFile('Dialogs.DLL')
import Dialogs

# Test the message box code.
TestMessages()

# Test the form code.
TestForm()

# Pause after the debug session.
raw_input('\nPress any key to continue...')
```

The code begins by importing CLR support and then uses the `AddReferenceToFile()` to add a reference to the `Dialogs.DLL`. The next step is to import the Dialogs namespace for use. The `__main__()` function calls two functions, `TestMessages()` and `TestForm()`, to test the content of the `Dialogs` namespace. It then pauses so you can see the results.

The `TestMessages()` function begins by creating an instance of `Dialogs.Dialogs`, `MyDialog`. It then calls the `MyDialog.__doc__()` method to output the help information provided by the `Dialogs` class. Normally you'd use this method at the interactive console, but it's good to see how the method works.

The next step is to test the `MyDialog.ShowMessage()` method. To keep you from clicking all afternoon, the test code uses just two forms of the method. The first form shows the simplest dialog box, while the second shows the most complex. The most complex dialog box (shown in Figure 17-13) contains a message, title, icon, and three buttons. Notice that the second button, rather than the first button, is selected by default. Normally, a message box selects the first button by default.

FIGURE 17-13: The complex message box can convey quite a bit of information for such a simple call.

The next step is to display an input box. In this case, the `MyDialog.GetInput()` method displays an input box that contains a simple prompt and a title, as shown in Figure 17-14. Notice the default message in the input box. The input box automatically highlights this default entry so that the first thing the user types will erase the default content. The output from the `MyDialog.GetInput()` method is the text that the user types in the input box.

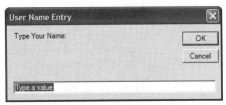

FIGURE 17-14: Input boxes are good for small amounts of custom user input.

The `TestForm()` function begins by creating an instance of the `Dialogs.TestForm` class, `MyForm`. The code then displays the dialog box shown in Figure 17-9 using the `MyForm.ShowDialog()`

method. Notice that the example code adds a call to `ToString()`, so that the entire method call is `MyForm.ShowDialog().ToString()`. This is a technique for converting the `System.Windows` `.Forms.DialogResult` to a simple string that you can compare with the desired output, which is `'OK'` in this case.

> *The hidden namespace provided with Visual Basic won't change names when you add the `TestForm` class to it. The namespace retains the same name as when you created the project and changed the name of the original class. Consequently, you access the Windows Forms class, `TestForm`, as `Dialogs` `.TestForm`, not as `TestForm.TestForm`.*

When the call succeeds (the user clicks OK), the code prints the user's name and favorite color. Notice that the code directly accesses both `txtName.Text` and `txtColor.Text` to obtain the required information. When the call fails (the user clicks Cancel), the code outputs a simple failure message. Figure 17-15 shows typical output from this example.

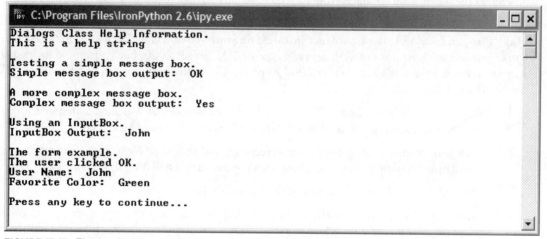

```
Dialogs Class Help Information.
This is a help string

Testing a simple message box.
Simple message box output:   OK

A more complex message box.
Complex message box output:   Yes

Using an InputBox.
InputBox Output:   John

The form example.
The user clicked OK.
User Name:   John
Favorite Color:   Green

Press any key to continue...
```

FIGURE 17-15: The IronPython output shows the results of the various dialog and form selections.

USING VISUAL BASIC.NET FOR DATABASE SUPPORT

Visual Basic.NET makes database management easy. Of course, there are all the handy designers that Visual Basic.NET makes available. The features of Server Explorer help as well. However, the fact that Visual Basic.NET tends to hide some of the details is what helps the most. The following sections provide a simple database management example that you could easily expand to help IronPython work with all sorts of data.

This example assumes that you have SQL Server 2008 installed on your system. Although the example will very likely work with older versions of SQL Server, it hasn't been tested with them. You could also download the SQL Server 2008 Express version from `http://www.microsoft.com/express/sql/download/`. *The example doesn't provide complex database connectivity, so the SQL Server 2008 Express Edition will work just fine. If you want to see the full version of SQL Server 2008 Express in action, download the trial version at* `http://msdn` `.microsoft.com/sqlserver/bb895906.aspx` *or* `http://www.microsoft.com/` `SQLserver/2008/en/us/trial-software.aspx`.

Obtaining and Configuring the Database

This example relies on an old standby, the Northwind database. Microsoft has passed this database by for significantly more complex examples, but Northwind remains unsurpassed in its ability to create useful examples with very little code, so it's the database of choice for this chapter. You can download the Northwind database from `http://www.microsoft.com/downloads/details` `.aspx?FamilyID=06616212-0356-46A0-8DA2-EEBC53A68034`.

Make sure you have a database manager installed on your system. The Northwind database works just fine with versions of SQL Server as old as SQL Server 2000, but you should at least try a newer version, even if it's SQL Server 2008 Express. The following steps tell you how to install the Northwind database.

1. Double-click the `SQL2000SampleDb.msi`. You'll see the normal Welcome dialog box for installing Microsoft products. Click Next. You'll see the licensing agreement.

2. Click I Agree after reading the license agreement, and then click Next. You'll see an Installation Options dialog box. There aren't any actual installation options.

3. Click Next. You'll see a Confirm Installation dialog box.

4. Click Next. The installer installs the files into the `C:\SQL Server 2000 Sample Databases` folder on your machine (you aren't given a choice about the installation folder). After the installation is complete, you'll see an Installation Complete dialog box.

5. Click Close. The Northwind database and its associated script are now loaded on your machine.

6. Open a command prompt in the `C:\SQL Server 2000 Sample Databases` folder.

7. Type **OSQL -E -i InstNwnd.SQL** and press Enter (the command line switches are case sensitive — make sure you type the command correctly). The OSQL utility will start building and installing the Northwind database. This process can take a while to complete — get a cup of coffee and enjoy. When the process is complete, you see a command prompt with a bunch of numbers on it and no error message, as shown in Figure 17-16.

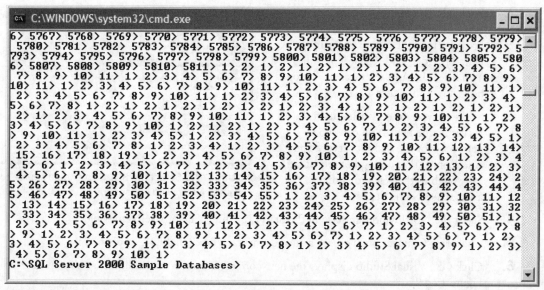

FIGURE 17-16: The output from the OSQL utility doesn't tell you much except if it encountered errors.

The OSQL utility comes with your SQL Server installation. If Windows tells you that it can't find the OSQL utility, make sure the \Program Files\ Microsoft SQL Server\100\Tools\Binn *folder (or equivalent for your version of SQL Server) is part of your path statement. To check the path, type* **Path** *at the command line and press Enter. To add the path to your path statement, type something like* **Path = C:\Program Files\Microsoft SQL Server\100\Tools\ Binn;%PATH%** *and press Enter at the command line.*

Creating the Database Support Module

Creating a database support module is a multi-step process. At a minimum, you must first create a connection to the database and then work with that connection using code. The example that follows isn't very complex. All that this example will do is retrieve some information from the database in the interest of keeping things simple. Even so, the basics shown in the example provide enough information for you to start creating database extensions of your own.

Creating a Connection to the Database

The first step in working with the Northwind database is to create a connection to it. The following steps describe how to perform this task.

1. Right-click on the Data Connections entry in Server Explorer and choose Add Connection from the context menu. You may see the Choose Data Source dialog box shown in Figure 17-17. If not, you'll see the Add Connection dialog box shown in Figure 17-18 and will need to proceed to Step 3.

2. Highlight the Microsoft SQL Server entry. Select the .NET Framework Data Provider for SQL Server entry in the Data Provider field. Click Continue. You'll see the Add Connection dialog box shown in Figure 17-18.

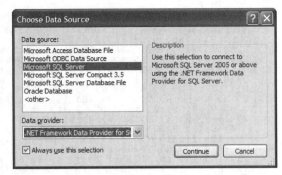

3. Select or type the server name in the Server Name field. You can type a period (.) for the default server. The Add Connection dialog box automatically enables the Select or Enter a Database Name field.

FIGURE 17-17: Select the SQL Server data source to make the Northwind connection.

4. Select the Northwind database in the Select or Enter a Database Name field.

5. Click Test Connection. You see a success message box (click OK to dismiss it).

6. Click OK. Visual Studio displays the new connection in Server Explorer, as shown in Figure 17-19.

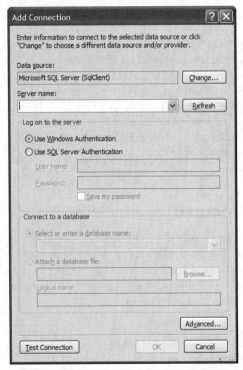

FIGURE 17-18: The Add Connection dialog box lets you create and test a connection to the Northwind database.

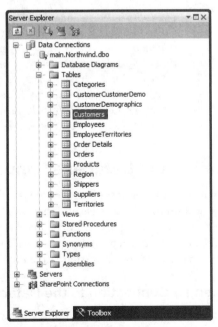

FIGURE 17-19: The new connection appears in Server Explorer where you can work with it directly.

7. Choose Data ➪ Add New Data Source. You'll see the Data Source Configuration Wizard dialog box shown in Figure 17-20.

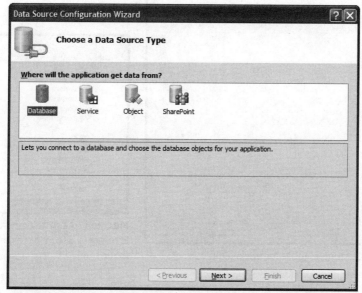

FIGURE 17-20: Use the Data Source Configuration Wizard to create a coded connection.

8. Highlight Database and click Next. You'll see the Choose Database Model page.

9. Highlight the Dataset option and click Next. You'll see the Choose Your Data Connection page. Notice that the Northwind database connection already appears in the connection field. The connection name will have your machine name, followed by the database name, followed by .dbo, such as `main.Northwind.dbo`. If it doesn't, make sure you select it from the list. If the connection doesn't appear in the list, click Cancel and start over with Step 1 because your connection wasn't successful.

10. Select the Northwind connection and click Next. The wizard will ask how you want to save the connection. There isn't a good reason to change the default name provided.

11. Click Next. You see the Choose Your Database Objects page shown in Figure 17-21.

12. Check the Customers table entry, as shown in Figure 17-21. The example relies on the Customers table and none of the other database content. Click Finish. The new data source appears in the Data Sources window, as shown in Figure 17-22. If you can't see this window, choose Data ➪ Show Data Sources.

Adding Database Manipulation Code

After all the work you performed to obtain access to the data, the actual database manipulation code is relatively easy. Listing 17-5 shows the small amount of code used to actually retrieve a particular record from the database based on the `CustomerID` field. Of course, you can add any level of complexity required.

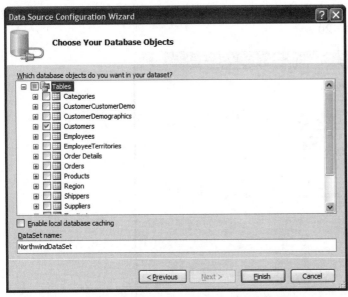

FIGURE 17-21: Select the Customers table for this example.

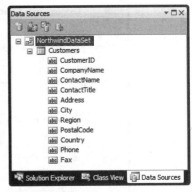

FIGURE 17-22: The data source is ready to use in the example extension.

LISTING 17-5: Retrieving data from the database

```
Public Function GetData(ByVal Customer As String) As _
    NorthwindDataSet.CustomersRow

    ' Obtain access to the table.
    Dim MyData As NorthwindDataSetTableAdapters.CustomersTableAdapter = _
        New NorthwindDataSetTableAdapters.CustomersTableAdapter()

    ' Create a DataSet.
    Dim DS As NorthwindDataSet.CustomersDataTable = _
        New NorthwindDataSet.CustomersDataTable()

    ' Fill the DataSet with data.
    MyData.Fill(DS)

    ' Find a particular record using the Customer ID.
    Return DS.FindByCustomerID(Customer)
End Function
```

The code begins by creating a `TableAdapter` object. Because the example relies on the Data Source Configuration Wizard, it has a specific `TableAdapter` to use in the form of the `NorthwindDataSetTableAdapters.CustomersTableAdapter`, `MyData` object. `MyData` provides the means to select information from the table. In addition, it can update, delete, and insert records. Essentially, `MyData` is the database connection.

The next step is to create a `DataTable` object. Again, the example has a specific version, `NorthwindDataSet.CustomersDataTable` class, `DS` object. `DS` contains all the data selected from the database through the `TableAdapter` object.

In order to get data from the database into the `DataTable` object, the code calls the `MyData.Fill()` method. Until the code calls this method, DS contains all of the information about the Customers table, but none of the records.

Finally, the code calls the `DS.FindByCustomerID()` method to find the record requested by the caller. The input argument to this method, `Customer`, is a string that contains the `CustomerID` field value. The output from the call is a `NorthwindDataSet.CustomersRow` object, which is a specialized form of the `DataRow`. Interestingly enough, IronPython can use the `DataRow` directly without having to translate it in any way.

Accessing the Database Module through IronPython

The example extension has a method, `GetData()`, that accepts a `CustomerID` as input and provides a `NorthwindDataSet.CustomersRow` as output. All you need now is some IronPython code to make the request and display the result. Listing 17-6 shows a typical example.

LISTING 17-6: Displaying a record onscreen

```
# Import the Common Language Runtime.
import clr

# Access the extension.
clr.AddReferenceToFile('Northwind.DLL')
import Northwind

# Create an instance of the Northwind access object.
MyData = Northwind.DBAccess()

# Fill a row with data.
Row = MyData.GetData('ALFKI')

# Display the data on screen.
print 'All the data for Customer ID ALFKI'
print '\nCustomer ID: ', Row.CustomerID
print 'Company Name: ', Row.CompanyName

print 'Contact Name: ',
if Row.IsContactNameNull():
   print 'Nothing'
else:
   print Row.ContactName

print 'Contact Title: ',
if Row.IsContactTitleNull():
   print 'Nothing'
else:
   print Row.ContactTitle

print 'Address: ',
if Row.IsAddressNull():
   print 'Nothing'
```

continues

LISTING 17-6 *(continued)*

```
    else:
        print Row.Address

    print 'City: ',
    if Row.IsCityNull():
        print 'Nothing'
    else:
        print Row.City

    print 'Region: ',
    if Row.Is_RegionNull():
        print 'Nothing'
    else:
        print Row._Region

    print 'Postal Code: ',
    if Row.IsPostalCodeNull():
        print 'Nothing'
    else:
        print Row.PostalCode

    print 'Country: ',
    if Row.IsCountryNull():
        print 'Nothing'
    else:
        print Row.Country

    print 'Phone: ',
    if Row.IsPhoneNull():
        print 'Nothing'
    else:
        print Row.Phone

    print 'Fax: ',
    if Row.IsFaxNull():
        print 'Nothing'
    else:
        print Row.Fax

    # Pause after the debug session.
    raw_input('\nPress any key to continue...')
```

This listing looks like a lot of code, but the process is relatively simple. The example begins as usual by gaining access to CLR, using the AddReferenceToFile() method to create a reference to the extension, and creating an instance of the extension class.

At this point, the code calls MyData.GetData() with a CustomerID of 'ALFKI'. The output is placed in Row. If you use the dir() function on Row, you see it provides a lot more than a listing of fields that appear as part of the output. Figure 17-23 shows the attributes Row provides.

The output fields come in two types. The first are fields that the row must contain. These fields always contain data. The second are optional fields that might not contain data. If you try to print these fields, you'll get an error. Consequently, the next section of code displays the mandatory fields first.

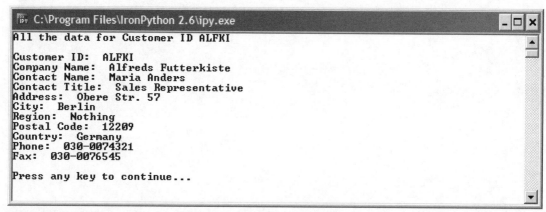

```
C:\WINDOWS\system32\cmd.exe - ipy

IronPython 2.6 (2.6.10920.0) on .NET 2.0.50727.3603
Type "help", "copyright", "credits" or "license" for more information.
>>> import clr
>>> clr.AddReferenceToFile('Northwind.DLL')
>>> import Northwind
>>> MyData = Northwind.DBAccess()
>>> Row = MyData.GetData('ALFKI')
>>> dir(Row)
['AcceptChanges', 'Address', 'BeginEdit', 'CancelEdit', 'City', 'ClearErrors', '
CompanyName', 'ContactName', 'ContactTitle', 'Country', 'CustomerID', 'Delete',
'EndEdit', 'Equals', 'Fax', 'GetChildRows', 'GetColumnError', 'GetColumnsInError
', 'GetHashCode', 'GetParentRow', 'GetParentRows', 'GetType', 'HasErrors', 'HasV
ersion', 'IsAddressNull', 'IsCityNull', 'IsContactNameNull', 'IsContactTitleNull
', 'IsCountryNull', 'IsFaxNull', 'IsNull', 'IsPhoneNull', 'IsPostalCodeNull', 'I
s_RegionNull', 'Item', 'ItemArray', 'MemberwiseClone', 'Phone', 'PostalCode', 'R
eferenceEquals', 'RejectChanges', 'RowError', 'RowState', 'SetAdded', 'SetAddres
sNull', 'SetCityNull', 'SetColumnError', 'SetContactNameNull', 'SetContactTitleN
ull', 'SetCountryNull', 'SetFaxNull', 'SetModified', 'SetNull', 'SetParentRow',
'SetPhoneNull', 'SetPostalCodeNull', 'Set_RegionNull', 'Table', 'ToString', '_Re
gion', '__class__', '__delattr__', '__doc__', '__format__', '__getattribute__',
'__getitem__', '__hash__', '__init__', '__new__', '__reduce__', '__reduce_ex__',
'__repr__', '__setattr__', '__setitem__', '__sizeof__', '__str__', '__subclassh
ook__']
>>>
```

FIGURE 17-23: Row contains more than just fields.

Notice the if...else structures that appear next. Every optional field includes an IsFieldNameNull() method. Before you print these optional fields, use the null check, such as Row.IsContactNameNull(), to verify that the field contains data. In this case, the code simply prints 'Nothing' when the field is null.

You need to consider one other issue when working through your database access methods. Notice that the _Region field has an underscore in front of it. This underscore doesn't appear in the database or in the Visual Basic.NET code — IronPython adds it for some reason. If you suddenly find that some fields aren't accessible, even though you're using the right name, check for an underscore. Figure 17-24 shows the output from this example.

```
C:\Program Files\IronPython 2.6\ipy.exe

All the data for Customer ID ALFKI

Customer ID:  ALFKI
Company Name:  Alfreds Futterkiste
Contact Name:  Maria Anders
Contact Title:  Sales Representative
Address:  Obere Str. 57
City:  Berlin
Region:  Nothing
Postal Code:  12209
Country:  Germany
Phone:  030-0074321
Fax:  030-0076545

Press any key to continue...
```

FIGURE 17-24: The extension provides data to IronPython to output.

USING IRONPYTHON CONSTRUCTIVELY

This chapter has helped you discover the wonders of the Visual Basic.NET extension. As with the C# extensions discussed in Chapter 16, the extensions described in this chapter follow certain rules and you must provide basic functionality when creating an extension in Visual Basic.NET before you can use it with IronPython. Visual Basic.NET extensions also follow the C# extension rules in areas such as method visibility. The two advanced examples in this chapter help you understand the areas in which Visual Basic.NET is the better choice when creating an extension.

If you really want to use extensions to their full effect, you really need to know which language to choose to get the job done quickly. With this in mind, you'll want to work through all the examples in this chapter so you understand the Visual Basic.NET strengths. After you complete the examples, take time to go back through Chapter 16 and the list you created of tasks you might want to perform for your organization using a combination of IronPython and C#. At this point, you can ask yourself whether all those tasks really will work best with C# as the extension language, or whether they'll work better using Visual Basic.NET. The whole purpose of this task is to help you start considering the importance of language choice when designing an application.

Chapter 18 takes you in another direction in working with IronPython — application testing. Some organizations spend as much time creating a test suite for their application as they do on the application itself. The scripting nature of IronPython makes it a perfect choice for some types of testing tasks. Chapter 18 describes how to perform testing using IronPython as the testing language. It also helps you understand when you might need to work with another tool to perform testing. Although IronPython is a great choice, it isn't the perfect choice for all situations and you need to consider this issue as part of developing your test suite.

18

Using IronPython for Application Testing

WHAT'S IN THIS CHAPTER?

➤ Considering IronPython for testing

➤ Defining the test environment requirements

➤ Performing tests on DLLs

➤ Performing tests on applications

➤ Testing applications at the command line

One of the things about IronPython that's exciting a lot of application developers is the ability to use it to write application tests quickly and easily. Now, you might wonder why you'd need yet another application testing tool, but IronPython has some significant advantages over other test tools, and these advantages will be discussed in this chapter.

Before you begin testing anything, you have to consider the kind of testing you want to do and the environment in which testing takes place. In short, you need to define the test environment. IronPython has unique capabilities that you should consider while devising the test environment. Because IronPython operates outside of the application, you can create a *test harness*, a set of routines that could possibly work on multiple applications in a particular way. Using the test harness approach means that you place the test on the application, perform the test, and then take the harness off for production-level testing.

This chapter looks at three main kinds of application testing: DLLs, desktop applications, and ad hoc testing at the command line. You can use IronPython for any sort of testing, but these three application types demonstrate a range of IronPython testing uses. The demonstrations in this chapter provide everything you need to create test harnesses for your applications.

The techniques in this chapter don't imply that your old testing tool is worthless or that IronPython is somehow superior to everything else on the market. Like any other tool, IronPython excels in some areas and not in others. As a good developer, you want to have multiple testing tools in your arsenal to ensure you create useful applications that won't immediately break under heavy usage. IronPython is simply another tool in your toolkit and you should treat it as such.

UNDERSTANDING WHY YOU WANT TO USE IRONPYTHON FOR TESTING

Every testing technique you've ever used has some drawback. For example, if you include debug statements in your code, you must ensure that you perform a release build to remove the statements before you release the code. Otherwise, the application will run slowly. In addition, using debug statements can cause the application to perform differently from the way it performs when you use it in a production environment, which makes it possible that the very tests that you depend on to check the application will actually hide problems from view.

Using IronPython for testing has a considerable number of benefits over other testing tools. The biggest benefit is that you don't have to do anything special to the application. The test harness you create exists outside the application and doesn't affect the application in any way. All the test harness does is monitor application behavior and report on it to you. As a result, if the test harness reviews every aspect of the application and verifies that it runs correctly, the application will run correctly in the production environment, too, because nothing will have changed.

As you've seen throughout the book, IronPython is an interpreted environment. That means you don't have to create the test harness in one piece — you can create it a little at a time as you try things out with the application. In fact, the very nature of IronPython makes it possible for you to play "what if" analysis on your application. You can see just how bad you can make the application environment and try things that users do, such as create unreasonable execution conditions.

Using an IronPython script for testing means that all the testing code is in one place. If you decide that you need to add another test, you don't have to delve into the inner workings of the application to add it and then create another build. Instead of using this time-consuming process, you simply add a few more lines to an external script using any text editor that you like. There's nothing complicated about the process — anyone knowledgeable about your application should be able to do it without any problem.

The external nature of IronPython also makes it impossible for your test code to add problems (such as errors, performance issues, or reliability concerns) to the application. In some cases, adding test code actually introduces an application error, making it hard to know whether the error is in the test harness or the application. If there's a problem in the IronPython test harness, you'll see an IronPython error telling you about it. In short, you have separation between the test harness and the application, which ensures one won't affect the other.

There are a few downsides to working with IronPython as a testing tool. The most important of these issues is that IronPython treats your application like a series of black boxes. It provides input to a method and expects a certain output. However, IronPython can't see into the method to test individual elements within it.

IronPython also can't see private members of your application, so it can't test absolutely every aspect of your application. If a private member is causing a problem, you need to use some other tools to find it. Of course, you can use IronPython to infer certain issues in private methods based on their effect on public methods, but this kind of logic can prove more troublesome than direct testing.

CONSIDERING THE TEST ENVIRONMENT

Before you begin writing your test harness, you need to consider the test environment. The test environment determines how you test the application, be it a DLL or a desktop application with user access. The following list provides some criteria you need to consider as part of the test environment.

➤ **Code access:** You must define how the test harness will access the code. It's important to determine whether the harness will test absolutely every method, property, event, and other application element individually, whether it will test elements in combination, or whether it will use a combination of individual and combined tests.

➤ **Test ranges:** A test harness must test both the possible and the impossible. For example, you might design a method to accept positive numbers from 0 through 5. However, the test harness must also test numbers greater than 5 and less than 0. In addition, it must test unexpected input, such as a string.

➤ **User emulation:** When working with some applications, you must determine how to emulate user activity. For example, you might write down a series of steps that the user will take to perform a certain activity and then execute those steps in your test harness. Of course, users are unpredictable; your script must also perform some haphazard and unpredictable steps and provide unexpected input. If you find that users are doing something you never expected, you must add it to the test harness.

➤ **Security testing:** If you don't try to break down the walls you erected for your application, someone else will most certainly sign up for the job. Because IronPython tends to treat everything as public, it actually makes a great tool for testing security. You'll find no artificial walls to keep things neat and tidy. Security is never neat or tidy — it's all about someone ripping away the veneer of the façade you called security when you put the application together. IronPython lets you test your application brutally, the same way someone else will.

➤ **System characteristics:** Even though you can't write code to ensure that your application will run on every machine in the solar system, you can do things such as add random pauses in your code to mimic activity on an overloaded system. You can also execute your application and its test harness on a number of different machine configurations to verify that the application will run as expected.

There are probably other criteria that you need to consider for your individual testing scenario. Take time to brainstorm scenarios, worst-case situations, and truly horrifying events, and then test for them. The following sections provide some additional insights about the test environment and the issues you must consider.

It's important to remember that IronPython can test more than just .NET code. If you can load some type of code into IronPython, you can test it. Of course, this means you can test IronPython code at a minimum, but you'll find that you can test other kinds of code as well. The point is that IronPython is a good environment for testing multiple kinds of code, which makes it an incredibly flexible testing tool.

Defining Access

The matter of access is an essential part of testing. The word "access" has all kinds of meanings and connotations. Of course, there's the access of your test harness to the code within the application. The black box nature of IronPython prevents access in depth, but careful programming can provide access to unprecedented amounts of information within your application and make testing relatively complete.

You must also consider the access the user has to the application as part of the test harness. For example, if you use external configuration files, you can count on some number of users accessing them. Even if you work out methods that are seemingly impossible to overcome, a user or two will find a way to overcome them. Anything you can devise will be overcome by someone (it's always easier to destroy than to create). Consequently, you must consider all forms of user access as part of your test harness — if for no other reason than to determine how bad things can get when a user meddles.

It's also important to consider external access. Whenever a system has access to the network or the Internet, you must consider the potential for outside sources to access your application (even if your application isn't designed for such access). Many vendors of shrink-wrapped software have gained notoriety for not taking this kind of access into consideration. The thought was that the application didn't access the outside source, so there wasn't any need to consider the outside source during testing. It turns out that any outside access opens avenues of influence and attack for all the applications on a system, so you must test this kind of access.

Access is a two-way street. As part of your testing harness, you must consider application access to external resources. For example, you must consider what happens when an application attempts to access a particular file on disk and can't find it. Even more important, you need to consider resources on the network or on the Internet. There are many forms of access that your test harness must consider as it tests the various methods inside the application. It isn't always possible to test simply for strict inputs or outputs; you must test inputs and outputs within the confines of an environment defined by various kinds of access.

Considering a Few Things IronPython Can't Test

Earlier, you learned that IronPython tests application elements using a black box approach — given a particular input, what should the element provide as output? However, there are other limitations you need to consider in the way IronPython performs testing. For example, IronPython can't perform stress testing. If you want to test your application in a memory-starved environment, then you need to combine IronPython with another tool. For example, you might want to read the article at `http://msdn.microsoft.com/magazine/cc163983.aspx` about a load-generating tool you can build yourself. Web application load testing requires other techniques that you can learn about at `http://support.microsoft.com/kb/231282`. If you need to stress test applications in combination with a particular server, check out the site at `http://blogs.msdn.com/nickmac/archive/2004/10/06/server-stress-tools.aspx`.

IronPython can perform diagnostic testing of your application with ease, but it doesn't make a good environment for performance testing. As with stress testing, you need to combine IronPython with another tool to check application performance in various conditions. In fact, you may very well need to combine IronPython, your stress testing tool, and your performance testing tool to obtain statistics for a range of test scenarios and environments.

The point of this section is that while IronPython is a good scripting tool or a good diagnostic tool, it can't do everything. In many cases, you must combine IronPython with one or more additional tools to obtain the desired information about your application. Your test plan should include all of these contingencies, and you should consider them before you create your test harness.

Creating the Test Harness

An advantage to working with IronPython is that you need not create the test harness in one sitting. You can use an iterative technique to create the test harness. It's possible to start with a small nugget of tests that you know you must perform, and then add to that nugget as other issues come to light. Eventually, you end up with a full-blown test suite.

Most .NET developers won't initially understand the benefits of using an interpreter for testing, but the realization will grow with time that interpreters make things easy. If you get an idea, you don't have to run a complete test or compile anything. All you need to do is open up the IronPython console, load the assembly you want to test, and then try out various tests until you come up with a perfect combination of items to use. At this point, you can click the system menu in the IronPython console, choose Edit ➪ Mark, highlight the text you want to copy from your experiments, and press Enter to copy it to the clipboard. Now you can paste the text you've created into your test harness and comment it. In fact, the IronPython console (and all consoles for that matter) provides a number of commands, as shown in Figure 18-1.

As an alternative, if you already have the beginnings of a test-harness check, but want to add to it, you can always paste the text directly into the IronPython console using the Paste command shown in Figure 18-1. The interpreter will automatically execute any statements that you paste into it, so you'll be ready to start typing new code after you paste it.

Modularity is the name of the game when it comes to a test harness. Try to place the individual tests into separate files so that you can reuse the code later. Simply have a centralized file where you call each of the tests in turn. The tests will output the information you need to screen, so the developer using the test harness need not even know that there are multiple files involved.

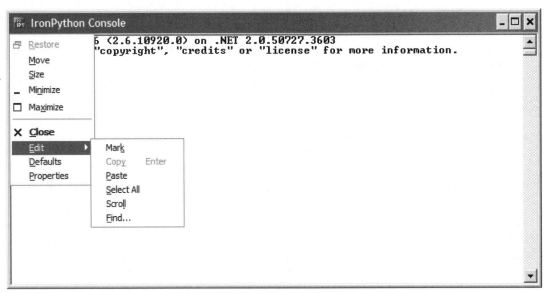

FIGURE 18-1: Use the text-editing tools to copy and paste text as needed.

TESTING DLLS

DLLs present one of the easier ways to begin using IronPython to test applications. In fact, you've already performed a kind of testing in Chapters 16 and 17 when you created the extensions and then used their content as part of an IronPython application. All that a test harness will do is formalize the testing process so that the output you receive speaks directly about the functionality of the DLL under test, rather than its use in an application. The following sections describe how to perform a test on a DLL using IronPython.

The examples in this chapter rely on the project construction technique shown in the "An Alternative Method for Adding the IronPython Project" sections of Chapters 16 and 17. If you're working with a C# application, use the procedure found in Chapter 16. Visual Basic.NET developers should use the procedure found in Chapter 17. Using a centralized build makes things simpler. Of course, in a real-world environment, you'll probably use a number of techniques to get the IronPython test script close to your application code.

Creating the Test DLL

The DLL used for testing purposes is extremely simple so that the section doesn't focus more on an interesting DLL than it does on testing techniques. All that this DLL provides is an account where you make an initial deposit to create the account and then make deposits, withdrawals, and transfers. The DLL includes a number of features so that you can try things out, but the code definitely isn't production quality. For one thing, most of the error-checking code is left out to keep the code clear so you can easily see what will happen next. Listing 18-1 shows the DLL code used for this example.

LISTING 18-1: Defining a DLL to test

```
public class Accounts
{
    // Contains the current account amount.
    private Int32 Total;

    public Accounts()
    {
        // Sets a default acccount amount.
        Total = 5000;
    }

    public Accounts(Int32 Initial)
    {
        // Set a user supplied initial amount.
        Total = Initial;
    }

    // Provides access to the account total.
    public Int32 GetTotal
    {
        get { return Total; }
    }

    // Adds a deposit to the account.
    public Int32 Deposit
    {
        set { Total += value; }
    }

    // Subtracts a withdrawal.
    public Int32 Withdrawal
    {
        set { Total -= value; }
    }

    public void Transfer(Accounts Account2)
    {
        // Place the money in the second account in the first account.
        this.Total += Account2.Total;

        // Withdraw the money from the second account.
        Account2.Total = 0;
    }
}
```

The example includes two constructors (something you didn't try in Chapters 16 or 17). The developer can create an account with a default value of 5000 or provide some other initial amount. In either case, you end up with a new Accounts object that has Total defined.

The GetTotal property is read-only and lets the developer obtain the total in the count from Total. Using a property enables you to perform checks before allowing people to have the information. For example, you could place a security code in this property to ensure that only authorized personnel received the information. If a developer were to take this approach, you'd need to write a test to check the GetTotal property using an account other than the developer account.

The Deposit and Withdrawal properties are write-only. The caller doesn't receive anything back from them. You could use a method to perform the task as well. Using a property makes the test code easier to read, but that's the only advantage. In both cases, the properties change the value of Total. Of course, you can perform checks in the properties, such as verifying that a withdrawal won't result in an account with a value less than 0.

The Transfer() method moves all the money from one account to the other. Typically, you'd provide some type of transaction support in a method of this type, but the example doesn't include it. This is one situation where IronPython can test the method's inputs and outputs, but can't test the internal workings of the method. You'd need another tool to test issues such as whether the transaction support actually worked as intended.

Creating the DLL Test Script

It's time to build an IronPython script to test the DLL shown in Listing 18-1. In this case, the test script is a bit short and doesn't test every contingency (such as starting with a negative amount in the account), but it demonstrates how you'd create a test script for a DLL. Listing 18-2 contains the code needed for this example.

Available for download on Wrox.com

LISTING 18-2: Developing a DLL test harness

```
# Creates a new heading.
def CreateHeading(Test, Title):
    print '\n#####################################'
    print 'Test ID = ', Test
    print 'Test Title = ', Title

# Displays the values.
def ShowValues(Expected, Received):
    print 'Expected Value = ', Expected
    print 'Received Value = ', Received
    if Expected == Received:
        print 'Test Passed'
    else:
        print 'Test Failed'

# Ends the test.
def CreateFooter():
    print '#####################################'
```

```
# Print out statements of everything the test is doing.
print 'Beginning Test'

print 'Loading clr'
import clr

print 'Loading test module'
clr.AddReferenceToFile('TestDLL.DLL')
from TestDLL import *

CreateHeading('0001', 'Creating Account1')
Account1 = Accounts()
ShowValues(5000, Account1.GetTotal)
CreateFooter()

CreateHeading('0002', 'Making a Deposit')
Account1.Deposit = 1000
ShowValues(6000, Account1.GetTotal)
CreateFooter()

CreateHeading('0003', 'Making a Withdrawal')
Account1.Withdrawal = 500
ShowValues(5500, Account1.GetTotal)
CreateFooter()

CreateHeading('0004', 'Creating Account2')
Account2 = Accounts(3000)
ShowValues(3000, Account2.GetTotal)
CreateFooter()

CreateHeading('0005', 'Transferring Money')
Account1.Transfer(Account2)
print '\nAccount1 = 8500'
ShowValues(8500, Account1.GetTotal)
print '\nAccount2 = 0'
ShowValues(0, Account2.GetTotal)
CreateFooter()

# Pause after the debug session.
raw_input('\nPress any key to continue...')
```

Let's begin with the three functions at the beginning of the script: `CreateHeading()`, `ShowValues()`, and `CreateFooter()`. It may seem a bit silly at first to create these functions, but they provide a method for changing the output of the tests quickly, should you need to do so. In addition, you don't want to write the same `print` statements hundreds of times as you create your script. It's far easier to simply call the functions.

The `CreateHeading()` and `CreateFooter()` functions don't have much logic in them — they simply display information onscreen. The `ShowValues()` function does have a bit of logic. In this case, it simply compares the expected value to the result and displays the appropriate output text. However, you could perform any number of checks required by your application. For example, if you're working with strings, you might need to check the string length and determine precisely how it differs from another string.

Notice that the __main__() code begins with print 'Loading clr'. It's important to describe every event that occurs in the test script. Otherwise, you won't know where a script has failed during testing. Make sure you describe the mundane acts of loading and unloading modules, as well as the actual tests.

The first test begins with a call to CreateHeading() with the test number and title. The code then performs a test, Account1 = Accounts() in this case, calls ShowValues() to test the result, and finishes with CreateFooter(). Almost all of the tests follow the same pattern.

The final test is a little different than the rest. To perform the test correctly, you must evaluate the content of both Account1 and Account2. This is a case where you can infer what is happening inside a method with the test code. The method, Transfer(), could perform the task correctly with Account1, but not with Account2, which would tell you something about the content of the method and where to look for the problem.

This final bit of script also shows the flexibility of using the three functions presented earlier. By separating the individual tasks into three parts, you can call the ShowValues() function multiple times as needed. You might also consider creating a second form of ShowValues() to accept a comparison string for output (the print '\nAccount1 = 8500' part of the script).

Performing the DLL Test

It's time to run the DLL test. If you configured your project using the techniques in Chapters 16 and 17, you should be able to click Start Debugging (or press F5) to start the build process. During the build process, the compiler checks your DLL for major errors.

After the DLL is built, the IronPython script runs. Remember that this script is running outside of the IDE, so nothing it does will actually affect the performance of your code. The diagnostic tests will run and provide the information shown in Figure 18-2.

Notice that the use of formatting, test numbers, titles, comparison values, and so on makes the test results extremely easy to read. Of course, a large DLL could overwhelm the capacity of the console to display information. In this case, you could just as easily send the output to a text file, HTML page, or an XML file. The point is that the script makes it possible to view diagnostics about your application almost immediately after you build it.

TESTING APPLICATIONS

You can use IronPython for more than DLL testing — you can also use it to test your applications. Applications are more of a challenge than DLLs because you have to find a way to emulate user input. Of course, many developers just aren't as creative as users. A developer would never think about putting text where a number is expected. Many developers discover, to their chagrin, that users will also try implanting scripts and doing other weird things to the application that aren't easy to test. Some users will even try odd character combinations looking for hidden application features or just to see what will happen. Tests will only work as well as your ability to outguess the user. The following sections show how to test a simple Windows Forms application.

```
Beginning Test
Loading clr
Loading test module

#########################################
Test ID =  0001
Test Title =  Creating Account1
Expected Value =  5000
Received Value =  5000
Test Passed
#########################################

#########################################
Test ID =  0002
Test Title =  Making a Deposit
Expected Value =  6000
Received Value =  6000
Test Passed
#########################################

#########################################
Test ID =  0003
Test Title =  Making a Withdrawal
Expected Value =  5500
Received Value =  5500
Test Passed
#########################################

#########################################
Test ID =  0004
Test Title =  Creating Account2
Expected Value =  3000
Received Value =  3000
Test Passed
#########################################

#########################################
Test ID =  0005
Test Title =  Transferring Money

Account1 = 8500
Expected Value =  8500
Received Value =  8500
Test Passed

Account2 = 0
Expected Value =  0
Received Value =  0
Test Passed
#########################################

Press any key to continue..._
```

FIGURE 18-2: The output shows a list of all of the tests run by the IronPython script on the DLL.

Creating the Test Application

The test application is very simple, but it does include some internal code you can use for testing purposes. The following sections describe the test application.

Defining the Form

A Windows Forms application need not be complex to test it using IronPython. All you really need are a few controls and some buttons with code for their event handlers. Figure 18-3 shows the simple form used for this example.

As with Windows Forms you use in a DLL, you must make an important change to test an application using IronPython. All the controls you want to access must have their `Modifiers` property set to `Public`. The default setting of `Private` prevents you from accessing them directly in IronPython.

Building the Code

You can see that the form in Figure 18-3 has three `Button` controls in it. Each of the controls has a `Click()` event handler associated with it, as shown in Listing 18-3.

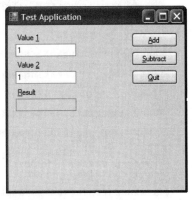

FIGURE 18-3: The simple form used for this example provides enough inputs to test.

Available for download on Wrox.com

LISTING 18-3: Defining an application to test

```
private void btnQuit_Click(object sender, EventArgs e)
{
    Close();
}

public void btnAdd_Click(object sender, EventArgs e)
{
    txtResult.Text = (Int32.Parse(txtValue1.Text) +
        Int32.Parse(txtValue2.Text)).ToString();
}

public void btnSubtract_Click(object sender, EventArgs e)
{
    txtResult.Text = (Int32.Parse(txtValue1.Text) -
        Int32.Parse(txtValue2.Text)).ToString();
}
```

The `btnQuit_Click()` event handler is as you might expect. It simply closes the form using the `Close()` method. You won't test this functionality using the IronPython script.

The `btnAdd_Click()` event handler converts the values of `txtValue1.Text` and `txtValue2.Text` to `Int32` values using `Int32.Parse()`. It then adds the numbers together, converts the result to a string using `ToString()`, and places it into `txtResult.Text`. Because IronPython needs to test this event handler, the visibility is set to `public`. If you don't change the visibility of the event handler, IronPython won't be able to access it. The `btnSubtract_Click()` event handler works the same as the `btnAdd_Click()` event handler, except that it subtracts the two numbers.

Creating the Application Test Script

As long as you're willing to make the required visibility changes to your application, you can use IronPython to test it. Creating a test project for an application works precisely the same as creating a test project for a DLL. Here's the short list of changes you must perform:

1. Change the build output location for both the Debug and Release builds to the solution folder.

2. Add IPY.EXE as an existing project to your solution.

3. Set the ipy project as the startup project so that the IDE executes it instead of the Windows Forms application.

4. Configure the ipy project to start your script and to use the appropriate working directory.

5. Add a new IronPython script to the solution folder.

This test script uses the three functions described in Listing 18-2 to provide output. It also adds the following two output functions:

```
# Verify the type.
def CheckType(Object, Type):
    if Object.GetType().__str__() == Type:
            print 'Test Passed'
    else:
            print 'Test Failed'

# Show initial values.
def ShowInit(Value1, Value2):
    print 'Value1: ', Value1
    print 'Value2: ', Value2
```

The CheckType() function compares the type of an object you create against an expected type. If the type is incorrect, then it displays a failed message. You can use this function when creating a form or other object that could fail for any number of reasons.

The ShowInit() function displays the initial values for a binary operation or perhaps just two values used for some other task. You could probably create a version of the function that accepts any number of arguments in the form of an array. The point is that you can create some specialized functions to display data for a particular test and then find that you can use it for other purposes later.

As previously mentioned, this test script also uses the three functions found in Listing 18-2. Listing 18-4 shows the actual test script for this application. It doesn't provide a complete test but does provide enough information that you could easily complete it if you wanted.

LISTING 18-4: Developing an application test harness

Available for
download on
Wrox.com

```
# Print out statements of everything the test is doing.
print 'Beginning Test'

print 'Loading clr'
```

continues

LISTING 18-4 *(continued)*

```
import clr

print 'Loading System assembly support'
import System

print 'Creating a blank event argument.'
EventArg = System.EventArgs()

print 'Loading test module'
clr.AddReferenceToFile('TestApplication.EXE')
from TestApplication import *

CreateHeading('0001', 'Creating a test form')
MyForm = Form1()
CheckType(MyForm, 'TestApplication.Form1')
CreateFooter()

CreateHeading('0002', 'Testing a default add')
MyForm.btnAdd_Click(object, EventArg)
ShowInit(MyForm.txtValue1.Text, MyForm.txtValue2.Text)
ShowValues('2', MyForm.txtResult.Text)
CreateFooter()

CreateHeading('0003', 'Testing a default subtract')
MyForm.btnSubtract_Click(object, EventArg)
ShowInit(MyForm.txtValue1.Text, MyForm.txtValue2.Text)
ShowValues('0', MyForm.txtResult.Text)
CreateFooter()

CreateHeading('0004', 'Testing add with one change')
MyForm.txtValue1.Text = '5'
MyForm.btnAdd_Click(object, EventArg)
ShowInit(MyForm.txtValue1.Text, MyForm.txtValue2.Text)
ShowValues('6', MyForm.txtResult.Text)
CreateFooter()

# Pause after the debug session.
raw_input('\nPress any key to continue...')
```

The test script begins by loading the required code for the test, beginning with clr. Because this test has to work with event handlers, it needs to load the System assembly and create a System.EventArgs object, EventArg. Because the event handlers in this application don't actually use the event arguments, EventArg is actually a default object with no content. The call simply won't succeed without it, however, so you must create it.

After the script finishes the prerequisites, it performs the first test, which is to create the Windows Forms object, Form1, as MyForm. The creation process could fail; you want to verify that MyForm isn't null, so that's the first test that relies on the CheckType() function. You don't have to show the form to test it, so the code doesn't call ShowDialog(). If you do decide to show the form, you'll actually need someone to work with it. The script is suspended during the time the form appears onscreen.

The next step is to perform some tasks with the form. The code performs a default add and subtract. The two value fields, MyForm.txtValue1.Text and MyForm.txtValue2.Text, contain default values that you can use for testing. Actually, it's good application design to always include default values for the user so that the user has some idea of what kind of content to provide.

The MyForm.btnAdd_Click() and MyForm.btnSubtract_Click() event handlers perform the actual addition and subtraction. In order to call these two methods, you must supply both a sender object and event arguments. The sender object can simply be an object because the code doesn't use it.

The final test in the example is to change one of the values and perform another addition. To perform this task, the script changes the value of MyForm.txtValue1.Text and calls MyForm.btnAdd_Click(). Normally, you'd provide a wealth of additional tests to check various values and see how they react with the code. For example, you might provide some negative values to ensure that the event handlers work properly with them. You might also test incorrect input, such as providing a string. The point is that you can completely automate any level of testing using this IronPython script technique.

Performing the Application Test

At this point, you have an application to test and the script to test it. It's time to run the application. One of the problems you could encounter is not making something public (such as an object, control, or property) that you need to test (the default is to create private objects, controls, and properties). Unfortunately, the need to make class members public is one of the problems of using IronPython for desktop application testing. It's not a big problem, but you need to consider it. When working with an extremely large application, changing the required member visibility could prove problematic. In addition, making some members public could pose security risks.

Let's hope everything works as anticipated when you run the test. Figure 18-4 shows typical output from this application.

As with the DLL testing script, this script outputs text that's easy to read and results that are easy to decipher. You know immediately whether certain tests have failed and precisely what inputs were used to conduct the test. As with DLL testing, you may need to use some other form of output, such as an XML file, when performing testing on complex applications because the content won't fit entirely onscreen.

Applications can present a number of problems for this kind of testing. For example, you wouldn't want to make the password field of a security dialog box public because someone else could possibly intercept user passwords as a result. It's always a good idea to return the members that you've made public to private status to ensure that the application works in a secure manner when you put it into production.

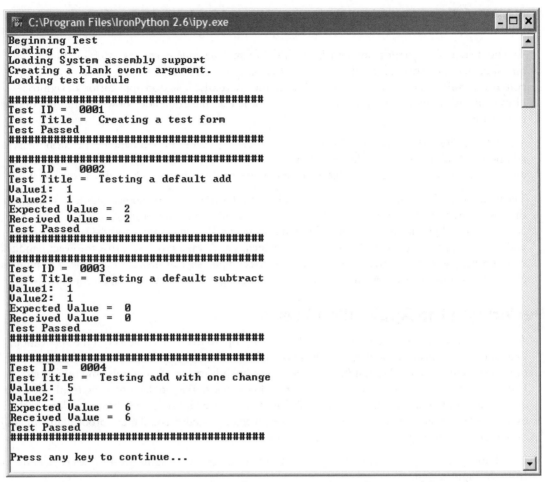

FIGURE 18-4: Desktop applications can prove difficult to test, but the results are worth it.

PERFORMING COMMAND LINE TESTS

For many developers, testing must be formal or it really isn't testing. Actually, ad hoc testing is sometimes better because you get to play with the application while you test it. Testing in an ad hoc manner at the command line is possible in IronPython because it's an interpreted environment. In fact, we've been performing ad hoc testing throughout the book. Every time you reviewed the content of an application, no matter what type it was, using the `dir()` function, you were performing a kind of ad hoc testing because you were reviewing the content of the application.

To provide a more concrete example, both Chapters 16 and 17 discussed the use of operator over-rides in the `Calcs` extension DLL. In this case, the `dir()` function showed that the + operator override resulted in the addition of the __add__() and __radd__() methods. The test demonstrated that the DLL had added the overrides correctly and that you should be able to access them from an application. In addition, you discovered that IronPython views the content of the DLL in a slightly different manner than another environment might view them.

Let's look at a specific test example, the TestDLL.DLL file. For the purposes of this example, you want to use the dir() function to determine whether the Accounts class contains everything it should (and nothing it shouldn't), as shown in Figure 18-5. Notice that there's no mention of Total in this list, but you can see all of the properties and methods described in Listing 18-1.

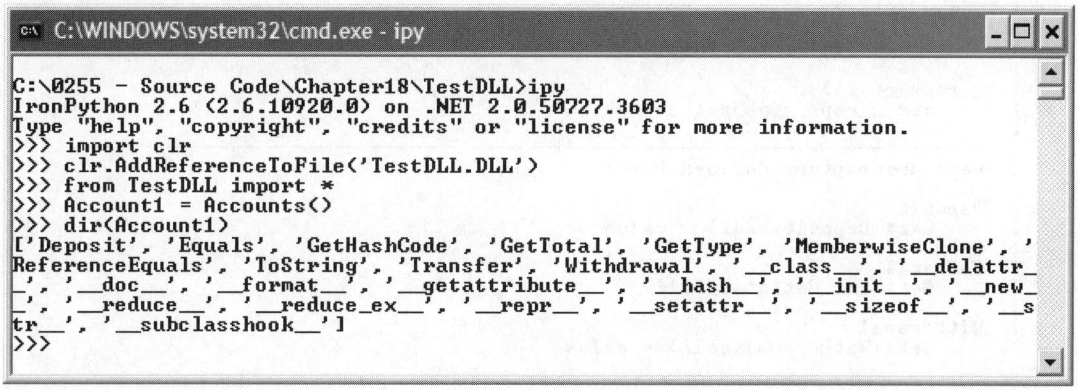

```
C:\WINDOWS\system32\cmd.exe - ipy                                    _ □ ×

C:\0255 - Source Code\Chapter18\TestDLL>ipy
IronPython 2.6 (2.6.10920.0) on .NET 2.0.50727.3603
Type "help", "copyright", "credits" or "license" for more information.
>>> import clr
>>> clr.AddReferenceToFile('TestDLL.DLL')
>>> from TestDLL import *
>>> Account1 = Accounts()
>>> dir(Account1)
['Deposit', 'Equals', 'GetHashCode', 'GetTotal', 'GetType', 'MemberwiseClone', '
ReferenceEquals', 'ToString', 'Transfer', 'Withdrawal', '__class__', '__delattr_
_', '__doc__', '__format__', '__getattribute__', '__hash__', '__init__', '__new_
_', '__reduce__', '__reduce_ex__', '__repr__', '__setattr__', '__sizeof__', '__s
tr__', '__subclasshook__']
>>>
```

FIGURE 18-5: Make sure you check the actual content of the DLL against the expectations you have for it.

If you remember from Chapters 16 and 17, the __doc__() function is undefined for an assembly that you import into IronPython, but the help() function does produce a result. One of the next checks you should perform manually is to verify that the assembly provides the kind of information you expect from help. Figure 18-6 shows the output of the help() function for the Accounts class. Notice that it contains all of the information you expect, including the fact that there are two forms of __new__(), the constructor, and the read/write state of the various properties.

Of course, you'll want to perform other sorts of manual testing that could eventually appear in your test script. For example, you might decide to check whether the Accounts class will let you create an account with a negative starting amount (it will).

It would be also helpful to know whether someone could circumvent some of the properties in the Accounts class. You wouldn't want someone to use code such as Account2 = Account2 + 20 to overcome the protections in the Deposit property. In this case, the test displays an error. Another check might include adding two accounts together, such as Acccount3 = Account1 + Account2.

By now, you should have the point of using manual testing. You can creatively think of ways that someone might try to overcome protections in your code. It probably isn't possible to find every avenue of entry into a DLL, but testing in this way helps you think through more potential problems that other forms of testing allow. Interactively probing your code is a unique method of testing the impossible.

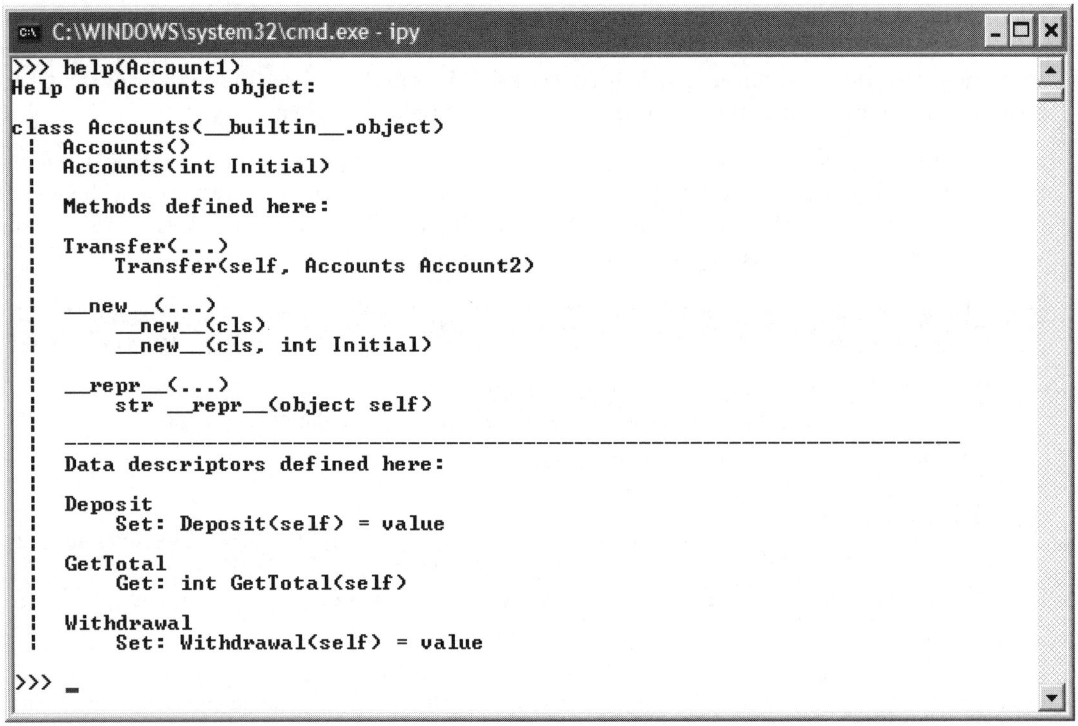

```
C:\WINDOWS\system32\cmd.exe - ipy                                    _ □ ✕
>>> help(Account1)
Help on Accounts object:

class Accounts(__builtin__.object)
 |  Accounts()
 |  Accounts(int Initial)
 |
 |  Methods defined here:
 |
 |  Transfer(...)
 |      Transfer(self, Accounts Account2)
 |
 |  __new__(...)
 |      __new__(cls)
 |      __new__(cls, int Initial)
 |
 |  __repr__(...)
 |      str __repr__(object self)
 |
 |  ----------------------------------------------------------------
 |  Data descriptors defined here:
 |
 |  Deposit
 |      Set: Deposit(self) = value
 |
 |  GetTotal
 |      Get: int GetTotal(self)
 |
 |  Withdrawal
 |      Set: Withdrawal(self) = value
>>> _
```

FIGURE 18-6: Verify that the help() function doesn't show any surprises about your assembly.

USING IRONPYTHON CONSTRUCTIVELY

This chapter has discussed and demonstrated some of the techniques you can use to work with IronPython for application testing. Because IronPython works outside the application, it tends not to interfere with the application's internal processing as some other testing tools can. In addition, you've discovered that IronPython can find errors quickly, especially those that tend to cause the most trouble. By creating a good test harness, you can possibly use parts of a test suite to work with other applications (depending on the purpose of that application and how you coded it).

It's time for you to try IronPython out as a testing tool. Begin with the sample applications in this chapter. Work through the examples to see how IronPython performs its job. After you get done with the example, try creating a test harness for some of the simpler applications you've created and then work your way up. You'll find that creating a test harness in IronPython is relatively fast, and the interpretive nature of IronPython makes it easy to create the test harness one step at a time.

Chapter 19 explores another exciting possibility for using IronPython — on another platform, such as Linux. That's right! You might initially think that IronPython is married to the .NET Framework (and it is, in certain situations), but you can do a great deal with IronPython using a .NET Framework alternative called Mono. Using Mono is interesting because it also lets you use IronPython on the one Windows platform that doesn't support a full implementation of the .NET Framework, Windows Server 2008 Server Core Edition.

19
Using IronPython with Mono

WHAT'S IN THIS CHAPTER?

➤ Defining Mono and its features

➤ Getting and configuring Mono

➤ Using Mono and IronPython together

➤ Using Mono with other .NET languages

If you buy into the idea that IronPython only works on the Windows platform, you're losing out on a lot of the power of IronPython. In fact, IronPython works fine on a number of platforms, including Linux and the Macintosh. The secret, as is the case in so many situations, is to think outside the box. There's a little product called Mono that Microsoft would rather you didn't think about too much. Mono is an alternative for the .NET Framework that runs many (but not all) .NET applications just fine. Because IronPython is mainly a character mode kind of an application development platform, you can use the vast majority of your IronPython applications on any platform that supports Mono.

Because Mono is such a big secret, this chapter begins with an overview of Mono. You won't get every detail about what Mono has to offer, but you'll obtain enough information to use IronPython comfortably with Mono. If you do decide that Mono is the product for you, you should probably obtain a Mono-specific book because Mono has too much to offer to discuss it in just one chapter.

Your system probably doesn't have Mono installed, so the next step is to obtain a copy and install it on your machine. Mono won't cost you a penny, so all you really need to invest is a bit of time to work through the examples in this chapter. (Mono is an open source product that is sponsored by Novell.) The next section shows how to work with IronPython using Mono. However, IronPython and Mono are such a good match that you'll find many of your applications will run just fine under Mono.

Many developers are worried that the extensions they create for IronPython won't work under Mono. Unfortunately, not every extension will run under Mono, but you'll be surprised to discover that Mono comes with fewer limitations than you might think. The section "Interacting with Other .NET Languages Under Mono" later in this chapter discusses a few issues you should know about when using your extension on another platform to support IronPython.

Finally, the chapter discusses application testing. Actually, there are fewer issues here than you might think. Mono provides good support for many of the testing techniques that you already use. However, you might find that you need to obtain a few additional tools to create a full testing solution. Some platforms simply require that you buy a testing tool for that platform, but take time to read this section before you come to any conclusions on your own.

WHAT IS MONO?

Mono (http://www.mono-project.com/) is a run time along the same lines as the .NET Framework, and it includes much of the functionality of the .NET Framework. In fact, with each release, Mono gets a bit closer to .NET Framework functionality. However, don't get the idea that Mono will ever exactly match the .NET Framework. Platform differences, Microsoft copyrights, and other issues will always keep Mono just a bit different from the .NET Framework. Even so, Mono can run a considerable number of .NET applications. The following sections describe Mono, its advantages and limitations, in greater detail.

An Overview of the Mono Family

You can obtain Mono for a considerable number of platforms. In fact, the makers of Mono add new platforms with every release. At one time, Mono worked on just a few Linux implementations, Windows, and the Mac OS X. Over time, Mono support has increased to the exciting list of platforms that follows.

➤ **LiveCD:** This is actually an openSUSE 11.2.1 (http://www.opensuse.org/en/) LiveCD (a CD or DVD that contains a bootable image — see http://en.wikipedia.org/wiki/Live_CD for details) that includes Mono 2.6.1.

➤ **Mac OS X:** You can use this installation on a number of Mac versions including Mac OS X Tiger (10.4), Leopard (10.5), and Snow Leopard (10.6) (it may work on other versions as well, but you're on your own for support). The download includes Mono, Cocoa#, and Gtk# (GIMP Toolkit Sharp). You need to download the Client Software Development Kit (CSDK), available on the Mono site, separately. There are separate downloads for the Intel and PowerPC platforms. You can learn more about Mac OS X at http://www.apple.com/macosx/.

 Computer acronyms and abbreviations often contain terms within terms. GIMP stands for GNU Image Manipulation Program. Of course, GNU is one of those fancy recursive abbreviations that stands for GNU's Not Unix. You can learn more about Gtk# at http://www.mono-project.com/GtkSharp. *You can obtain a .NET Framework version of the Gtk# library from* http://ftp.novell.com/pub/mono/gtk-sharp/; *simply download* gtk-sharp-2.12.9-2.win32.msi.

➤ **openSUSE:** You can use this download for the openSUSE 11.0, 11.1, and 11.2 platforms. You must have your own system with openSUSE installed to use it. You can download openSUSE at `http://software.opensuse.org/`. Just in case you're interested, the SUSE part of the name stands for Software und System-Entwicklung, which translates to software and systems development.

➤ **SLES/SLED:** You can use this download for SUSE Linux Enterprise Server (SLES) or SUSE Linux Enterprise Desktop (SLED). SLES and SLED are the paid versions of SUSE from Novell. As with openSUSE, you must have your own system with SLES or SLED installed to use this version of Mono. You can find out more about SLES and SLED at `http://www.novell.com/linux/`.

➤ **Virtual PC:** This is actually an openSUSE 11.2.1 virtual PC image that includes Mono 2.6.1. You could use this download to check out Linux functionality for your IronPython application on your PC without leaving Windows. Of course, performance won't be very good, but it will get the job done.

➤ **VMware:** This is actually an openSUSE 11.2.1 VMware image that includes Mono 2.6.1. You'd use it to check your application for Linux functionality without leaving the host operating system.

➤ **Windows:** You can officially use this download for Windows 2000, XP, 2003, and Vista. Testing shows that it also works fine for Windows 7 and Windows Server 2008. The download includes Mono for Windows, Gtk# (a graphics library to display a user interface onscreen), and XSP (eXtensible Server Pages, an alternate Web server for serving ASP.NET pages). You can also get the Mono Migration Analyzer tool as a separate download.

➤ **Other:** This is a group of less supported platforms including Debian and Ubuntu. At least these two platforms have supported packages. You can also get Mono in an unsupported form for Solaris, Nokia, and Maemo. Theoretically, you could support yet other platforms by compiling the source code found at `http://ftp.novell.com/pub/mono/sources-stable/`.

Of course, this list contains only a summary of the main Mono downloads. There are a large number of Mono add-ons a well. For example, you can obtain Mono Tools for Visual Studio (`http://go-mono.com/monotools/download/`) if you want to work with Mono directly from Visual Studio. Unfortunately, the current version of this product only works with Visual Studio 2008. The developer should provide a Visual Studio 2010 version soon. You can obtain a trial version of Mono Tools for Visual Studio (registration is required), but you must pay for the full version.

You might also decide that you want to eschew Visual Studio for something specifically designed for Mono. In this case, you should at least look at Mono Develop (`http://monodevelop.com/`). Mono Develop comes in a form for most platforms that Mono supports, so you can use the same IDE on any platform you require. For the time being at least, Mono Develop is free, so download it and give it a try.

IronPython does include support for Silverlight development. If you plan to use IronPython for Web applications and need to support multiple platforms, you might want to look at Moonlight (`http://mono-project.com/Moonlight`) instead. This Silverlight replacement works on the same platforms that Mono does and should also work fine with IronPython.

Some of the extensions to Mono are well outside the scope of this book, but are interesting to contemplate. For example, you can get Mono Touch (`http://monotouch.net/`) to develop applications for the iPhone and iPod Touch devices. The point is that you can probably find some form of Mono to meet just about any need, but using Mono fully means learning some new techniques, such as creating user interfaces using Gtk#.

Considering the Reasons for Using Mono

You already know the reasons that you're using the .NET Framework and this chapter isn't about changing your mind. The .NET Framework is stable and many developers love the functionality it provides them for building great applications. However, you could think of Mono as another tool to extend the range of your applications. If for no other reason, the fact that you could run your IronPython application on Linux or the Mac OS X makes Mono a good choice for some forms of application development. In sum, the main reason for using Mono in place of the .NET Framework is flexibility.

As previously mentioned, Mono and the .NET Framework aren't precisely the same. The first thought that most developers will have is that compatibility issues will be bad, and to a certain extent, they do cause problems. However, Mono also provides functionality that you won't find when working with the .NET Framework. Features such as Gtk# actually make Mono a better product. In addition, with Mono you have a lightweight Web server for ASP.NET pages, XSP, that works on every Mono platform. Therefore, the differences between Mono and the .NET Framework aren't always bad — sometimes they become downright useful.

Mono does provide direct support for IronPython, but you need to use a newer version of Mono (see `http://www.mono-project.com/Python` for details). The support isn't all that good. The section "Running the Application from the Command Line" later in this chapter demonstrates the problem of using the Mono implementation of IronPython. Even so, you do get IronPython support that will likely improve as Mono improves, so this is an area where you can expect Mono to grow as an IronPython platform. In reality, the Mono community is quite excited about IronPython. You can find tutorials for using IronPython in a Mono environment at `http://zetcode.com/tutorials/ironpythontutorial/`. If you want to see IronPython running under Mono on a Linux system, see the screenshot and description at `http://www.ironpython.info/index.php/Mono`.

Understanding Mono Limitations

Don't get the idea that every .NET application will instantly run on Mono. For example, while Mono includes support for Language Integrated Query (LINQ), the support isn't perfect. The LINQ to SQL support works fine for many applications, but not all of them. The Mono developers realize that the support isn't complete and they plan to work on it (see the release notes at `http://www.mono-project.com/Release_Notes_Mono_2.6.1` for details).

There are some obvious limitations for using Mono that should come to mind immediately. Because the purpose of Mono is to work across platforms, the P/Invoke calls in your extensions aren't going to work. A P/Invoke call causes your extension to provide Windows-specific support, so using it on Linux wouldn't work no matter what product you tried. The previous chapters in the book have emphasized when a particular technique is unlikely to produce useful cross-platform results.

 The Mono developers want you to be able to move your applications from the .NET Framework to Mono so they've provided some assistance in the form of the Mono Migration Analyzer (MoMA). You should check any application you want to run under Mono using this tool. The download is free from http:// mono-project.com/MoMA. *There's also a version of MoMA for openSUSE users available on the Web site.*

The current version of Mono doesn't work with .NET Framework 4.0 applications. The applications won't start at all — you see an error message instead. However, Mono does work fine with older versions of the .NET Framework. It's only a matter of time before Mono supports the .NET Framework 4.0, so this is a short-term limitation that you can easily overcome by using an older version of the .NET Framework when building your application. Given that IronPython doesn't currently support the .NET Framework 4.0 in many respects, this particular problem isn't much of an issue for IronPython developers.

In a few cases, you have to look around to determine whether you'll encounter problems using Mono for a particular task. For example, if your ASP.NET application uses Web Parts, you can't use Mono (see http://www.mono-project.com/ASP.NET). You also can't use a precompiled updateable Web site.

Using Mono on Windows Server 2008 Server Core

Early versions of Windows Server 2008 Server Core (Server Core for short) don't come with any form of the .NET Framework. Consequently, you can't run any form of .NET application on early versions of Server Core unless you use Mono. The lack of .NET Framework support on Server Core led some people to come up with odd solutions to problems, such as running PowerShell (see the solution at http://dmitrysotnikov.wordpress.com/2008/05/15/powershell-on-server-core/).

Fortunately, Microsoft decided to provide a limited version of the .NET Framework for Windows Server 2008 Server Core Edition R2. You can read about it at http://technet.microsoft.com/ library/dd883268.aspx. However, this version of the .NET Framework still has significant limitations and you might actually find it better to use Mono for your .NET applications. For example, while you can now provide limited support for ASP.NET on Server Core, you might actually find the Mono alternative, XSP, to provide the solutions you need for your application.

Mono has generated quite a bit of interest from the Server Core crowd, especially anyone who uses Server Core as their main server. Server Core has a number of advantages that makes it popular with small- to medium-sized companies. It uses far less memory and other resources, runs faster, runs more reliably, and has a far smaller attack surface for those nefarious individuals who want to ruin your day by attacking your server. You can find a complete article about running applications on Server Core using Mono at http://www.devsource.com/c/a/Architecture/ Mixing-Server-Core-with-NET-Applications/.

OBTAINING AND INSTALLING MONO

It's time to obtain and install your copy of Mono. Of course, the first step is to download the product. You can find the various versions of Mono at `http://www.go-mono.com/mono-downloads/download.html`. This section assumes you're installing Mono version 2.6.1 on a Windows system. If you need to install Mono on another system, follow the instructions that the Mono Web site provides for those versions. After you complete the download, follow these steps to perform the installation.

1. Double-click the `mono-2.6.1-gtksharp-2.12.9-win32-1.exe` file you downloaded from the Mono Web site. You see a Welcome page.

2. Click Next. You see a License page.

3. Read the licensing information. Select I Accept the Agreement, and then click Next. You see the Information page shown in Figure 19-1. Unlike most Information pages, this one actually contains a lot of useful information. Make sure you review the information it contains and click on the links it provides as needed. Especially important for keeping updated on Mono is joining the mailing list (`http://www.mono-project.com/Mailing_Lists`) or forums (`http://www.go-mono.org/forums/`). You can find these links at the bottom of the Information page.

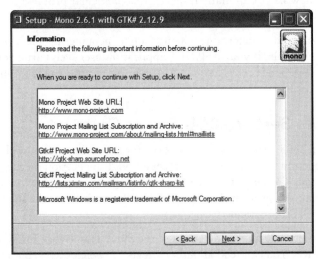

FIGURE 19-1: Make sure you review this Information page because it contains useful information.

4. Read the release information and then click Next. You see the Select Destination Location page shown in Figure 19-2. Normally, you can accept the default installation location. Some developers prefer a less complex path to Mono, such as simply C:\Mono, to make it easier to access from the command line. The chapter uses the default installation location.

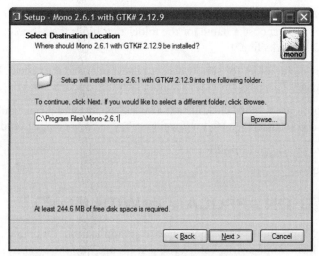

FIGURE 19-2: Select an installation location for Mono.

5. Provide an installation location for Mono and then click Next. You see the Select Components page shown in Figure 19-3. The components you select depend on what you plan to do with Mono — you can always change your setup later if necessary. If your only goal is to try Mono for your existing .NET applications and to create some simple IronPython applications, you really don't need the Gtk# and XSP support. This chapter assumes that you perform a Compact Installation to obtain a minimum amount of support for working with the IronPython sample application.

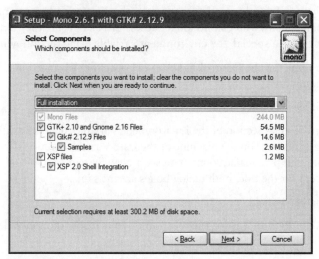

FIGURE 19-3: Choose the Mono components that you want to install.

6.   Select the components you want to install and then click Next. You see the Select Start Menu Folder page. This is where you choose a name for the folder that holds the Mono components. The default name normally works fine.

7.   Type a name for the Start menu folder (or simply accept the default) and then click Next. You see the Ready to Install page. This page provides a summary of the options that you've selected.

8.   Review the installation options and then click Install. You see the Installing page while the installer installs Mono on your machine. After a few minutes, you see a completion dialog box.

9.   Click Finish. You're ready to begin using Mono.

CREATING AN IRONPYTHON APPLICATION WITH MONO

It's time to begin working with Mono and IronPython to create an application. Of course, you'll want to know a bit more about how Mono works before you just plunge into the project, so the first step is to look at Mono from a command line perspective. The first section that follows shows how to create an IPY environment variable and use it to open the IronPython console using Mono whenever you need it. The sections that follow show how to create a project, build a simple IronPython application, and then test the application in a number of ways.

Working at the Command Line

Mono works differently than the .NET Framework. When you want to use the .NET Framework to execute an application, you simply double-click the application and it starts. The same doesn't hold true for Mono. If you want to execute an application using Mono, you must open the Mono command prompt and start it by specifically specifying Mono. Unfortunately, this limitation has an unusual effect on working with IronPython because you can no longer access IPY.EXE using the Path environment variable. Instead, you must create a special IPY environment variable using the following steps.

1.   Double-click the System applet in the Control Panel and choose the Advanced tab. You see the System Properties dialog box.

2.   Click Environment Variables. You see the Environment Variables dialog box.

3.   Click New in the System Variables section of the Environment Variables dialog box if you want to use IronPython from any account on the machine or the User Variables section if you want to use IronPython only from your personal account. You see a New System Variable or New User Variable dialog box. Except for the title, both dialog boxes are the same.

4.   Type **IPY** in the Variable Name field.

5.   Type **C:\Program Files\IronPython 2.6** or the location of your IronPython installation in the Variable Value field.

6.   Click OK three times to add the new environment variable, close the Environment Variables dialog box, and close the System Properties dialog box. You're ready to begin working with IronPython.

At this point, you're ready to begin working with Mono. Choose Start ➪ Programs ➪ Mono 2.6.1 for Windows ➪ Mono-2.6.1 Command Prompt to display a Mono command prompt. When you see the Mono command prompt, type **Mono "%IPY%IPY.EXE"** and press Enter. You'll see the usual IronPython console.

The first thing you should notice is that the .NET Framework version reporting by the IronPython console is slightly different from the one you normally see. There isn't any problem with this difference. In fact, it's the only difference you're going to notice as you work with the IronPython console. Let's give it a try so you can see for yourself. Type the following code and you'll see the standard responses shown in Figure 19-4.

```
import sys
for ThisPath in sys.path:
    print ThisPath
```

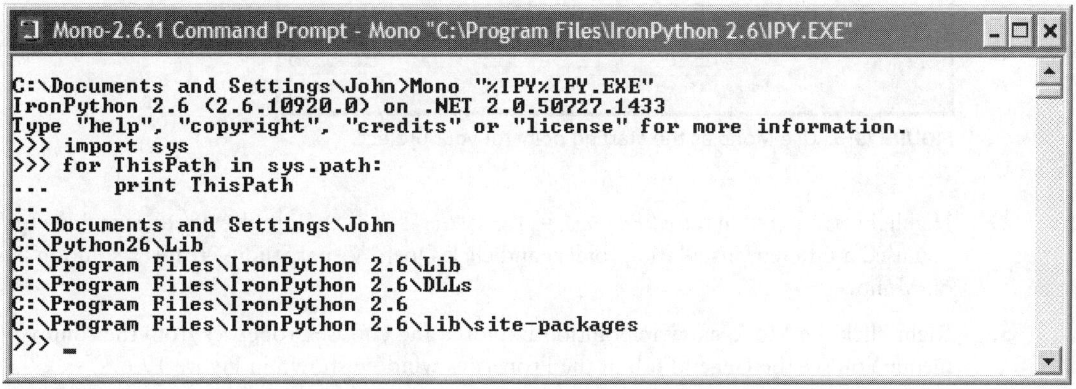

FIGURE 19-4: Running IronPython under Mono doesn't really look any different.

If you compare the results you see when running IronPython under the .NET Framework with the results you see when running IronPython under Mono, you won't notice any differences. In fact, you can try out the applications in this book, and you won't see any differences at all unless you need to work with an extension or other outside code source (and you might not even see any differences then). Working with Mono simply means you have access to more platforms when working with IronPython, not that you have more limitations.

Defining the Project

The project you create for working with Mono is going to be just a little different from the one you create when working strictly with the .NET Framework. You'll still start up IronPython using the Visual Studio IDE, but there's an extra step now: you must start Mono first. The following steps describe how to create the project for this chapter.

1. Choose File ➪ Open ➪ Project/Solution. You see the Open Project dialog box shown in Figure 19-5.

page 414 chapter 19

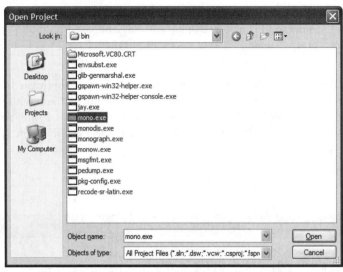

FIGURE 19-5: Use Mono as the starting point for your project.

2. Highlight `Mono.EXE` in the `\Program Files\Mono-2.6.1\bin` folder of your machine (unless you used a different installation folder) and click Open. Visual Studio creates a solution based on Mono.

3. Right-click the Mono entry in Solution Explorer and choose Properties from the context menu. You see the General tab of the Properties window shown in Figure 19-6.

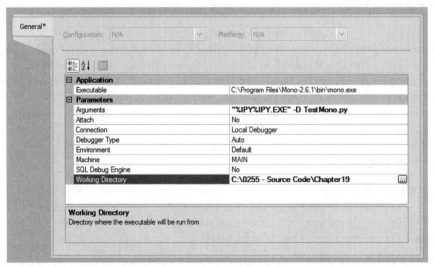

FIGURE 19-6: Set the Mono configuration for your project.

4. Type `"C:\Program Files\IronPython 2.6\IPY.EXE" -D TestMono.py` in the Arguments field (change the folder location to match your IronPython installation).

5. Click the ellipses in the Working Directory field to display the Browse for Folder dialog box. Locate the folder that contains the project you're working on and click OK. The project folder appears in the Working Directory field of the Properties window.

6. Choose File ⇨ Save All. You see a Save File As dialog box.

7. Type the solution name in the Object Name dialog box and click Save.

8. Right-click the solution entry in Solution Explorer and choose Add ⇨ New Item. You see the Add New Item dialog box.

9. Highlight the Text File template. Type `TestMono.py` in the Name field and click Add. Visual Studio adds the Python file to your project and automatically opens it for you.

Creating the Code

It's time to add some code to the IronPython file. This example provides a listing of the modules that IronPython is using. If you compare this list to the one that IronPython provides when you run the application using the .NET Framework, you'll see the modules in a different order, but otherwise the output is the same. Listing 19-1 shows the code used for this example.

Available for download on Wrox.com

LISTING 19-1: Creating a simple Mono test program

```python
# Obtain access to the sys module.
import sys

# Output a list of modules.
print 'IronPython Module Listing\n'
for ThisMod in sys.modules:
    print ThisMod, sys.modules[ThisMod]

# Pause after the debug session.
raw_input('\nPress any key to continue...')
```

This example demonstrates a simple `for` loop to iterate through the list of modules found in the `sys.modules` dictionary. In this case, the code prints out two items. First, it prints out the module name. Second, it prints out the module information, which normally includes the module location. As always, the code ends with a pause, `raw_input()`, so that you can see the output before the window closes.

Running the Application from the IDE

Running the application is the first place you see some potential problems with using Mono. If you click Start Debugging, you see the No Debugging Information dialog box shown in Figure 19-7. If you click Yes, the program will run, but you won't get any debugging support. This is one of the problems with using Mono exclusively. You'll probably want to use the normal .NET Framework setup to debug your application first, and then move on to the Mono configuration described in this chapter to test the application under Mono.

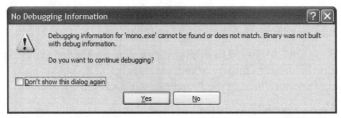

FIGURE 19-7: Mono doesn't provide any debugging support that Visual Studio understands.

 If you really do need Mono debugging, then you should consider adding Mono support to Visual Studio or using one of the alternative Mono IDEs. The "An Overview of the Mono Family" section of this chapter provides additional details about these alternatives.

To start the application successfully, choose Debug ⇨ Start Without Debugging or press Ctrl+F5. The program will run normally and you'll see the usual message at the end. Pressing Enter displays a second pause as shown in Figure 19-8. It seems that Mono provides its own pause so that you can see the results of executing the program, which is a nice touch for those times when you forget to add a pause of your own.

```
C:\WINDOWS\system32\cmd.exe                                          _ □ X

IronPython Module Listing

os.path <module 'ntpath' from 'C:\Python26\Lib\ntpath.py'>
__builtin__ <module '__builtin__' (built-in)>
site <module 'site' from 'C:\Python26\Lib\site.py'>
copy_reg <module 'copy_reg' (built-in)>
stat <module 'stat' from 'C:\Python26\Lib\stat.py'>
abc <module 'abc' from 'C:\Python26\Lib\abc.py'>
os <module 'os' from 'C:\Python26\Lib\os.py'>
errno <module 'errno' (built-in)>
UserDict <module 'UserDict' from 'C:\Python26\Lib\UserDict.py'>
warnings <module 'warnings' from 'C:\Python26\Lib\warnings.py'>
_abcoll <module '_abcoll' from 'C:\Python26\Lib\_abcoll.py'>
_warnings <module '_warnings' (built-in)>
genericpath <module 'genericpath' from 'C:\Python26\Lib\genericpath.py'>
sys <module 'sys' (built-in)>
__main__ <module '__main__' from 'TestMono.py'>
nt <module 'nt' (built-in)>
types <module 'types' from 'C:\Python26\Lib\types.py'>
ntpath <module 'ntpath' from 'C:\Python26\Lib\ntpath.py'>
linecache <module 'linecache' from 'C:\Python26\Lib\linecache.py'>

Press any key to continue...
Press any key to continue . . .
```

FIGURE 19-8: IronPython displays the list of modules found in the current setup.

Running the Application from the Command Line

Interestingly enough, Mono does come with direct support for IronPython, but Mono supports IronPython 1.1, and the IronPython console supplied with Mono seems to do odd things. Open a Mono command prompt, type **IPY**, and press Enter. When you see the IronPython prompt, you'll see that it differs considerably from the one used throughout the book. Now try typing **1+1** and pressing Enter. You'll probably see results like those in Figure 19-9.

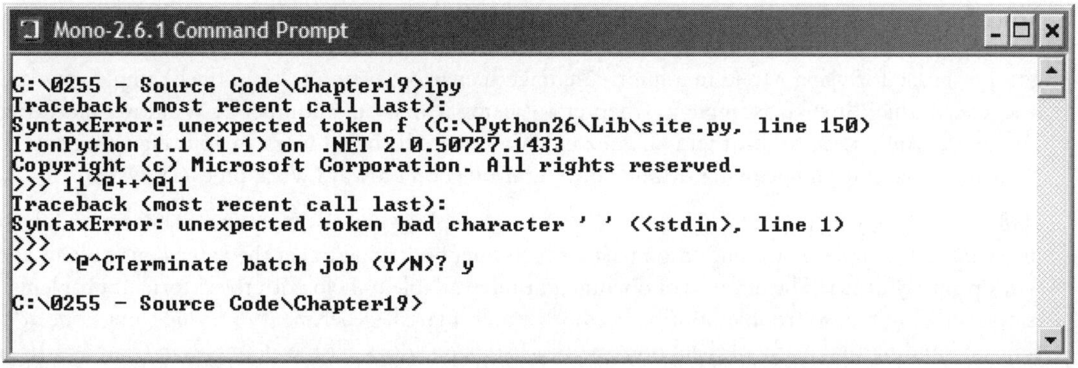

```
Mono-2.6.1 Command Prompt                                    _ □ x

C:\0255 - Source Code\Chapter19>ipy
Traceback (most recent call last):
SyntaxError: unexpected token f (C:\Python26\Lib\site.py, line 150)
IronPython 1.1 (1.1) on .NET 2.0.50727.1433
Copyright (c) Microsoft Corporation. All rights reserved.
>>> 11^@++^@11
Traceback (most recent call last):
SyntaxError: unexpected token bad character ' ' (<stdin>, line 1)
>>>
>>> ^@^CTerminate batch job (Y/N)? y

C:\0255 - Source Code\Chapter19>
```

FIGURE 19-9: The IronPython console provided with Mono leaves a lot to be desired.

Of course, the question isn't about the IronPython console, but whether it can run the example application. Press Ctrl+C to break out of the mess you're seeing onscreen. Type **Y** and press Enter when you're asked whether you want to stop the batch file. Then type **IPY TestMono.py** and press Enter. You'll see that the application does indeed work, as shown in Figure 19-10. The number of modules is far smaller than the list shown in Figure 19-8, but it's correct for the version of IronPython provided with Mono.

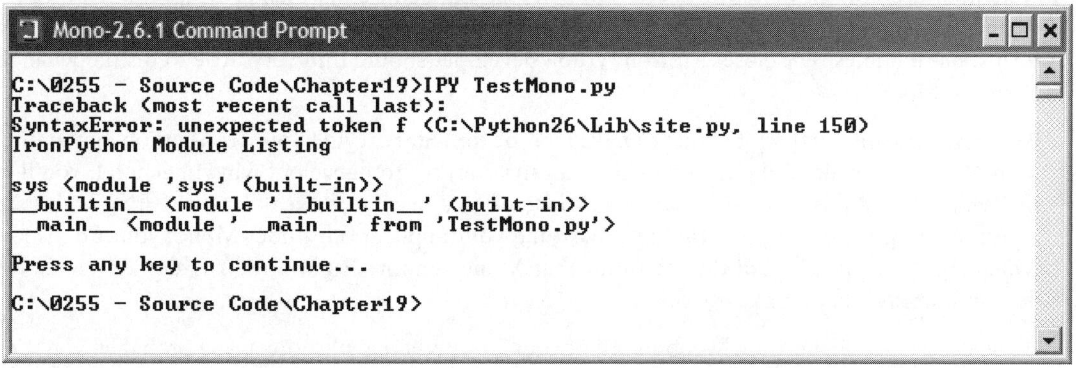

```
Mono-2.6.1 Command Prompt                                    _ □ x

C:\0255 - Source Code\Chapter19>IPY TestMono.py
Traceback (most recent call last):
SyntaxError: unexpected token f (C:\Python26\Lib\site.py, line 150)
IronPython Module Listing

sys <module 'sys' (built-in)>
__builtin__ <module '__builtin__' (built-in)>
__main__ <module '__main__' from 'TestMono.py'>

Press any key to continue...

C:\0255 - Source Code\Chapter19>
```

FIGURE 19-10: You can run the test application using the Mono version of IronPython.

The picture isn't completely gloomy. Developers are constantly trying new solutions for working with IronPython. You can find a potential fix for the problems described in this section of the chapter at `http://ironpython-urls.blogspot.com/2009/06/mono-can-now-compile-ironpython-20` `.html`. The solution comes with the caveat that it might not work for you.

INTERACTING WITH OTHER .NET LANGUAGES UNDER MONO

Mono originally focused its attention on C# development, but later added support for Visual Basic .NET as well. At this point, you can run any Visual Studio 2008–created application written under C# or Visual Basic.NET using Mono within the limitations described in the section "Understanding Mono Limitations" earlier in this chapter. Even DLR code appears to run fine in Mono within the current limits of the product, which aren't many.

The question for this book is whether Mono will work with your IronPython application and its extensions written in C# or Visual Basic.NET. The extensions found in Chapters 16 and 17 are a good test case for using Mono in a multi-language scenario. During testing, the examples worked fine (except the P/Invoke example in Chapter 16) using Mono on a number of Windows platforms. Of course, you'll need to test them on your machine to see if they'll work in your environment. As with anything new and growing, Mono configurations don't always work on every system.

Unfortunately, trying to get the Chapter 16 and 17 examples to work on an openSUSE setup didn't prove quite as simple. The IronPython part worked fine, but trying to get the extensions to load and work properly didn't. The amount of documentation available to help with these sorts of problems is currently limited, so troubleshooting becomes a nightmarish experiment in trying things one at a time and finding that many of them don't work. If someone does get the examples in Chapters 16 and 17 to work on Linux, I'd be really interested in knowing. Please contact me at JMueller@mwt.net. The point is that you'll probably find situations where your multi-language application won't work on other platforms as you originally intended.

USING IRONPYTHON CONSTRUCTIVELY

This chapter has helped you understand Mono as it applies to IronPython. By now you're probably thinking about all the possibilities of running your IronPython applications on a Macintosh, Linux system, or even under Windows Server 2008 Server Core edition (which provides limited .NET Framework support). Using Mono isn't a perfect solution for applications that run on multiple platforms, but it comes very close. An IronPython developer should find very little to dislike when it comes to Mono.

Before you go any further, it's time to have a bit of fun. Start trying your IronPython applications with Mono. If you do find one or two that doesn't run, try to figure out why. In general, you'll find the limitations imposed by Mono are few, so it's often a matter of tweaking something a bit here or a bit there to get it to run. The thing is, by trying your applications under Mono, you can discover which ones can run on all of the platforms that Mono supports right now. You don't even have to do anything special to make it work.

If you get serious about using Mono for all of your IronPython applications, you probably won't get quite enough information from this chapter to do everything. Make sure you take time to look through the Mono sites presented in this chapter. It's also important that you obtain a Mono-specific book and start working through it. Now that your appetite for things Mono has been whetted, take some time to get the full Mono experience.

Congratulations! You've finished the book. Of course, you'll want to check out the two appendices as you have time. Appendix A tells you about the differences between IronPython and CPython. This information is invaluable when you try to use applications created by CPython developers. In most cases, these applications will work fine. In a few cases, you can tweak the application to work with IronPython. You'll definitely run into a few instances where IronPython simply won't run the CPython application. Appendix B provides you with a list of CPython extensions that will work with IronPython. Using these extensions can save you considerable time and effort. Please be sure to contact me if you have any questions or comments about this book at `JMueller@mwt.net`.

IronPython Differences
with CPython

WHAT'S IN THIS APPENDIX?

➤ Considering standard types, functions, and behaviors

➤ Defining which CPython libraries are missing

➤ Defining which extension modules are changed or missing

➤ Working with custom CPython extensions

➤ Using the interpreter and environment

➤ Using garbage collection

IronPython has a lot of functionality, but throughout the book you've probably noticed that it isn't precisely like CPython. In fact, there are more than a few differences between IronPython and CPython. Some of these differences occur because of the way IronPython is written. (IronPython is a managed application, CPython is written in C.) However, some of the differences result from Microsoft's interpretation of the specification or its decision not to follow the specification in order to make IronPython interact with the other .NET languages with greater ease. Whatever the differences, you need to know about them in order to avoid potential problems when working through your applications.

IMPLEMENTING STANDARD TYPES, FUNCTIONS, AND BEHAVIORS

Whenever you have two different teams working on a software product, some differences will occur in implementation and behavior. The IronPython team is currently working on these differences, but you can probably expect some of them to remain long-term. For example, you might see different error messages when working in IronPython than when you work with CPython. The error number is the same, but the message is different. Other than making it harder to search for information about the error online, the difference in wording really doesn't cause a show-stopper problem. Both IronPython and CPython carry on as before. However, the differences can prove confusing to developers who are used to looking at the error message rather than the error number, so it's important that both products begin to display the same error messages.

 It would be easy to beat up on one party or another when it comes to language implementations. The problem is that the Python language specification found at `http://www.python.org/doc/current/reference/` *isn't always as clear as it could be about certain language characteristics. The lack of clarity has translated into different implementations of some features. Of course, now that these problems are clear, the specification should get an update to clarify them. Unfortunately, past experience shows that no matter how well the specification is written, there will always be some wiggle room for different implementations so you need to learn to work around them when building your application.*

You'll find other cases where IronPython and CPython behave differently. For example, when displaying a traceback after an error, IronPython provides a caret (^) to show the origin of the error. CPython doesn't provide the functionality.

There are a few cases where IronPython and CPython react differently to code. The following list contains the most common issues that you'll encounter. (Because the IronPython developers are constantly fixing issues and developers are finding new ones, you'll also want to review the issue list at `http://ironpython.codeplex.com/WorkItem/List.aspx`.)

➤ IronPython doesn't support use of __reduce__() or __reduce_ex__() on the None object. The problem is that IronPython doesn't think it has an instance in which to use either method.

➤ IronPython supports the use of _slots_ on a tuple, whereas CPython raises an error if you try to use _slots_. For example, the following code runs fine in IronPython.

```
class foo(tuple):
    _slots_ = 'abc'
```

➤ Sometimes IronPython fails to show all the members of a type that has a metaclass. The most common missed members are __delattr__(), __getattribute__(), __hash__(), __setattr__(), and __str__(). You can still call the members.

➤ If you attempt to get a method from a class that hasn't been instantiated in IronPython, you get an unbound method, while CPython returns a function.

➤ Some IronPython modules have a __dict__() attribute defined that displays a list of the module content. CPython modules don't have this feature.

➤ The sys.version value is different between IronPython and CPython.

➤ The maximum recursion limit is unlimited in IronPython by default. You can call `sys.setrecursionlimit()` to set an appropriate value. As an alternative to coding the recursion change, you can use the `-X:MaxRecursion 1000` command line switch to give IronPython behavior similar to that of CPython.

➤ IronPython tends to be more lenient about the use of keyword arguments in many cases. For example, IronPython will accept `[].append.__call__(item='abc')` as usable code, but CPython will raise an error. In fact, IronPython is less restrictive in a number of ways. The following code raises an error in CPython but works fine in IronPython.

```
x = ''
x.center(1, fillchar='*')
```

➤ The address returned by the `socket.socket()` method differs between IronPython and CPython. Given an address of 0.0.0.0, IronPython returns 0.0.0.0 and CPython returns 0.

There are many other differences between IronPython and CPython that you can read about at `http://ironpython.codeplex.com/wikipage?title=Differences`. Make sure you check the differences for each IronPython version because the Web site doesn't relist differences. In addition, some of the difference entries aren't complete. The version 2.0.x page at `http://ironpython.codeplex .com/wikipage?title=IPy2.0.xCPyDifferences&referringTitle=Differences` is an example.

MISSING CPYTHON LIBRARIES

IronPython isn't a full implementation of CPython. Yes, it has most of the pieces, but some pieces are missing. A few of these pieces are written in C. IronPython relies heavily on pure Python modules, so the C modules don't appear in IronPython unless someone has written an alternative for them. In some cases, the IronPython team simply hasn't written the required module yet, but will in the future. Table A-1 provides a list of the missing CPython libraries and what they do for you.

 The IronPython team is constantly adding new functionality to IronPython. This section lists the missing CPython libraries at the time of this writing (using IronPython version 2.6.10920.0), but the IronPython team will add at least some of these modules in the future.

TABLE A-1: Missing CPython Libraries

LIBRARY NAME	PURPOSE
ast.py	This module provides Abstract Syntax Tree (AST) support in CPython. The purpose of this library is to parse the current grammar for each Python version since the grammar can change with each new version. You can read more about this module at `http://docs.python.org/library/ast.html`.

continues

TABLE A-1 *(continued)*

LIBRARY NAME	PURPOSE
cProfile.py	Python provides a number of profilers that developers can use to determine the runtime performance of their application. The standard recommends using the `cProfile` profiler because it has low overhead and is suitable for long running programs. You can find out more about the Python profilers at `http://docs.python.org/library/profile.html`.
csv.py	One of the most common methods for storing database and spreadsheet information in text format is Comma Separated Value (CSV). This module provides Python support for CSV files. Because there's no CSV standard, this module provides generalized CSV support that will work on a range of file formats. You can read more about this module at `http://docs.python.org/library/csv.html`.
dbhash.py	Originally, this module provided access to the Berkeley Software Distribution (BSD) database library for Database Management (DBM)-style databases. In order to use this module, the application must have access to the `bsddb` module. This module has been deprecated and will probably be removed in Python 3.0. You can read more about this module at `http://docs.python.org/library/dbhash.html`.
gzip.py	This module provides support for GNU ZIP (`.gzip`) files, a kind of compression commonly found on Linux systems, but not found very often on Windows machines (although you might see it when downloading open source files). In order to use this module, the application must have access to the `zlib` module. It's also possible to use the `bz2`, `zipfile`, and `tarfile` modules to compress and decompress files. You can read more about this module at `http://docs.python.org/library/gzip.html`.
pty.py	You can use the Pseudo-Terminal (PTY) utilities to start another process, and then read and write from its controlling terminal. This module currently works reliably only on Linux systems, even if you use a CPython implementation on Windows, so it isn't surprising that IronPython doesn't implement this module yet. You can read more about this module at `http://docs.python.org/library/pty.html`.
sre.py	The Support for Regular Expressions (SRE) module provides support for Regular Expressions under Python. The level of support is similar to that found in the Practical Extraction and Report Language (PERL). You can read more about this module at `http://docs.python.org/library/re.html` and `http://pydoc.org/2.3.3/sre.html`.
ssl.py	Web applications of all types require security, especially with the rampant abuses on the Internet today. The Secure Sockets Layer (SSL) module provides support for SSL security within your Web (and other network) applications. In order to use this module, you must have OpenSSL (`http://www.openssl.org/`) installed on your machine because the module makes low-level calls to this software. You can find out more about this module at `http://docs.python.org/library/ssl.html`.

LIBRARY NAME	PURPOSE
stringprep.py	Provides methods for preparing Unicode strings for Internet use according to the requirements of RFC 3454 (`http://www.faqs.org/rfcs/rfc3454.html`). You can find out more about this module at `http://docs.python.org/library/stringprep.html`.
subprocess.py and subprocess .pyc	Allows a Python application to spawn subprocesses and then interact with them through their input, output, and error pipes. The host application also receives the subprocess's return code. This module replaces several older modules including `os.system`, `os.spawn*`, `os.popen*`, `popen2.*`, and `commands.*`. You can read more about this module at `http://docs.python.org/library/subprocess.html`.
symtable.py	The `ast` module generates symbol tables right before Python generates byte codes. This module provides access to the symbol tables so that you can examine them in detail. You can read more about this module at `http://docs.python.org/library/symtable.html`.
tty.py	This module provides terminal mode support. In order to use this module, the application must have access to the `termios` module. This module currently works reliably only on Linux systems, even if you use a CPython implementation on Windows, so it isn't surprising that IronPython doesn't implement this module yet. You can read more about this module at `http://docs.python.org/library/tty.html`.
webbrowser .py and webbrowser .pyc	This module provides Web browser controller support for applications. In most cases, all you need to do is perform a little configuration and then open the file for viewing. The behavior of this module varies on different platforms so you need to exercise some care when using it. This module doesn't directly support Internet Explorer, but does support the other major browsers. It does indirectly support Internet Explorer through the `WindowsDefault` option. You can read more about this module at `http://docs.python.org/library/webbrowser.html`.

CPython includes a number of compiled (`.pyc`) modules that don't appear in IronPython. Even though these are technically missing modules, the fact that you have a source code original makes it possible to access the functionality these modules provide. Table A-2 provides a list of the missing compiled modules.

TABLE A-2: Missing Compiled Modules

__future__.pyc	_abcoll.pyc	abc.pyc	BaseHTTPServer.pyc
bdb.pyc	bisect.pyc	code.pyc	codecs.pyc
codeop.pyc	collections.pyc	ConfigParser.pyc	copy.pyc

continues

TABLE A-2 *(continued)*

copy_reg.pyc	dis.pyc	fnmatch.pyc	functools.pyc
genericpath.pyc	getopt.pyc	heapq.pyc	inspect.pyc
keyword.pyc	linecache.pyc	locale.pyc	mimetools.pyc
ntpath.pyc	opcode.pyc	os.pyc	pkgutil.pyc
pydoc.pyc	Queue.pyc	random.pyc	re.pyc
repr.pyc	rfc822.pyc	shlex.pyc	site.pyc
socket.pyc	SocketServer.pyc	sre_compile.pyc	sre_constants.pyc
sre_parse.pyc	stat.pyc	string.pyc	struct.pyc
tabnanny.pyc	tempfile.pyc	threading.pyc	token.pyc
tokenize.pyc	traceback.pyc	types.pyc	UserDict.pyc
warnings.pyc			

MISSING OR CHANGED EXTENSION MODULES

Chapters 16 and 17 demonstrated the benefits of extension modules. With the proper extension modules, you can perform amazing feats with IronPython. Unfortunately, some CPython extension modules don't work with IronPython for various reasons (some of which have to do with the fact that the extensions are written in C). In other cases, IronPython does provide an alternative extension that doesn't work quite the same as the original CPython extension. Table A-3 provides a list of missing and changed extension modules. See Table A-1 for a description of the associated libraries.

 Early versions of IronPython were missing a lot of extension modules, but support for extension modules has improved greatly with recent releases. This section lists the missing CPython extension modules at the time of this writing, but the IronPython team will add at least some of these modules in the future.

TABLE A-3: Missing and Changed Extension Modules

MODULE NAME	MISSING OR CHANGED?	NOTES
_bisect	Missing	Maintains lists in sorted order. You can read more about this module at http://pydoc .org/2.5.1/_bisect.html and http://docs .python.org/library/bisect.html.

MODULE NAME	MISSING OR CHANGED?	NOTES
_csv	Missing	Provides support for the `.csv` file format. You can read more about this module at `http://pydoc.org/2.5.1/_csv.html` and `http://docs.python.org/library/csv.html`.
_heapq	Missing	Provides support for the heap queue algorithm. You can read more about this module at `http://pydoc.org/2.5.1/_heapq.html` and `http://docs.python.org/library/heapq.html`.
_hotshot	Missing	Provides high performance logging profiler support. You can read more about this module at `http://pydoc.org/2.5.1/_hotshot.html` and `http://docs.python.org/library/hotshot.html`.
_multibytecodec	Missing	Implements the multi-byte encoder and decoder. You can read more about this module at `http://pydoc.org/2.5.1/_multibytecodec.html`.
_subprocess	Missing	Allows subprocess management. You can read more about this module at `http://docs.python.org/library/subprocess.html`.
_symtable	Missing	Returns symbol and scope dictionaries used by the compiler. You can read more about this module at `http://pydoc.org/2.5.1/_symtable.html` and `http://docs.python.org/library/symtable.html`.
_testcapi	Missing	Incorporates Python testing functionality. You can read more about this module at `http://pydoc.org/2.5.1/_testcapi.html`.
_winreg	Missing	Allows Windows registry access. You can read more about this module at `http://docs.python.org/library/_winreg.html`.
audioop	Missing	Manipulates raw audio data. You can read more about this module at `http://docs.python.org/library/audioop.html` and `http://pydoc.org/2.5.1/audioop.html`.
binascii	Changed	Performs conversions between binary data and ASCII. Some methods don't work as anticipated or produce different error information. You can read more about this module at `http://pydoc.org/2.5.1/binascii.html`.

continues

TABLE A-3 *(continued)*

MODULE NAME	MISSING OR CHANGED?	NOTES
codecsiso2022	Missing	Provides ISO 2022 codec (`http://en.wikipedia.org/wiki/ISO/IEC_2022`) support. You can read more about this module at `http://docs.python.org/library/codecs.html`.
codecsjp, codecskr, and codecstw	Missing	Provides various types of codec support. You can read more about these modules at `http://docs.python.org/library/codecs.html`.
doctest	Missing	Creates a framework for executing examples found in document strings. You can read more about this module at `http://pydoc.org/2.5.1/doctest.html` and `http://docs.python.org/library/doctest.html`.
imageop	Missing	Manipulates raw image data. You can read more about this module at `http://pydoc.org/2.5.1/imageop.html` and `http://docs.python.org/library/imageop.html`.
md5	Missing	Implements the Message Digest 5 (MD5) hash algorithm used for security purposes. This extension module is deprecated, and you should use `hashlib` instead. You can read more about this module at `http://pydoc.org/2.5.1/md5.html` and `http://docs.python.org/library/md5.html`.
mmap	Missing	Provides memory mapped file support. You can read more about this module at `http://pydoc.org/2.5.1/mmap.html` and `http://docs.python.org/library/mmap.html`.
msvcrt	Missing	Allows direct access to a number of useful Microsoft Visual C++ runtime functions including those that affect file operations and console access. You can read more about this module at `http://docs.python.org/library/msvcrt.html`.
parser	Missing	Provides access to Python's internal parser for parse trees. You can read more about this module at `http://pydoc.org/2.5.1/parser.html` and `http://docs.python.org/library/parser.html`.

MODULE NAME	MISSING OR CHANGED?	NOTES
pickle	Changed	Provides access to the Python method for serializing and de-serializing its object structure. The IronPython version doesn't support fast mode. You can read more about this module at `http://pydoc.org/2.5.1/parser.html` and `http://docs.python.org/library/pickle.html`.
regex	Missing	Performs Regular Expression manipulation within Python. You can read more about this module at `http://docs.python.org/library/re.html`.
rgbimg	Missing	Defines a method for reading and writing Silicon Graphics, Incorporated (SGI) Red-Green-Blue (RGB) graphics files. You can read more about this module at `http://pydoc.org/2.5.1/rgbimg.html` and `http://www.python.org/doc/2.4/lib/module-rgbimg.html`.
select	Missing	Waits for I/O operations of various types to complete. This module only works for sockets on Windows systems. It works for a range of other file types, including pipes, on other platforms. You can read more about this module at `http://pydoc.org/2.5.1/select.html` and `http://docs.python.org/library/select.html`.
sha	Missing	Implements the Secure Hash Algorithm 1 (SHA-1) hash algorithm used for security purposes. You can read more about this module at `http://pydoc.org/2.5.1/sha.html` and `http://docs.python.org/library/sha.html`.
signal	Missing	Defines handlers for asynchronous events. The .NET Framework doesn't support signals. You can read more about this module at `http://pydoc.org/2.5.1/signal.html` and `http://docs.python.org/library/signal.html`.
socket	Changed	Provides low-level support for the BSD socket interface used for network communications. Some methods don't work as anticipated or produce different error information. You can read more about this module at `http://pydoc.org/2.5.1/socket.html` and `http://docs.python.org/library/socket.html`.

continues

TABLE A-3 *(continued)*

MODULE NAME	MISSING OR CHANGED?	NOTES
strop	Missing	Provides support for common string operations. This module is optimized for speed. You can read more about this module at `http://pydoc.org/2.5.1/strop.html`.
xxsubtype	Missing	Presents an example of how to subtype built-in C types. You can read more about this module at `http://pydoc.org/2.5.1/xxsubtype.html`.
zipimport	Missing	Defines a method for importing modules from ZIP files. You can read more about this module at `http://pydoc.org/2.5.1/zipimport.html` and `http://docs.python.org/library/zipimport.html`.

USING CUSTOM CPYTHON EXTENSIONS

Getting your CPython extension to work with IronPython could prove difficult. In fact, you can't ever make compiled extensions, those with the `.pyc` file extension, work with IronPython because it simply doesn't provide the required support. If your custom extension is written in pure Python and doesn't rely on any of the missing modules found in Table A-2, then it may very well work with IronPython.

> *You don't need to slog through the process of creating a solution for a custom CPython extension alone. The Google group at* `http://groups.google.com/group/c-extensions-for-ironpython` *can provide assistance with your custom CPython extension needs. In addition, some companies such as Resolver Systems are looking for ways to make using CPython extensions a lot easier (see the press release at* `http://www.resolversystems.com/news/?p=17`*).*

It's important to consider, however, that direct access limitations need not mean a complete lack of access. For example, you could always write an extension wrapper using C# or Visual Basic.NET using the technique found in the "Using C# for Win32 Support" section of Chapter 16. Using P/Invoke makes it possible to access code that IronPython couldn't ordinarily access. For this solution to work, however, you must have a detailed knowledge of how the CPython extension works.

In some cases, you might find a third-party alternative for the CPython extension you want to use. This solution is becoming more common every day as other developers find that they require access to a particular CPython module that IronPython doesn't support.

INTERACTING WITH THE INTERPRETER AND ENVIRONMENT

The IronPython setup focuses more on .NET usage, rather than strict Python uses in some respects. For example, IronPython doesn't provide access to the Standard Library by default. Chapter 6 explains techniques you can use to access the Standard Library and why this access is important in some situations.

IronPython and CPython also behave differently in some situations. In some cases, this behavior is by design or a necessity given the differing goals of the design teams. In other cases, the IronPython team plans to fix the error or has asked the Python community about the issue and the Python community has found it acceptable. In fact, some of the following behavior issues might be fixed with the next release of IronPython.

> ➤ The actual error output might not be changed in response to a change to `sys.stderror`.

> ➤ IronPython and CPython use different forms of command line editing support.

> ➤ IronPython and CPython use differing command line options, which means that batch files created for one won't necessarily work for the other.

> ➤ Some `sys` module hooks may not work at all or may work differently than those in CPython. For example, IronPython doesn't implement the `sys.getrefcount()` method.

> ➤ It's possible to access `__dict__()`, `__module__()`, `__class__()`, and `__init__()` at the global level, where CPython doesn't allow global access.

USING GARBAGE COLLECTION

CPython relies on an older method of keeping track of objects, reference counting, which is similar to the technique used in older Component Object Model (COM) applications. IronPython uses a newer garbage collector. Relying on a garbage collector is actually an advantage for the IronPython developer. The Python community as a whole has decided that using a garbage collector is acceptable. However, using a garbage collector has the following implications for the IronPython developer.

> ➤ No need to worry about circular references because the garbage collector ensures that such instances are properly collected.

> ➤ There's no guarantee as to when finalization occurs or system resources are freed. This has implications for people who constantly create and then free resources. The system could very well slow down when garbage collection occurs at inconvenient times.

> ➤ Invoking the `__del__()` method doesn't immediately delete the affected resource. The deletion occurs during the next garbage collection cycle.

> ➤ Calling `sys.getrefcount()` returns an `AttributeError` because the `sys` module doesn't implement this feature.

> ➤ CPython reuses `tuple` objects in some cases, but this behavior doesn't occur in IronPython.

B

CPython Extensions for IronPython

WHAT'S IN THIS APPENDIX?

➤ Finding extensions that work

➤ Fixing extension problems

➤ Finding third-party solutions to fix problems

In many cases, there's code that's already written for CPython that also works for IronPython. You've already experienced using CPython code in Chapter 6 when working with the Standard Library. The material in Chapter 6 also applies to third-party extensions. Some of these extensions will work just fine, especially if they're written in pure Python and there aren't any odd IronPython behaviors to consider (see Appendix A for details).

The sticky part comes when you try to work with CPython extensions that rely more heavily on the C basis for CPython. In this situation, you need to create your own tool to make the extension work, rely on a third-party tool to perform the heavy lifting, or simply emulate the behavior of the CPython extension using .NET code. All of these solutions have problems.

The purpose of this appendix is to provide you with some tips and techniques for making your CPython extensions run in IronPython. However, you need to face the fact that not every CPython extension will work as you'd like it to, and some won't work at all.

OBTAINING THE EXTENSIONS

You can find more than a few Python extensions on the Internet. For the most part, you see them listed simply as Python extensions — not specifically IronPython or CPython extensions. A number of these extensions are simply `.py` files and probably work fine for IronPython or

CPython without any changes. However, when you see an extension listed as providing support for Python, it's better to assume that the person created it specifically for CPython. IronPython extensions typically state that the developer created them for IronPython.

There are a number of places where you can find extensions specifically for IronPython. However, sometimes you have to take the source code and build the module yourself. Fortunately, Chapters 16 and 17 tell you how to perform the task. The following list provides information about various sites to try in order to obtain extensions for IronPython tasks, such as debugging your application or configuring a Web server.

➤ **Debugger:** You might not be very impressed with the debugging features that IronPython provides natively. Some people have decided to start looking at the problem and doing something about it. You can find a start for a debugger at `http://blogs.msdn.com/jmstall/articles/Sample_Mdbg_IronPython.aspx`. If you need an explanation of how such a debugger would work, check out the article at `http://devhawk.net/2009/02/27/Writing+An+IronPython+Debugger+MDbg+101.aspx`.

➤ **Web Server Gateway Interface (WSGI):** There wasn't an IronPython version of the WSGI until Jeff Hardy (`http://jdhardy.blogspot.com/`) put one together. The NWSGI (.NET Web Server Gateway Interface) provides the functionality you need to provide full WSGI support in your IronPython application. Download this extension at `http://nwsgi.codeplex.com/Release/ProjectReleases.aspx?ReleaseId=36268`.

➤ **ASP.NET Dynamic Language Support:** You'll probably want to try IronPython with ASP.NET at some point. Fortunately, you can get the information and software you need to perform the task at `http://www.codeplex.com/wikipage?ProjectName=aspnet&title=Dynamic Language Support`.

You may have found that Visual Studio isn't precisely hospitable toward IronPython. Fortunately, you can find some Visual Studio extensions that make the life of an IronPython developer easier at `http://jdhardy.blogspot.com/2009/11/ironpython-extensions-for-visual-studio.html`.

Some CPython extensions are must haves. Here's a list of extensions that you might want to get for your IronPython configuration with suggestions on how to make them work.

➤ `numpy.py` **and** `scipy.py`**:** The original `numpy` (`http://numpy.scipy.org/`) and `scipy` (`http://scipy.org/`) combination provides the resources needed for scientific numeric computations. You can download the `numpy` extension and associated `scipy` tools from `http://scipy.org/Download`. You need to use IronClad to make these extensions work.

➤ **pygames:** If you ever thought you'd like to perform game development using IronPython, you can do it using pygames, which is more like an entire platform than a single module. Learn more about pygames at `http://www.pygame.org/news.html`.

➤ **Python for Windows:** A number of extensions specifically designed for Windows developers that are packaged together (some developers might know this package as pywin32). You can download this package from `http://sourceforge.net/projects/pywin32/`. The majority of this package will very likely run without extra help.

There are some situations where you should consider not using an extension. For example, you could easily download the `pymssql` extension found at `http://pymssql.sourceforge.net/`. However, it's probably easier to write your own extension using Visual Basic.NET using the technique shown in Chapter 17. The resulting extension will probably run faster and provide precisely what you need with a lot less work. For that matter, you could always decide to import the required .NET assemblies and directly access your database from IronPython (assuming you want to pursue the task without designer support). When in doubt, consider at least trying to obtain the results you want using the simplest and most direct approach possible, which often means writing your own extension.

OVERCOMING POTENTIAL EXTENSION PROBLEMS

If you have a CPython extension that you really must use and there isn't an IronPython alternative, you have a number of solutions you can try. Of course, the first solution is to get someone else to fix the problem (see the section "Obtaining Third-Party Solutions" later in this appendix for details). Unfortunately, duping someone else into performing your work for you isn't always possible, so you might have to fix the problem yourself.

When you have the source code for the CPython extension in the form of a `.py` file, you can sometimes fix the issue directly. Try importing the extension and then working with it. Often, the error information you receive from the interpreter is enough to help you locate and fix the problem. Some CPython extensions will work fine once you overcome the compatibility issues between IronPython and CPython.

 One company that has a lot of experience fixing problem extensions is Resolver Systems. You'll find blogs and articles about the experiences of their developers in a lot of places on the Internet. Most important, Resolver Systems has created a spreadsheet application, Resolver One, which relies on IronPython as its base language. You can learn more about Resolver Systems at `http://www.resolversystems.com/`. Another example of Python in action is the Python Extension for Mozilla developers found at `http://pyxpcomext.mozdev.org/`. You get the power of Python within Firefox, Thunderbird, and XulRunner. In short, there are lots of examples of Python in use on the Internet.

The issue that will give you the most trouble is that some CPython extensions rely on C code. These extensions contain a combination of Python code and DLLs written in C because using C provides certain advantages (much as C# and Visual Basic.NET provide certain advantages for the .NET developer). In this case, you need to access the code within the DLL, but you probably can't do it from IronPython. The fastest way to overcome this problem is to use a third-party solution such as IronClad (see the section "Working with IronClad" later in this appendix).

Another technique you can use to overcome extension problems that involve C code is to work through the issue using P/Invoke. The section "Using C# for Win32 Support" in Chapter 16 provides a quick view of how powerful a P/Invoke extension can be. However, sometimes it's the detective work required to obtain the information you need to use P/Invoke that proves the most difficult to obtain. I've written a series of four articles that show some of my techniques for performing this task:

➤ "Working with Windows Messages in .NET" (`http://www.devsource.com/c/a/Using-VS/Working-with-Windows-Messages-in-NET/`)

➤ "Hooking Windows Messages in .NET" (`http://www.devsource.com/c/a/Using-VS/Hooking-Windows-Messages-in-NET/`)

➤ "Globally Hooking Windows Messages in .NET" (`http://www.devsource.com/c/a/Using-VS/Globally-Hooking-Windows-Messages-in-NET/`)

➤ "Special Windows Message Hooking Techniques for .NET" (`http://www.devsource.com/c/a/Using-VS/Special-Windows-Message-Hooking-Techniques-for-NET/`)

There's a point where you do need to give up on using a particular CPython extension with IronPython. These situations are becoming fewer as developers come up with new tools for addressing problems and IronPython itself becomes closer to CPython in implementation. It would be overly optimistic to say that there will ever come a time when you can run any CPython extension using IronPython.

OBTAINING THIRD-PARTY SOLUTIONS

Third-party solutions are definitely easier, in many respects, than creating your own solutions. Of course, you have to find a third-party solution that actually performs the required task. In addition, you can't accept that third-party solutions come without potential problems. If you use a third-party solution, even one that works, you always run the risk that you won't be able to obtain help when you need it or that the third party will choose not to update the software as needed. Even so, third-party solutions can be very beneficial, especially when you're on a tight time schedule. The following sections describe some third-party solutions in general and one specifically, IronClad.

Considering Some of the Better Solutions

There are a number of quick and easy fixes for your CPython library problems. In most cases, all you do is download the alternative you need, place it into the right IronPython folder, and you have the support you require. The following list provides information about a number of these third-party solutions.

➤ **ZLib Module for IronPython:** Download this solution from `http://bitbucket.org/jdhardy/ironpythonzlib/overview/`. After you download the ZIP file, simply unzip it and place the resulting files in your `\Program Files\IronPython 2.6\DLLs` folder to obtain `zlib` module support. (You'll probably have to create the DLLs subfolder because it doesn't exist by default.)

➤ **subprocess.py:** Download this solution from `http://bitbucket.org/jdhardy/code/src/`. This same page has `sqlserver_backend.py`, which is a SQL Server backend for Trac. After you download the `subprocess.py` file, add it to the `\Program Files\IronPython 2.6\Lib\site-packages` folder to obtain `subprocess` module support.

➤ **pyexpat.py:** Download this solution from `https://fepy.svn.sourceforge.net/svnroot/fepy/trunk/lib/`. This same page has a wealth of other `.py` files you can use with IronPython. After you download `pyexpat.py`, copy it to the `\Program Files\IronPython 2.6\Lib\xml\parsers` folder and rename the file to `expat.py` to obtain `expat` module support.

Working with IronClad

There's a third-party tool available on the market from Resolver Systems that could make it easier for you to work with CPython modules, IronClad (`http://www.resolversystems.com/products/ironclad/` or `http://code.google.com/p/ironclad/`). As the tool's author states, it's a work in progress. The tool currently works only on Windows 32-bit platforms, so this isn't a good tool to try if you need 64-bit support for your IronPython applications. The Web site provides a download link. After you download the file, simply unzip it into a folder on your hard drive, as suggested by the author.

One of the changes that you'll probably want to make to the author's instructions is to create an IRONPYTHONPATH environment variable like the one described in the section "Accessing the Standard Library from IronPython" in Chapter 6. However, in this case, set the environment variable to provide access to the full Standard Library and to IronClad as well by including `C:\Python26\DLLs;C:\Python26\Lib;C:\Python26\Lib\site-packages;C:\ironclad-v2.6.0rc1-bin` as directories. (You'll need to change the paths to match your system configuration.) When you open the IronPython console, you'll be able to access all of the Standard Library and IronClad as well. Use the following code to verify that you have the required access:

```
import sys
sys.path
```

When you execute these commands, you should see the output shown in Figure B-1. At this point, you should be able to follow the IronClad directions for a fully functional setup that can import many, but not all, of those CPython modules you want to use.

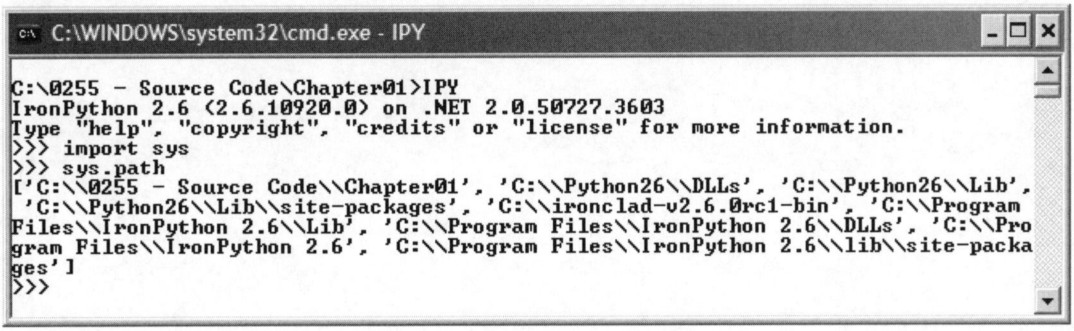

FIGURE B-1: Make sure you have the path to IronClad set correctly.

INDEX

D